# ULTIMATE DECEIT

## OF THE HUMAN RACE

### THE EZZRATH THEORY

EZZRATH BAHT SHEM

ANATH'S PUBLISHING COMPANY

**Published by Anath's Publishing Company**
A division of Anath Enterprises Incorporated

**ANATH'S PUBLISHING COMPANY**
P.O. Box 3132
Marion, Indiana 46953 USA
1 (800) 363-0799
www.ultimatedeceit.com
ezzrath@comteck.com

First printed in January 2001

10 9 8 7 6 5 4 3 2 1

Edited by Teddy Kempster

Book and cover design by Lightbourne

Manufactured in the United States of America by BookMasters, Inc.

**Hardcover ISBN: 0-9702227-2-6**
**Softcover ISBN: 0-9702227-1-8**

**LCCN: 00-092791**

*Dedicated*
*In Loving Memory*

*of*

George Black Jr., my Father
Yohanathan Ben Israel, my Son

*and*

Queen Betty Shebazz and Mother Teresa
*My Inspiration*

If Christ were here there is one thing
he would not be . . .
**a Christian**.

—Mark Twain

# The Life You Don't Remember

The life you don't remember surely exist nonetheless.
Just because you can't remember it don't miss out on pure
    bliss.

The life you don't remember is truly there for you.
It is what it is that keeps you, and guides you through and
    through.

Humans live the experiences of life on the edge,
    in the raw, never knowing what's comin' or goin'.

We live then we die: that is the one sure guarantee.
Whether we find joy or life's hell, is up to you and me.

We will throughout eternity live life's experience, you see,
    going here and going there, touring various galaxies.

Whether we choose here or if we choose there it is all
    the same for us.
For once we understand, we know life is sweet and just.

I wish I could, I know I should, help all humanity,
    for if only we all could choose this wonderful
    philosophy, we wouldn't have such hate you see.

We would grow strong, powerful in love and unity.
    We would possess all the riches inherited instinctively.

We would know that there is no end and in reality we
    never began.
We would know all the secrets existing inside us
    from within.

We would find peace, joy, and happiness, in every
    breath we took.
If only we would learn that our memories we forsook.

Our memories, they hold the key to all that ever was.
    Let's tap inside and discover life, like in the *Wizard of Oz*.
Let's learn how real it is to journey deep within.
    The characters from Oz all discovered this fact therein.
The Tin Man needed a heart, and found it there within
    The Lion needed courage, he, too, found it there within.
Alas there's the Scarecrow, the wittiest of them all,
    And he, too, had his need—a medulla in his skull.

By now you should know where he found his answer true.
From the greatest to the least of all, you'll find it there
    with you.
Flabbergasted they will discover, that it is actually
    nothing new.
For finding all your needs within is all you have to do.

Besides that's what it's all about, learning not to go without.
    Think about this rhyme, that I send to you from me.
Without love, understanding, and peace: that's the reward
    of going without.
So, my friends, you have the choice to go within or
    eternally without.

Nonetheless, I want you to know that whatever choice you
    choose, you are bound to never lose, in this journey we
    choose to cruise.
You see, my friend, that's how perfect a world we
    chose, before our physical trip imposed, all of life's
    incredible no-nos.
Now its time that we all arose, and claimed the crown
    before our nose.

For without a doubt the winning has begun. Just because
    you see racial colors doesn't mean we aren't all one.

Although you kill the red, the black, or the yellow,
    "Regardless, we are one," the Universe will bellow.
Though you kill the white, or the brown, whichever,
    when you wake from your dream you will find
    it not so clever.
You see, you will see yourself truly as you are—
    not physical bodies, but all one big STAR.

                    — Ezzrath,
                      *For peace on earth*
                      *good will toward life*

# Acknowledgments

There are no words within the human vocabulary which I can use to express the depth of gratitude in which I wish to acknowledge the Creator foremost for entertaining the awesomely creative idea of creation. The mere idea of creation (nature) totally soothes the human soul with a terrible awe of love, revelation, and self-control. For all this I give thanks to my Creator and Redeemer, for surely God has begun saving me from hell—"self destruction."

The next thanks belongs to my beloved mother, Mildred Barber, who has supported me through a dynamic metamorphosis. She plunged into the waters of salvation (reading information for herself, and discovering hidden truths) with me as a last recourse to win me back to Christ's grace. Thanks, Mom, for being there through thick and thin with me. The next appreciation goes out to my lovely children, Alicia, Yetunde, and Kemuel. My Uncle Kenny Barber and my Aunt Orine Johnson have both inspired me to quit procrastinating through their unwavering belief in Jesus and the traditional plan of salvation. They made me remember that at one time I, too, was in ignorance.

Numerous friends have inspired the production of this book, the most faithful being Alonzo Johnson. When we decided to partake of friendship he inspired me with the fact that he had lived with a broken neck in a wheelchair since 1975 and was still one of the happiest souls on the planet. Another friend who has been my best friend since college and has never ever let me down is Jennifer Morrison of South America Guyana. Thanks also to my Chicago friends who helped me through the transformation: Tonya King, Pearl Washington and her husband Jim, Kennedy Fuse, Ruth

Timmons, Katy Gray, Harry Else, Joseph Newman, and Banji Ayoola.

Special thanks goes out to my final proof readers Shanta and Jewel Nadratowski.

You may be surprised to find that I would choose to include my shadow figures with a sincere, "thank you." For it is through my shadows that I have made it to this point in life and they, too, must be given gratitude. The foremost shadow and thanks to Azzur Israel, many of the City of Chicago Water Department management, and Yeshayahuwa. None of who I am today could have happened without you and for all your efforts—I SIN-CERELY THANK YOU.

# Preface

I was born in 1960, and raised in a small midwestern city in the state of Indiana by two loving parents, Mildred and George Black Jr. My entrance into the physical world was somewhat extraordinary given the fact that my mother had been married previously to another man and could not produce children. A doctor told her that she would never have children because she was born with a tilted uterus and therefore would be incapable of producing a pregnancy. She accepted her fate and eventually gave birth to me. I was born into the Baptist faith. From as far back as I can remember, my home church, St. Paul Baptist Church, has been my first love even unto this day. My church was never harsh to my soul; loving kisses, hugs, and praises were all that I can ever remember experiencing from my church. Even though one of the sister's harsh discipline and rumor of the clothes hanger beatings haunted me, I still felt love and the spirit of God. This was just the way things were.

From as young as I can remember, the Spiritual, and God, has always consumed my thoughts. I spent many days outside, supposedly playing, but actually pondering away and daydreaming of how it all fit together. One recurring notion in my mind was if I died, where would I wake up. I remember thinking and comparing falling asleep and waking up to dying and—"But will I wake up?" Somehow that was an unthinkable question. It always turned into, "where will I wake up, and what will it be like there?"

As a young teenager, God became more and more important in my life until a time came when I had become totally consumed. "Jesus" was the only way for the world, and I had decided to become fanatical about my worship of Christ. I lived in the church. Literally every day, if the doors of the church were closed, we would gather for home Bible classes. In the name of Jesus, I watched many miracles and participated in healings by the laying on of hands. I prayed to my God that He should never let me live to see the day that I would turn from Jesus. I told Him that if He foresaw any way that I would be tempted to sin in college, that he please send a sign to intercept my decision to further my education. My entrance into college would change all of the fanatical healings and miracles that I used to practice.

I attended the University of Tuskegee, (originally Tuskegee Institute) as an undecided major, which eventually turned into a deferred Bachelor of Science degree in chemical engineering. Like most Americans, programmed by religious doctrines, I saw my actions as sinful, yet saved by the grace of Jesus. I felt my prayers had been answered when the opportunity for marriage arose.

The marriage failed. Relationship after relationship failed, and then I met Hebrew Israelites, who reshaped my religious thinking forever. I became fanatical for Yahweh, the God of the Hebrews, my **only** salvation. The hells that would come along as baggage with this religion will make another entire book in itself. Nonetheless, I soon discovered that the Israelite religion too, was a fabrication of personal agendas.

All my life, I had accepted religions as they were presented to me without ever actually delving into the origin of the religion. I read only the information that supported the belief that I was given, and it would seem as if it were the only way. These types of behavior lead me into a perpetual *ULTIMATE DECEIT*—the deceit of worshipping Satan (the Enemy) as my God.

Discovering the "Ultimate Deceit," I had come face to face with reality, that there was so much more to God than I could have imagined. My obsession was to know God in the fullest degree attainable—760 degrees of knowledge. I retrieved pieces of the puzzle, leading me to find that the Creator of worlds, universes, and species seen and unseen was unknowably immense. I will never, in this current human form, fully understand all there is to know about our magnificent Creator and all His/Her Glory and plan for creation. (Please keep in mind that if God is male only in your perspective, then you are represented in the He part of He/She.) How can there be a true and rewarding relationship with God if we do not possess a real understanding of who God is? The majority of those who follow the Bible will tell you that they do not have a thorough understanding of both the Old and New Testament. Yet they will base their entire belief system around the assumed hypothesis:

*The Bible is God's complete word and contains everything that mankind needs to know regarding God.*

Likewise, followers of Islam assume that to know God all you need is the Koran. In Judaism, all one needs for the truth of God is the Torah and the prophets (Old Testament). All the religions of the earth have their own book, writings, oral traditions, and so forth as the *absolute* guides from God.

Unfortunately, I too have had to set one hypothesis that can not be proven, which states:

"God is."

The difference is that I do recognize the fact that this statement is my belief and that it is hypothetical, no one can prove that "God is." Most religions do not recognize the difference between belief and fact. I eliminate one hypothesis assumed by all religions, that is, "that God has only one book or sets of books" (Bible, Koran, Torah, Vedas . . .) and "one religion for the world" (Christianity, Islam, Judaism, Hinduism . . . ).

Furthermore, another difference is the fact that I am conscious of the realization that I am starting out with information based on a hypothesis (accepted theory without proven validity) which allows flexibility in retrieving information from others. Those bound in religion suffer great difficulty overcoming tunnel vision or receiving information contradictory to their beliefs. The information you are about to receive is not absolute. It may in time prove to be immaterial. Every person searching for the reality of "absolute truth" must understand: Any assumptions may prove false. I have selected this premise as basis, consistent with most every believer in God:

1.  There exists a Creator (force or person), who is living, who is in complete control of the universe as He/She wills it to be, and who is all knowing. (There is nothing that God does not know.)
2.  The ultimate "will" of the Creator will never change.
3.  God gave us common sense and more importantly "*God or divine sense.*" We should use it!

Approximately seven years ago I could not have imagined myself asking the unthinkable question: "Did the Creator authorize the writing of the Bible?" I did not have the slightest desire to ponder the question, let alone actually answer the question: "How do you know that God gave us the Bible?" The question would often create anxiety and frustration, because it was simply a known fact that God would not give us the Bible in error, and besides, there was no way that God would allow so many to be deceived. Furthermore, so many people, myself included, felt the words of the Bible must be absolutely trustworthy. Therefore, the Bible absolutely must be God's word; case proven and justified in faith. Or is it?

To base one's total faith in a book as God's word merely because it feels right and has been accepted from our childhood is outrageously ludicrous. The only thing more ludicrous is saying to oneself, "I don't accept the Bible just because it feels right, 'cause I read the Bible, and I know what God has revealed to me"; but in actuality they are doing just that. They do not know why the Bible was written originally, nor do they have the faintest clue about the cycles (plagiary of predated material) and stages (translations with additions and deletions) that produced the Bible of today.

In order for you to follow my complicated and controversial

material, as your parents gave you all the answers before you knew what the questions would be, likewise, I too would like to give you the answers to what actually happened regarding the Bible. Then I will attempt to prove these answers with both Bible verses and historical data. If you are of the "norm," you probably will find this hypothesis unbelievable in any way, but please be patient and complete your studies. You will enhance your knowledge, even if you learn nothing more than some of the crazy mindsets of your fellow human beings. If I am wrong, then you can also point out my mistakes and perhaps help others to distinguish truth from fiction. The answers are as follows:

1. The Bible is not an authorized book from God.
2. The Bible does state conflicting passages that were written for personal agendas of that period.
3. Both Yahweh, (the names Yahweh and Jehovah are both the name of the God of the Old Testament in Hebrew and English respectively, and are used interchangeably throughout this book) and his Israelite people were black and against spiritual humanity.
4. Yahweh was/is (depending on whether or not he still lives) an alien or a man with super intelligence (like Hitler), but not God and perhaps not immortal.
5. If indeed Yahweh/Jehovah is not God, then Jesus is not the Son of God, due to the fact that without the Old Testament God, there is no New Testament Son of God.

Now let's take a moment to digest this hypothesis. If you have an open mind, you will say to yourself, "Let's see if the hypothesis can be proven." Those who have closed minds are saying to themselves as they read this writing that this is all impossible. "There is no way!" "Why should I listen to this confused and imaginative mad woman?" "What a bunch of crock . . . bull . . . bologna . . . !" It is my hope that you will be patient enough to look up scriptures and references that are presented, and begin your own investigation. After all, let's face it, we Americans believe in becoming well-informed consumers. The average one of us would never go shopping for a car and simply buy the first car they show us. Never! Yet how many of us ever take the time to investigate the origins of our religion, let alone other religions and their origins (we take the first God given to us from birth)? Many of us choose the same religion as our parents, never considering the possibility that they may be wrong. When we give our hearts to a religion, we must constantly defend and justify our beliefs when contradictions occur within our doctrines. When we are in a true relationship with God all humans can come together and believe that there is a Supreme Being greater than the physical self. We will want to be *one* with God. On the other hand, the religions were created to divide and conquer the human race. They create fractions even within the very same religion due to all of the double talk, which no one (enslaved to their belief) will admit that the double talk actually exists. They prefer taking one side of the double talk and making a religion out of it. They were created to cause war, and make one group believe that their particular belief system (the double talk) is absolute truth, while everyone else's religion is false. For example, the Seventh Day Adventists believe that they have the closest, truest path to God because they prioritize the Sabbath, as the Bible requires, while the Jehovah's Witnesses know that they have the most-true religion on the earth because they follow the requirements for prioritizing Jehovah's name and building his kingdom on earth, just as the Hebrews taught. The Baptists are actually more righteous than any of the other denominations, for they are baptized, and have the faith, and are saved by grace just as the Bible requires. Without a doubt each of the denominations know that they have the closest walk with God—absolute truth. Yet none of them are the same. Is it possible to have perfect truths all absolutely different regarding the same Person (God) and subject (His Will)? But this is what religion offers the human race.

However, if indeed our relationship to God is of a greater priority than our religions, then we should attempt to know whether or not we have chosen the right belief system. We should challenge all religions to an inquiry, and decipher after a detailed investigation what tends to be fictitious and what appears truthful. This is the purpose of these writings. I would like to see more of humanity place time into the investigation for the validity of their faith. If this book is taken as the only possible truth, without seeking one's own personal conclusions and convictions, then all of my efforts would be in vain. This book was written to inspire thinkers and researchers for the truth of God and creation. It is not designed to seek converts or believers. For God's sake, please, I beg of all my readers, *don't accept anything I say as absolute truth, but instead search out history and scripture for your self!*

Is it not common sense that each individual should be responsible for learning and becoming knowledgeable about his Creator? Or does it make more sense that we should just accept what our preachers and parents have taught us, assuming that it is impossible for them to be in error? If you believe the latter, then there's no rewarding information in this book for you. However, if the first statement rings true, then this book is an absolute requirement of information to decipher, modify (or delete as necessary), and adjoin to your current knowledge.

— Ezzrath Baht Shem
*Sept. 13, 2000*
*Marion, Indiana*

# Contents

# SEVEN
## Ancient Mythology

# EIGHT
## The Philosophy of Ezzrath on Illusions

# NINE
## Salvation

# TEN
## People on the Path

# ELEVEN
## The Ezzrath Theory

# TWELVE
## Real-Life Biographies

# Introduction

It has been said that beauty is in the eye of the beholder. But I have found more profound, the statement that truth is nothing more than the perception of the thinker. Why do we simply accept that the grass is green? That's simple; it takes too much time and bother for the average person to research the color spectrum and discover the actual wave frequencies on the color spectrum that make green, green and then to study chlorophyll and its characteristics. The entire purpose of this book is to point out truths/falsehoods that you may have simply accepted without knowing anything about where the information originated, and to prove that what we believe, perceive, think, and unfortunately know may be erroneous. Undoubtedly, there will be skeptics, skeptics who would no longer exist or in the very least would find themselves saying "hum" if only they read the references presented here and research the origin of each idea presented.

It is easy to throw up both hands and say that so much research is impossible and time consuming and to simply except what has been handed to us as truth. If that had been the way of all mankind throughout history we would all KNOW that the world is flat. Many of us would KNOW that life began less than six thousand years ago, according to our Bible, with one man named Adam and one woman named Eve. Prior to modern technology, we KNEW that the earth was the center of the universe and that the sun revolved around it. Now the majority of all people know that the accepted truth of the past is not always valid.

Most of the information in this book will probably be new

to many readers. To provide some important background for understanding the religious doctrines and biblical quotes, I offer this list of ten important references. At the end of the book are many more references supporting my premise; also the first few chapters include supporting references due to the religious controversial content.

The primary references for fully understanding the Hebraic scriptures known as the Torah and the Pentateuch, now located in the Bible, are as follows:

1.  *King James Version* of the Bible. All Bible verses quoted in this book are from the King James Version.
2.  *Strong's Exhaustive Concordance of the Bible,* by James Strong, Madison, N. J. (Try to get the oldest version attainable. Later versions tend to cover up and lose important data and information. Try the one published by World Bible Publishers, Inc. in 1992, ISBN 0-529-07235-1. Any version with Hebrew and Greek translations will be better than none.)
3.  *Young's Analytical Concordance to the Bible.* Hendrickson, ISBN 0-917006-29-1.
4.  *The Anchor Bible Dictionary* (all six volumes), Doubleday, 1992, ISBN 0-385-19351-3.
5.  *The 12th Planet, Earth Chronicles, The Stairway to Heaven, The Wars of Gods and Men, The Lost Realms,* all by the Zecharia Sitchin. Avon, ISBN 0-380-39362-X.
6.  *The Gods of Eden* by William Bramley, Avon Books, 1993, ISBN 0-380-71807-3.
7.  *The Webster's Dictionary*
8.  *The Antichrist Teitan 666,* by William Josiah Sutton, W. F. G. Inc. 1980.
9.  *Sex and Race,* by J. A. Rogers, Helga M. Rogers, Vol. 1-3.
10. *From Babylon to Timbuktu,* by Rudolph R. Windsor, Windsor Golden Series, ISBN 0-962088-11-0.

The books are not absolutely necessary as I will provide background for my arguments; however, a true devout researcher of the truth will never simply accept another person's word without cross-checking.

You will discover that the human race has one common ancestry, and that this ancestral lineage originated through the gods. The god species lies dormant in each of us today with out regard for race, sex, color, or creed. We will then begin to recognize that we are truly *one* with God, not under God. We will then take responsibility for all the hells we create for ourselves instead of looking for some outside force to blame. We will ultimately find the *God within.*

I too have been a victim of receiving all the answers way before I KNEW what the questions would be. Being born into a Baptist family, one answer I KNEW, as far back as I can remember is that, "Jesus is the answer for the world today." I KNEW this at the tender age of three without ever asking any questions or even having the slightest idea that there could be any possibility whatsoever that perhaps my mom, dad, or preacher could be capable of making a mistake in their perceptions. After all, at the age of three, moms and dads never make mistakes, and it is against every law conceivable for ministers of God to make a mistake in their perceptions. So I KNEW that Jesus was the answer for the world and ultimately me. When I was a young teenager, anyone who would even mention anything other than Jesus dying for our sins would at first be a target for conversion. If I failed to win that soul for Jesus, it would be tossed into the condemned-to-hell list with no hope of survival unless that soul at some point in the future repented and accepted Jesus Christ before leaving this world. That soul appeared to be ridiculous, stupid, and outright uninformed. What could be easier than letting the Lord Jesus carry all of your sins and inherit salvation by His death? Without Jesus there is no recourse other than hell; and I KNEW it. How dare anyone have the audacity not to accept my precious Lord Jesus, whom I had learned to KNOW that He died for the sins of the world, and now they want to deny Him of His glory as the Son of God! Some of them reduced my savior to simply a prophet like Moses or Elijah. Yet others denied that there was ever a remote possibility that a man called Jesus ever existed. I was taught that the only way to heaven was to accept Jesus as my personal savior and without this personal relationship with Jesus, I would be doomed to hell. HELL! How could anyone not accept Jesus? After all, we all KNOW that hell is a *living* nightmare of consuming and absorbing eternal flames, in which the non-believer receives condemnation of a fiery, burning, everlasting life from God. How could anyone not accept Him to be the messiah, the Son of God? The very moment you stop believing you are headed to hell.

Well, one day I discovered that I had been taught many false and misleading concepts. I found myself in a heated anguish. My world had totally disintegrated. I was positively headed for hell and I didn't KNOW how to stop it. All that I KNEW was that the Jesus story couldn't hold water, once I realized that the Bible was intended to be taken mostly literally. For the greater part most Bible readers interpret the Bible as metaphors and not literal. (The only way to make sense of the contradictions and destruction of human life is to believe that there is a deeper message than the one presented—we many times call them metaphors.) Historically speaking it was nothing more than a copycat of an earlier Babylonian and Canaanite epic of creation. The Bible literally shows that the Jesus story is impossible in its entirety. If we simply use common sense as the Bible says we should in II Timothy 2:15, while properly dividing the word of truth, then we will indeed *discover our misconceptions.* Did you know that the Bible actually tells you to divide it? That is, unless you do *not* believe that the Bible is the word of truth. All that I could do was to roam the streets of Chicago in pure agony for my soul when I discovered the deceit. I KNEW that I did not KNOW how to find salvation! How was I going to receive salvation now that Jesus was no longer real for me? IMPOSSIBLE!

I began a seven-year intensive research into the Bible, history, languages, and all the religions and myths of the world, gathering bits and pieces of information here and there and filling in the puzzle as I went along. I would rarely sleep before 3 or 4 a.m. again. This book is the result of that intensive fact-finding process, and includes information on the following topics:

1.  Countless mysteries of the Bible
2.  Reliability of the Bible
3.  Who are the ancient Hebrew Israelites?
4.  What is the origin of the Bible?
5.  What is the origin of Christianity?
6.  Who was the God of the Hebrews?
7.  A comparison of religions
8.  Who are the Hebrew Israelites today?
9.  How did human life begin?
10. Is there life after death?
11. How does one obtain salvation?
12. Who are the idol gods and where are they today?
13. Why is there so much suffering on earth?
14. How did holidays begin?
15. How do we distinguish reality from falsehoods?
16. Who are the races today in comparison with ancient times?
17. Why do we have religion?
18. What is hell about?

After reading this book you should be able to decipher the origins and reasons for many of our earthly beliefs and religions. Rely more on the information that our mother earth has given us and a little less on handed-down information, passed on from generation to generation. You will never think the same again! FOR YOU WILL BE ENLIGHTENED. You will KNOW that you did not KNOW.

# Bible Test for Knowledge and Wisdom

This Bible test is designed to test one's ability to see reality according to what is depicted in the Bible. For example, if the Bible says in several accounts that Jesus was quiet, and slow to anger, but in one account Jesus gets into a fight, then the question stating, according to the Bible, true or false: Jesus was a man who got into fights easily, would be false. This test is designed to use a common-sense analysis of the Bible based on *all* its content and the overall character and behavior portrayed. Suppose you are given a situation such as, I kick you over and over again, and then beat you and steal your money, and then I state, "I am doing this because I love you." Then you are asked, "I love you," true or false? Based on what I have just told you, if you answer true because I said that I love you, then your answer is considered wrong. The weights of actions and deeds are counted ten times higher on this test than an actual statement or a belief. I have stated that I love you, but my actions show you that I don't.

## TRUE OR FALSE (from a biblical point of view)

1. God never does wrong.
2. God instructed the Israelites to kill babies.
3. God creates good.
4. God creates evil.
5. From the beginning of time God has always loved all of mankind.
6. God caused the Israelites to take another person or persons as possessions.

7.  The Israelites' covenant with God is everlasting.
8.  Jesus did away with the law and now we are under grace.
9.  Jesus came to save the world.
10. Jesus was racist.
11. God ordered a man stoned to death by the Israelite community for picking up sticks.
12. Solomon was a very wise king.
13. God and Adolf Hitler have similar actions and concepts of life.
14. Jesus sent his disciples out into the world to give his message to everyone they met regardless of nationality.
15. Moses was a Jew.
16. If Jesus' father would punish an act by death, then Jesus, being like his father, would also punish the same act by death.
17. The god of the Old Testament and Jesus share the same purpose for they are one.
18. Job blessed God.
19. Jesus implied that a Greek woman was a dog.
20. Jesus wept.

### Answers to the Test

1.  **False**—In fact, God was continually committing violent acts of murder, genocide, and extermination. If the god of the Old Testament were to be in front of the American judicial system for his crimes he would qualify for the death penalty! Humans justify the god of the Old Testament by saying, "If He is God, then He can do whatever (crimes) He wishes and it is righteous because He is GOD." But, the problem is the fact that no one questions the possibility of whether or not the god of the Old Testament is indeed GOD.

2.  **True**—The god of the Old Testament found it easy to give

the order to kill babies. The chapter on the god of the Old Testament talks about this fact and gives the actual verse where Jehovah gives the order to kill infants.

3. **True**

4. **True**—Just as god said he was capable of creating good, the god of the Old Testament states that he creates evil, also.

5. **False**—According to the Bible, the god of the Old Testament loved no humans but Israelites. But he proved not to love the Israelites either, forcing his prophets to eat feces, marry whores, and murder men, women, children, and babies.

6. **True**—The god of the Old Testament directed the Israelites to take the land of another people, the Canaanites. After having races of people killed off, he instructed the Israelite men to take their virgin daughters for themselves.

7. **True or False**—According to all the verses, Jehovah's statement is that his covenant is everlasting. However, in actuality, Jehovah turns against these people, delivering them into the hands of their enemies permanently before making his grand exit. Thus biblically speaking the answer is true; however in reality it is false.

8. **True or False**—This depends on whether you take Paul's point of view or Jesus'. Paul did away with the law. Jesus states that until heaven or earth pass away nothing shall pass away from the law. (See Matthew 5:18.)

9. **Same As #8.**

10. **True**—See the chapter "Origins of Christianity."

11. **True**—God had an Israelite man stoned to death for picking up sticks on the Sabbath. See the chapter discussing the god of the Hebrews for explicit details.

12. **False**—It was mentioned in the Bible that Solomon was a very wise king, but if we analyze the actions of Solomon one would see him as a foolish king. Some of his foolish

acts were the marriage of over 300 wives solely for the purpose of political propaganda; his orgy in his "god's" temple also was gravely unwise due to the wrath he knew that would come upon the people. Using common sense we know that Solomon could not have possibly pleased all these women.

13. **True**—See the chapter discussing the god of the Old Testament.

14. **False**—Jesus sent his disciples to the lost sheep of Israel only and specifically told them not to go to the Gentiles. Although there is a second piece of information in the Bible that begins "For God so loved the world . . ." this section of scripture is the only one which, when taken literally, makes sound Christian doctrine. However, once you really know the Hebrew God, then you will know beyond all doubt that the only answer close to Hebrew (Jewish) practice is the practice of *isolation from the world.* Also, to choose to recognize a few verses in support of your belief over the majority is not considered sound judgment. Without doubt, for every one verse in which Jesus states that he came for the world, I can give three that state that either God or his Son came for the Israelites *exclusively.* Neither biblical Israel, nor her god, would ever include the world in its culture except to consume it! The proof of this statement lies inside the text of this book.

15. **False**—Moses was a Levite, not of the tribe of Judah (or the Jews).

16. **False**—The god of the Old Testament had a man killed for picking up sticks on the Sabbath. Jesus justified his disciple's action of picking corn on the Sabbath. The Old Testament god said an eye for an eye and a tooth for a tooth; but Jesus requires forgiveness instead of pay-back. The Old Testament gives provisions for which a man may divorce his wife, but Jesus was against this teaching.

17. **False**—The god of the Old Testament had a personal agenda to destroy all of mankind, including the Israelites. Jesus came to save the lost Israelites from the lies of Baal and the god of the Old Testament. Paul, on the other hand, had a totally different agenda from either Jesus or the god of the Old Testament.

18. **False**—Job in the Old Testament offered sacrifices to a higher god than Yahweh of the Old Testament to seek forgiveness for the possibility that his sons may have blessed Yahweh. Therefore, clearly Job was against the worship of Yahweh. According to the Bible, Job was against blessing Yahweh and offered a sacrifice to God in case his sons had blessed Yahweh. Proof of this fact is in this book, guaranteed or your money back!

19. **True**—Jesus refused to help a Greek woman because she was of another race. He compared her to a dog, and the Israelites are compared to children. He states that it is not good to give the food (teachings and healings) meant for the children (Israel) to dogs (other races, the case in mention were Greek).

20. **True**

*A score of 17 to 20* answers right means that you are not only knowledgeable about the Bible, but also very wise. You are able to give the acts and deeds more value than mere words alone. You have a very open mind to seeing the world as it is and not as you wish it to be.

*A score of 10 to 16* means that you are knowledgeable about the Bible, but somewhat lacking in the wisdom of giving the acts and deeds a higher priority than talk alone. You have a moderately open mind for investigating total situations that are given. You will certainly benefit from the information contained in this book.

*A score of 5 to 9* tends to show that you have average to below average Bible knowledge. You tend to have very little open-mindedness. You will take for granted whatever is told to you about the Bible and may care less about researching the evidence for yourself. You will tend to believe that you know much about the Bible when in fact the opposite is true. If you don't believe one way or the other about the Bible, then this test is invalid for you. If you have not based your faith on the Bible, then you may be open-minded with little Bible knowledge.

*A **score less than 5*** shows that you may or may not be easily persuaded by the thoughts and beliefs of others. If you believe that the Bible contains ***all*** the necessary information to acquire a close walk with God, then you may also tend to be immoral and lacking in spirituality. (Parts of the Bible teach racism, hate, rape, murder etc.) Without doubt, you do not live a reality of what you actually believe your stance to be if you are not immoral. If you do not kill a person who you know breaks the Sabbath day, then you do not follow the Old Testament orders, and thus only believe in part of what the god of the Hebrews requires.

---

If you received a score of 17 or above, then you may wish to skip the chapters regarding the Bible and the origins of Christianity. It would appear that you already have an excellent background on this information. You may choose to simply browse through some of the ideas presented in later chapters.

---

# ONE

## The Origin
## of the Holy Bible

### Did the Creator Authorize the Bible?

Until about five years ago, I did not have the slightest desire to ponder the question (Did the creator authorize the Bible?) in my mind, and, moreover, I couldn't have formed my lips to even speak the question aloud. How do you know that God gave us the Bible? The answer was ALWAYS clear and without doubt. I accepted as fact that God would not give us the Bible in error. Like so many others, I knew that there was no other way possible, because we were taught that the Bible was the only creditable source of God from childhood up, and we knew that it felt right. When someone would say, "Were you there?" or "Did you see the making of the Bible?" it would feel like an insult because we all know that none of us were there.

Nonetheless, to base your entire faith in a book as God's word solely because "it feels right," "it says many things that feel right," and "this is the way we were taught for generations" is by far more ludicrous than the question, "Were we there?" Every soul on the planet will agree that the current physical bodies we now possess were not present when the Bible was written. You will learn that the Bible also says many things that do NOT FEEL GOOD NOR ARE THEY RIGHT!

Many of us would say that our religion is the best thing for our souls, but mean in our hearts to say that our relationship with God is best for our souls. These two statements are vastly different. We can choose any religion on earth and, as long as we connect to the Creator, have an absolutely wonderful and meaningful relationship with God. However, when we give our hearts to a religion, we must constantly defend and justify our beliefs when contradictions occur within our doctrines. We will not care how stupid or how impossible our belief system sounds. We will justify it with faith. We will instruct our fellow believers and our children never to listen to what any other religion has to say, for others may confuse them and lead them to the devil or hell. In a religion, same as in a cult, one must continually keep the faith and avoid listening to any contrary information outside the cult/religious belief systems, such as the information in this book.

Humans should seek to remember their spiritual origins more than their religious beliefs, because spirituality includes the entire human race or unites us as one, the act that Satan (our enemy) despises. Satan has taught us that unity is evil. When we are in a true relationship with God all humans can come together and say that there is a Supreme Being greater than the physical self. However, if indeed our relationship to God is our first priority, it should be well worth our time to investigate all religions or beliefs claiming to know God. Then we will know that we are equipped with all the information available to us, to structure our belief systems more on actual evidence, instead of hopes and beliefs.

The greatest mystery of the Bible begins with the general acceptance of its authenticity as "God's words" without true intense research by believers into its history, and the history of the people who wrote it. How many have heard of the *Enuma Elish*? How many of us know of the Sumerian people (according to the Bible, they were perhaps the people of Shinar) or of their cuneiform language of symbols and wedges? Their cuneiform language and its appearance are unimportant to anyone not searching for the ultimate truth. However, those of us who are searching for truth must develop an understanding of the languages, cultures, political stances, and belief systems which the ancient people who wrote the scriptures practiced. More important, that biblical history should be investigated, knowing that the entire basis of the Bible as *"God's word"* stems from the so-called "chosen people" or "God's people," who we believe were given the authority directly from GOD. If we choose to believe that the Bible is God's word, and that the Israelite people are His chosen, then we must study their origins without bias to obtain the highest truth possible. We must research these people to prove to ourselves that there is absolutely no conflicting evidence on which we base our belief. It should be noted that Christianity, Islam, and Judaism do not even exist without the Hebrew God of Abraham, Isaac, and Jacob.

## The Derivation of the Bible

Our first exploration will begin with the Bible. According to the *Webster's New Universal Unabridged Dictionary*, the word "Bible" stems from the Greek language. The Israelite language was Hebrew. The word "Bible" in Greek stems from the word *biblio-* or *biblion*. It is a fact that all modern languages stem from a predecessor language. What is the predecessor of the Greek language? Could it be the Babylonian or Phoenician language? Let's look at the similarities. Bible or Babel . . . Biblion or Babylon. In the Phoenician language the word "Babel" for a book would have been chosen to name a book of confusion. If you look up "Babel" in Hebrew it means confusion. How many times do you hear the excuses, "Oh, the Bible is too complicated to fully and completely understand"? We so quickly shelter our beliefs in the Bible through justifying statements such as: "The Bible was not meant for everyone to understand," and "God hid many secrets so that only His elect would be able to decipher the truth." If the latter be the truth, then without doubt not one person shall be the elect of

God for no one who is true to herself will state assuredly that she knows everything in the Bible. And then there is my personal favorite: "God will help us understand it better by and by." This is another one of the major reasons that I have been led to write this book. I would like to end much of the confusion.

The Hebrew Israelites were in complete destitution and hard bondage. They were starving and just about as low as a community of people could conceivably go. They had been in prayer and meditation for a god that would deliver them from their suffering. Now imagine a being cloaked in light all around saying, "I am thy God, I have come to deliver thee." Do you think that the Israelites in that state would demand proof so as not to be deceived by the devil? Do you think that they would hesitate and say "No, not until we see more than mere tricks, that you are the creator God of the Universe"? For example, the God of the Universe could have delivered Israel from Egypt in harmony and in peace, but a deliverance from any other force would have been chaotic and caused the Egyptians resentment.

In the days of the Israelites each nation had its own individual culture and gods of worship. For the most part, tradition had been tolerant for all nations to be at peace and tolerant of one another's belief systems. For example, in pre-Israelite existence, when a man married a foreign woman she was permitted to bring her gods with her. This was the tradition of the lands, which is one of the reasons why the God of Israel banned foreign marriages.

Contrary to the story told in the Bible of only Abraham's father, Terah, being a worshiper of many gods, so was it true also with Father Abraham himself, Job, Noah, all three sons of Noah, and so forth. Later chapters will give insight into this statement. Originally, from as far back as Adam in the Bible and "Adapa" in the Babylonian scriptures predating the Bible, the gods have manipulated mankind like marionettes, every which way except close to the Creator of his soul. Many ancient civilizations recorded the epics of creation as it appeared to their people.

## CHRONOLOGY OF ANCIENT LANGUAGES

**Group I—Sumerians and African India.** Possessed the first known written communication: *Cuneiform* (Mesopotamian area, "the cradle of civilization") and *Sanskrit* (India, recorded in Hindu religion dating over two million years old). Were the first writings according to history, generally documented at around 5000-3000 B.C.

**Group II—Egyptian, Phoenician-Canaanite, Chinese, Ethiopian, Hattic, Assyrian, Babylonian, Akkadian, etc.** First writings recorded as dating sometime around 4000-2400 B.C. This group may have initiated the alphabet.

**Group III—Aramaic, Hebraic, Hittite, Early Greek.** (The beginning of the end of the black man in authoritative power. The black man becomes more and more barbaric with his traditions and laws, yet he is accepted as civilized.)—First writings around 2400-1500 B.C. The period of the so-called beginning of the dark ages of mankind. Prior to this period the humans were known to be more than mere humans: **THEY WERE GODS**.

**Group IV—Arabic, Later Greek, Latin, Scandinavian, etc.** (The beginning of the white man ruling the planet, which signifies the end of the DARK AGES (the age in which blacks {dark-skinned people} ruled the earth unscrupulously.) Dated around 1200-800 B.C.

**Group V—Roman, French, German, Spanish, English, etc.** The age of invention; perhaps toward the end of this age we will return to our original state of peace and harmony.

Note: Some of the above languages overlap from group to group.

The story of a sole survivor of a flood was told by many different nations, some were predating the Bible. The religion of monotheism (the worship of one god as the sole Creator Deity) was relatively new, relative to the period of time that man has been in existence.

### The Bible Is A "Copycat," Not God's Word

How do we know for a fact which nationality or culture predates which? The first clue or evidence that can be taken with surety is the language of the documents. For example, we know without doubt that Hebrews wrote the books of the Old Testament Bible in the Hebrew language for the most part and the book of Daniel in Aramaic. The New Testament was first written in Aramaic and Greek. Languages that predate Hebrew by far are the cuneiform and Sanskrit languages. If tablets were written in these languages, we determine the close proximity of the age of the writings based on that era. Moreover, added accuracy in calculating age comes with the use of modern technology—carbon dating. Take a trip to your local library and verify whether or not these statements are true. Look up dates for the oldest written languages and you are guaranteed to find that Hebrew is not the oldest of nationalities or languages. (See the chart on page 16.)

Why is this information important to know? Because many religions will teach that they are the oldest on the planet when in fact they are relatively very new in comparison with the human race. Today's Christianity is one of the newest religions practiced on the planet. The reason why it is important to know when incidents occur is because we are trying to establish the highest truth. Seeing that the *Enuma Elish* and Sumerian epics predate the Bible by far, shouldn't we hear the testimony of these people? It is true that some of the clay tablets weren't discovered until after 1903, long after our religions were well grounded and established, but is that an excuse not to know what was said before the Bible?

The Bible contains information handed down from an earlier

period. It appears that the Sumerians had the original creation story, which was adapted and altered by the Assyro-Babylonians, which was adapted and altered by the Canaanites/Phoenicians, which was adapted and altered by the Hebrews/Arabians, which was adapted and altered by the Greeks, which was adapted and altered by the Romans (Latin), which was adapted and altered by us (the English-speaking nations) and still others. Now we call it an authoritative writing from God even though the Hebrews themselves did not revere the scriptures as such. Just as we today would appreciate the book, *Conversations with God*, by Neale Donald Walsch, who adamantly testifies that he is talking with God, so is the way that the nation of Israel revered the writings of the Bible. The people who originally wrote the creation epics before the Hebrews never called these scrolls (which simply contained information copied from earlier clay tablets and adapted into Hebrew culture) the word of God. The Bible as we have it today was a myth taken from an earlier source and used to validate the Israelite god as God almighty.

How can we be certain of this statement? There is but one way to know for certain that the Bible is a copycat of an earlier period and that is to read the stories told before the Bible. Read the accounts told by the Sumerians. The Sumerians, Babylonians, Assyrians, Canaanites, and Phoenicians all told the same stories that we read now in the Bible, a slightly altered version of the original epic. The primary alteration lists Yahweh as the sole deity who did the things that were written earlier as done by gods called Anu, Ishtar, Enlil, Enki, Shamash, Marduk, and many others. In the Bible the original Sumerian name of God changes from Anu into Ea (Babylonian)/El (Canaan), transferred into Yahweh (Hebrew). Furthermore, the name of the god Enlil/Marduk (the enemy of humans—Satan) transferred into Baal (Canaan) transferred into Yahweh also. El was the benevolent god whose mercy endureth forever, and Baal was the god of destruction, jealousy, and vengeance; both of these gods became known to the Hebrews as

Yahweh as they broke up into factions. Some worshipped the Creator as El (Yahweh) and others worshipped the Creator as Baal (Yahweh), but neither of these gods was God. Note that the word "myth" from the Greek language did not mean false as we take it to mean in English. The word myth actually meant stories. Therefore, when we read about creation myths we are reading about creation stories. A myth, just like any other story, can be either true or false. It is of the utmost importance for us to read the accounts predating the Bible that we may not err. This is the only way that we can begin to see that man fabricated the Hebrew myth as God's word. Read the "Bible" predating the Bible. Read the Sumerian epic of creation and the Babylonian epic of creation, and the Canaanite epic of creation. Note the similarities and differences. *Use your common sense.*

## Translations of the Bible

Given the translations that the Bible has undergone, it is reasonable to assume that the Bible of today cannot perfectly be the same message of the original people. The original Hebrew scrolls appear to have been found as early as the third century B.C. and pieced together by seventy-two scholars. The patchwork became known as the Septuagint, the Latin word for seventy. These scholars never professed to be divinely inspired nor at that time was their work taken by the masses to be divinely inspired.

Over time, legends grew into a story of a miraculous divinely translated work. It was said that seventy individuals worked separately and all came up with the exact same translation from Hebrew into Greek. The average Christian has never heard the reason why they simply accepted the translations as God's words. I believe that the original people believed the legend and the modern people today could not care less how the Bible became "God's word." Most Christians were simply told it was God's word and accepted it as truth.

The books originally were separate and written in a different order than the version we have today. In the making of the Septuagint, the Ptolemy of Philadelphia, by the name of Demetrius, sent for the Jewish scholars to come to Alexandria for the purpose of broadening the selection of literature in their library. These scholars decided what order would be the best presentation of the Bible and compiled it into one book instead of the sixty-six separate writings. The translators (the seventy-two scholars) also decided which **scrolls to exclude** as God's word and which they would deem worthy of inclusion in the Bible as we have it today. Yes, people who have never been deemed authorities on God's word *have removed and added books* as they desired and saw fit. If you truly read the Bible as a scholar, instead of being spoon-fed by the preacher, you will find that many Bible verses direct you to OTHER BOOKS THAT WERE LEFT OUT OF THE BIBLE. I will list a few of them here:

1. **The Book of Wars of Yahweh.** This book may attempt to prove Yahweh's barbaric behavior far more than any of us would have ever imagined. Therefore the original translators had to get rid of it. I would imagine that the original book would have revealed man's strife against Yahweh. Numbers 21:14.

2. **The Book of Shemaiah.** Unknown reason for throwing it out. II Chronicles 12:15.

3. **The Book of Remembrance.** This book would most likely teach about reincarnation. The church had decided that the barbaric attitude of the people would be encouraged if they believed in reincarnation for they could do whatever they wanted and get a second chance in the next life. The church wanted people to believe that their sin would disconnect them from God and cause them to burn in hell forever. Malachi 3:16.

4. **The Book of Jehu.** Unknown reason for throwing it out. II Chronicles 20:34.

Not only were books added and taken away, but entire meanings that were not acceptable to translators were changed, softened in severity, or deleted/added to suit the beliefs of the translator. So this is the first translation of the Hebrew Old Testament into Greek, the Septuagint.

The next translation occurred in Rome. Commissioned by the pope, Jerome set forth to prepare the Latin version of the Greek Old and New Testament. The first Latin version was later revised, with many alterations to the original meanings of the Bible. The next translator would be John Wycliffe, who is credited with the first English Bible. This Bible was expensive and prepared for only the elite. William Tyndale sought to prepare a translation for commoners. The personal belief system of Tyndale was that "*men were better off without God's law and should substitute the Pope's law in its stead.*" This shows that the Old Testament (the law) was done away with through Christianity ("the Pope's law"). The Bible would be translated over and over and over again before the development of the authorized King James Version of the Bible in 1611. This is the widely accepted English version. Many later versions have been developed, just as all previous versions, by the desecration of man and as man saw fit. Some names of various versions of the Bible are the Good News Bible, The Jerusalem Bible, American Standard Bible, New American Bible, New International Bible, Revised Standard Version of the Bible, and The Living Bible, just to name a few.

## King James

The average Christian today would not have accepted King James I of England as a born-again Christian had they known of his personal reputation. King James was born to a father suffering of a disease most widely accepted as syphilis. His mother, Mary Queen of Scots, was considered a harlot and suspected of her husband Henry Stuart's death. The paternity of King James raised grave doubts about his parentage among the subjects. James' father suspected his wife of being unfaithful with a man called Darnely. Queen Mary refused to marry Darnely and was again accused of affairs with her cousin, and her secretary, David Riccio, who was murdered.

James Stuart was orphaned as an infant. With his father dead, and his mother imprisoned, signing away all her rights to be queen, James was left with a strict, shrewd relative, the Earl of Mar. Any mistake that James made was quickly blamed on the bad blood in his veins.

As James grew into young adulthood, he found little love and compassion from his guardians. Although he received all physical, material, and mental things necessary to develop into young adulthood he lacked the emotional comfort of warm, compassionate, loving parents. He was mentally challenged with the best education of that era. But, as with all children who are raised without love, our beloved King James developed a severe emotional imbalance. He never acknowledged his mother publicly, despite the fact that she had written him in hopes of support. When the days of Queen Mary were numbered due to her enemies among the nobles, King James offered no public support whatsoever for his mother for fear of losing popularity with the Queen of England, who hated his mother. He silently stood by for the execution of his mother to be fulfilled. King James found popularity, indeed, for this act of denial.

King James was reported to have delved into witchcraft and demonology with sincerity all throughout his life. He had taken a fancy to studying the occult and at some point it appears that the king discovered a plot against his life through the use of witchcraft.

King James did not like the idea of feminine company because in his upbringing it was imbedded into his mind that women were worth just about as much as two dead flies. He felt that they were brainless and that men seemed to have by far much more to offer in communication and social activity. Nonetheless, the issue of offspring forced him to marry Anne, the fourteen-year-old daughter of the King of Denmark. James' marriage to his young bride could do little to replace the strong desire within himself for a man. King James' homosexual tendencies became public knowledge in his affair with Robert Carr. It was reported that King James fell head over tail in love with Carr after he had suffered a broken leg in a tournament. King James was seen in public romantically fondling, pinching, hugging, and kissing his male favorites. Did he have sex with them? Again, common sense must prevail. Let's ask ourselves how many people we know in a long-lasting relationship having the above behavior without sex?

An excellent book of information on King James is *King James VI of Scotland—I of England* by Antonia Fraser, published by Alfred A. Knopf, Inc. Other additional reading for this chapter:

1. *The English Bibles From KJV to NIV, A History and Evaluation,* by Jack P. Lewis, Baker Book House Company
2. *The Interpreter's Bible, A Commentary in Twelve Volumes,* Volume 1, Abingdon Press
3. *The Anchor Bible Dictionary,* Volume 4, Doubleday (Look up languages.)
4. *Before Writing, Volume I, From Counting to Cuneiform,* by Denise Schmandt-Besserat, The University of Texas Press
5. *Reading the Past, Ancient Writing from Cuneiform to the Alphabet,* by J. T. Hooker, Barnes and Noble
6. *Is It God's Word?* by Joseph Wheless, Kessinger Publishing Company

# TWO

# Who Was the
# God of Israel?

## Introduction of the Name Yahweh

In order to grasp the concept of Hebrew thought in the Old Testament, one must first acquire the primary information missing from the original Hebrew text—that is, the name of their god. First of all, I would like to clarify that the name of Yahweh was purposely removed from the King James Version of the Bible. The name originally appeared over and over in the Hebraic text as a revelation of how important and powerful the name would be to the Israelites, but in the King James Version god's name was removed and now appears as the capital letters "the LORD." I counted the name of god, Yahweh (Jehovah) in the original text from the Strong's Concordance. It appears by far over 6,000 times, and not once does the name appear in the New Testament. In fact, the god of the New Testament is totally nameless. He is referred to as God and Lord only. Why would an All Knowing God make His name so important that it appears far over 6,000 times in the Old Testament, and then that same deity is later represented nameless in the New Testament? Hint for the wise. Is the god of the Old Testament and the god of the New Testament the same god? We will discuss this further in later chapters, but give it some serious thought. If you want the full understanding of what was being said in Hebrew always substitute the name Yahweh for "the LORD" wherever you see it in the Old Testament. In Hebrew there is no need to write the vowels so the name of god in Hebrew looks somewhat like this:

How ironic it is that so many of us feel that we know God, but have never seen what the name of the god we worship looks like. Those four letters as you see them are called the Tetragrammaton. In English they correctly look like YHWH. However, due to European influence you will also find it as YHVH and JHVH (Jehovah). The YHVH comes from the Yiddish influence on the Hebrew language. Yiddish combines the Hebrew and German languages. (Have you ever noticed how a German pronounces Volkswagen? They say, "Folksvagen." Germans pronounce their W's with a "V" sound. For example, *Was ist das* is German for "what is that," {in German pronounced "**v**as ist das."} This explains the change from YH**W**H to YHVH. Ok, enough of the German lesson.)

Once we really begin to decipher the Bible we find that the Old Testament god was called by various names and titles, including *El Shaddai* (God almighty), *Eloah*, *Elah/Allah*, *El*, *Adonai* (Lord), *Elohim* (Gods), and *Ayil*. According to Islam, Christianity, and Judaism, all these names represent one deity whose name is Yahweh/Allah. The New Testament refers to God as *Kurios*, and *Theos*, Greek words for God. We are familiar with the Greek word "theology," meaning the study of God. All these names can be found in the Strong's Concordance for the King James Version of the Bible.

## A Racist God

The Old Testament of the King James Version of the Bible leads its readers to believe that God "Yahweh" chose one nation of people to be His chosen people above all the other people of the earth. In Amos 3:1-2 the god of Israel is talking to the Israelites, "*Hear this word that Yahweh hath spoken against you, O children of Israel, against the whole family which I brought up from the land of Egypt, saying, **you only have I known of all the families of the Earth.***" What happens to all the other races of the planet? Clearly god is showing himself to be a racist. The race of people that this god recognizes is Israel only. A racist loves one particular race, usually his own, and finds his own race superior, yet all others inferior. What of all the billions of people before Israel? Did they all go to hell? According to archeological findings the Hebrew Israelite nation in comparison to all the nations prior is very new and, comparatively speaking, not ancient at all. Deuteronomy 7:6-8 states, "*For* (you) *are a holy people unto Yahweh* your (Israelite) *God: Yahweh* your *God has chosen you to be a special people unto himself, **above all people** that are upon the face of the Earth. Yahweh did not set his love upon you nor choose you, because you were more in number than any people: for you were the fewest of all people: But because Yahweh loved you, and because he would keep the oath **which he had sworn unto your fathers**.*" However in Deuteronomy 5:3, we find that Yahweh states that he did **not** make this covenant with Israel's fathers. Did you catch the contradiction? Deuteronomy 7:14 states, "*you shall be **blessed above all people;** there shall not be male or female barren among you, or among your cattle.*" This is racism at its best. Yahweh is promising to bless Israel above all nations, but there is much more going on than meets the eye. Notice that Yahweh seems as if he has to suck up to Israel and literally bribe the Israelites into doing as he wishes. Yahweh is telling the Israelites that they are going to have it all far better than any other race. I can imagine in my mind the Israelites, cheering . . . "Ehh, Yahweh, you be da man, You got it

— 26 —

going on, bro." Now put yourself into the shoes of the Israelites. Remember that Yahweh was face to face with Jacob (Genesis 32:30) and Moses (Exodus 33:11). Here, Yahweh talks to Moses *as a man talks to his friend*! The Bible emphasizes how important it is that we know that god is literally talking face to face. But what we should question is whether or not we believe that it is possible for a true Creator of the entire Universe to sit face to face with a man. Moreover, the entire Israelite congregation is with god face to face (Deuteronomy 5:4). Numbers 14:14 states, "*And they will tell it unto the inhabitants of this land: for they have heard that you **Yahweh are among the people**, that you Yahweh are **seen face to face**, and that your cloud stands over them, and that you go before Israel, by daytime in a pillar of a cloud and in a pillar of fire by night.*" Here, the Israelites are describing Yahweh's spaceship, but we will discuss this more later. Moses is interceding for Israel's continuous rebellion against Yahweh as their god. Yahweh was within minutes of pushing the button to give Israel the same fate as Sodom and Gomorrah, a nuclear blast. On the other hand, the Bible clearly tells us that **no man has seen god at any time!** See I John 4:12.

Now, as I stated earlier, to decipher this text you must use just a little common sense and place yourself in the actual situation place in Israel. Let's imagine ourselves in this situation. We have a god telling us that he is the Supreme one and only Creator God. He has supposedly exclusively rescued us from bondage while placing pestilence, fire, plague, death, and more on our enemies. Above all, we literally see Him face to face. I want you to feel this story as if you are really a Hebrew experiencing God, I mean Gaaaaaaaawd, Great GOD working all of these miracles right before your very eyes. These miracles are nothing like the miracles we pray for today, "trust, and have faith, type deals." According to the Bible, God personally reveals himself to the Israelites and manifests great miracles, powers, and wonders. Don't count physical healings or a blessing of money here, which are today's great miracles of God. We are talking the Red Sea opening, and every firstborn of a nation dropping dead just for your religion/nation, **a manifestation to other nations of God's power,** not by faith, but by GOD Himself. How many of us, don't be shy to speak up, ministers, have had this type of relationship with God? NONE OF US! No, not one! Even though none have seen god many remain faithful to him, but think about it. If you had sat face to face with God and seen all the wonders prophesied in the plagues against Egypt (see Exodus 7, 8, 9, and 10), can you imagine forsaking God and preferring a cow made of gold instead because one man (Moses), the leader, disappears for forty days? Common sense knows that something stinks here. I can hear it now, "Yeah, those stupid Israelites, they were about as ignorant as they come." If we want to blame the Israelites, then god still is at fault for choosing such a retarded, non-conforming (according to the Bible, Israel is continuously turning against god) people. They would witness this magnificent display of power only to turn traitor at a mere snap of the fingers and worship a cow of stone. The fact that we know that no race can claim this type of relationship with God, nor has any other nation seen this famous god who talks face to face with his chosen people today, makes it questionable as to whether this god is God. Please note that I am stating that this one fact makes it questionable: we have only touched the surface of the issues at hand. Automatically, we can conclude beyond a shadow of a doubt that something is happening differently in ancient times than can possibly occur today, assuming that the Bible is reasonably accurate in its accounts of ancient Israel.

Further accounts of racism executed by the black god Yahweh can be found in Deuteronomy 26:17-19, *"Thou hast avouched Yahweh this day to be thy God, and to walk in his ways, and to walk in his ways, and to keep his statutes, and his commandments, and his judgments, and to hearken unto his voice: And Yahweh hath avouched thee this day to be his peculiar people, as he hath promised thee, and that thou shouldest keep all his commandments; And to make* **thee high above all the nations which he hath made, in praise, and in name, and in honor; and that thou mayest be a holy people unto Yahweh thy God as he hath spoken.**" It is clear here that a marriage-like ceremony is taking place between Israel and its god. This would have been a great day for Israel, considering that many gods were among man in those days and were fighting wars and blowing away entire races with one nuclear blast with no regard for innocent life. If we examine the word "avouch" we can determine that this relationship between Yahweh and Israel was not a one-way street in the beginning where Yahweh chooses Israel, but that there was a requirement in this ceremony for Israel also to choose Yahweh. Israel vouches that Yahweh is their choice of representation before the nations and likewise so does Yahweh choose Israel. Yahweh agrees to make Israel a great people and Israel swears to be loyal to him. This is a recording of an event similar to the electoral vote for presidency, but in this case it is for Yahweh as the god of the Hebrews. In the end (Yahweh) Yah claims that Israel doesn't uphold its end of the bargain because it turned to other gods for help.

But my question is if he was keeping up his end of the bargain why would Israel turn to other gods? They would have everything they needed within Yah. Is it remotely possible that perhaps Israel as a people realized that they had signed up with the devil (Baal) himself? Could they have on their own decided that it is not nice to go around killing people, especially innocent babies as Jehovah commanded them to do? Maybe they realized that it was not so very nice or godlike to covet (be jealous of) their neighbor's (Canaan's) property. What if it were those ridiculous laws that Yah made up to force Israel into killing one another over the most trivial incidents? Whatever the case may be, the Israelites must have in their hearts decided that Yah was not god enough for them as a people. Yet, now many people are eagerly ready to sign Yahweh up just like that. They have all agreed to avouch for him without ever knowing who he really is and how much he hated all humanity. He was only using Israel as a tool for ancient ethnic cleansing and many of the Israelites got smart and saw through his personal agenda.

Yahweh throughout the Bible swears allegiance with Israel as his only people. It is always Israel that will be above every other race; no wonder there is anti-Semitism. If the world were to believe all of this garbage that Yah was trying to hand down, that is, that my people, ancient Israel, were above every one else, why wouldn't they be justified in the desire to wipe my race off the face of the earth? It would stand to reason that perhaps then, god would have to bring forth another race of superiority. Perhaps the German race? Do you see what the Bible's god teaches the human race? Of course, Christianity totally changes the ideas and desires that Yah has for his people, and drafts Christians in through the redirection of Yah's intention. So it may be hard for them to truly feel the god of the Hebrews' nature, giving rise to an infectious disease of racism on the human race. After all, where does the Ku Klux Klan justify most all their beliefs? It is all there in the Old Testament of the King James Version of the Bible.

Let's continue with this racism issue. In Deuteronomy 28:1 and Hosea 4:6 we have more examples of god showing his true racist self, not very much like God. *"And it shall come to pass, if thou shalt hearken diligently unto the voice of Yahweh thy God, to observe and to do all his commandments which I command thee this day, that Yahweh thy God will set thee **on high above all nations of the Earth.**"* Again Yahweh is trying to drill it into Israel that they are superior to all other races, but only, of course, because gaaaawd says so.

In Hosea, god pouts like a big baby, saying his people are destroyed for the lack of knowledge. He continues on to say that since his people have rejected knowledge he would in return reject them. In other words, it is just like a father acting like an over-grown kid pouting to his son, and saying, "Since you don't want to play my way" sniffle, sniffle, "I ain't gonna play with you no more. Furthermore, since you have forgotten me, I'm gonna forget you, too." Come on, god, GROW UP! Mere humans have sense enough to know that you don't treat your children like that. If he had acted like a God maybe he would have been treated like God. Yah should have realized that Israel wasn't going to buy that bologna for long. God continually boasts of how he recognized Israel alone, but through the Israelites' travel back and forth to Ethiopia and Egypt, individuals would eventually find out that god spoke the most incredible untruths to Israel. He did not only know Israel as his people, for he went to Egypt and gave them that self-same jive turkey line—"Egypt, you my peeps." See Isaiah 19:25, which states, *"Whom Yahweh of host shall bless, saying blessed be **Egypt my people** and Assyria the work of my hands, and Israel mine inheritance."* Clearly this god is not devoted to one race or, at least, let's say that his people here are clearly the Egyptians. Israel is mentioned a distant third place on god's list of nations. Why? What's happening here to this Israelite, (can't make up his mind) Egyptian, Assyrian god? This is a clear example of several gods (to name two, El and Baal) manifesting themselves in scripture. El loved all the humans and did not want to see any die or suffer in any way. Baal hated humans and sought their destruction any way he could find it. The upcoming chapters will shed a little light on this subject. More than likely here, where Egypt is shown compassion, and in the passage Amos 9:7, where the Ethiopians are shown compassion by pleading with Israel to accept the Ethiopian race as their own, we can assume these passages to contain El's influence. For Baal had taught the Israelites to hate all other nations, just like the KKK. As stated before, the KKK is one of the most accurate worshippers of the Hebrew god's religion.

## Blessing Yahweh (God?) Is a Sin

In those days, many gods walked on the earth; they were seeking the souls of mankind to possess them as their own for the next world or "heaven." They began enslaving mankind to worship them. A good reference for this point can be found in the *Oahspe,*

*A New Bible in the Words of Jehovah and His Angel Ambassadors.* This Bible proclaims to consist of a sacred history of the dominions of the higher and lower heavens on the earth for the past twenty-four thousand years. These gods were not the Creator, but they did play a vast role in the physical existence of humans today. These gods used the earth as their playground and mankind as their toys. They played us (humans) like a piano, and we fell hook, line, and sinker for all of their folly.

Both Isaiah and Job offer some insight into the deceit planned by these gods. Isaiah 14:12-16 states that there would be a god who pretends to be God, who will say, *"I will be like the most high."* But the prophesy continues on to say that those who look up to this god in the end will say is this the **man** that caused all the confusion and division of all the nationalities. It appears that the god who visited Israel was an impostor of the Supreme Creator, and there is far more evidence that the Old Testament god was an impostor than there is to support that he was the Creator. If, and only if, we read the Bible and apply II Timothy 2:15, which requires that we properly divide the word of truth, then we can expose the trickster impostor who deceived the nations. The word of truth was considered to be the scriptures or the Bible. In other words, clearly here the Bible is telling you that you are required to divide out the truth. How do we properly divide the word of truth? The answer is to find out what is true and what is false in this so-called *"word of truth."* This brings us to information that I will share with you in a light that I have never seen in writing before.

The original Bible (before translations), in the book of Job, clearly states that it was considered a sin to worship the god of the Old Testament. Job 1:5: *"And it was so, when the days of their feasting were gone about, that Job sent and sanctified them, and offered burnt offering according to the number of them all: for Job said, It may be that my sons have sinned and cursed* (**blessed**) *God in their hearts. This did Job continuously."*

Here it will become clear that Job did not want his sons worshipping god or Elohim. The *Enuma Elish* predates the Bible and is a copycat of a still earlier Sumerian version of the creation epic. In the *Enuma Elish* this same god Jehovah, then by the name of Marduk, decides that he will take on the personality of all the gods and he will become the God of the gods, just as Yahweh did. In this text, as you will learn later, all the gods submit and agree to allow Marduk to reign supreme as God over all the gods, just as Yahweh did.

Job knew of Marduk's desires to reign as the creator god who was in actuality Ea/Enki in the more ancient text. Job knew that Marduk hated humans just as much as his uncle Enlil did and the only way they wanted to see humans were as slaves for their personal greed and corruption. (Enlil is mentioned in the Hebrew Bible as Satan or adversary. Look up Ellil/Enlil in the Hebrew concordance.) Enlil was the Jehovah in the garden asking Adam and Eve who had told them that they were naked. On the other hand, Ea wanted to see humanity uplifted. In the most ancient text it is Ea who helps man (Noah) escape the flood and it is Enlil who wants man destroyed. In the Bible it is God almighty who saves Noah and it is God almighty who wants to see man destroyed. In the ancient text it is Ea who creates the first man and takes him to his father, Anu, to receive immortality. However, man is tricked out of it. According to the Bible it was a sin to eat from the tree of knowledge of good and evil, and the serpent tricks Adam and Eve into doing wrong. Genesis 2:17 states, *"But of the tree of the knowledge of good and evil, thou shalt not eat of it: for in the day you eat thereof you will surely die."* WHY?

Again, I am requesting the use of our common sense: What is wrong with knowledge? I will tell you what is wrong with it. Through knowledge man can liberate his soul from the forces of self-created hell. But if man is liberated will he remain enslaved to the gods? No he never will, for he will learn the true divinity within. Job felt indebted to Ea/Yahweh in the same way that we are indebted to our parents. Ea/Yahweh was apparently the God that Job worshipped and served. Job was blessed immensely with the help of Ea/Yahweh and great knowledge until Marduk/Baal/ and Enlil/Satan noticed how perfectly Job served Ea/Yahweh. They became jealous and Enlil/Satan dropped some agitating remarks in Marduk's/Yahweh's ears by explaining that, yes, Ea/Yahweh is getting all the praise and glory. After all, look at how Ea has blessed him with all the riches of the earth; but if you take all that he has, he will begin blessing (worshipping) you. Once you know the story of these gods of old times you can just about tell who is who by their actions, as you will see in a later chapters. See Job 1:11, *"put forth thine hand* (your hand, Yahweh/Marduk) *now, and touch all that he (Job) has and he (Job) will BLESS YOU to your face."* They were trying to FORCE Job to bless god (Marduk).

The King James Version of the Bible was mistranslated from the original Hebrew text. Ministers will not teach these facts from their pulpits. The Hebrew word "baruch" meaning "bless" was disregarded and the word "curse" was put in its place. You can look this fact up yourself in the *Strong's Concordance* of the Bible. Look up the word curse and you will find the corresponding number representing the Hebrew word of the text. You will find "baruch." Now look up the word for bless in the concordance you will find the **same word "baruch" or bless.** You can also find reference to this information in the *Anchor Bible Dictionary* under Bible, Euphemism and Dysphemism (**substitutions** of vague or harsh statements with harsh or vague statements).

Without a doubt Job did not want his sons blessing Jehovah. On the other hand, Jehovah wanted to find a way to make Job begin to worship him so Jehovah began making good his threats to torture Job. Marduk/Jehovah would continually torture Job by having his sheep and servants destroyed. Job would not bow to Yahweh, so Yahweh had his daughters and sons killed. It gets quite complicated when many personalities takes on the character of one person as has happened in the name of Yahweh. The Hebrew

Israelites, or mistranslation, used Yahweh's name to describe the same actions taken by Ea, Marduk, Enlil, Snake, Serpent, and even Satan. The complicated part is the fact that this impostor hated man and was against his spiritual evolution so he invented the snake and the serpent characters, who I believe to be Ea. Then he made up this ridiculous lie that man may gain anything but knowledge (the tree of knowledge) and unity (the tower of Babel). And we all fell for it! I will explain more in detail later. Let's get back to Job.

Persistently, Job would not bow down to Yahweh even after the curses carried over to his health and he was near the brink of death. I believe that Yahweh/Marduk was using what some new age participants call magic and others may term voodoo on Job. Although Job knew that he was fighting a no-win situation he still would not bow to the mighty magic of Yahweh/Marduk. Surely Ea would come to rescue him. But Ea, being of flesh just like Marduk/Yahweh and Job, had problems of his own to take care of. Even Job's wife saw him there on the brink of death and pleaded with her husband to bless Yahweh. Job refused, accusing her of talking foolish (IT IS FOOLISH TO BLESS JEHOVAH, Job is saying this) and it is in your Bible in Job 2:9! She asks Job to give up his integrity: "*Dost* (do) *thou* (you) *still retain thine* (your) *integrity? Curse* (**bless**) *god and die.*" That word curse again was mistranslated and should be bless. Yahweh /Marduk had tormented Job within inches of his life through the help of Satan/Enlil, yet Job vowed to stay committed to his forefather/creator, Ea.

In the book of Job, Job states that he is concerned that his children may have **sinned and blessed Yahweh.** Reflecting a desperate yearning to be enslaved and loyal to Jehovah, who hated us, the few who are aware of this fact will try to justify this statement by saying it is the same as in English to bless out. They will try to say that it is like when we say a beautiful color TV is bad, meaning the TV is good. There is no way this could be the case if we apply common sense. First of all, in the ancient languages they did not have the play on words like bad meaning good or to bless meaning to curse. One way for the layman to apply a common sense approach to research the word "bless" in Hebrew is to take note that in the Bible you will never find baruch/bless used to mean curse except in the book of Job. Why out of the entire Bible did it appear only in this case that the word bless actually meant curse? BECAUSE JOB WAS A PERFECT AND UPRIGHT MAN WHO HATED EVIL. How can this perfect man not want to worship/bless Yahweh (the God of the Old Testament)? Many in the human race continually bless Yahweh as their god. These verses stand alone in testifying that Yahweh was not the Creator, because a perfect upright man is saying that it is a sin to bless god (Jehovah). If nothing more than hmmmm, we as intelligent beings should now wonder what is going on here, for there is yet much more to come.

## The God of Israel
## Was First the God of Canaan

All around the world, in both ancient times and in the present, man has professed to know or hear the word of the lord. In Canaan, they heard the voice of El and Baal, who were constantly at war with each other. Sound familiar? The difference between the Canaanite religion and the Hebrew religion is that the Canaanites recognize El as the Supreme Creator God, but not as the one and only Creator God. The Canaanite religion had a polytheistic belief system where the Supreme God was El and had a consistent personality that was benevolent, merciful, and loving to humans. Another powerful deity was called Bel/Baal and he was consistently full of destruction for the human race in view of Israel, but in Canaan he brought forth fertility and was a resurrection god. Likewise in the Hebrew text, Yahweh, who is also called El (using the same name for god as did Canaan— coincidence?), was both benevolent and capable of destruction.

Sorry, but I've got to do it again. Let's use a little common sense. How many nice mass murders do you know? How many benevolent evil people do you know? How many merciful rapists do you know? Do you get the picture of what is happening here? It's kind of confusing, but what has happened here in the Old Testament is that one or more gods decided that he wanted to be worshipped as God alone and solely, thus establishing monotheism in a polytheistic universe. The Hebrews were not the first race to begin practicing monotheism. To the best of my knowledge Egypt's king Amenhotep IV was one of the first in human society to create a monotheistic religion. Just like Egypt, the Israelites, too, rolled all the deeds, incidents, and roles of various gods into one god that Israel would worship as the Supreme Creator God. However, what we do not know is what types of influences the gods put on Amenhotep or Moses and the Hebrews to force compliance. Just like Canaan, Israel described its primary gods as benevolent and destructive. Israel called her good god Yahweh or, in accordance with the Canaanite pantheon, *El,* Yahweh, Elaoh. Israel calls her evil god *Baal,* Satan, Lucifer, also like Canaan. But this is where the confusion comes in. Many times when the destructive god had visited Israel, as an angel of light, he identified himself as Yahweh/El. It is recorded over and over again that Israel would always fall prey to Baal. Why would we trust the Israelites to record only that which came from the Creator when Israel continually fell to worship other gods? This is absolute fact according to the Bible. How can we verify without doubt that Baal is not the one ruling Israel all along? Does it really make a difference? Only if it makes a difference as to whether you serve Satan or God. If indeed the destructive character of Yahweh is Baal, then Satan has impersonated god and tricked millions of humans.

## The Conflicts of God and His Human Nature

The Old Testament would have you believe that Yahweh is the Creator, Supreme God of the universe. Yet this Supreme God has human-like characteristics such as being jealous and vengeful. He has a backside, feet, hair of wool, and so forth. This God can give the order to kill and then write the commandment not to kill. He can wipe out all of mankind with a flood, and at the same time His mercy endureth forever.

In Exodus 15 we find "*Then sang Moses and the children of Israel this song unto the LORD,*" (to understand the original intent we should try to say exactly what the ancient Hebrews said. We should substitute the name Yahweh here.) "*And spake, saying, I will sing unto the LORD* (Yahweh) *for he hath triumphed gloriously: the horse and his rider hath he thrown into the sea. The LORD* (Yahweh) *is my strength and song, and he is become my salvation: he is my God, and I will prepare him an habitation* (a hotel or lounging); *my father's God (more than likely Ea), and I will exalt him. Yahweh is a MAN of war: Yahweh is his name.*"

This verse alone yields much information about the God of Israel. First, it is reported that Yahweh is his name. We know that the words "the LORD" are a title. Use of the words, the LORD, in this manner is the same as saying your daddy's name is daddy. No, daddy is a title and your daddy is called by a name. Second, it appears that Yahweh is going to receive a habitation prepared by Moses or one of His worshipers. Third, it is plain to see here that Yahweh is a **man**, yet not just any type of man, but a man of war. Isaiah 42:13 also states, "*Yahweh shall go forth as a mighty **man**, he shall stir up jealousy like a man of war, he shall cry, yea roar; he shall prevail against his enemies.*" (We already know that Yah **is** a man of war from the previous verse.) Now with just a little common sense let's take a human illustration of God versus the evil/satan as painted here in this verse.

Imagine that you are God and Israel is a nation of ants, for with our God sense we all know that God to Israel is like infinitely huge to small. Because we cannot with our human imaginations see infinitely huge, let us compare ourselves in size and intelligence (as God) to the ant (as Israel). Imagine telling the ants of how you created their ant farms and without you they would not be there in your room. Now can you imagine griping, roaring, complaining, and going to war, and boasting at the ants how you will conquer them damn ants? Can you imagine telling the ant that you will no longer hold your peace and that now you are going to devour and destroy?

If the ants piss you off enough, you will simply take out a can of Raid and call it a day. How many wars, complaints, frustrations do you think you will conduct? More than likely, you will pay the ants' evil thought no attention whatsoever. (This is not to say that God doesn't care for us.) You just would not care one way or the other as to whether the ants are worshipping you, or plotting at how they will become human like you, or conspiring with a rat, called Satan (a title meaning the enemy, could be a sinner, evil plot, or the devil) as to how they will overthrow you as the owner of your home. Using common sense, we know that ants (sinning Israel) and a rat (Satan) can not upset you (God) by merely acknowledging the conspiracy to overthrow your (God's) home with anything more than amusement at such little creatures actions or thoughts. They are just too small and it is inconceivable for you to began to imagine that ants and a rat would have the capability to destroy your plans for your home. Especially noting that as God you are perfect, therefore the ants can never escape their enclosed habitation anyway. This illustration is God-inspired. If my writing were to be in the Bible, I would be quoted as saying thus saith the Lord God unto Ezzrath, and the above parable. Get it?

How many of us ever considered God being a man or requiring habitation? Our common sense tell us that no supreme, omnipotent God could be considered a man or a being in need of room and board or a place of rest. But, then, of course, now that this verse does not fit our belief patterns we will add it to our soon to be never-ending list of verses where the Bible is saying what it really doesn't mean. Of course, it doesn't mean that god is a man even though this is what the Hebrews called Yahweh. Let's be honest with ourselves: When is the last time we called God a *man*, let alone a *man of war?* Since we have a wrong hypothesis of the Bible as God's word, we reject the truth that it might be possible for all the nations to be weakened (deceived) by a being who would set himself up as the most high. We will have the opportunity if the prophecy in Isaiah 14:12-16 is true—to look upon this man's face and say is this the man that made the earth to tremble, that did shake kingdoms. Yahweh was not Yahweh the Creator, but a god impersonating God, pretending to be God. A wannabe God—not God.

This is a God who one minute requires all his writings of the law to be in Hebrew by His chosen people. He demands that these Hebrews follow his laws and statutes, then he states that he has made an **everlasting covenant** with His chosen people merely to totally change his entire plans and do away with the law and introduce grace through Greek writings. His chosen is now the world through Jesus' blood instead of the Israelites and the law. This wonderful God supposedly allows His own son (who was miraculously born through a virgin) to be murdered for a species known as mankind. Already right in front of us are facts that are commonly accepted in blind faith by most Bible readers, yet none of it appeals to our common sense. If a young lady came before us pregnant, and swearing that she has never had sex, everyone would roll over laughing. How absurd! It is impossible for a woman to be pregnant without ever having sex. However, when it comes through our religion and tradition we must make an exception. "God works in mysterious ways," we say, "We can not understand the ways of God." "God's ways are higher than ours." I say let's get down to the nitty gritty and really decipher the Old and New Testament god, Yahweh.

The gods of the Old Testament can be discovered as just that—gods, not the Creator. Isaiah 54 speaks only of a god with an everlasting love for Israel. This god at times is required to be in places other than Israel, leaving Israel feeling forsaken and abandoned. He explains in verse 7 that it is only for a moment, *"For a small moment have I forsaken thee; but with great mercies will I gather thee. In a little wrath I hid my face from thee for a moment* (**notice that in wrath this god walks away, not destroys!**)*; but with* **everlasting kindness will I have mercy on thee,** *saith the LORD thy Redeemer.*" It would be safe to assume that this would be El/Enki talking here for this god is promising everlasting kindness and mercy for Israel. Using common sense, it is actually a **fact** that this verse was alone shows that either there was indeed two or more gods of the Old Testament, or that indeed God is a liar. Because in other places in the Bible god promises to utterly destroy Israel if they do not heed his instruction. Either way you choose to believe distorts the credibility of the Bible tremendously.

Furthermore, the god of the Hebrew Israelites loved to hate and spoke highly of his capacity to do evil. Due to human nature, (common sense or God sense) we automatically know that God the Creator does not hate and is not evil. Unfortunately, due to another fine quality that we humans possess, loyalty, we cannot give up an empty faith that has been passed down for centuries and millennia regardless of the fact that it just doesn't hold water. Thus many will be trapped in a religion with a god who boasts of his glory to create evil. Although right now as you read this passage my average reader will say, "Noooooooo, God does not hate," "NO way can God be evil." Yes, you will swear and swear that this is an impossible conclusion for everyone knows that God is merciful, kind, and generous. After all, he said so himself that, "*His mercy endureth forever.*" Let's look at what the god of the Old Testament has to say about his capacity to create evil and to hate. Turn to Isaiah 45:7, "*I form the light, and create darkness: I make peace,* **and create evil**: *I Yahweh do all things.*" And again in Isaiah 42:16, "*and I will bring the blind* (anyone who has not studied to show himself approved), *by a way that they knew not*" (religions that worship others instead of God, others like Jesus, Buddha, Mahdi, Muhammad, Krishna, all the ways that the Israelites knew not). REMEMBER, THEY ALWAYS KNEW THE WAYS OF BAAL

AND OTHER IDOL GODS (aliens). They did not worship the masters and enlightened souls as we do today. Here Yahweh/Baal is threatening the Israelites that he will take the blind on the wrong path. How evil can one be? He clearly states that he is going to the ignorant blind people to mislead them. Why pick on the ignorant? Yahweh goes on to say *"I will lead them in paths that they have not known."* Clearly these people are to follow a false religion that none of them have known. Can you name the religions that were developed after the Hebrew Israelite religion? *"**I will make darkness** light before them, and crooked things straight."* Aren't our religions light for us and in our minds aren't they the straight and narrow? Here Yah is promising to make wrong things right for the people. Sooooo, what seems right to all the people of the earth? RELIGIONS!!! All religions teach that we must go outside ourselves to seek prophets, messiahs, teachers, legends, traditional rituals (such as the mock eating and drinking of Jesus' flesh, ceremonies, and so forth). *"These things will I do unto them, and not forsake them."* The word forsake means help in Hebrew. In the *Strong's Concordance,* the Hebrew word for forsake was *azab,* a prime root to loosen, relinquish, permit, etc. Surely this god is promising to mislead people permanently and will not help them. Does this all sound merciful to you?

I can hear it now: "But God loved His people, and they would not worship Him." Well god should get a life and stop torturing people into worshipping him. Just as I would tell you to get a life and quit bugging those ants.

In addition to Yahweh being a man, it appears that Yahweh and his Israelite servant (with whom Yahweh physically fought side by side) were in fear for Yahweh's life and believed that Yahweh might die. Refer to Habakkuk 1:12: *"Art thou not from everlasting, O Yahweh my god, mine holy one? We (**YOU**) will not die."* Reference the *Anchor Bible Dictionary,* under Bible, Euphemism and Dysphemism. The word "you" was taken out, and replaced with the word "we" due to the fact that nobody would ask God, if He was indeed God, whether or not He would die. In the original text, as some believe "the word of God," it is clear that a Hebrew subject of god's was worried and dismayed, asking his god if he was going to die. He asks in modern terms: *Are you not an immortal god? Will you die?* God appeared to be fatally wounded. So it is written, what will you believe? Here the Bible again doesn't really mean what it is saying. Remember also that for God to be a mortal he may not have even been one of the ancient idol gods. This Israelite is clearly talking with a mortal man or alien idol god at the highest evolution. Remember Exodus 15 where Yahweh states himself that he is a man of war. Just as Moses and the prophets have been saying all along. We will just keep the faith in spite of the fact that using common sense we know that no human would ask God if he were going to die.

## God Practices
## Malicious and Hideous Acts

Let's consider many of the inferior and perhaps barbaric characteristics of the god of the Hebrews. For starters, he was a jealous and vengeful god. Exodus 20:5 states: "*Thou shalt not bow down thyself to them, nor serve them: for I Yahweh (the LORD) thy God am a jealous God, **visiting the iniquity of the fathers upon the children** unto the third and fourth generation of them that hate me.*" I don't think that most people deny that the god of the Bible is jealous and vengeful. In Exodus 20:5, he is vengeful to the point that he decides to take out his jealous rage on the children's children of whoever betrays him. Our common sense will tell the average sane being that just because you are mad at the parent doesn't mean that you should seek vengeance on their children. Yet the god of the Old Testament states right here that he is going to do just that. Again . . . let's throw away common sense, this is God. He can be vindictive and hurt the innocent if he chooses. This is just the reality of the type of God we have. After all, He is God! Or is he actually god?

Moreover, he gives the commandment to murder innocent people. How do I know that they are innocent? Because this god that so many love and worship commands the murder of babies. Numbers 31:17-18 states, *"Now therefore **kill every male among the little ones**, and kill every woman that hath known man by lying with him. **But all the women children**, that have not known a man by lying with him, keep alive for yourselves."* (God gives the order to rape.) Yahweh goes on to command Saul in I Samuel 15:3, *"Now go and smite* (kill) *Amalek, and utterly destroy all that they have, and spare them not: but slay both man and woman, infant and suckling* (toddlers and babies still breast feeding), *ox and sheep, camel and ass."* How cruel! This god is not happy with just killing men, women, and toddlers; he is requiring the deaths of the babies on the breast (suckling). In the other case he instructs Israel to use the young female virgins for their own purposes, but everyone else must die. COME ON PEOPLE, is this what we call a merciful God? One who encourages rape, murder, racism, hate, destruction and every vile consideration the human imagination can possibly conceive? Perhaps we should consider why we find it necessary to make excuses for the acts of this god. Let's end wars by realizing that these gods have manipulated the entire human race into believing the most ridiculous of lies and deceit: "I am all right and you are all wrong, and let's go to war and prove whose god is God." No, no, no—this is not what we want to believe, but we have been tricked into believing that this is actually the way things are.

Our hearts and souls know that our wonderfully merciful Creator could not be guilty of such revolting criminal acts that totally mutilate human consciousness of the every essence of a merciful God. Nonetheless, without any justification other than a feeling and handed down tradition we MUST believe that the Hebrew god is GOD. Therefore, we say to ourselves that we cannot reject God. We don't understand why to save humanity He had to allow His son to be murdered, but we just believe. The more selfish and ignorant of our society would say that this is the only way that God with all his majestic God power could save man. That is, through the innocent blood of His only begotten son, Jesus. Why should we take pride and glory in needing someone to be murdered for our sins? How selfish! And where is the justice in this action? Then they complete the justification cycle, by saying, "But that is just the way of the Creator, and we can't go against His plan for our world." "Without the spilling of blood redemption is impossible." AND WE BELIEVE IT? Where is our proof? Is it our feelings? Whose plan is it really? Do we really care to know the truth? Will we seek answers to all these questions? Do we prefer being spoon-fed and just believing?

Yahweh is using the leader of the group of people known as Hebrew Israelites to establish a brainwashing technique by which failure to sit and do absolutely nothing but meditate on Yahweh once per week would result in certain death. Can you imagine living in a society where if you worked on the seventh day you would be put to death? Put yourselves in the shoes of the Israelites. The idea of dying automatically forces mental adaptation to Yahweh's rules without question. Some might say, well, if he is God, and he desired to treat these people in a special way, we should accept it.

Years ago I would have totally agreed with this statement, and perhaps would have been the first in line to justify this god's actions. Now I realize that the justifying statements, like the one just mentioned, have conditions which we never sought to validate. For example, if He is God? **If He Is God**? **IF HE IS GOD**? Nobody, in blind faith, ever challenges this condition (if Jehovah is God) with written evidence establishing that indeed the Hebrew god is or is not God. We never put all the pieces together as to who the races were then, and who they are today. We never gave any conclusions or suggestions as to why or how this god and other gods could deceive so many. We never pondered what would be the criteria set by Jehovah for choosing a favorite nation of people. We could never understand, if not Jehovah, then what replacement or alternative God, since having common sense/God sense we automatically assume that there is a Source/Creator/Force which has caused the world's existence as we know it today. All is not lost in the fact-finding discovery process, because in the end of all this, I have come to find that the true God of our universe really is merciful and kind. If salvation·becomes an issue for you at any point in reading, please skip ahead to the chapter that deals with salvation.

Let's continue looking at the reasoning used by the Bible believer. It is funny how we misuse the English language and make false statements based on the evidence. For example, it is fact that this god wants to have people put to death for working on his day. Then we (the Bible believers) come alone and justify this barbaric action by saying God desired to treat these people in a special way. Get REAL! This is a positive and loving statement to an English-speaking person's ear to receive "special treatment." You and I would have loved a special treatment from God, but how many of us are ready to die for working on the Sabbath? **NOT ONE.** We never thought of putting ourselves in the Israelites' position, for if we did, we would not feel so special for being put to death solely for a mere religious violation. Israel never received special treatment from their god. How special do you think the daughter of the Hebrew judge Jephthah felt when she learned that she was to be sacrificed to Jehovah to honor her father's vow? Her father had vowed to Jehovah to offer a sacrifice of the first thing to enter his door when he returned home victorious from war. The first to enter was his daughter dancing with glee for her father's victory. (See Judges 11:29-31 and 11:34-37.) Unlike in Father Abraham's days when the evil Yahweh requested the sacrifice of the young Isaac, none was wise enough to see through the barbaric gesture, and the young girl was put to death. The same fate would have befallen young Isaac had not Father Abraham seen through the evil Jehovah. This is written in the Oahspe Bible, pages 330-331, verses 10-19. How special do you suppose the poor Israelite man gathering sticks in Numbers 15:32 may have felt? It states, *"And while the children of Israel were in the wilderness, they found a man* *that gathered sticks upon the Sabbath day. And they that found him gathering sticks brought him unto Moses and Aaron, and unto all the congregation. And they put him in ward, because it was not declared what should be done to him. And Yahweh* (God) **said unto Moses, The man shall be surely put to death:** *all the congregation shall stone him with stones without* (outside) *the camp. And all the congregation brought him without* (outside) *the camp,* **and stoned him with stones, and he died; as Yahweh** (God) **commanded Moses."** If we are to believe that the Bible is a perfect translation of God's word, what do we make of what occurred next? Directly after the order to kill the man was an order on how to dress with fashion designs to suit Yahweh's sanctification of Israel. The dress was important so that all would know by the dress code that Israel had signed allegiance with Yahweh Elohim.

In the New Testament, we have an identical situation, changing only the characters and objects. The Pharisees find Jesus' disciples picking corn on the Sabbath. Sound familiar? They bring the issue to Jesus, just as they brought the issue of the man who picked up sticks to Yahweh. However, the answer that this Son of God gives is totally opposite of what god would have done. Jesus states that the Sabbath was made for the Son of Man, and then throws in some corrupt deeds of the kings in the past as why it was *acceptable for the disciples to break the Sabbath law.* (See Matthew 12:1-8.) Clearly we have the exact same violation of the Sabbath. A man picks up sticks and *God says he must die.* And men pick corn and *God (Jesus) says it is acceptable* (note that Jesus has not died for anyone's sins so the law is intact for Christian belief, also). A religious person will say without failure that there are no contradictions whatsoever in this book, the Bible. They will say that it is in perfect harmony. They will come up with such things as "you must just believe." Others will insist that you are confused to have the gall to think that the Bible could possibly contradict itself. Still others would tell me that in this particular situation God didn't change, but that man changed for they were worshipping the Sabbath instead of the

Creator so Jesus had to teach the Pharisees a lesson. But if we know the God of Israel, and we assume that His words are truth, we learn that Yahweh consistently without exception insisted on the worship of the Sabbath, as we will see. In Deuteronomy 5:12-14, *"Keep the Sabbath day to sanctify it, as Yahweh thy God hath commanded thee. Six days thou shalt labor, and do all thy work: But the seventh day is the Sabbath of Yahweh, thy* (your) *God: in it thou* (you) *shalt* (should) *not do any work, thou* (you) *nor thy* (your) *son, nor thy daughter, nor thy manservant, nor your maidservant, nor your ox, nor your ass, nor any of your cattle, nor your stranger that is within your gates; that your manservant and your maidservant may rest as well as thou."* Their god was trying to establish a cult through the Hebrew nation using a method similar to the one Hitler used in his attempt to establish his cult over the world. Similar verses can be found in the following, *and so many more:*

1. Exod. 16:23, 25, 26, 29
2. Exod. 20:10-11
3. Exod. 31:13-16
4. Exod. 35:2-3
5. Lev. 19:3, 30
6. Lev. 26:2
7. Num. 15:32
8. Deut. 5:12
9. Deut. 5:14
10. Deut. 5:15
11. Neh. 13:22
12. Isa. 56:2,6
13. Jer. 17:24
14. Jer. 17:27

The people were brainwashed daily about Yah's Sabbath policy and the penalty for violating this statute was severe: DEATH. Both Yahweh and Hitler used racism and murder to both control and mesmerize their followers into accepting the most heinous of ideas humanly conceivable. Both emphasized their violence as righteous, and it seems that it is even possible that both Yahweh and Hitler ended their fates in a similar manner. (See the chapter about god's human nature where God appears to be dying.)

Furthermore, there is overwhelming evidence of vile, disgusting activities that Yahweh forced his Israelite subjects to take part in. For example, Hosea (the prophet of God) was forced into a marriage with an unfaithful partner, labeled in the Bible as a whore (Hosea 1:2). As a Christian I was taught that this was the only way that God could show Israel and perhaps the other nations how whorish Israel was in the sight of God. I won't even comment on this act of god.

Moreover, in Ezekiel 4: 12-14, God forces his holy prophet and his chosen people to eat cow manure in front of the Gentiles as the only way to make an atonement for the iniquity of the Israelites. Hey, who was it who said that the only redemption of sin is in the blood? We can eat feces for our salvation, what a caring god? Starting at the fourth verse God explains why this was necessary. He gives Ezekiel instructions to lie down for so many days on one side and then the other. Ezekiel must prepare food for this task because it will require many days. The instructions for preparation of the cow manure begin at verse 12: *"Bake it with dung* (feces) *that cometh out of man."* Ezekiel protests, and then God makes it easier on him by giving him cow manure (get real) in verse 15: *"I* (God) **have given thee cow's dung** (manure) **for man's dung** (feces) **and thou shalt prepare thy bread therewith."** This god has so many characteristics that show without doubt he is not our Supreme Creator God. My people (the Israelites) served Baal at first because he pretended to be the most high, showering them with miracles, gifts, favors, etc., but later when they discovered their gross mistake it was too late; their service to Baal was without choice. Baal had begun by using germ warfare and infecting those who would rebel with disease, itching, burning, and severe stomachache (painful bowels). Thus Yahweh created a self-fulfilling prophecy to devise a tactic of control and intimidation of the small Israelite community. In Job 30:27, we read, *"My bowels boiled, and rested not: the days of affliction prevented me,"* one account of poisoning. Likewise in Psalm 22:14, *"I am poured out like water, and all my bones are out of joint: my heart is like wax; it is melted in the midst of my bowel."* Also in Jeremiah 4:19, *"My* *bowels, my bowels! I am pained at my very heart."*

Surely after murder, rape, hate, racism, destruction, biochemical warfare, and forcing people to eat dung, and marry prostitutes, it can be deduced that god, Jehovah, was not such a nice guy to hang around. But on a serious note, surely this god should be held under investigation. Look at what is being said here: One should try the spirit by the spirit to see whether or not it is of God or NOT. But how will one know whether or not a spirit is of God? My answer is through unconditional love. Any spirit that loves unconditionally does it only by the spirit of the true God. Any spirit that fails to love UNCONDITIONALLY is guided by satanic energy or in reality in service of the lower worlds. Stop and take time to think about it. This is what I would love to have happen, people actually researching for themselves; without relying solely on being told by the preacher or one special book, or hoping to feel the right way, to truly know God.

If a dog is told that it is naked, it will just be spoken words of no value. The dog will be at peace in its ignorance of the fact that it is naked, for it knows no difference. Likewise is the veil of all the religions of the earth that bind the souls of mankind. Man will be at peace, like a naked dog, never for a second considering the possibility of being misled by his religions into ignorance.

I would like to share a story with you from my life that is very similar as to how religions of blind faith manipulate us by forcing the believer to be caught in a perpetual lose-lose situation. When my children were small, one of my friends told them that there was no such thing as Santa, and that their mom was the person responsible for the gifts under the tree. When my children came home and told me this, I was furious, needless to say. I was taught to practice the traditional lie of Santa's customs at Christmas, and I put it off on my children. I let the lady have it with both barrels. I told her that I couldn't care less as to what she instilled in her children, but my children were to be hands off. Her family came from a Muslim background. Then I told my children this. "Honey, for Tammy and her children Santa does not exist. That is why her children do not get gifts from Santa. Santa only comes to the good children who believe hard in him," I explained in all sincerity, desperate to keep the myth alive. "The moment you stop believing is the moment that Santa will no longer visit you because you have forced Santa to no longer be real for you," I insisted. Santa does not have the power to make it to the children who don't believe in him. I explained that Santa doesn't visit Tammy's children because they don't believe. "So it is your choice." "Are you going to believe or turn your backs on Santa?" I asked the children. We celebrated Christmas for two more years before I had to come clean with my children after becoming a Hebrew Israelite. After learning that Christmas was actually a pagan holiday, I had a nightmare to straighten out before my children. They were not happy campers at all.

I tell this story only to illustrate how when believing appears not to hurt anything, but great is the reward (Christmas toys) for the believer, the believer will not care whether there is any merit to the belief. It is hard to look for truth when your mindset is that you will lose everything in finding it. How can you desire to know whether or not I speak the truth when you will lose the concept of grace? Grace is a beautiful notion, that is for the born-again sinner. Nonetheless, that is all that it is—a notion just like Santa. My kids were told the truth two years prior to my telling them, but since I had added my fictitious story of, "WITHOUT FAITH, ALL IS LOST," they didn't care about the truth, for the hope of the gifts. Likewise Christianity does not want the truth, for there is a promise of salvation in Jesus' resurrection. Why should we desire or risk the truth when we can dump all our load of guilt, shame, and mistakes on Jesus and make them His burden? What if this guilt, shame, and sin game was made up, and just as a bitch in heat does not sin against God as she has sex with every male dog in sight neither does mankind sin against God? Let's just keep the faith whether it can be proven or not, for we want the gift of salvation. I

remember the drama of visualizing all the suffering that an innocent Christ had undergone for my wretched soul. What is the
difference between this lie and the one that I told my children? You
want to say that your belief is truth? I will guarantee you that my
children would have said the same, that their belief in Santa was
TRUTH! At least with my children believing the lie they did see
physical evidence of Santa's gifts.

## God Despises Women

Continuing on, there remains quite a bit to discover about our
wonderful god's relationship and philosophy regarding women.
Given the opportunity to go back in time to the period of ancient
Israel, most every Bible-conscious American woman of today
would refuse. Although the average woman knows that the way of
ancient Israel was baneful toward women, most of them never
take the time to investigate why they feel so thankful to have been
born now instead of then. After all God was in person back then.
It is common knowledge that the woman's role in the creation of
the Hebrew and Greek text was at best a minimal one. Women
were trained from infancy to be homemakers and devout servants
to their husbands. Many times the women referred to their men as
lord. In Genesis 18:12 Sarah calls her husband, Abraham, lord.
Rachel calls her father lord in Genesis 31:35. Under no circumstances is the woman referred to as lord.

Yahweh encouraged multiple sex relations for the men in
Israel. He worked on causing division within the families of the
Israelites by pitting the man against his woman. What better way
to gain division in a household than to prophesy that one day
seven women will happily seek out one man to share for their
husband (Isaiah 4:1)? Men have been waiting ever since for this
prophecy to be fulfilled. If there had to be sex with multiple partners, by physical design it should have been the woman with extra
marital sex. She is far better equipped to handle many more
rounds of sex and longer. If we studied Tantra as did kings of Israel

Solomon and Ahab (I Kings 16:32) in the temple of God, we would know that a woman could be more capable and sexually adequate for multiple partners than her male counterpart. Ahab is considered the worst king of all kings because he practiced Tantra (religious orgies with drugs and strong liquor) in a temple raised to Baal. Solomon practiced his orgies in the temple of Jehovah and therefore he is ranked as a much higher king of Israel for being more loyal to Jehovah. Nonetheless, in Jehovah's temple Solomon called upon Ashtoreth (Astarte) and other gods as he partook of mass sacred sex. But that's another book.

Why was Solomon searching for the Queen of Heaven? You should research this one on your own. But I will tell you about the Queen of Heaven. She was the Mesopotamian fertility goddess Inanna of Sumeria, Ishtar of Assyro-Babylon, and Ashtoreth of Canaan-Israel (today's worship of her fertility is observed by Christians on Easter day [Ashtoreth's day] through the fertile bunny). She was known by various names with respect to her ancient cult locations. See I Kings 11:5: *"For Solomon went after Ashtoreth the Goddess of the Zidonians."* In Tantric salutations to the real God within (not Jehovah) various rituals used exotic sexual arousal on multiple partners (a type of orgy) in search of losing one's physical self in bliss. Study forms of East Indian rituals.

According to *Inanna Returns* by V.S. Ferguson, Marduk/Yahweh was imprisoned inside the pyramids at Giza in Egypt by Ashtoreth. Marduk/Yahweh was a god whose only ambition was to *rule* and *control.* He had set up his cousin Inanna's/Ashtoreth's husband's death and she was determined to avenge her husband. Ashtoreth set up Marduk with the permission of the royal/god family of Anunnaki's. She had her assailant incarcerated, sealed behind the walls of the pyramid without food or water.

Marduk's father, Enki, persuaded his niece Ashtoreth, who liked her Uncle Enki, to free Marduk for the sake of Enki. She bargained with Enki that her cousin Marduk/Yahweh would have to make offerings at her temple and plead to her for mercy. Jehovah was forced to succumb to the whims of Ashtoreth.

Anyone with even the slightest background of Jehovah's behavioral patterns would know that this incident would be the worst nightmare of Yah's life. Imagine Yahweh imprisoned by another god; worse, a goddess. A goddess has forced Yahweh to beg and plead for his life. Beyond all imagination, a mere female.

According to Ferguson, this event places Marduk/Yahweh on the warpath of all women, especially targeting Inanna's temples and priestess. Inanna reports, "Marduk (God/Jehovah) went out of his way to slander me. He claimed *I was an evil witch* who devoured men and *turned innocent women into whores.* Coveting (jealous of) my temples and all the lands owned by my priestesses, Marduk embarked on a campaign to slander and destroy these women. My priestesses, who were highly trained in business and the arts, were accused of *black* magic, of casting *dark* spells over the land. Whenever anything went wrong, if there was a bad storm or a crop failure, my women were blamed. And *Marduk saw to it that plenty went wrong.* My beautiful priestesses were imprisoned, beaten, tortured, raped, and burned alive. All of their property was confiscated. Marduk was taking his revenge on me, the one who had ordered him buried alive." (Ref. V. S. Ferguson, starting from page 125.)

Biblical records also show that this report was in all probability accurate. The Bible mentions that Israel should have a witch put to death (Exodus 22:18 and Leviticus 20:27). Who would determine whether or not an individual was a witch and how that determination would be made is not mentioned. However, the burning of witches (any woman of societal nonconformity) has been practiced in our recent history where many innocent women were burned at the stake. This claim by Inanna should not be shocking to most anyone who knows their history and the biblical references. In Jeremiah 8:21 it states that, **"For the hurt of the daughter of my people am I hurt"** and in verse 19, *"Behold the voice of the cry of the daughter of my people because of them that dwell in a far country."* Jeremiah doesn't specify exact details of incidents that take place to cause the daughters of Israel so much grief. But if we read various sections in the Old Testament we will be able to see that good ole trusty Yahweh has got his hand in the pot stirring up dung. Yahweh began manipulating the Israelite community into abusing its women and casting them into a category of second-class citizens at its best. In Isaiah 3:12, Yahweh establishes that it is a curse that women rule over the people. Yahweh is using a common technique used today to pit the husband against his wife. Even today women experience their husbands' male friends advising their husbands to stand up and wear the pants in the house, to make sure the women know who is the boss. Of course, that will lead to one of two things: an unhappy marriage or divorce. This shows the Israelite mentality; one of the worst things that could happen to them was for a woman to rule or have authority. It is true today. Being of a former Israelite/Levite consciousness, I could have never perceived of the idea that a woman could direct a man—impossible. If you love God, then you must be willing to present yourself in a way appealing to God, I convinced myself. The most agonizing years of my life were during the time I believed in Jehovah as the God of my life. I knew that God saw me as unimportant, and only required as a source of repopulating the earth. God placed the man to rule over me. God said that the man had a right to forsake my needs and cater to his own with as many wives as he could take care of. God said that if I was the oldest sister and had brothers, that my brothers would inherit property before me based solely on the fact that I am female. God counted me so insignificant that my husband was given authority to correct any wrongs that I spoke, he would be responsible and would bear my sins. (See Numbers 30:15.) A woman could not bear the sins of a man. God stripped me bare of all the essentials that classified me as an intelligent, independent individual and made me a slave for the men of my family. As a Hebrew woman my only desire was for when I could exit this plane of existence. I am so thankful to have found the truth about the *Ultimate Deceit*—when a physical being sets himself up as the Most High, Creator of the

Universe. It has been biblically established that God was doing exactly as Inanna describes to the ancient women.

In Isaiah 3:16, Yahweh accuses the daughters of Zion of being haughty and proud, with their heads lifted high. For punishment, Yahweh strips the women of their jewels, ornaments bonnets, and fine clothes. *He promises to make them widows in verse 25.* Also the Bible states that the women's "mighty" (priestess/leaders) shall die in the war. It appears that the Israelite women were trying not to buy into Yahweh's intimidation tactics (threatening to kill their husbands and leaders). In Isaiah 32:9 Yahweh/Marduk vindictively lashes out on the women; he curses them in verse 10 with many days and years of trouble. He curses the Israelite women's crops to fail and promises to strip her bare. Is this a wonderful and merciful God that we serve and love? It shouldn't be a wonder that women are abused today. God started all the tyranny and oppression of women. And as the Bible would have put it, it has been like that *even unto this day.* Why should men have respect for women when their god does not? Their god killed the Israelite woman's husband as punishment for a proud woman. Surely a man should beat his wife and conceivably kill her if he ever finds out that God kills the husband of a proud, stretched neck wife. Think about it. We teach our children daily that the Bible is God's word and that it is flawless— PERFECT! Our children will turn to this flawless word in their moments of trouble as adults, perhaps when going through a rough divorce. I was taught that the Bible never contradicted itself and that anytime people made the mistake of thinking that there was a contradiction, it was due to not being led by God. If I asked a Christian, "Should we try to be godlike?" he would quickly answer, "Yes." If I said, "Without doubt?" he would say, "Without a doubt, it is good to be godlike." Then if I said, "God doesn't like proud women and he kills their husbands; is it all right for me to do it, too (being godlike)?" The Christian would answer immediately without pause to consider, "No way!" But I can't understand why they would say it is acceptable for God to do it, but not me. They will answer me with a question; "Do you think you're God?" "I know that I am not God," I will tell them, but if we are supposed to be godlike how do they (followers of the Bible) get to pick which things we do like God and which things we don't. If I did the exact same act that God did by killing the proud woman's husband, I would be labeled ungodly. Perhaps that is the label that mankind should considered putting on this mass murderer of the Old Testament.

I can hear many of you right now as you are reading. This is one crazy lady headed for nothing but the fiery pit of hell and the dummy talks as if she has no idea of how ridiculous she sounds. After all, anyone with common sense should know that the Bible speaks the truth. God inspired his prophets and scribes to write nothing but the truth and I believe and know that the Bible is God's word. **Or is it?**

## The Prophets Confess to Writing Lies

According to the scribes and the prophets, the Israelite nation was nothing more than a bunch of liars, along with **their kings, priest, and prophets**. Proof of this statement can be found through out the Old Testament. Let's take a look at Jeremiah 8:7, 8: *"But my people know not the judgment of the LORD"* (here it is clear that Israel does not know the desires or plan of God). The prophet continues, *"How do ye say, we are wise and the law of the LORD is with us? Lo, certainly **in vain made he it**; the pen of the scribes is in vain."* (**The pen of the scribes writes falsely.**) (See the international version of the Bible.) It is clear that the prophet is complaining that Israel boasts of knowing and possessing the law of God when in fact it does not, but what's worse is the **fact that this false belief is being recorded**!!! SCRIBES WRITE FALSELY! In Isaiah 59:8 a prophet again confesses that the people are making wrong judgments. *"The way of peace they know not, and there is no judgment* (choosing of the right God) *in their goings: they have made them crooked paths* (they have chosen the way of Baal)*: whosoever goes therein shall not know peace."*

Even today we humans have tried to follow the ways of Baal through the Torah, Koran, and the Bible. Continuing in Isaiah, "*Therefore is judgment* (choosing the right God) **far from us**, *neither does justice* (doing right) *overtake us: we wait for light, but behold* (cling to) *obscurity* (Baal); *for Brightness* (in the place of God), **but we walk in darkness** (we choose Baal/Satan the enemy)." Notice that the word "we" is used here, not "they"! The prophet clearly states that we walk in darkness. In plain everyday words Isaiah is saying that the Israelites had mistaken Baal for God and that they were totally incapable of discerning when God appeared to them and when Baal appeared as God. Look at Isaiah 30:8-14, "*Now go, write it before them in a table and note it in a book, that it may be for the time to come for ever and ever: That this is a rebellious people, lying children,* **children that will not hear the law of the Lord**: (How do we justify accepting their writings as God's words?) *Which say to the seers, See not; and to the prophets,* **Prophesy not unto us right things;** (**Therefore, common sense should tell us that they had to prophesy wrong things or die.**) *speak unto us smooth things prophesy deceit: Get you way out of the way, turn aside out of the path, cause the Holy One of Israel to cease from before us.*" The righteous god of Israel ceased from being among them. Here Isaiah is speaking of El not Baal.

The way I devised this notion is by the Holy One's behavior and reaction to Israel's choosing Baal (another god over himself over the god El). Let's continue and you will see that El simply allows Israel to continue in its folly. He does not, however, curse the Israelites with threats of how he would destroy them utterly, as does Baal. "*Wherefore thus saith the Holy One of Israel, Because ye despise this word,* **and trust in oppression and perverseness,** *and stay thereon: Therefore this iniquity shall be to you as a breach ready to fall, swelling out in a high wall, whose breaking cometh suddenly at an instant.*" The phrase "the Holy One of Israel" is quite different from "the LORD thy God" which was so often used by the Hebrews. Why are they using a different name in this instance? Notice the fact that Israel chooses oppression and perverseness. Many Christians do this daily. They will pray to Jesus: If it *takes all the worldly things* from my life, make me better, if it means that I will have a *lot to sacrifice,* make me better. Do what ever it takes to get me straightened out. Then as they suffer dismay, dis-ease, discontent, dis-harmony, they say to themselves and everyone around them that they should please be patient for God is not done with me yet. Worse yet they continuously pray in a perpetuating summons of the Universe to make their lives horrid so that they might be better people.

Not only did the Prophets admit to telling lies, but also Jehovah himself comes out with the fact that if a prophet be deceived he indeed deceived that prophet. In Ezekiel 14:9, Jehovah states, *"And if the prophet be deceived when he hath spoken a thing,* **I the Lord have deceived that prophet,** *and I will stretch out my hand upon him, and will destroy him from the midst of my people Israel."* Jehovah hardened Pharaoh's heart to inspire the Egyptian army against Israel and blocked them by a fire, only to let them loose to drown in the Red Sea. Likewise he tricked his own people and admitted that the prophet that is deceived is **deceived by Jehovah** himself. Why would the true Creator God deceive His own beloved people? And where are the writings of praise to false gods? Where are the writings of the bad Israelites who were whoring after other gods? Where in Israel is the word of God, thus saith Baal, or Ashtoreth, or Asshur (a few of the other gods)? I am trying to get you to see that if Israel was truly turning to other gods (which is the one statement that all Bible readers agree upon as fact) then there should be documentation of this account showing Israel's lifestyle with Baal in the same way that the Bible supposedly shows Israel life with El/God. We can assume that these misled Israelites were proud of their God Baal. We know that Israel wrote prophecy and worshipped Baal even more than God according to the Bible! Baal's Bible by the Israelites has to exist; the prophets confessed this fact in our Bible. Where's the book of the prophets of Baal, Judges of Baal, Kings of Baal?

Take a big, deep breath for I am going to tell you where the worship of Baal is recorded in full detail. The worship of Baal, also known as Marduk of earlier worship and Enlil of more ancient worship, also known to the Israelites as Yahweh, **was knitted and woven right into the Bible as if it were God's word.** Yes all the murders, rapes, stealing of land, and destruction raps placed on God were not of God. Backsliding, whoring after other gods, Israel recorded these destructive acts of Baal as the acts of God Supreme Creator of the Universe. I will give you several other references to hopefully get you started searching out the truth for yourself. See Jeremiah 8:10, *"Therefore will I give their wives unto others, and their field to them that shall inherit them: **for every one from the least even unto the greatest** is given to covetousness, **from the prophet even unto the priest everyone dealeth falsely.**"* Once you really develop a personal feel for what God would do in any given situation by using even the slightest of common sense you will know whether or not this is the Creator. The Creator is not vindictive, but Baal is. The Creator is not jealous, but Baal is. The Creator does not instruct man to kill, but Baal will. The Creator does not instruct a man to covet and take another man's land, but Baal will. The Creator will never tell any man to take on any vile acts such as eating feces, marring whores, raping young women of other nations, but Baal will.

There were so many gods on the planet in those days that no race would subscribe to any one god. They turned to the most convenient god of that particular period. If El was busy in Egypt, they would make do with Baal; if Baal was taking care of some destruction in Babylon, Israel would call on Ashtoreth, and so forth. Think now about the plagues god sent to force Pharaoh to let the Hebrews go and how when Moses left their sight for forty days, Israel turned to other gods. It makes a lot of sense if there were many gods performing the plagues, trying to intrigue Israel to sign them up as sole deity of Israel. This explains why it was so simple to leave Yah and turn to other gods. It was not solely Jehovah who helped Israel escape, but Baal and sons of Baal, and El and sons of El, Ashtoreth, and other gods. Each god would bring a plague on behalf of Israel seeking to become the national god of Israel. So when Moses left with his deity, the next convenient god available was called up on. There were many gods working the plagues of Egypt so as to win Israel as their cult, making it easy for Israel to call on any of the other gods immediately available. The gods were pretty much treated as out of sight out of mind.

In Jeremiah 27, Baal prophesies to the Israelites saying, thus saith the God of Israel, place shackles and chains around your necks and go into the lands of all your enemies telling them that the God of Israel has spoken. Tell the kings of Edom, Moab, Tyrrus, and Zidon that God said to all you masters of your lands; I have made the earth, man, and the beast. Therefore, God says in verse 5, I will choose who shall have and the shall have-not. I have chosen the king of Babylon as my servant, rationalizes god. In verse 6 god says that he has taken all the lands from everyone else and given them to Babylon. **He continues to state that all the nations shall serve the Babylonian king,** (KEEP IN MIND THAT BABYLON IS SUPPOSEDLY THE LAND OF EVIL AND ENE-MIES OF GOD AND THE CHILDREN OF ISRAEL) **and his son, and his son's son, until the very time of his land come: and then many nations and great kings shall serve themselves of him.** In verse 8 god says that anyone who refuses to serve Babylon will be punished with the sword, with famine, and with pestilence. Therefore in verse 9, Baal continues his taunting instructions, telling the masters not to listen to El in his words to the prophets, or his vision to the diviners, or in any dreams or other forms of magic that El/Yahweh might send their way. Then as usual Baal states that El's prophecies and divinations are lies, in verse 10. Marduk's cult center was located in Babylon. **His personal agenda was to rule the planet earth from his cult base in Babylon.** What better way than to appear to the prophets of all the nations as God, the Supreme Creator and give the command? Thus saith Yahweh, thy God, "Enslave yourselves unto Babylon, and spread it unto all the nations that they do the same," as it has been *unto this day.*

The information in this chapter is but the tip of the iceberg. There are many writers who have devoted entire books to explain how impossible historically, archaeologically, and biblically that it is impossible for Jehovah to be OUR MAGNIFICENT MERCIFUL SUPREME CREATOR GOD. Let no one who has not read from cover to cover a vast majority of information referenced here in this document say that they know God. If the true origins of a belief system are unknown, how can we assure ourselves not to err, as did the Israelites?

## Evidence that God Is an Alien

Starting in the Bible for clues as to god's origin, we must first take all the puzzle pieces and place them together with common sense and logic. We have already discovered that god is manlike according to the Bible. It is stated that he has hair of pure wool (Daniel 7: 9). God has hair! His garment was white as snow. Thus god has a physical body which he must put clothes on. The throne on which he sits has a fiery flame, and god has wheels that are as burning fire. There is no doubt the verse is stated literally. The only physical truth that we know of where a being sits on fiery flames without being destroyed would be a rocket ship. Both the Mayans and Sumerians drew pictures of their gods riding in spaceships with some type of breathing apparatus attached to the nose.

If this were the only clue, then of course it could not stand alone. However, the actual Hebrew of the Bible in Genesis 6:4 refers to beings who arrived on earth from the sky. The word "giants," which was literally "Nefilim," was mistranslated by Jewish scholars who were not actual biblical Hebrew-speaking people. According to Sitchin, a Jewish scholar, the term "Nefilim" was mistranslated as "giants" when its actual meaning was "those who were cast down," who had descended to earth. He devotes an entire series of books proving that the god Jehovah and the mythical gods of the ancients were parallel in their trends of events and that they were beings from outer space.

Other traces of biblical evidence lies in the stories of the prophets themselves. Ezekiel witnessed god's spaceship from both the inside looking down on the earth and the outside looking up at the ship. In Ezekiel 1:4 the spaceship is described as a whirlwind from the north, making a great cloud. The whirlwind has a great fire the color of amber in its midst. Now, the question we must ask ourselves is what have we seen that can create a whirlwind with a bright amber-colored fire in its midst. The only thing that blows wind up while kicking fire out of the middle from the sky would be a rocket or a spaceship. Even if you decide that a spaceship is impossible, then we are still left with the dilemma as to what caused the whirlpool of wind with the fire in the middle. Also we must remember that this event is occurring at a time when, supposedly, no flying crafts exist. So how do we explain them?

Yet even more overwhelming evidence are the pyramids, Sphinx, Stonehenge, and large heads in Mexico. The fabrication of the pyramids is so precise and economically complex that even today's technology barely dares to compete with the ancients. Each block of the Egyptian pyramid weighs over two tons and was set in place with great accuracy. The degree of accuracy in with which each block was placed into position, would be next to impossible to remake today. How were the huge, heavy blocks installed on the pyramids? The ancient people did not have the technology, but the pyramids were built. Scientists and the general public call the building of the pyramids a mystery. Even their purpose is not fully known although some speculate that they were used for burial tombs of the elite of Egypt. However in the *Opening of the Way*, by Isha Schwaller de Lubicz, and in other documented material, various scholars argue the point that even still today there are various areas of the pyramids that no modern man has ventured through. These scholars state that the pyramids were built by Enoch to escape the prophesied flood yet to come of Noah's deluge. Still others like Zecharia Sitchin state that the pyramids in both Egypt and Mexico were built as some type of landing towers, closely resembling the use of the pyramids in the movie *Stargate*. The most fascinating find that I have made, which I have not read in any book to date, is comparing the Egyptian and Mexican pyramids in respect to location on the earth. The pyramids are on the same line of latitude, the Tropic of Cancer. From space, with primary focus placed on the pyramids and earth would look somewhat like this. Note that the pyramids are exaggerated in size so as to show positioning and clarity of the pyramids.

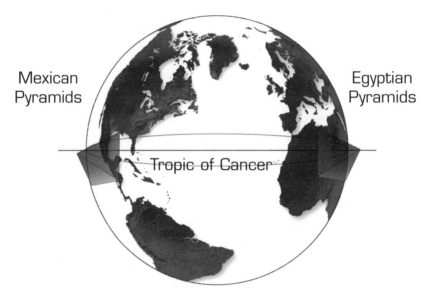

Surpassing the mystery of the pyramids are the Sumerian and Mayan cultures themselves, for their origins are absolutely unexplainable. All the other races appear to have migrated from one place to the other, but not the Sumerians or the Mayans. They both simply appeared to have materialized from nowhere and then vanished into nowhere. How is it possible to have instant civilization from nowhere? It is not! The scientists will admit that they do not have any theories as to how the Sumerians arrived in Sumer and yet they hold firmly to the idea that their civilization appeared out of the blue from nowhere, but this is when our common sense should kick in. In our physical reality nothing appears physically from nowhere. Therefore the land of Sumer was cultivated and civilized by people from somewhere. But where?

The answer lies within our ancient mythology. Ancient mythology and the Bible both reveal a physical world that operates on an entirely different basis than does our physical world today. In ancient times the civilizations could pop up from nowhere, but not today. The gods of various ancient civilizations are reported as having talked face to face with the people and even fighting in battles with the people of their cult centers. This type of activity does not happen today. Let me rephrase that: this type of activity does not openly happen today.

More evidence that the gods were extraterrestrial comes to us via our language itself. Men spoke of having "shems" (a space ship) or requiring a "shem" to become as the gods. Again Sitchin makes it clear that these men are referring to a ship. Job 30:8 clearly states that the men had suffered some vile fate due to the lack of possession of a shem. Most interpretations falsely interpret the word "base" as "name," thus they interpret the meaning here to have meant that these men are "men without a name." Besides, if it meant that they had no name, how would not having a name reduce a person to becoming lower than a dog? However, those without a spaceship to escape nuclear fallout from the atomic blasts generated by the gods would be labeled; especially seeing that they mutated and became incapable of producing melanin (social misfits of that era), basemen (men without the spaceship). We should know that no human being has an excuse to hate another human being, no matter what the circumstances. But even today we reduce AIDS victims to the point where we would rather sleep with our dogs than one of them. It is apparent that Job's prejudices against the men without a shem caused him to treat them the same way many today out of ignorance treat AIDS victims. It also appears that the feeling was a mutual dislike between the people.

Where one has to rationalize with logic is to ask the question, what terrible fate could have taken place by not having some gadget called the shem? We give up so easily, throw up both hands and think that it is impossible to really ever know what took place. That is fine as long as you are willing to admit that you don't know; however, most of us need closure as to what is actually happening within our lives and our universe. Those of us must press on toward the mark by climbing the towering puzzle pieces of life and snapping them into position piece by piece, eliminating the falsehoods and placing a conscious thought within the mind that the falsehood was once taken as truth. What other falsehoods are there within my belief system that I need to eliminate or at least examine? Supporting references are as follows:

1.  *Is it God's Word*, by Joseph Wheless, Kessinger Publishing Company
2.  *The Twelfth Planet*, by Zecharia Sitchin, Avon Books
3.  *The Wars of Gods and Men*, by Zecharia Sitchin, Avon Books
4.  *Deceptions and Myths of the Bible*, Lloyd M. Graham, Carol Publishing Group
5.  *Forgery in Christianity*, by Joseph Wheless, Kessinger Publishing Company
6.  *The Antichrist 666*, by William Josiah Sutton, W. F. G., Inc.
7.  *Gods of Eden*, by William Bramley, Avon Books
8.  *Why I Am Not a Christian*, by Bertrand Russell, Simon and Schuster
9.  *The Almost Forgotten Day*, by Mark A. Finley, The Concerned Group Inc.
10. *Losing Faith in Faith: From Preacher to Atheist*, by Dan Barker, Freedom from Religion Foundation

# THREE

## Origin of the Hebrew Israelites

### Process of Elimination

The day that I discovered who, in fact, the ancient Israelites were annihilated my entire Baptist belief systems. I was taught and I believed that the Jewish people now in Israel were God's chosen, and that I was a descendant of the Gentile nation. However, the Bible contradicts that there is any way that I could be Gentile. According to the Bible, after the flood there were only three men responsible for all the races of people on earth. Those men were Shem, Ham, and Japheth. Keep in mind that we are coming strictly from a biblical viewpoint. That is not to say that I am saying this is truth but that the Bible says that all life was destroyed with the exception of Noah and his three sons in the great flood. You will find this story in Genesis 6-8, and in Genesis 6:13 we read: "... *and God said unto Noah, the end of all flesh is come before me.*" Now if Shem, Ham, and Japheth replenished the earth, one of these men must be responsible for creating the Gentile people. Again, the Bible tells who the people would be in Genesis 10, which identifies each of the sons of Noah's sons. It explains how these sons of sons went on to become nations. It begins, "*Now these are the generations of the sons of Noah, Shem, Ham, and Japheth: and unto them were sons born after the flood.*

*The sons of Japheth; Go'-mer, and Ma'-gog (Russians), and Ma'-dai, and Ja-van (Greeks), and Tu'-bal, and Me'-shech, and Ti'-ras. And the sons of Go'-mer; Ash'-ke-naz, and Ri'-phath and To-gar'-mah. And the sons of Ja'-van; E-li'-shah, and Tar'-shis, Kittim, and Do'-da-nim.* **By these were the isles of the Gentiles** *divided in their lands; every one after his tongue, after their families, in their nations."* The Bible goes further to give the same family tree structures of both Shem and Ham. However there is no mention in the Old Testament of a race of people being Gentiles other than the Japhetic race. So then I pondered on the idea of who this Japhetic race could be. According to what I was taught these people had to be my ancestors. So next I was off to visit my old friend Webby, the Webster Dictionary. If you look up the Japhetic nation in the dictionary you will find that Japheth was Indo-European. Now I knew the Bible said so; I could not possibly be a Gentile for I knew that there was no way that I was Indo-European. Now my mind was racing for answers like never before. I applied every waking moment searching for what else had been hidden from me. For thirty-three years of my life the pastor or the Baptist faith had deceived me into just accepting that I was a Gentile even though the Bible that we supposedly believed in said differently. My every essence of my total being lived and strived for what discovery would next be found contrary to my beliefs.

## The Biblical Testimony of Black-Skinned People

After discovering that I was not a Gentile, I began searching and researching for who this Israelite nation might be. My first discovery was the fact that these people made continuous mention of having black or dark skin: Job, Jeremiah, King Solomon, Moses and his sister, and God Himself. Job 30:30 says, *"my skin is black upon me."* Since some interpreters of the Bible did not want it known that Job said his skin is black you must refer to the King

James Version. Other Bibles have replaced the word black with disgraceful words like mournful or dirty. Now you and I know that a white person would not mention that their skin is black from mourning. How many white people have we ever seen turn black from mourning? Job had to have already been a dark person or, as some say, blue-black. Jeremiah states in Jeremiah 8:21, *"For the hurt of the daughter of my people am I hurt; **I am black.**"* Further mention of blackness in the Bible can be found in Lamentations 5:10, which states that their (Israelites) **"skin was black** like an oven."* Also, Lamentations 4:8 states that their (Israelites) faces (the word visage means face) are blacker than a coal. No white, red, brown, or yellow men would compare themselves to a coal, but here in the Bible these peoples' skin is compared to the color of a coal. Do you know any whites that compare their skin color to a coal? In the Songs of Solomon 1:5 it is stated, *"I am black, but comely, o ye daughters of Jerusalem."* Some say that this is Solomon himself bragging to the ladies of his harem and others say it is one of his mistresses or concubines bragging that she is black and beautiful. Let's take the latter to be truth. Even so, added with all the information, it points to a black people. Yahweh, the god of the Israelites, compares Israel to the Ethiopians, asking in Amos 9:7, *"Are you not as the Ethiopians?"* How many of you would today compare modern Israelis to Ethiopians? Can you find a document anywhere that shows a comparison of the white Jews being similar to Ethiopians?

Moses marries an Ethiopian woman in Numbers 12:1, also yielding association to black people. The miracle that god uses to prove to Moses His power is found in Exodus 4:6, *"Put now thine hand into thy bosom. And he put his hand into his bosom: and when he took it out behold, his hand was leprous as snow."* The passage does not refer to any rising of the skin or sores. This was a condition of losing skin pigmentation, which to a racist god and people, changing skin color is the worst thing in the world to happen to them. Furthermore, what would be so devastating about a white man's hand turning white? The snow represents skin color, and there is a passage that supports this statement in Numbers 12:10, *"and, behold, Miriam became leprous, **white as snow**."* It goes on to say that Aaron witnesses Miriam turning white and runs to Moses to beg him to intercede to Yahweh on Miriam's behalf. He tells Moses of what he witnessed and then begs in verse 12, *"Let her not be as one dead of whom the flesh is consumed when he cometh out of his mothers womb."* Comedy actor Bill Cosby in his comedy show *Bill Cosby: Himself,* also makes a similar joke about a baby being born half done and that the doctor should put it back, it's not done yet because of its skin color. The vast majority of all newborn black babies are indeed born with far lighter complexions than what their natural complexion will become within weeks after their birth. So this comparison of Miriam looking like a newborn baby would probably be the closest skin color to the likeness of Miriam and Aaron's experience. Being black myself, I can imagine that if there were nothing but black people around me, then the only comparison I could use to describe a white person would be a newborn black baby.

Furthermore, Yahweh, God Himself, is depicted with black attributes. Daniel 7:9 states, *"I beheld till the thrones were cast down, and the Ancient of days did sit, whose garment was white as snow, and the hair of his head like the pure wool."* Here the Bible uses the adjective "pure" to describe wool. Have you ever seen an old black man with a gray Afro? The closest adjective to describe this man's hair would be pure wool. How do we know that the Bible refers to the ancient of days as Yahweh? Refer to Daniel 7:22 which states, *"Until the Ancient of days came, and judgment was given to the saints of the most high; and the time came that the saints possessed the kingdom."* Here it appears that the judgment of the saints cannot take place without god or the Ancient of days' presence. Finally in verse 13 Daniel states, *"I saw in the night visions, and behold, one like the Son of man came with the clouds of heaven, and came to the Ancient of days, and they brought him near before him. And there was given him dominion, and glory and a kingdom that all people, nations, and languages, should serve him; This dominion is an everlasting dominion, which shall not pass away, and his kingdom that which shall not be destroyed.*" Many people confuse this person who is like the Son of man to be Jesus because this person receives all glory and an everlasting kingdom from the ancient of days or god. They throw out the fact that Jesus is referred to as the Son of man not *like* the Son of man, making it impossible for Daniel to have been talking about Jesus.

## The African-American Slavery Predicted by the Old Testament

Several prophecies appear to predict the predicament of the African-American slaves. God informs Abraham that his seed would be enslaved in a land that wasn't theirs. (See Genesis 15:13-16.) Many insist that these passages refer to the Egyptian captivity. However, that is impossible since Genesis 15:16 states that the Amorites are the people who enslave Abram's descendants. In I Samuel 7:14, the Amorites were at peace with Israel, thus having never begun the iniquity spoken of in Genesis 15:16. The Hebrew word used in the Bible for Egyptians was "Mizraim"; refer to the chapter on races for evidence showing this fact. Moreover, also given was a time period when this would happen: in the fourth generation. If we decipher the fourth generation with a literal meaning we could count down four generations from Abraham down. Abraham is the first, Isaac second, Jacob third, Joseph fourth; after Joseph would be the fifth generation.

The Bible clearly shows that Joseph's generation of Israelites were welcomed and shared in prosperity with Egypt, thus they were not slaves until after the fourth generation. Exodus 1:6 states, *"And Joseph died and all his brethren and all that generation."* Clearly, the fourth generation is gone when Egypt enslaves Israel. But let's examine Genesis 15:16 more carefully. It is clearly stating that in the fourth generation Israel leaves enslavement (the

Exodus) in that foreign land and returns to Israel.

For the commonly assumed reasoning of the passages in Genesis 15:16 to be true, the Israelites would have had to be enslaved before they existed, and leave Egypt sometime during Joseph's life span. This never happened.

Next I looked for a slavery in history where Israel was in bondage, being afflicted 400 years. It was already evident that for the prophesy in Genesis 13:15 to be true it would surely be an event that would take place after the writings of the Bible.

| Chronology | Hebrew Event |
|---|---|
| 2500 B.C.? | **Eber** is the first Hebrew. The name means "he who crossed over." |
| 2000-1800 B.C. | **Father Abraham** The first recorded Hebrew contacted by Yahweh—asked to kill his own child |
| 2000-1800 B.C. | **Father Isaac** Considered the second patriarch; son of Abraham and father of Jacob—first biblical recording of different nations born simultaneously |
| 2000-1800 B.C. | **Father Jacob** The first Israelite—father of Israel, name meaning power with god |
| 2000-1800 B.C. | **Joseph** Son of Jacob—by living in abundance in Egypt allows his eleven brothers (the children of Israel) to move to Egypt also |
| 1800-1500 B.C. | **Israel in Egypt** becomes a large community—Egyptians place Israel in bondage. |

| | | |
|---|---|---|
| 1500 B.C. | **Egyptian plagues**—Exodus from Egypt, Moses leads the children in the wilderness—Jehovah is forced on Israel. | |
| 1400-1100 B.C. | **Joshua** fights the battle of Jerico and establishes Yahweh's order—Judges set over Israel. | |
| 1100-931 B.C. | **Israelite Kingdom**—Israel chooses first king, **Saul,** with Samuel as the prophet; **David** with prophet Nathan reigns as second successor over Israel; **Solomon** reigns as third successor over Israel; Nathan. | |

| **Israel is divided into two kingdoms:** | | |
|---|---|---|
| | **South** | **North** |
| 931 B.C. | Rehoboam | Jeroboam I |
| 875 B.C. | Jehoshaphat | Ahab/Elijah & Elisha |
| 790 B.C. | Uzziah/Isaiah | Jeroboam II/Hosea |
| 722 B.C. | Fall of Sumaria | |
| 716 B.C. | Hezekiah/Isaiah | |
| 640 B.C. | Josiah/Jeremiah | |
| 586 B.C. | Fall of Jerusalem to the Babylonian Empire | |

| | |
|---|---|
| 539 B.C. | Tribe of Judah re-established in Israel |
| 520-515 B.C. | Haggai, Zechariah, and the rebuilding of the second temple |
| 486-465 B.C. | Queen Hadassah (Hebrew)-(Persian) Esther—saves Israelite provinces from genocide |
| 457-444 B.C. | Ezra, Nehemiah, and Malachi the last prophets in the Old Testament |
| 7 B.C. | Prophecy of John the Baptist birth |
| 5 B.C. | John the Baptist's birth |
| 5-4 B.C. | Birth of Jesus |
| A.D. 25-27 | Ministry of John |
| A.D. 27-30 | Ministry of Jesus |
| A.D. 70 | The final fall of Israel—scattering the tribes to the four corners of the earth |

I also looked up the word "generation" in Hebrew with a paperback version of *Strong's Concordance.* I discovered that perhaps the Israelites were not speaking of a father-to-father-to-father situation. But apparently in this particular instance, the word "generation" is talking about a period of time, a revolution or cycle of one thousand years.

Now it all would fit into place. The African-American slavery and affliction still in effect lasted closest to the four hundred years prophesied and the fourth generation or four thousand years after the time of Abraham click right into place. It even appeared as if

Father Abraham is shown directly when and why the slavery will come to an end. But the end of this period would not happen until the iniquity of the Amorites (white Americans) was fulfilled according to the Bible.

These conclusions could seem somewhat far-fetched if this was the only prophecy of the African-American slavery, but there is so much more as I will show you. In Deuteronomy chapter 28 it will be clearly evident that the only slavery in history meeting all the requirements and conditions of the prophecy will be that of the African-Americans.

Yahweh informs the Israelites in Deuteronomy 28 of all the blessings that will come if they will do his laws, statutes, and commandments. He says in verse 1, *"And it shall come to pass if thou* (Israel) *shalt hearken* (listen and obey) *diligently unto the voice of Yahweh thy God, to observe and to do all his commandments which I command thee this day, that Yahweh will set thee on high* (cult brainwashing techniques similar to those of Hitler) *above all nations* (racism) *of the Earth: And all these blessings shall come on thee, and overtake thee, if thou shalt hearken unto the voice of Yahweh.*

***"Blessed shalt thou be in the city, and blessed shalt thou be in the field. Blessed shall be the fruit of thy body, and the fruit of thy ground, and the fruit of thy cattle, the increase of thy kine, and the flocks of thy sheep. Blessed shall be thy basket and thy store. Blessed shalt thou be when thou comest in and blessed shalt thou be when thou goest out."***

On the other hand, for Israel's disobedience to Yahweh's law and statutes, quite the contrary is true. In Deuteronomy 28:15 we read, *"But it shall come to pass if thou shalt not hearken* (listen, obey, be my perfect slave) *unto the voice of Yahweh, thy God, to observe to do all his commandments and his statutes which I command thee this day; that all these curses shall come upon thee, and over take thee.*

***"Cursed shalt thou be in the city, and cursed shalt thou be in***

*the field. Cursed shall be thy basket and thy store. Cursed shall be the fruit of thy body, and the fruit of thy land, the increase of thy kine, and the flocks of thy sheep. Cursed shalt thou be when thou comest in and cursed shalt thou be when thou goest out."*

Let's stop and focus on the fact that according to the Old Testament, Israel rarely obeyed Yahweh's laws and statutes. Therefore if we are firm believers in the Old Testament, then we know that the Israelites of today should receive these prophecies of a curse from Jehovah. That is, they should in general live out vexation, curses, and rebuke. They must definitely not be wealthy or generally excepted as a "well-off race of people" in comparison to the world. This eliminates the Jewish race, for they can trace their ancestral tree back only to Japheth and Esau (later discussion in the chapter dealing with races) Indo-European. Furthermore, they are considered a wealthy people, not poor.

Deuteronomy 28:21 states, "***Yahweh shall make*** *the pestilence (plague, disease) cleave unto thee.*" African-Americans and blacks throughout the world are on the bottom of the social ladder within any country where they dwell. Blacks in larger numbers than other races die younger from hypertension, stroke, kidney failure, heart attack, and diabetes. "*Until he have consumed thee from off the land* (the real Israelites are not on the land) *whither thou goest to possess.*" Furthermore, in verse 30, an act that was commonly practiced within African-American slavery was the white master's seizure of the black female's virginity before she was allowed to marry her husband. It states, "*Thou shalt betroth a wife, and another man shall lie with her: thou shalt build a house and thou shalt not dwell therein: thou shalt plant a vineyard, and shalt not gather the grapes thereof.*" The African-American slaves built their master's buildings and raised his crops from which they reaped no reward for their labor, just as prophesied. When the African-American slaves (Israelites) gave birth to their babies they belonged to their masters; no such lifestyle ever took place with the modern-day Jewish parents. Verse 32 states, *"Thy sons and thy daughters shall be given unto another people, and thine eyes shall look, and fail with longing for them all the day long: and there shall be no might in thine hand."* Finally, in verse 64-65 we find that the Israelites are no longer located in Israel. It states, *"And the Lord shall scatter thee among all people, from the one end of the Earth even unto the other; and there thou shalt serve other gods, which neither thou nor thy fathers have known, even wood and stone. And among all these nations shalt thou find no ease, neither shall the sole of thy foot have rest: but the Lord shall give thee there a trembling heart, and failing of eyes, and sorrow of mind."* An example of this fact existing even today can be found in the belly of America's prisons. More than 70 percent of the American prison population consists of blacks while general population is less than 15 percent black. This too was prophesied in Isaiah 42:22 which states, *"But this is a people robbed and spoiled; they are all of them snared in holes, and they are hid in prison houses they are for a prey, and none delivereth; for a spoil,* **and none saith, restore.**" Certainly this passage could be referring to a period in ancient Israelite history of the distant past, but just as all the distant captivities haunted the Israelites into the current present life so it would seem part of the perpetuating circumstances of this particular nation of people. The karma (energy) is passed down from generation to generation through the DNA, consciousness, and universal memory of the species. Just as man chose the state of perpetual amnesia or loss of self into a state of deaths and rebirths, so have the species (reptilian, snake, dragon, man/Ape, Pleiadian, Sirius, Orion, Arcturus) within the various nationalities of humans lost parts of themselves into perpetual life cycle of events. These life cycles can never be quenched as long as the life force (soul/spirit) fails to recognize the reality of its *true* existence. Therefore, with our current knowledge of biblical prophecy we conclude the following with regard to the biblical Israelites today:

1. They began enslavement approximately four thousand years after Father Abraham's vision of prophecy. (The African-Americans' history reasonably satisfies this prophecy.)

2. They were enslaved for four hundred years and afflicted. (The African-Americans' history reasonably satisfies this prophecy.) Until today African-Americans have lost their names, language, and entire cultural identity. Today the vast majority of blacks service America in remedial jobs for lower pay than their white counterparts.

3. After enslavement is banished, they are to remain with their captors until the iniquity ("evil deeds"—such as oppression, racism, killing and so forth) of the Amorites is full (complete). (The African-Americans' history reasonably satisfies this prophecy).

4. The Amorites (Americans) must enslave them. (The African-Americans' history reasonably satisfies this prophecy).

5. They must not live as a nation in the land of Israel. (The African-Americans' history again reasonably satisfies this prophecy.)

6. These people must according to prophecy be on the bottom of the social ladder with a higher mortality rate than other races (Again the African-Americans' history reasonably satisfies this prophecy.)

7. They should be the majority of people within the prisons. Their cyclic universal existence is one of self-destruction, which causes them to fall prey to victimization by other nationalities. (All karmic energy can be broken once the intent to do so is manifested.)

There are so many clues in the prophecies establishing that the African-American people are the only people in history that can satisfy all the requirements, thus leading to the conclusion that the

African Americans are a part of the true lost tribes of Israel. For example, Deuteronomy states 28:25, *"Yahweh shall cause thee to be smitten before thine enemies: thou shalt go out one way against them and flee seven ways before them: and shalt be removed into all the kingdoms of the Earth."* Here we have Israelites in all kingdoms (nations) and kicked out of Israel. See the chapter on who the Israelites are today. Verse 26 continues, *"And thy carcass shall be meat unto all fowls of the air, and unto the beast of the Earth, an no man shall fray* (chase) *them away."* The most vivid picture of this prophecy is sung in a song by Billie Holiday called "Strange Fruit." The fruit in the trees makes one visualize the vast quantities of beaten, bloody, black bodies lynched and hanging for the vultures, buzzards and other scavengers to devour. In the 28th verse, *"Yahweh shall smite thee with madness, blindness, and astonishment* (amazement and wonder) *of heart."*

With this verse in mind let's look into the eyes of the starved, big-bellied African babies, and the drug- and poverty-infested slums of America. These wonders are typically shown weekly on TV at some point or another. They constantly remind us that AIDS is growing at a much faster rate for African-American women than for white women. I am not saying that every African baby or the majority of Africans are starving. I am simply saying that for one reason or another poverty, starvation, homelessness, drugs, child abuse, etc. are shown far more with black faces in white media. White child abusers, criminals, homeless people, etc. are not shown nearly as often as the black faces, therefore causing the world to look on the black race with astonishment, thus fulfilling the prophecy.

My white co-worker asked me why our people live in such deplorable conditions there in Chicago. His exact words were "Why are your people living like this?" I explained to him that his question was out of order, insulting, and offensive. I informed my co-worker that if he asks the right black person a question in such manner he could lose a couple of teeth behind that question. I quickly brought up rich black members of our race such as Oprah Winfrey and Michael Jordan.

They are the exceptions to the rule, he insisted. And then he went on even to insult them, wondering how can they be happily caught up in their little world of fortune while a devastating number of African-American people (their people) suffer in poverty. I realized then, that this was a form of madness among my people, because he was right; we do have the few wealthy within our race who could purchase factories and businesses to place many of our own people in jobs. Instead, many of them give to organizations like the United Negro College Fund and the sort, which contribute very little to the cause. Most people are not aware that non-profits are required by law to place only a minimum of 10 percent of the funds toward the cause for which they were created. Thus, if Oprah gives one million dollars to the United Negro College Fund, by law they have every right to distribute $900,000.00 for anything other than funding black colleges, such as positions, research, grants to other organizations, and so forth as they see fit.

If our wealthy African-Americans are wise in their business strategies they should become even richer while lifting up their fellow man in the black community simultaneously. This Romanian white man, whom I will call Dan, was quick to inform me that in his race each person is taught to feel responsible and to seek out a way of lifting up his fellow man. He said that if a person seemed sincere, and promised to pay him back, he could easily loan them thousands of dollars. Dan went on to explain that it was incomprehensible as to how the Oprahs and Jordans of our race did not use their fame and wealth to build businesses and jobs within the black communities. He went on with an example and said that Michael Jordan allows restaurants, shoemakers and so forth to use his name to make billions while he gets only pennies in comparison. Dan felt that as long as we have black people begging in the streets and homeless on Chicago's lower Wacker Drive, all efforts and finances should be pooled to remedy these situations.

I was speechless, but I knew that our wealthy people are also victims of being told where they should put their money for the purpose of charity. They are told that they cannot save the world, and then there are the endless beggars that force them to feel that there is no end and that indeed the information they are fed is truth. They cannot change the world. I can tell when I hear them speak out that they are constantly being reminded that they cannot save the world. Why not? The world has put them where they are today. I could be wrong, but I do not believe any white charities formed for the sake of poor unfortunate blacks has ever advised our rich people to build businesses to make our poor people wealthy, while at the same time making themselves richer than imaginable. Blind madness.

Without a doubt all races have their poverty-stricken, unfortunate outcasts of society, but the world targets blacks in the limelight of destruction in general. Before we sidetrack, let's return to our Bible verses and deal with the issues as they are stated there. Deuteronomy 28:29 says: *"And thou shalt grope at noonday, as the blind gropeth in the darkness, and thou shalt **not prosper** in thy ways: and then shalt thou be only oppressed and spoiled (robbed) ever more and **no man shall save thee**."* Today Africans are being raped and robbed of their natural resources. Excellent accounts of this fact can be found in *The Unseen Hand*, by A. Ralph Epperson, and *How Europe Underdeveloped Africa*, by Walter Rodney. An activist and political leader who publicly speaks out against the rape and destruction of Africa is Lyndon LaRouche. He prints information on worldwide deceits, trickeries, and tragedies resulting in millions on top of millions of deaths unknown to the common everyday person. I keep myself informed through his organization and its publication, *The New Federalist*. The only caution to my readers is that he does teach that he is the only leader who can make a difference and all his followers fanatically believe that Lyndon LaRouche is the only man who can save the world. I do not support this belief, for it is when we believe that one man, and one man only will save our souls, that we lose our souls. The only way that the human race can be saved is by the human race, NOT AN INDIVIDUAL LEADER.

Refocusing biblically, we should pay close attention to the final part of this particular verse for "*NO MAN SHALL SAVE THEE.*" If there is any validity to these words spoken by God (according to the Bible), only a woman, angel, some unknown force or God, can change the conditions of this race of people. Of course here we are dealing with the assumption that the Bible is completely factual.

Verse 33 has serious implements requiring that another nation be placed in Israel **whom Israel does not know**. Up until now many of these prophetic curses could be confused with instances of other races or even earlier times in ancient Israel. But now we are narrowing the margin of possibility considerably. Most all Bible scholars know and do not argue that apparently the Israelite people were highly civilized and educated. Many Israelites not only knew of a vast number of nationalities surrounding them, but also spoke diverse languages. So now we can see it was impossible for the neighboring races to have enslaved Israel in this particular instance. Israel knew of Egypt, Babylon, Assyria, Persia, and all the people in their area to whom at various times, according to the Bible, they have fallen into captivity. So now we can completely eliminate these captivity periods from consideration of this prophecy with assurance only if God's word is valid. The African Israelites knew the nationalities that subjected them to slavery in biblical times; however, the Israelites knew next to nothing about the Northern Europeans or **the Jewish/Israeli people who are in their country today.**

The Jewish people are not the Ancient Hebrew Israelites, nor did the Ancient Hebrews practice Judaism. However, Judaism is a branch of the Ancient Hebrew religion. No nation today can practice the strict morbid laws of my ancient ancestors due to the fact that this barbaric energy of mass participation in self-annihilation and destruction has partially dissipated. The last time that we humans with world power practiced anything close to the Ancient Hebrew religion was during World War II with Adolf Hitler. Ever since then the masses have not supported such actions knowingly, although this is not to say that even at this very moment genocide and mass murder are not taking place. There are a select few who have taken it upon themselves to fulfill Yahweh's prophecies in heaven. That is, they are working to destroy the human race for their own enemy, and haven't got a clue that they are being used like puppets.

There are biblical examples of people portraying themselves as Hebrew Israelites when indeed they were not. The first can be found in the book of Kings, where we find that Israel is taken away captive to serve another race of people. The land of the Israelites is replenished with another people *(people who are not Israel)* who learn the Israelite language and customs in order not to be destroyed by the magical incantations of Jehovah/Baal. Look in your Bible at II Kings 17:24-28, *"And the king of Assyria brought men from Babylon, and from Cuthah, and from A'va and from Ha'math, and from Sepharva'im, and* **placed them in the cities of Samaria instead of the children of Israel** (THIS IS WHY JESUS TOLD HIS DISCIPLES NOT TO GO INTO THE WAY OF SAMARIA, BECAUSE THEY WERE NOT ISRAELITES): *and* **they possessed Samaria** *and dwelt in the cities thereof. And so it was at the beginning of their dwelling there, that they feared not the Lord: therefore the Lord sent lions among them, which slew some of them. Wherefore they spake to the king of Assyria, saying, the nations which thou has removed, and placed in the cities of Samaria, know not the manner of the God of the land: therefore he hath sent lions among them, and, behold, they slay them, because they know not the manner of the God of the land. Then the king of Assyria commanded saying, Carry thither one of the priests whom ye brought from thence; and let them go and dwell there, and let him teach them the manner of the God of the land* (**The Israelites have**

recorded that the king of Assyria took them captive while placing several other nations in their land and commanded their
priests to teach the foreign people the Israelite culture). *Then
one of the priests whom they had carried away from Samaria came
and dwelt in Bethel and taught them how they should fear the Lord."*
I am sure that these people did not go on to become the Jewish
people of today, but this is a biblical account of how it is possible
for a foreign people to live in the Israelite land and practice in part
the Israelite customs, **yet they are not Israelites**.

Another biblical account in which there are foreign people
living in the land of Israel can be found in the New Testament as
stated by Jesus Christ himself. In both Revelation 2:9 and 3:9, *"I
know thy works, and tribulations, and poverty."* The King James
Version adds in *"but thou art rich."* (Note that Jesus did not say
this—the original writings did not say this!) In an attempt to
make the modern Jews, who are considered rich, appear to be the
same poor ancient Israelites, the translators had to insert their
own words. For King James' translators knew that the Jewish
people are rich. Again the translators try to help the Bible make
sense by paralleling what was actually said (the Israelites are poor)
with what in reality existed (rich Jews). Anytime you see phrases
in parentheses know that this is the mind of a translator, it was not
there originally in "God's Word." The translators were so kind to
let you know when they added their own words to the Bible. The
same verse continues, *"And I know the blasphemy of them which
**say they are Jews, and are not**, but are the synagogue of Satan."*
Here Jesus' racism rears its ugly head again. Racism during the
ancient time was systematically instilled into people. It would have
taken a miracle for one to recognize the mistake of racism in Jesus'
day, and even he fell victim to it.

He repeats this again in Revelation 3:9: *"Behold, I will make
them of the synagogue of Satan, which say they are Jews, and are not,
but do lie; behold, I will make them* (Jewish people) *come and worship before thy feet* (the ancient African Hebrews who followed

— 84 —

Ancient Christianity {**not today's Christians**}. Jesus made the same mistake of most all religions and that is cutting off all humanity that was not exactly like himself) . . . *and to know that I have loved thee.*" The Bible continuously mentions that there are people living amongst the Ancient Hebrews who could not possibly be Hebrews. For example, we find in St. John 8:31-33: "*Then said Jesus to those Jews which believed on him, If ye continue in my word, then are ye my disciples indeed; And ye shall know the truth, and the truth shall make you free. They answered him, We be Abraham's seed, and were never in bondage to any man: how sayest thou, Ye shall be made free?*" To get the gist of what has been said imagine someone saying that he is the direct descendant of Harriet Tubman, but later on in conversation admits that his people had never gone into slavery. You would know that either this person isn't an African-American or they are lying about not having been enslaved. Likewise, in this verse, either these people are not Jews or they are lying when they say that they have been enslaved to no man. It is very probable that these people are telling the truth and that they are the direct descendants of Father Abraham through Isaac's favorite son, Esau.

Jesus called the Jewish people Satan because his father god did the same thing and stated that he hated Esau. Jehovah states that he hates Esau in Malachi 1:2-3, "*I have loved you saith the Lord, Yet ye say, Wherein hast thou loved us* (the nation of Israel)? *Was not Esau Jacob's brother, And I hated Esau, and laid his mountains and his heritage waste for the **dragons** of the wilderness.*" Jacob and Esau are nations of opposition. Theory has it that again manipulation of human DNA produced twin babies born to Rebekah, one a black child and the other a white child. For biblical reference see Genesis 25:23-25, "*And the Lord said unto her, '**Two nations** are in thy womb, and **two manner of PEOPLE** shall be separated from thy bowels; and the one people shall be stronger than the other people; and the elder shall serve the younger.' And when her days to be delivered were fulfilled, behold, there were twins in her womb. And the* *first came out red all over like an hairy garment; and they called his name Esau."* More than likely, if this Bible verse is true regarding two nations coexisting in Rebekah's womb, the only way that this could have happened is through genetic manipulation. One other possibility would be that during the time that Rebekah was ovulating her husband, Isaac, may have had intercourse and then hours or even moments later Rebekah could have freely or forcibly had sex with another human or species, thereby producing two separate races within one pregnancy. The offspring would have to be fraternal twins, where the mother releases two eggs. One egg could have been fertilized with Isaac's sperm while the other egg received the sperm of someone other than Isaac. Whether this action took place in a scientific clinic, as it appears to have taken place here in the Bible, or naturally, is not clear. But the only way to have two nations in one womb is to place TWO NATIONS IN ONE WOMB!

I believe that the Bible is giving a corrupted account of an event that did indeed take place. It appears to me that if Jacob was black and Esau white (or another race), that there could have been even a third way and this way happens even today. I have witnessed it for myself. Twins can be born to a black mother and father with one being white and the other black, if the white one is actually albino. So, whichever the case, maybe it is scientifically possible for this event to have taken place. Manipulation of human DNA seems much more logical when one has a sound understanding of ancient mythology and history.

Therefore it appears that god had blessed the barren couple to conceive and in this conception he purposely created a source of friction to be raised up amongst the human race. These boys, according to Yah's plan, would grow and destroy the human race or at least help keep the animal population of man to an all-time minimum through continuous wars. He inspired Japheth to migrate north so that he would lose color pigmentation. And he later nuked (radioactive blast) the Canaanites so that they two would lose melanin. The prophecy given to Father Abraham regarding the American slavery in Genesis 15:13-16 Jehovah self-fulfilled, keeping the Israelites in racist ignorance against their brothers (fellow humans), the white race. Many preachers deceive people either on purpose or out of ignorance themselves and they teach that this was the prophecy of the Egyptian slavery. But don't you let them fool you. It is impossible for this to be the Egyptian slavery and you will see why.

Deuteronomy 28:36-37 states: *"The Lord shall bring thee, and thy king which thou shalt set over thee* (in West Africa), *unto a nation* (America) *which neither thou nor thy fathers have known: and there shalt thou serve other gods, wood and stone. And thou shalt become an astonishment, a proverb, and a byword* (gibe—to mock, jeer, or make fun of), *among all nations whither Yahweh shall lead thee."*

For this verse to be a true prophecy Yahweh must have been talking of various enslavements and exile states of existence throughout the history of the African Israelites. In his book *From Babylon to Timbuktu,* Rudolph R. Windsor superbly illustrates and documents historical migrations of the ancient Hebrew Israelites of the Bible up through to the Hebrew Israelites of today. He shows how and where the Israelites scattered to the four corners of the earth. One group of our people migrated to west Sudan and established an empire that extended into Ghana, West Africa. The native Africans accepted the Israelite community due to its ability to establish creative economic wealth through the high-tech knowledge that they brought with them. The Israelites established civil growth, with engineering, agricultural, and architectural influences. They constructed crossroads for trading goods, customs, and ideas. Every country the Israelites settled into would soon owe a large part of its economic success to them. Even here in America, though oppressed and destitute, many from the Israelite (African-American) community built America with blood, sweat, tears, and, yes, technical resources. Look up the true founder of Chicago, the first successful heart surgeon, and numerous inventors in *100 Amazing Facts about the Negroes with Complete Proof* by J. A. Rogers, and other literature that gives information about famous blacks.

We cannot devote much time to proving the fact that there are many successful blacks for it would require an entire book. My point is that the Israelites have blessed all the nations most everywhere they dwelt, thereby becoming an astonishment and a proverb. None of these nations feel indebted to Israel in any way. Indeed, they all have developed bywords such as niggers, coons, darkies, and spooks, etc., when they refer to them. We are blessed nowadays to have sweeter-sounding bywords that even we as a people accepted, such as Negroes, coloreds, blacks, and African-Americans. All of these words and so many more have been used to refer to a part of the ancient Israelite race (the only race to fulfill the prophecy [more accurate: a psychic reading] of the ancient Hebrew Israelites from Yahweh) now in America and scattered all over the planet, which is the tribe of Judah. Let's make an assessment of many of the other races here in America.

*The people are:*
1. from a land called Germany, with a language called German and a people called Germans, possessing German names.
2. from a land called Great Britain or England, with a language and a people called English, possessing English names.
3. from a land called France, with a language and a people called French, possessing French names.
4. from a land called Italy, with a language and a people called Italians, possessing Italian names.
5. from a land called China, with a language and a people called Chinese, possessing Chinese names.
6. from a land called Nigeria, with a people called Nigerians, possessing Nigerian languages and names.

7. from a land called Ghana, with a people called Ghanaian, possessing Ghanaian languages and names.
8. from a land called Sudan, with a people called Sudanese, possessing Sudanese languages and names.
9. from a land called India, with a people called Indians, possessing Indian languages and names.

These examples make up but a few of the nationalities that live here in America today. Every last nationality has a country, language, and a name for their people that recognizes and legitimizes their inheritance (their land), Mother Earth, with the exception of the African-American. These nations of people can return to the land of their forefathers. There is no African-American land for us to return to, none of us speak African-Americanese, or African-Americanish. As a matter of fact, this language and people does not even exist if you look them up prior to the past few decades.

A nice Israelite community in Harvey, Illinois, had the most wonderful song that they sang there which still brings sentiment to my heart: "I Can See Everybody's Nation, But Mine." It was written and sung by such a beautifully, sweet, older African Israelite lady. She sang the lyrics so graciously: "Ever since my nation died, all I can do is hang my head and cry, cause I can see everybody's nation, but mine." What a tragic fact, that even the majority of the blacks here in America have never realized. Even the black tribes originally in Africa turned against us in the end and took part in helping the white man catch us to place us into bondage. Truly, Israel has been utterly destroyed and no man has saved her.

Continuing on, in Deuteronomy 28:41,we find: *"Thou shalt beget sons and daughters, but thou shalt not enjoy them; for they shall go into captivity."*

We can see that the proverb stating that a man who does not know his history is doomed to repeat it certainly appears accurate for the African Israelites. Verses 43-45 continue, *"The stranger that is within thee (a race of people with Israel but not Israel) shall get up above thee very high* (This happened during and prior to the Roman conquer of Israel in 70 A.D.): *and thou shalt* **come down very low**. *He shall lend to thee, and thou shalt not lend to him: he shall be the head,* (on top, ruling, with power) *and thou shalt be the tail* **(on the bottom, lead about, without power)**. *Moreover all these curses shall come up on thee, and shall pursue thee, and overtake thee, till thou be destroyed; because thou heakenedst not unto the voice of Yahweh thy God, to keep his commandments and his statutes which he commanded thee: And they* (curses) **shall be upon thee** (Israel) *for a sign and for a wonder, and upon thy seed for ever."* According to the Bible, the chosen children of Yahweh, because they had not kept God's commandments, are today in general a race of people suffering in poverty: the last hired and the first fired, the dwellers of the slums, the highest mortality rate among new-borns, with the shortest life expectancy. Many of them never live long enough to receive social security benefits These verses alone make it impossible for the Jewish people to be the ancient Hebrew Israelites. The Israelites went from world renown to the bottom of the social ladder wherever they are found unto this day.

Furthermore, ladies and gentlemen, pay close attention to this one if you still have not seen the African-American slavery in any of these prophecies. Now you will! Deuteronomy 28:47-50 states (please brace yourself for this one), *"Because thou servdest not Yahweh thy god with joyfulness,* (which Israel was going to do regardless of anything Yahweh said) *and with gladness of heart, for the abundance of all things; Therefore shalt thou* **serve thine enemies** *which Yahweh shall* **send against thee**, *in hunger and in thirst, and in nakedness, and in want of all things: and he* (America) *shall put a yoke of iron upon thy neck* (see the movies *Roots* or *Amistad*) *until he* (America) *have destroyed thee* (forced Israelites to no longer exist as Israelites). *Yahweh shall bring a nation* (America) *against thee from far,* to describe how far Yahweh continues, *from* **the end of the Earth**, (now to describe the symbol of that nation, Yahweh continues) *as swift as the eagle flieth; a nation whose tongue* *thou shalt not understand* (**remember Israel knew the languages of her neighbors and other captors**). *A nation of fierce countenance, which shall not regard the person of the old* (of all nations of the world, which throws her elderly in nursing homes more than any other?), *nor shew favor to the young.*" There are no other races in all of history other than the African-Americans and the white Americans, where one race would come from the end of the earth (the other side of the earth) and enslave the other race of people for four hundred years except for the African-American people. Knowing Yahweh's character, and that failure to adhere to the commandments always meant enslavement for the Israelite race, which two races do you know of that captured and enslaved the other race from opposite ends of the Earth?

The fact that Yahweh was able to predict this prophecy, however, is nothing new. Many individuals even today can predict the fate of another individual; they are called psychic. Accessing information from other dimensions and levels of consciousness has been done since the beginning of time. Jehovah simply altered his consciousness to look into the possible destiny outcomes of Ancient Israel, thus predicting Deuteronomy 28. In all actuality when we read the so-called biblical prophecy, it should be called— fortune telling. To read about people who have done the same type of work as Jehovah (predicting the future) look up the names Edgar Cayce and Nostradamus.

## Biblical Account of Hebrew-Israelite Origins

Most Bible readers do not have a thorough knowledge of how the Israelites came into existence. Anyone who would say that Father Abraham was an Israelite grossly misunderstands where and how the term Israelite came about. Many will say that Moses was a Jew, which is totally false. Now I will break down for you the origin of the Nation of Israel and the Jews.

It all starts, according to the Old Testament, with Abraham.

That's why they say that Father Abraham is the patriarch of the Hebraic race. We find the first mention of a Hebrew person in Genesis 14:13, *"And there came one that had escaped, and told Abram the Hebrew."* We know that Abram the Hebrew is actual Abraham from Genesis 17: 3-5, which states, *"And Abram fell on his face: and god talked with him, saying, as for me behold, my covenant is with thee, and thou shalt be a father of many nations. Neither shall thy name anymore be called Abram, but thy name shall be Abraham, for a father of many nations have I made thee."* However Abraham was not the first Hebrew. Strong's Concordance says that "Hebrew" in the Hebrew language was the word "Ibriy" pronounced "ib-ree" coming from the name E-ber, implying that the Hebrew race began with a patriarch known as Eber and his name meant one who crossed over. Eber can be found in Genesis 10:21-25 and 11:14-17.

Now, Abraham brought forth Isaac and Isaac brought forth Jacob and Jacob gave birth to the name of Israel in Genesis 32:28: *" And he said, thy name shall be called no more Jacob, but Israel: for as a prince hast thou power with God and with men, and hast pre-vailed."* Now, we can see where Hebrew-Israelite originated and if we use biblical meaning the name does appear to mean "he who crossed over with power, with God, and with man."

Let's recap: Abraham, Isaac, and Jacob were three Hebrew patriarchs. See Deuteronomy 1:8, *"you go in and possess* (an act of robbery) *the land which Yahweh sware onto your fathers, Abraham, Isaac, and Jacob."* Jacob becomes the first Israelite. The twelve sons (Nation of Israel) are recorded in Genesis 46:8. You will find that Reuben was his first born, second born was Simeon; third born was Levi; fourth, Judah; fifth, Issachar; and sixth, Zebulun, all by Jacob/Israel's first wife, Leah. Leah also had a daughter named Dinah of whom very little is mentioned, and that which is discussed in the Old Testament appears tasteless and unfruitful. I believe the only reason for her brief mention was to criticize her tasteless acts that she and her brothers (for her sake) are accused of. I leave this one up to you to look up. However, for us to believe that Jacob made four women pregnant, as the Bible states, and had twelve boys and only one girl is statistically improbable. It is without doubt in my mind that had Dinah had an untarnished record she would have never been mentioned since she was considered nothing—a woman. Jacob had two sons by Zilpah, Leah's handmaiden: Gad and Asher. His second wife, Rachel, gave birth to two sons: Joseph, (Jacob's favorite) and Benjamin, the last-born child. Her handmaiden also had two sons for Jacob, Dan and Naphtali.

So, these are the tribes of Israel: Reuben, Simeon, Levi, *Judah*, Issachar, Zebulun, Gad, Asher, Joseph, Benjamin, Dan, and Naphtali. Out of all the Israelites, only one son went on to become a Jew. The word Jew is a shortened form of the tribe of Judah. Therefore, the only way to be a Jew is to come from the tribe of Judah. Moses was a Levite and therefore he could not have been a Jew or from the tribe of Judah. Many people never realized that the majority of Israelites were not Jews (the sons and daughters of Judah). If you still can't make out the difference between a Hebrew Israelite and a Jew, you should start back at Father Abraham and read the beginning of this section carefully again. Even if you have a feel for what is happening it won't hurt to read this part twice so that you can fully grasp what groups of people we are talking about. Later on, for example, Yahweh admits that Father Abraham never heard the name Yahweh, Exodus 6:3, *"And I appeared unto Abraham, by the name Yahweh was I not known."* A god named Yahweh according to the Old Testament did not exist until the days when Israel became large in its numbers. The whole verse says, *"And I appeared unto Abraham, unto Isaac, and unto Jacob, by the name of God almighty* (Hebrew translation of god almighty is the name of a god–"El Shaddai") *but by my name Yahweh was I not known."*

Read your Bible and check out the character of the Israelite god, who sits face to face with them. He boasts continuously that his name is Yahweh, but he forgets to mention his name or decides not to mention his name to Father Abraham and we are just supposed to believe that he appeared to Father Abraham with a title and no name? The god who deals with Israel is egotistical over the importance of his name, using it over six thousand times when dealing with Israel's written accounts. Common sense convinces one that father Abraham did not worship Yahweh. However, he did appear to Abraham when he tried to get him to murder his son Isaac in a human sacrifice to his cause. This is why Yahweh could not get Israel to commit to him only.

I believe that Israel knew that Yahweh was not God, but a god at best, just as today's followers of Yahweh Ben Yahweh know that he is not God, but they call him god because he delivered great wealth and many wondrous things before them. He received a prison term for racketeering, and many of his followers left Florida and moved to Atlanta. They reside there in Atlanta today to my knowledge. The followers are highly intellectually focused, in the hope of re-establishing the Ancient Israel, like the Christians not knowing the origins of their religion. Just as Yahweh-Ben-Yahweh is not GOD, Yahweh is not GOD, but became the Israelites, leader and king, until Saul took his place as king. Israel used Yahweh's advanced technology to escape the bonds of Egypt, but our elders never intended that he would be a god over Israel. Yahweh's plan was set in heaven way before Yahweh contacted the Israelites. Several other gods just like Yahweh planned a conspiracy for the souls of mankind. Many of these gods are known today by the names of Baal, Ashtoreth, El, Anu, Enlil, Enki, Zeus, Apollo, Ptah, Ra, Isis, Horus, Osiris, and so forth, to name only a very few. Who were these gods and where did they come from? Why did they target the human race?

Many books have been devoted to proving that the ancient Israelites were black. That is not the purpose of this book. This book was written to hopefully create a desire to want to know more about the origins of our religions. For more information, read these books:

1. *From Babylon to Timbuktu,* by Rudolf R. Windsor
2. *God, the Black Man, and Truth,* by Ben Ammi
3. *They Came Before Columbus,* by Ivan Van Sertima
4. *The Valley of Dry Bones,* by Rudolf R. Windsor
5. *Stolen Legacy: Greek Philosophy is Stolen Egyptian Philosophy,* by George G.M. James
6. *Destruction of Black Civilization: Great Issues of a Race from 4500 B.C. to 2000 A.D.,* by Chancellor Williams

Remember that there is so much evidence out there. I am giving you just enough for you to know that information like this exists. Go find it.

# FOUR

## A Comparison of Biblical Ancestry to Today's Races

### Hebrew Israelites and the African-Americans

We see similarities in the cultures of the Hebrew Israelite and the African-American in various ways. African-Americans, like the Hebrews, must continuously grease/oil their scalp and hair. The Hebrews called it anointing their heads. Of all the races of the planet it is only the black Africans with woolly hair who are unable to manage their hair without the addition of oils. Some say that it is due to the curl of nine ethers (for kinky hair) and six ethers (for straight hair) which is like the antennae of a ant, but used for connecting to the ultimate source, God.

Whites know that they must wash their hair daily. None of them could consider going for two or three weeks without washing their hair due to their natural oil build up. I can go for up to three weeks without washing my hair, as long as I am leading a relatively sedate life, without any bad odors or impossible-to-manage hair. (Lots of sweating can require blacks to wash their heads weekly to avoid odor.) I will, however, need to add oil (anoint my head with oil) continuously to maintain a well-groomed head of hair. The more modern African-American hairstyle with straight hair (relaxers) may require less oil and more frequent shampoos.

However, this is due to a chemical process to straighten the natural curl of black hair. All throughout biblical history the Hebrews anointed their heads with oil—NOT THEIR FOREHEADS.

It may be fairly difficult for whites to understand the cultural difference in the discipline of our children. African-American children in general are reared from infancy to respect adults and there is little tolerance, in general, for exceptions to this rule. If an African-American child goes too far out of line, he is likely to receive a beating. Black comedians often exaggerate the differences between how blacks and whites discipline their children. They poke fun at how a white child can be rebellious to his parents by telling them to shut up without getting much more than a time-out. The average black child who makes this grave mistake by the age of four or five will never make it again. I believe that the importance of respect for elders and discipline of our children is part of the culture that we brought from Israel to West Africa to America.

The average black person from the Deep South knows that greens should be eaten with the fingers instead of a fork, just as we ate our African foo foo dishes of long ago. There was nothing like a good ol' down south batch of greens on the plate with its trimmings in full. We would take a portion of corn bread between the fingers and sop up a bit of greens, boiled eggs, and onion; with a topping of good ol' fat back/salt pork all in the mouth at one time! And without any conscious effort we would lick every finger clean.

Then we have our old folklore, where it appears that the African slaves were pleading with Yahweh the best way they knew how, to rescue them from bondage. "Swing Low Sweet Chariot, coming for to carry me home," they sang. They were secretly calling out to their alien god to bring his spaceship to take them home. Think about it, what type of chariot do you know that would need to swing low? All the ones that we know of for that day were already on the ground. True? Much of the old Negro folklore seemed to be calling out to the Old Testament god. "Kum Ba Ya," or "Come by here, Yahweh" was another way the slaves would worship their Israelite god in secret. In the Tuskegee Institute choir we sang a song entitled "Ezekiel Saw Da Wheel," again encouraging the African slaves to remember their heritage and their god's characteristics: a god with a flying chariot having wheels in the middle of a wheel—a spaceship.

## Amorites/Canaanites and the European-Americans

In my opinion, as stated before, the white American ancient ancestry goes back to the Amorites/Canaan-Ham/African. Proof of this is a bit more difficult but discernible to anyone looking for the most practical viewpoint. One physical proof that we have among us today is the name of the land, America. We were taught in school that America was named after Amerigo Vespucci, a navigator. That he was a navigator and explorer is about all you will ever hear about the guy. However, Christopher Columbus is given the credit for discovering America in 1492. The land that Columbus "discovered" had no English name at the time. Columbus led great expeditions here and for a time was considered the first to arrive on these shores. Why is it that our country is not called Columbus land? Or better yet, how is it that Amerigo, a nobody in history who never ever gets more than a line or at best a paragraph's mention in the chronicles of history, receives the historical recognition in the future world power, America?

One reason given is that Amerigo claimed discovery of the Americas while Columbus was wandering around America not knowing that he had discovered the land first. Yet, Columbus had chapters after chapters, books after books written on his accomplishments and setbacks both here and abroad. Many dictionaries and encyclopedias omit any mention whatever of Amerigo. Yet we are all willing to accept this concept of Amerigo Vespucci as the predecessor of the name for North and South America. Even if we buy that it is true that a nobody should be given credit for the naming of America, biblically, we must accept that the name by divine order reflects a nation from the end of the earth, which the Israelites did not know, afflicting them for 400 years (combining both Deuteronomy 28 and Genesis 15:13-16).

Do research on American history and you will find that in North America, the United States was populated with the rejects of Europe. The descendants of the outcasts banded together and vowed loyalty to a brotherhood, a secret society, in the forming of America. The Masonic lodge pledged never to forget the evil crimes that the builders of the pyramid or the black people committed against their people. They built a reminder of this fact in their money on the back of the dollar bill. You will see both symbols of the modern (eagle) and the ancient (pyramid) powers. The eagle has thirteen stars above its head, a branch of thirteen leaves in its left foot and thirteen arrows in his right foot. These were all to represent the thirteen American colonies of that time. The All-Seeing Eye, which some call God's eye, can be found above the pyramid. Also on the back of the dollar bill, there are eleven number ones. The eleven ones represent the brotherhood unity of the eleven Canaanite brothers.

Presidents George Washington and Thomas Jefferson and their ancient secret brotherhood of Masonic Order vowed that when the modern powers ("forces of the riders of the goat"—eagle) caught up with the ancient powers ("forces of the riders of the camel"—serpent) some sort of Armageddon-type god/race war would take place. According to the Masonic experts, the Masons were known as worshippers of Lucifer. The thirty-three degrees were considered the highest level that a freemason could obtain. Albert Pike and Manly P. Hall are the most widely publicized and recognized Masons for their participation in the Masonic Order. Hint for the wise: Keywords like Freemasonry, Masons, New World Order, the Illuminati (brothers of the light), Albert Pike, and Manly P. Hall can all be used to research this information. None of this information above will make sense unless you investigate for yourselves; enough is given for you to conduct your own research into these ancient secret societies. (Hence, they are not so secret.)

The early Masonic founders of America claimed to possess the secrets from the temple of Solomon. They vowed an oath to remember how the black brothers turned against the white brothers and roped them out from civilization as lepers and caused them to go backward. Currently, they conduct an initiation ritual in which the initiate is blindfolded and led about with a rope. This ritual keeps it within their memory as to how the African brotherhood (riders of the camel) roped them off and sent them into illiterate darkness. Without civilization they were forced to revert to living in caves and eating juniper berries. They were considered a bastard race without a god all due to the "CURSE OF CANAAN." The Africans **(the entire human race)** had been manipulated by the self-serving gods into separating/dividing for the first time in human existence. Whether by chemical/biological warfare or magical incantations I am not sure, but the gods caused some of us to mutate and lose melanin. The gods told the blacks that those who had become mutated and are now white were the scum of the earth, inferior, low class, and needed to be quarantined from civilization. That is where Europe got its name, explained later.

In Job 30, Job is quoted as saying, *"But now they that are younger than I have me in derision, whose fathers I would have disdained to have set with the dogs of my flock. Yea, whereto might the strength of their hands profit me, in whom old age was perished?"* (Here I believe that Job is speaking of the ancient nuclear radioactive blast or magical spell that caused a minority of the human race to loose melanin by producing albinos or whites.) Job continues, *"For want and famine they were solitary; fleeing into the wilderness in former time desolate and waste: who cut up mallows by the bushes and juniper roots for their meat.* **They were driven forth from among men** (roped off to Europe), *they cried after them as* *after a thief, to dwell in the cliffs of the valleys,* **in caves** *of the Earth, and in the rocks. Among the bushes they brayed* (they have lost their language and grunted like animals) *under the nettles they were gathered together. They were children of fools, yea, children of* **base-men** (according to *Strong's Concordance,* 'for lack of shem')." You must read *The 12th Planet* to realize that here is ABSOLUTE PROOF, that other men left in a shem (a spacecraft) to escape the devastating holocaust. These basemen had no shem in which to escape (during Babylon's confounding of the languages and therefore were "nuked"). Job finishes: *"they were viler than the earth."* The Hebrew word for viler was "naka" meaning smitten, broken up, or driven off. The comparison of the basemen to the earth shows direct comparison to the *Enuma Elish* epic of Tiamat's (Earth's) broken and smitten body after the war against Marduk. They vowed never to forget the savagery of their black brothers and their god. In order to remember they named their country after the black brother's deeds. "You roped us off from civilization" or "Europa/Europe."

In the days of Solomon there were Freemasons and secret societies, but the knowledge and wisdom of that day and period were vastly different from what Albert Pike and his fellow Illuminati had touched on. The black Masons of Solomon's time were vastly into the Qabbala or Qabbala/Kabbala (another keyword, with various spellings.) The Qabbala was the study of the tree of life. It has been reported that the possessor of its fruit will possess the power of transformation. This is what I believe happened to Enoch and many others—including Moses—who studied the Qabbala. All of the magical miracles displayed by Moses and his god were produced through the use of the Qabbala. The white modern Masons were left only with the information of the Qabbala's existence and power, but not a practical or applicable use for its power. I am convinced that these people sat on the information and are unsure how to decipher it, like in the movie *Stargate.*

The fears of the gods of the dark-skinned people (the serpent,

Ea) and the gods of the light-skinned people (the eagle, Enlil) and Armageddon causes all the information and archaeological findings to become hush-hush. After all, we can see that these gods were anxious to stimulate war. They caused death, droughts, famine, and dismay among whomever they chose to team against. The black-skinned people were Ea's pets and he played them like a piano. Enlil hated all humans and felt that the only good humans were the humans who would willingly be enslaved. He knew that our spirits would never hold up to what he wanted of us so he decided to assist with the division of humans into the lighter- and darker-complexioned people as a plan to keep humans perpetually suppressed, and to raise a mighty, barbaric nation of light-skinned people who would fight against the reconditioned Baal worshipping (barbaric) dark-skinned ancients.

This is the scary part: Both the dark and light skinned people never really know which gods they will team up against or for. Just as Yahweh/Baal was supposedly against the Egyptians in support of the Israelites and . . . prepare yourself. After all my research, I have found that Ea/El/Yahweh (the merciful god Yahweh for the blacks) had plotted one last genocidal fight against the whites. To counter his brother Enlil's plan of total human extermination by creating division and ultimately (human) self-annihilation, Ea and his fellow supporter gods, the Enkites, all began biochemical warfare against the Europeans beginning in the thirteenth century. Unbeknownst to the Europeans, Ea (or gods who supported the dark-skinned people being in authority) had begun gassing their environment, causing what has become known today as the **black** or bubonic plague. The gods ultimately destroyed uncountable lives. People were dying by the millions. The Europeans never understood how the plague would simply break out from nowhere. They knew that the disease was usually caused from rat-infested, unsanitary conditions where people were crowded. But this disease would pop up from nowhere in sanitary conditions in the rural areas of Europe. Furthermore it was reported that there were increased sightings of UFO activity during this period. The people reported smelling a stench and later the god-awful disease would break out. It was also reported that a strange man in black was seen in the area prior to breakouts. Historians teach that the children's song of "Ring around the Roses" was about smelling flowers, to counter the repulsive odor caused by the chemical warfare on the Europeans during the era of the bubonic plague.

Furthermore, because of the stench, death, and deplorable conditions set forth on the people they began to add new dogma to their religion. Those who engaged in such activity were known as Flagellants. They began beating and scorning themselves for being such terrible sinners in having made the disease materialize in the first place. They felt that this was the only way to truly atone for the sins. The Flagellants had began to believe that they were born disgusting, filthy, the vile of the earth. SOUND FAMILIAR? Just because we have been told such god-awful lies all of our lives do we have to make them our reality? WE OF THE HUMAN RACE ARE NOT VILE DISGUSTING CREATURES FROM BIRTH! It is simply the most deplorable untruth that various races of people were told to hold us in submission for the personal agendas of the gods. With the Israelites, it was how Baal controlled them. For the Europeans, it was the way to make them destroy themselves. But must we be enslaved forever by this lie of being born sinners and disgusting?

Several scientists have established the fact that all human races trace back to one common African ancestral DNA. Allan C. Wilson, professor of biochemistry at the University of California at Berkeley, is quoted in the *Chicago Tribune*, Thursday, January 19, 1989, as saying that he found the African female common ancestor back in the mists of time. He states, "somewhere in Africa 200,000 years ago, Eve, is the sole mother of us all." This can be found also in the *Chicago Sun Times*, dated Sunday, October 29, 1989: "All the world's populations **are just twigs on an African tree,**" Wilson says. "Basically we are all !Kung." The !Kung are an

African tribe claimed to be most closely related to the Eve. Thus far the oldest remains found on the planet are solely of African ancestry. Therefore, although originally black, the Amorites (America named after their father) and the majority of the black Canaanites were turned white. (Genesis 9:25 says, *"cursed be Canaan."*) The Africans (especially Nimrod of Babylon) tortured the unfortunate whites and sacrificed many of them to their gods. It was such an unfortunate situation to have been conquered by the oldest cliché known to man: **DIVIDE AND CONQUER.** The gods had won the taste of sweet victory. Humans have been at war with one another ever since over land, religion, and race, all of which the gods set in place and we (YOU AND I) gladly oblige them the victory.

## Mixing of Noah's Sons and the Indians, Hispanics, and Asians

The Indians, Hispanics, and Asians are the only true mixed races of the planet. They are not made up of a majority of either one of Shem, Hem, or Japheth. In complexion they are made up of browns, reds, and yellow. Many times we confuse the offspring of black and white children as mixed breeds when in all actuality they are black children. However, the mixing of the races for centuries and perhaps millennia will create a new race of people, which evidently appears to have happened to these races. Now I am going to throw some really far-out information to you. Please be seated. Prepare for reception. Let's go!

It is my understanding that a master race of aliens from a star in Orion's belt (which Hitler had become obsessed with) landed in Europe around 1500 B.C. and migrated to the Himalayan Mountains of Tibet. They mixed in primarily with the humans of that area who had already been affected by the mutation of melanin deficiency. They produced a race of humans known as the Aryan race. They taught the people just the opposite of what the blacks had been taught about race superiority. They taught that the whites and lighter complexioned people were superior to all the other races. The lighter the skin pigment the better quality of human one would become. If you were a very good human, then maybe in the next life you would be fortunate enough to come back as a lighter-skinned individual. They were taught that the blacks were untouchables. The people of Hindu religion were swayed to develop the caste system in which the darker-skinned and woolly-haired people would be at the bottom of the social ladder. The lighter the skin pigments the closer to god one became. One of the religious goals of a Hindu was to be an upright and good citizen so that in the next life they would receive the blessing of lighter skin pigment.

Much of what you will discover in this chapter is pieced together using my own spiritual intuitiveness. There are some books that hint a little about the ancient races but for the most part I have put together my own synopsis of what actually happened based on all the data that I have before me. Is it possible for me to be wrong? The answer is without a doubt yes. However, based on biblical and true historical data I know of no contradictions to the information provided here.

## Ham and the Egyptians of Kemet, Ethiopians, and Africans

The biblical name for the Egyptian people was **Mizraim**, son of Ham. Their land was known as Kemet, in reference to their black skin. Their name refers to their black faces, like the Sumerian people (the most ancient people, that documented themselves as being "the black headed ones"). It was almost as if somehow they knew that one day it would be important to refer to themselves as being black. Just as it is throughout the Bible, throughout the pages of ancient history the people continually referred to themselves as "**black**."

Without doubt no one denies the blackness of Ethiopia, the children of **Cush** in the Bible. The god of Israel compared Ethiopians to Israelites and said that there was no difference between the races. Even today Ethiopia has managed to maintain her blackness and her ancient language and some of her culture. As a matter of fact, According to *Who's Who in the Old Testament*, by Joan Comay, the Ethiopian people have passed down through the generations a legend implying that the Queen of Sheba bore Solomon a son by the name of Menelek. Today's Emperor of Ethiopia bears the title "The Lion of Judah." The Hebrew Israelite Ethiopians and many of the Jamaican Rastafarian recognized Haile Selassie as "The Lion of Judah" until he lost his position in 1974 and died later in 1975. Although in general, Ham is given the credit as the father of the black nationalities, we must remember that Ham also has a son by the name of Canaan, who has a son that brought about the Amorite nations—whites that founded America of today. Furthermore, credit must be given to Ham for his contribution of languages and civilization to the human race. To the best of my knowledge the only reason why the development was first given to Ham was due to the stubbornness of his children. They did not take god's word which stated that man shall not eat of the tree of knowledge or that man must not become one like the gods. They partook of the tree of knowledge thus becoming as the gods with the ability to communicate in written languages and build exorbitantly designed buildings. They became in tune with the Adam Kadmon, the soul of Adam when it fell ten consciousnesses into a state of amnesia as it entered the animal known as man. They knew that they could be god's equal thus waging wars with the gods. You should really check into this one. God almighty doesn't have to war with His created (man), but those gods of ancient (Yahweh included) were given a run for their money. We humans were holding our own for a while, until we allowed them to divide and conquer from with in our very own souls.

Egypt has one of the richest recorded ancient histories on the planet. Or should I say that Egypt is the most widely publicized ancient civilization on the planet for all of its amazing wonder.

According to ancient Egyptian epics, the god Ptah ran parallel with the god Anu or Enki/Ea of Sumeria and parallel with the god El of the Old Testament and Canaanite pantheon in the Bible. He was considered the Father god and was mentioned more in ancient Egypt than later. Ra was the ultimate creator god of the Egyptians. Son of Ptah; he was worshipped as the sun god and supreme ruler over heaven and Earth. This god appears to have been the same as the Babylonian god Marduk and the Bible's (Evil Yahweh God) Baal. The black Egyptians today are on the bottom of the social ladder and are scarcely seen in public documentaries. The Egyptians today have yellowish-brown complexion with dark straight hair. These people represent race mixing and do not reflect the original appearance of the ancient Egyptians of Kemet.

## Ishmael with a Mixing of the Sons of Noah and the Israelis, Iraqis, Arabians, Iranians, and Modern-Day Egyptians

Like the modern-day Egyptians, the Israelis are a mixed breed coming from many years of interracial marriages. I believe that that the modern-day Israelis, Iraqis, Arabs and Iranians all stem from a common ancestral background of the latest Arabian-Ishmael (black) and Caucasian (Japheth, Canaan, and Esau). My conclusion is based on the languages they now speak. The Indo-Iranian language appears to stem from the ancient Hurrian and Urartian (Caucasian languages). Also, Arabic has influenced the peoples there. Because of strong race mixing, we can only speculate which races are in this category. The original Arab was also black with woolly hair and in his Koran he called the white man a blue-eyed devil. The god of the Koran was the same bad god of the Old Testament who required racism in order to follow his law. According to scripture, the Arabs are direct descendants of Ishmael, also black with woolly hair. In Genesis 9:27 it states, "*And God shall enlarge Japheth, and he shall dwell in the tents of Shem and Canaan shall be his servant.*" Currently, Japheth rules the world. This verse also implies that some of the Canaan brothers are mixed in with the Shemites (Ishmael) serving Japheth. These races of people raise more questions as to their origin than all the others due to excessive mixing of the races.

## Japheth and the Greeks, Germans, Slavs, Etc.

The most reliable source that reveals the sons of Japheth is a standard Webster's Dictionary. The entry for Japheth states that he was the son of Noah, and then it goes on to define the Japhetic race to be Indo-European. We should note that it is not just European, but Indo-European. This implies a specific category of Europeans. I believe that the Europeans consisted of two groups or actually that two ancient brothers fathered them.

The most ancient race is the Indo-European due to Japheth's ancient migration into the Caucasus Mountains, and his being the first African to have lost black skin pigment.

One may also investigate Bible dictionaries and encyclopedias, which shed more light on the fact. They state that Javan, the son of Japheth, was Greek, and that Magog, another son of Japheth, was Russian. The biblical quote on the sons of Ham, Shem, and Japheth can be found in Genesis 10.

The second family to later join the Caucasian race would be Canaan's son the Amorites, who are from the children of Ham. These people were victims of genetic warfare by the gods in an attempt to create friction in the human population and establish a division among humans where the blacks would quarantine the whites away from civilization (to Europe) and offer those left behind as sacrifices to the gods. They were considered less than animals by their Hamitic black brothers, because of their white skin; refer to Job 30. Read the Willie Lynch letters, *The Making of a Slave*.

## Mixtures of Japheth and Edom (Esau) and the Jewish (Modern-Day Jews)

There are quite a few historical events that prove the white

Jews are not the ancient Israelite people. The first proof is in their Yiddish language itself. The Jewish people do not speak ancient Hebrew, but a combination of Hebrew and a German dialect. There are several biblical prophecies that prove it impossible for the current Jewish race of people to have been the children of Israel. First, as stated before, biblically the stubborn Israelites have been prophesied to be poor and destitute. They have been enslaved to many other nations. If you ask the white Jews to trace back their heritage the majority will tell you the same thing they told Jesus, "Our forefathers have been enslaved to no man."

Let's take a look at St. John 8:31-33: *"Then said Jesus to those Jews* (some of the natives before the 1948 re-population) *which believed on him, 'If ye continue in my word, then are ye my disciples indeed; And ye shall know the truth, and the truth shall make you free.' They answered him, 'We be Abraham's seed, and were never in bondage to any man: how sayest thou, Ye shall be made free?'"* Without realizing it, these Jews were confessing that they were not Jews. We know biblically that the people of the tribe of Judah (Jews) suffered bondage often. Here, these so-called Jews suffered no bondage to any man. Another case of national identity is in the verses dealing with the birth of Esau and Jacob. Genesis 25:23-26 states, *"And the Lord said unto her, Two nations are in thy womb, and two manner of people shall be separated from thy bowels; and the one people shall be stronger than the other people; and the elder shall serve the younger. And when her days to be delivered were fulfilled, behold, there were twins in her womb. And the first came out red, all over like an hairy garment; and they called his name Esau. And after that came his brother out and his hand took hold on Esau's heel; and his name was called Jacob."* Furthermore, the average Jew cannot trace his ancestral tree back to Israel, because Japheth lost his African heritage before the great Babylonian confusion of languages (when the gods changed skin color, thereby causing division among the people). The Jewish people can trace their roots to Indo-European only. But we know that the Indo-Europeans were Japhetic.

Therefore they are not Semitic (children of Shem), thus they are not the Ancient Israelites. Get it?

In Revelation 2:9 and 3:9, twice, Jesus calls the Jews liars (the so-called chosen children of God all called ourselves Hebrew Israelites, not Jews) and he states that there is a race of people calling themselves Jews, but they are not Jews. Then Jesus' prejudice takes over and he calls the Jewish (name meaning **like a Jew** or *Jewish*) people of the synagogue of Satan. Jesus takes the same stance as the one taken in the Koran when the white man is called a blue-eyed devil.

Furthermore, if we simply investigate the history of both the Jewish people and ancient Hebrew Israelites, we will know that these two races are not related. Today's Jewish people trace their inheritance through their females due to mixing with remnants of people who called themselves Jews (who I believe to be Edomite or maybe actual African Jews). Whichever the case, maybe it is through Esau or Judah's women that the Jewish people mixed to inherit brown eyes and brown hair. It was this part of their genealogy that Hitler tried to destroy. Also, today's Jewish culture will not use the name of YHWH (Jehovah) due to their mixing agreement with the original followers of Jehovah. Remember that these people were taught that they were inferior and less qualified to use the name of God. The newer Jewish people, called Goldberg, Blum, or _____berg, with blond or lighter hair and fairer skin NEVER mixed with ancient African Edom/Israel. Their skin and hair characteristics tell the story. Their names confirm the fact. How many times do you find a Goldberg in the Bible or for that matter any of the Jewish/Yiddish names? Again, when we apply linguistic history to the cultures of a people, it sheds light on their ancestral tree. The names of people, their genetic character, their history, and their cultural practice tell a story once it is investigated. We may venture to place the pieces of the puzzle together.

On the other hand, descendants of ancient Israel would **never** portray their heritage through their women, who were considered by far inferior to males. This would be an unthinkable practice in ancient Israelite culture. Israelite children were named after their fathers and would have the father's first name as their last name. For example, if Shem practiced Israelite custom his full name would be Shem Ben Noah. Ham's full name would be Ham Ben Noah, and Japheth would be Japheth Ben Noah, meaning Shem son of Noah, Ham son of Noah, and Japheth son of Noah respectively. I changed my name to reflect my culture: Ezzrath Baht Shem, meaning Ezzrath daughter of Shem. I took my lineage back to Shem in defiance of my corrupted recent ancestral line through the Israelites, which would have caused my name to be Ezzrath Baht Israel or Ezzrath Baht Judah. Furthermore, the god of the Hebrews was always called by his name YHWH by his people! This was a rule without exception; refer to the first section of the chapter "Who was the God of Israel" regarding Jehovah. These two vastly contrasting cultural distinctions between the Jewish people and the children of Judah raise the red flag that the people are NOT one and the same people.

As before I will give you all the resources for this chapter, with the most informative literature first. You should be able to find at least 80 percent of the information in this chapter in the following books. As I had said before, this chapter and some of the following chapters contain inspired information. In other words, I have taken a lot of what I know to be facts and spent much time in meditation with the Creator, The Universal All That There Is. Therefore, not more than 20 percent of this chapter is of inspiration. However, one must keep in mind that all the inspired information is that which the average reader will find difficult to believe. One example is the white Americans being the biblical Amorites; although it does add up there is no sound physical proof, therefore it MUST be impossible. This information was inspired to me primarily from Genesis 15:16. I had already known that Canaan having been "cursed with leprosy" (a condition of turning white) was in reality god's manipulation of both the black and white races. As always I must remind you that NOTHING, not even the Bible, is 100 percent factual and I will make you a promise that I have made a mistake or two here or there, so please, please, please study for yourself, and evaluate history for yourself. You should always seek your higher guides and the Creator for confirmation of truth in all things!!! Anyone who tells you that they know the one and only way, RUN LIKE HELL! This person is a liar. Those who feel that they are on the path of wisdom and who profess to have insight to a higher truth, give an ear. Simply listen using your common sense and properly decipher all information given to you. You will know whether or not you are choosing truth, if you can imagine the doctrine in your life and how well it works for the entire universe as a whole, meaning all who are concerned. For example, if your God requires the death of his son would you require the death of your son? Not to say that this alone would dismiss the issue, but these criteria send up the alert signal to say to yourself, "Self, I must examine all relevant information so that I do not make a mistake." So I must compare how my sources (like the Bible, Koran, Torah etc.) holds up within the reality of the universe. I have come to learn that the statement, "Ye shall know the truth and the truth shall set you free" is ULTIMATE TRUTH. The quest for truth, knowledge, and wisdom is like a healthy diet and exercise program. They are both lifetime investments into ultimate human preservation throughout eternity. Without the conquest for ultimate truth the mind and soul will vegetate. For more information on the origin of the races read the following:

1. *Sex and Race: Negro-Caucasian Mixing in All Ages and All Lands: The Old World,* by J. A. Rogers, out of print
2. *The Antichrist Teitan 666,* by William Josiah Sutton, W. F. G., Inc.
3. *From Babylon to Timbuktu,* by Rudolph R. Windsor, Windsor Golden Series
4. *African Origins of Major Western Religions,* by Yosef Ben-Jochannan, Black Classic Press

# FIVE

# The Origins of Christianity

## My Christian Life

This will be the most difficult and heartbreaking chapter of this book and my life. As an individual whose first love was Jesus and the Christian religion, this ultimate truth has been a hard pill to swallow. As you know now, my Christian path ended the day I discovered that the Bible could not in general support what my soul held as ultimate truth with regard to the Creator. That day of bleak awareness did not come all in one day. After learning less than 5 percent of what I have presented in this book over a period of three weeks, I knew that my entire belief system had been built upon the *ultimate deceit*. The deception of my God—the god of the Old Testament fraudulently pretending to be the Creator, Most High God of the Universe—was an *ultimate deceit*, which had caused me to live in an illusion for at least one-third of my life.

I knew the New Testament forward and backward. There wasn't anything in it that I didn't know existed. Some of it I did not quite understand, like the part where it says that Jesus and God never change, but yet God changes his desire for man to obey the law for salvation and then turns around and saves man by grace. I couldn't understand how on God's green earth any person could find peace in serving Allah, Buddha, or any other god in those God-forbidden religions. Questions like these I kept on a little shelf in the back of my mind and told myself that I would better understand it by and by. I would continually thank God for my faith and my belief in His Son.

As a teenager I was what some of us Christians then called "holy rollers." I was saved, born again, and washed in the blood of Jesus. In my prayers I continually begged Jesus to keep me covered in the blood. I was a lover of Paul and the majority of all my prayers were like his. I always put myself down as a filthy wretch who never deserved a good sacrifice like the one made by Jesus, but of course I was thankful to receive the gift of his salvation. The one major verse (not saying that there weren't others) of my Baptist religion was Romans 10:9, "*That if thou shalt confess with thy mouth the Lord Jesus, and shalt believe in thine heart that God hath raised him from the dead, thou shalt be saved.*" My world was built around this one verse for as long as I can remember. Years later, at the age of eight, I took the big plunge and was baptized in the name of the Father, and of the Son, and of the Holy Ghost. I remember waiting for my parents and brothers to go to sleep so that I could have my quiet time with God. I remember crying so hard that I made myself sick while watching a movie about the crucifixion of Christ on Easter. How could they do this to my Lord Jesus? I would say to myself. I would envision the blood dripping from the cross to the point where I would physically reach my fingers up to place them in Christ's wounds.

This was a personal ritual that I put myself through, never telling a soul until now. To question whether or not this really happened never remotely crossed my mind. I think that for me to ask it was too tragic, for Jesus' death was my only answer, my all in all, my way out of no way! The idea that Jesus was like God Himself helped me to perpetually focus my attention more on Jesus than God, although I did not know this at the time. Jesus only wanted people to accept him as their personal savior. It was so easy to just believe, as I had believed. There was no religion on earth easier than my religion, so I thought. How could any God show more love than my God could by sending his Son to earth to be put to death so that I (a Gentile) could have a chance at salvation? I remember telling God that I was so thankful for his consideration for my group of people, the Gentiles, for salvation. I told him in all humility and sincerity that I would be happy to receive just a corner in paradise. I would take my place as a servant to the 144,000 Israelites (whom I thought were white Jewish people) who Revelation said would get their act together and finally accept Jesus as their Christ and Savior. I would sweep out whatever corner in heaven that God would give me for accepting Jesus, thereby escaping the fiery pit called hell. I was taught that if I didn't keep my belief system just as it had been all my life the fiery pit of eternal hell's damnation would be my reward, for the wages of sin is death. At this point, had anyone asked me if I would give up my Christian beliefs I would have told him that he was crazy to even think it; let alone speak such a ridiculous question. I would have said I would rather die, than to give up my beloved Jesus. I do not know for sure, but I think that I would have been the one in the pews at church who, if the pastor told me that *Ultimate Deceit* was blasphemous against God, would not go buy the book. I remember when the film *The Last Temptation of Christ* came out and my pastor told us that they were blaspheming against Jesus, by showing Him in an affair with Mary Magdalene. I never went to see that movie, because of what my pastor said, until after I had found this truth out many years after the fact. I just couldn't stand the mere thought of Jesus being mocked by the entertainment industry.

I would like you to know what type of Christian background I came from because there are so many various types of Christians. My favorite Christian speakers at the time were Kenneth Copeland and Frederick Price. My celebrity Christian mentor was Billy Graham, because I could feel his sincerity about God, it was just like mine. Tammy Faye and Jim Bakker used to receive some of my time also. I remember trying to get into *The 700 Club*, but found it sort of dry to my taste. I still ordered tapes from them, though.

I had read the New Testament three times front to back, and knew the majority of it word for word. Eventually I turned to the emotional side of Christianity, seeking the Holy Ghost, the laying on of hands, and speaking in tongues. I was a genuine force to reckon with for my Baptist pastor, who seemed to tolerate the radical changes our teenage/adult Bible study was bringing about. The display of power from the Holy Spirit, which I later learned was nothing more than the raising of Kundalini through the emotional seat, would truly take my soul to new heights of experiences. My testimony was that I was high on Jesus, and nothing could ever make me turn from my beloved. So how did I learn about the deceit?

I began attending a black history class. As I approached the building that the class would be held in I could see three guys entering, dressed from head to toe in all-white African garb. When I got there, I learned that they were going to present the lesson. I was leery of hearing anything contrary to my belief system so I quickly told the brothers that I was told previously that this would be a history class. I informed them that I would not be interested in anyone else's religion for I was very content with what I had, Christianity. The brother said that this was not about a religion, but the history of the black race of people. "For example," he asked, "Did you know, my sister, that you are a direct descendant of the children of God, the Israelites?" Impossible, I quickly told him, and he came back with, "I can prove it." I remember telling him that, "You can't prove nothing to me for I was raised in the Bible and I can't accept anything the Koran may have to offer." Then he informed me that it was in the King James Version of the Bible. Our dialogue to each other went as follows: "no," "yes," "no," "yes," "no" and, "yes." It went on and on before I finally said, "Okay, prove it." Once I learned that I was an Israelite, that was it. Of course, it took much more than one night of teaching, but now I was ready to listen. I spoke with my pastor immediately and informed him as to what I had learned. By this time my mom was frantic with fear that I was going to burn in hell and my pastor, the Rev. C.L. Adams, was on the phone attempting to straighten out all of this mess that I had discovered. I cited verse after verse to my pastor, and he finally admitted that he couldn't help me with my questions. He informed me that I would need a Greek theologian to straighten out all my errors. "But," I told him, "If you have a doctorate in theology, why can't you tell me why these verses all point to a fabricated lie in Christianity?" I will never forget it. My pastor then told me that he didn't know how I was coming up with all these questions, and that if I couldn't talk about Jesus Christ, him sacrificed and risen again, then we had nothing to talk about. That conversation took place back in August 1993, when I pledged never to serve a lie and denounced my Christian beliefs. This is what I found.

## Jesus' Name Represents the Idol Gods

First of all, the Christianity that we now embrace and hold true to our souls was not what the real Jesus would have wanted. Let's start with the name of Jesus. Every time we call up this name we are calling up on two idol gods at the same time. The first god is the Mesopotamian god Ea and the second is the Greek god Zeus. We can easily find this out. Did you know that Jesus' Hebrew name was Yeshua and if we did not choose to call upon Zeus we would call him Joshua in English? Yes, Jesus' name was really Joshua, but he was called Jesus to keep the names of the idol gods of the Greeks alive. You can use the dictionary and look up the truth. Look up "Jesus." My dictionary says, "[LL, Fr. Gk. **Iesous**, (*Ea and Zeus*) Fr. Heb. Yeshua] 1: the Jewish religious teacher whose life, death, and resurrection as reported by the evangelists are the basis of the Christian message of salvation." The Fr. Gk. Iesous part tells us that the word originated as the Greek word "Ie-(Ea) sous-(Zeus)." Furthermore, Jesus' name could not have been Jesus because the letter J was not used until after the sixteenth century, over 1,500 years after his birth. Find yourself a good encyclopedia and look up the letter "J." It can be traced all the way back to symbolic lettering. It did not exist when Jesus was alive and for a long time afterward. In the Greek name of Jesus it is so plain to see the idol god which brought it to its current place in history. Compare Iesous to Ea and Zeus. Ea and Zeus are the same god. The first one, Ea, is the Mesopotamian name for the same god in Greek named Zeus. Zeus was the head of all the Greek gods, but to the Mesopotamian people Ea was simply a major deity and to the Romans he was Jupiter.

Furthermore, there are a vast number of verses that give conflicting statements as to what Christianity should actually be about. On one hand, we are continually told that Jesus died for our sins, we are saved by grace, and that salvation came through believing in the name of Jesus. But, on the other hand, salvation is for the Jews only, the law is intact, we must worship only the father, and little emphasis is placed on the name of Jesus. As matter of fact, Jesus says that he does not know those who do work in his name. Of course, the Christians are happy with the verses that support their claim and I do not contend that these verses are not there in the Bible. However, I do believe that by now there should be at least a question as to the legitimacy of the Bible as "God's word." And it is by that claim that I agree that there are some verses that do support the Christian belief. These are the verses that were spoken about in II Timothy 2:15, where Christians are instructed to properly divide the word of truth (the Bible). When Paul wrote this he was referring only to the Old Testament lies and not his own. It is a fact that the primary supporting documents of the Christian belief system are the verses that Paul wrote. We Bible readers should properly divide out the lies of Paul in the New Testament and Yahweh in the Old Testament and keep the truth. The bottom line is that Paul admits that he lied and made the religion up, but his problem was the fact that the old Hebrew religion of law kept coming back to haunt him. Paul had pretended to choose the God of the Israelites to gain validity for a Creator from the beginning of Creation (without the Old Testament god, who claims to be the Creator of the Universe, Paul's religion would appear to be more of human origins than divine), but he hated every thing that Yahweh stood for. Therefore, he had to write II Timothy 2:15 for all the people who would present facts against Paul's religion as to how it can justify cutting out the law for grace, yet recognizes Jehovah the creator of the law as his god. When we take the Bible in its entirety there are far more verses against Christian beliefs than for them. So I will divide out the truth now from the New Testament.

## The First Christians

The first truth is the fact that Jesus never wanted people working in his name. See Matthew 7:22-23, *"Many will say to me* **in that day** (He can't be speaking of hypocrites, because he had hypocrites IN HIS DAY! But Jesus did not have today's form of Christianity in his day.), *Lord, Lord, have we not prophesied in thy name? and in thy name have cast out devils? and in thy name done many wonderful works?* **And then will I profess unto them,** *I never knew you: depart from me, ye that work iniquity."* It is clear that whoever these people are THEY ARE COMING TO JESUS EXPECTING HIS KIND EMBRACE! Would you expect Jesus' kind embrace? And are **YOU** doing everything in Jesus' name instead of recognizing the Father only? Jesus continuously tried to take the focus off himself for **none is good but the father** (Matthew 19:17, Mark 10:18, and Luke 18:19)! Jesus was a great prophet and seer. He knew just as some psychics would have known, that one day people would confuse everything he stood for and take the name of Joshua for the pagan gods. Jesus was strictly for uplifting the father and not himself as some verses in the Bible make it appear. But man has to decipher.

Christians will tell you that Jesus did not refer to their doing works in Jesus name. They will say that this verse refers to the hypocrite Christian. Doesn't the fake know that he is a fake? Let's reason. A KKK member smiles to my face, but hates me to my back. He knows that I know he's a hypocrite, and that I have the power to order him destroyed on the spot. Yet because I hit the lottery (Jesus' so-called resurrection with all glory in his hand) he continues to smile in my face with his hand held out **expecting** some great reward, giving me the opportunity to tell him to go to hell. In reality, do we know **many people** like this (remember that Jesus says that **MANY** IN THAT DAY!) or would people with this nature be FEW? For the Christians to be justified there would have to be **many** hypocrites (that is people like the KKK begging blacks for a reward) **begging** Jesus (many will COME TO HIM IN THAT DAY) for a reward who did wonderful works in his name. It just doesn't happen if we put it in perspective.

If we are honest we know that the majority of people who are praying in Jesus' name are sincere. Yes, there may be a few hypocrites who could not care less about Jesus' purpose and yet pray in Jesus' name, **BUT NOT MANY!** We cannot count as many hypocrites praying in the name of Jesus as we can the ones who appear sincere praying in the name of Jesus. But, according to Jesus he says, "**in that day**," clearly meaning not during his own time, **MANY** will perform the act of doing works in his name. In Jesus' time Christians did not do work in Jesus' name. As a matter of fact, the name Jesus did not even exist in his time. In this verse Jesus is clearly talking to someone who is to be startled, and shocked that Jesus does not know him simply because he did good work in Jesus' name. **There are MANY Christians who do work in Jesus' name and plan to stand before him justified . . . BEWARE!**

How many of you will have the shock of your life to discover that Jesus was talking to you and meet him face to face telling you that **he never knew you**, you idol worshipper? Yes, even though you are making Jesus your idol he still says he wants nothing to do with you. And he is harsh enough to mean it. Furthermore he clearly depicts in "that day" the people will do this, which clearly implies that they were not doing it during Jesus' own time. Jesus' complaint was not about the hypocrites, but about idol worshippers like Paul who would establish a new religion and cause many others who would establish a new religion and cause many others to follow his false teachings. That is why he is saying that he doesn't know them: They are followers of Paul, not Jesus. Remember the other verses that tell you to turn to the father only (Matthew 19:17, Mark 10:18, and Luke 18:19). They all say virtually the same thing, *"And he said unto him, 'Why callest thou me good'? There is none good but one, that is, God: but if thou wilt enter into life keep the commandments* (laws of God)."

In all three gospels Jesus is quoted as having raised objection to men praising him. Jesus is putting this young man on the spot in a harsh way. In other words, He is saying, "Dammit, why are you calling me good? Don't do that shit! Give praises to God the Father only." Of course, our New Testament character would never use bad words, but I know that the average Christian cannot get the gist of what Jesus is trying to tell his followers. So I am trying to help make his point by saying exactly the same thing with emphasis. **He is trying to get them to go within to seek the kingdom of God and His Righteousness, all from within.** But they never knew him. And like the naked dog, they are ignorant of the fact or "ignoring-the-fact." Jesus never meant to be the center of attention, He was trying to establish his **belief system** as primary focus for salvation only for the nation of Israel.

Many Christians totally misunderstand the passage of St. John 3:14-21 which states, *"And as Moses lifted up the serpent* (the talisman) *in the wilderness, even so must the Son of man be lifted up: That whosoever believeth in him* (that is the message that he brought forth) *should not perish, but have eternal life. For God so loved the world, that he gave his only begotten Son* (deceit—King David is begotten also), *that whosoever believeth* (believes in his message) *in him should not perish but have everlasting life. For God sent not his Son into the world to condemn the world; but that the world through him might be saved. He that believeth on him is not condemned: but he that believeth not* (believing in the deceit of Baal/Jehovah) *is condemned already, because he hath not believed in the name of the only begotten Son of God. And this is the condemnation, that light is come into the world, and men loved darkness rather than light, because their deeds were evil. For every one that doeth evil hateth the light, neither cometh to the light, lest his deeds should be reproved. But he that doeth truth cometh to the light* **(this is the secret code to salvation, he who is willing to *research* and then *accept the truth*)**, *that his deeds may be made manifest, that they are wrought in God."* This verse is among one of the most favorite used for today's Christian inspiration. It does without doubt support worshipping in Jesus' name (if taken literally), salvation to the believer, and moreover condemnation (Christians believe this is hell) for the non-believer. This is the verse that Christians use to say that God condemns the non-believer and not themselves. However, if they would take into consideration the origin of the Bible would Christians truly want to be apart of prejudging a soul for hell, just because the Bible says so?

The Gospel writers are clearly writing these passages as if they were presently happening. However, it is a fact and accepted by all the Christian scholars that the writers of the Gospel, wrote it well over thirty years after the death of Christ. Do you people out there hear what I am saying? These people are quoting Jesus thirty years later. Christian scholars believe that the writers of the New Testament remembered word for word everything that Jesus said thirty years later. But those of us who choose to use our God sense know that we can barely remember a complete story word for word that we heard only a week ago, let alone thirty years ago. It's just impossible. So if indeed any of the New Testament stories took place at all they had to become part of an oral tradition of storytelling through the years, and someone later decided that it might be good to write them down.

Let's begin with the first sentence regarding lifting up the Son of man just as Moses lifted up the serpent in the wilderness. This verse is literally saying that we should see Jesus in the same light as the Old Testament Moses when he had to save the Israelites from dying. Now remember we are given a for instance as to how Jesus should be lifted up. Look up the passage in Numbers 21:9 and see exactly how Jesus is saying he should be lifted up. It states, *"And Moses made a serpent of brass, and put it up on a pole, and it came to pass that if a serpent had bitten any man, when he beheld the serpent of brass he lived."* Moses had been trained extensively in the priesthood or what is known today as secret society brotherhood or fraternity. Moses was known to be an alchemist. You see, once you become well-rounded with information from not only the Bible, but all sources that are available, you will begin to realize that there is no such thing as a miracle. Miracles are only a justification and explanation of an actual event that an ignorant person has no idea how to explain what happened or how the event came about.

An excellent example of this theory would be if we were to strike a match before a caveman who has never seen fire. He will marvel and think that he has just witnessed the impossible (a miracle), that is a fire on a stick. He might even have tendencies to worship this almighty person producing fire on a stick as a god of great powers. The average reader of this particular verse would insist that Moses was working miracles in saving his Hebrew brothers from the poisonous venom of the snakes when in truth Moses was applying what he had learned in alchemy. It appears that he had made a talisman, an inanimate object with a combination of both symbolic and personal imagery revered as magical and holy. In this particular passage Moses is lifting an "idol" brass god (talisman) made in the image of a serpent, more than likely symbolic of Ea/Enki, the Mesopotamian god given credit for the creation of human beings. There is so much going on here that one would need a strong background in alchemy to fully understand the gist of what is actually happening. You can go to any occult bookstore and find information on alchemy. An alchemist is simply a metaphysician (beyond the physical), or esoteric practitioner creating the greater from the lesser. There are many diverse avenues of discipline that one may practice.

Although it is used constantly and consistently throughout the Bible from the beginning to the end, the Bible condemns the use of alchemy by any other nationality. The Wicca practitioner (a witch) is given a bad rap for using their God-given right to practice the human experience in the way that they see fit. Many have an imaginary green hooked-nosed old woman character on a broom in mind every time they hear the word witch. The Old Testament god was an egotistical, self-centered, pompous ass who wanted sole attention on him. Therefore, he used the common ordinary words to describe anyone who practiced seeing the future (seers, psychics, fortune tellers), reading the stars (astronomers, astrologists), casting spells (witches), talking to the dead (familiar spirits, necromancers) and so forth as EVIL. But the sad thing is that the majority of all the prophets possessed many of these identical powers, and they were considered good. Why? Because they worshipped Yahweh/Baal, therefore it was OK to practice all of the above. But if you were called a Sufi Muslim, watch out. If you were called a psychic or a fortune-teller, god forbid. However, called a prophet of god/Baal, now you have his blessings.

Therefore, clearly the salvation for mankind that Jesus was talking about was that any man might find Jesus' **teachings and practice** of alchemy and the tree of life or the Qabbala, then ultimately finding the secret keys transforming flesh to spirit without death (the keys of Enoch). That is, Jesus was teaching his disciples as he, too, was learning the secrets of the universe and Universal God Power, the power to become gods (see Psalms 82:6). Jesus was trying to establish and convince the Jews only (he may have changed his racist approach to his teachings later in his ministry) that they were not supposed to die like the ignorant men and princes. The verse states, *"I have said, **Ye are gods**; and all of you are children of the*

*Most High.* **But ye shall die like men** *and fall like one of the princes."* According to the Bible these people did not have to die.

The power to become immortal through transfiguration of the flesh was taught in the Qabbala, the discipline used by the Hebrew alchemists. People today could study Ifa mysticism, Chinese mysticism, Indian mysticism, Egyptian mysticism, and Celtic mysticism just to name a few. They should choose a path in accordance with what suits their individual needs, if they desire to have any true concept of what Jesus was trying to establish; they may wish to study the Kabbala and Indian/Persian Mysticism. My personal favorites, which I utilize today, are the Chinese, Ife, and Indian philosophies and practice. I suppose that I have chosen these because there is so much information available about their practical side as well as the theory. Theory is great, but if you can't make things happen and feel the results of evolution of the soul gravitating to the Great All That There Is, what have you profited? Yet, I do read theories from a wide range of belief systems. I apply the theories that align with my soul. This will be discussed in more detail in a later chapter.

So far I have talked about St. John 3:14-15. Let's continue to the verse 16. Jesus is supposedly quoted as saying, "God so loved the world that he gave his **only** begotten son." This is a blatant lie. According to the Bible, god had many sons, Christians will complain that yes, but only *one begotten son.* Now, either Jesus is a liar or the writers of the Bible have added their own beliefs and desires. I assume that Jesus was a seeker of the truth, so lets assume that the writers made the mistake. To prove that this is a lie, (assuming that there are truthful parts in the Bible and that this part that I am going to quote is truth) turn to Psalms 2:7 which states, "*I will declare the decree: the Lord hath said unto me, Thou art my Son; this day* **have I begotten thee**." Now for Pete's sake, surely everyone can see that something is wrong here. God tells David that he has become his begotten son. Now the authors of the Bible would have you believe that Jesus is the **only** begotten son years after David was already begotten. I can hear it now. There goes the grumbling and let's change this part. Again the Bible is not saying what it really means. Jesus' begotten is a different begotten than David's begotten. After all, Mary got knocked up by God Himself through the Holy Ghost. Common sense, where are you now? Out the window?

See Genesis 6:2: *"That the **sons of God** saw the daughters of men that they were fair; and they took them wives of all which they chose."* Now the Bible is saying that there are sons of God. So clearly God had many sons. How is it possible for God to have many sons and yet only one son? They will say, well, the sons in Genesis were angels and were not begotten of God. What, other than their own imagination, gives Christians the authority to establish that these sons were fabricated any differently than the begotten Jesus and David? Well, God says that David became begotten. Did he lie? Another verse that they will use is Luke 1:35: *"And the angel answered and said unto her, the Holy Ghost shall come upon thee, and the power of the Highest shall overshadow thee: therefore also that holy thing which shall be born of thee shall be called the Son of God."* So scripture is simply saying that the Holy Spirit will visit Mary. Does that mean that the Holy Spirit does not visit us today? And if the Holy Spirit does visit us today why aren't women still getting pregnant? How do we know that the Holy Spirit didn't visit the mothers of the Sons of God in the Old Testament? For that matter, where and who are the mothers of these sons of God in Genesis 6:2? Furthermore, if God had the capability to make a son without an earthly mother (Genesis 6:2) and who would have the power to come to earth in the flesh just as Jesus did, why did God all of a sudden lose this power and need to impregnate Mary?

Let's face it, it just doesn't add up. Or out of fear of condemnation from the puppeteer, let's just believe and have faith whether or not the story makes no God sense at all. The only begotten Son of God is tossed out the window for those of us using common sense. The everlasting life that Jesus is talking about (the only ever-lasting life that I believe does exist) is the tree of life, the power of the Qabbala or such disciplines, when applied. Knowledge and application of these teachings will result in immortality of the individual. Or as Jesus said it, the individual receives everlasting life.

Jesus shows that he is totally against grace and insists that the law is still intact. He tells his believers not to even think that he wants to see the law done away with or destroyed. And because he could see into the future, when men would say that the law is no longer in effect because of the death of Jesus, **Jesus set a time,** when the law could be done away with in the New Testament. Matthew 5:17-19 states, *"Think not that I am come to destroy the law, or the prophets: I am not come to destroy, but to fulfill. For verily I say unto you, **Till heaven and Earth pass,** one jot nor one tittle shall in no wise pass from the law, till all be fulfilled."* So . . . Jesus tells when the law can be considered over. He says when heaven and earth pass. Christians says that the law ended when Jesus died on the cross for their sins, but Jesus says not till heaven and earth passes. **HAS HEAVEN OR EARTH PASSED AWAY?** It is just so easy to see once we open our eyes. We must understand what will be intact until heaven and earth pass away. Jesus goes on to say not an *iota* (the ninth letter of the Greek alphabet) or *yod* (the tenth letter in the Hebrew alphabet). The *iota* and the *yod* are the same letter, making it clear that: "Not the smallest letter, NOR "the tiniest part of the smallest letter shall in no wise pass from the law." (See diagram below.)

He    Wah    He    Yod

The arrows point to the title on each letter in the
Hebrew YHWH.

Now, since the preachers haven't taught you what is actually being said, I will. Jesus is saying that none of the law can be done away with by showing which part of the law cannot be done away with. He has said not one of the smallest letters of the alphabet (jot), nor even a minute piece of a letter (tittle) that is written in the law can be done away with until all be fulfilled, that is not until heaven and Earth pass. So again I ask, *have heaven and earth passed away or been destroyed/ended?* You can prove to yourself that this is truth by taking your Hebrew concordance and looking up "jot." It will verify all that I am telling you. Know that the Greek and Hebrew languages are very similar. In Hebrew, the alphabet starts with Aleph, Beth, and Gimel; and in Greek, we have Alpha, Beta, and Gamma. It continues in this same manner throughout the (alpha beta) alphabet. You see I am sticking with this verse a little longer because this one alone according to Jesus gives you no choice, but the law; that is if we intend on being biblically correct. So all those who thought that his death and resurrection ended the law, sorry, but not according to scripture. But why does it appear that we are now saved by grace? The answer is deceit, I mean, D E C E I T big time !!!

The original Christians were solely Israelites. Jesus had been to Egypt and India to learn the ways of the ancient people. Jesus learned that salvation came from the God within, not any character who would order killing, raping, and destruction. He knew that his people had been led astray and recorded the laws of Baal (found in the Bible) instead of the laws of God. What are the laws of God? I guarantee you that we are all still learning them, but I will give you an example of a law of God. Thus saith the law of God that if a man without any equipment whatsoever climbs to sixth floor of a building and jumps, falling onto a concrete surface, the physical ramifications will most certainly cause death. We named that law of God the law of gravity. If a man keeps not the Sabbath (getting rest) he will surely die. I know of no man with the power to go without any sleep for a period of seven days and live. So it is true that without rest (a Sabbath) man will surely die. But, all praises to my Great and Mighty Creator, in all the laws of God that cause death, not one requires the aid of man to murder another human at any time past, present, or future. God doesn't need the help of man to kill off nations of sinful people. Jesus spent his youth away from his people to learn this and much more.

From all the evidence that is available about Jesus, it appears that he became a great master of the metaphysical and esoteric teachings of the All-highest Light, and he intended to give this gift of life to his people. So Jesus established a ministry to awaken the Jews, "the lost tribes of Israel," out of killing people who broke Baal's laws and out of following the many teachings of Baal/Satan (the enemy). Jesus taught them how to activate and discharge the universal laws of science that the ignorant man would call miracles. He developed a following based on these teachings, establishing **the first Christians.** It is important to keep in mind that the first Christians were solely African Jews (not Gentiles) breaking away from the corrupted Jewish laws, which were influenced by Baal/Satan. The Gentiles were strictly a hands-off, do-not-touch-or-have-anything-to-do with race of people.

## Jesus Discriminates Against Non-Israelites

Jesus was lacking somewhat in knowledge with regard to his desire to help only the Israelite people. He had learned that the teachings of Baal/Yahweh such as an "eye for an eye and a tooth for a tooth," (Matthew 5:38); and the acceptability of divorce, (Matthew 5:31-32); and killing people for working on the Sabbath, (Matthew 12:1-8), were all universal **LIES.** Jesus wanted to establish that this belief system was new (not the original way of mankind) and contradicts spiritual evolution. Jesus taught his followers that these beliefs did not exist from the beginning of time. Because Jesus did away with the evil part of the law that Baal combined with El's law, modern Christians have mistakenly believed that Jesus did away with all the law. This is NOT TRUE, according to Jesus. Jesus kept all Israelite laws that he believed uncorrupted by Baal. Throughout the scriptures, Jesus observed the Passover, and kept the Sabbath. He also took part in various feast celebrations and rituals in Hebrew tradition.

Jesus held firm the laws of the God of his people, but did not recognize Baal's laws that had been indoctrinated in many of his people. Jesus believed in the oral laws given to Father Abraham, which still fell short of universal truth. Proof of his ignorance can be seen in Matthew 10:5-6, *"These twelve Jesus sent forth, and commanded them, saying. Go **not** into the way of the Gentiles, and into any city of the Samaritans **enter ye not: But rather go to the lost sheep of the house of Israel.**"* Jesus clearly wanted nothing to do with helping anyone other than his own race. This is the part of Jesus that I believe was his failure. When you possess absolute truth you will voluntarily give it to anyone willing to receive it, not your race exclusively.

Another verse that shows just how ruthlessly prejudiced Jesus was can be found in Matthew 15:21-28, *"Jesus went thence, and departed into the coasts of Tyre and Sidon. And, behold, a woman of Canaan came out of the same coasts, and cried unto him saying, Have mercy on me, O Lord, thou son of David* (NOTE: she does not say **thou only begotten son of God**); *my daughter is grievously vexed with a devil. But he answered her not a word. And his disciples came and besought him, saying, Send her away, for she crieth after us. But he answered and said, **I am not sent but unto the lost sheep of the house of Israel**."* Jesus is refusing to help this woman SOLELY because she is of the white race/NON-ISRAELITE. More than likely Jesus would have turned down any race, black or white, due to his cultural traditions. *"Then came she and worshipped* (no, this woman is begging not worshipping) *him saying, **Lord, help me.** But he answered and said, **It is not meet to take the children's bread, and to cast it to dogs.**"* Clearly this woman is begging Jesus on her hands and knees to please help her save the life of her child, and Jesus replies by calling the white woman a dog. Yes, he is calling this woman a dog because of her race. He is telling her that it is not good to take the knowledge meant for the children (Israelites) and give it to the dogs (white people). How sad that he didn't know that it was not good to feel so poorly of another race even to the point of calling the other race of people dogs.

But what is worse is yet to come: "*And she said,* **Truth, Lord**: *yet dogs eat of the crumbs which fall from their master's table.*" It had been so solidly established that whites were the scum of the earth that even the average white person in their circle believed it of themselves, similar to the low self-esteem of blacks during American slavery. This woman agreed with Jesus that she was a dog, but informed him that even dogs are allowed small rations from their superiors/masters. Jesus was proud that this woman could humble herself to the point of acceptance that in deed she was a dog, and yet knowing that all her needs on earth would be granted from some source. How could we Israelites and the other great civilizations have done this to a race of people and expect nothing in return? Especially when that race was your IMMEDI-ATE BROTHER, not half brother, like the Chinese and Indian people. How could we have been deceived by Baal, and followed his deceit in one way or another even unto this day? The things that we humans do to one another the average dog owner would nearly lose his mind to see it done to his pet.

"*Then Jesus answered and said unto her, O woman, great is thy faith:* **be it unto thee as thou wilt**. *And her daughter was made whole from that very hour.*" Even as humble as the woman made herself to Jesus he would not get up off his lazy duff and go out to help her. It was because of her faith in the power of the Universal Power (Creator) through the alchemist, not Jesus, that her daughter was healed. Jesus refuses to lift a finger to the bitter end. Remember that the mere utterance of words is a practice of alchemy; we all practice it to some degree. The difference in the alchemist/magician and the majority of most of us is that he practices at will. The majority of us randomly practice alchemy without ever knowing that we are directing universal energy for healing or causing the body to dis-ease. We create order and chaos constantly with this practice. (See the chapter entitled Salvation.)

For definite proof that this woman was white read the story again in Mark 7:26. It literally says the woman was Greek instead of using the name of an ancient race for which most of us do not know the appearance of the people. Either the writer possessed little knowledge of ancient races or he may have been using the word Greek to say that she was a white woman. A Greek person is not a Canaanite, for the Greeks are descendants of Javan, son of Japheth. Nor can one associate the Syro-Phoenicians with the Greeks.

Furthermore, the scriptures show that Jesus avoided Gentiles like the plague. Can you name one Gentile disciple? Why do we suppose that Jesus shows next to zero concern and love for the Gentiles throughout the New Testament? The few cases that might be regarded as casual acquaintances never turned into a friendship or an ongoing relationship. Why? Telling the disciples not to work with other races, calling the Greek lady a dog, and finally the fact that he accepted no Gentiles in his circle of worship, and taught his disciples to do the same are all proofs of Jesus' prejudices against non-Israelite people.

Now that we have a feel somewhat for the mindset of a true Christian, let's take a look at the various sects of the Israelite faith during the early Christian era. The Hebrew Israelite religion developed numerous sects, just as all religions of the planet have. Each sect feels that its produces the highest order of truth. The primary sects during the first millennium comprised basically of five different groups:

1. Christians
2. Sadducees
3. Pharisees
4. Zealots
5. Essenes

We have already become familiar with the first group; let's take a look at the belief systems of Israelites following the Sadducee ways of life. The Sadducees believed that the strict laws followed by the Pharisees were unnecessary and that some were not the law of the Creator. They believed that the law was important, but developed a canon for their laws just as the Bible was canonized. They chose the laws that they believed were of God and may have practiced them leniently (similar to the Conservative Jew). They are very **similar** to the first Christians. However, one large difference in their belief and that of the Christians' was that the Sadducees' believed that reincarnation did not exist. Jesus believed and taught reincarnation. Moreover, the Sadducees placed more emphasis on immortality than rebirths. This explains the conflicts that Jesus encountered in the New Testament.

The Pharisees were the sect identical to the religious teachings of Moses. They would have been considered the true "Orthodox Jew." Unlike the Orthodox Jews of today, if a follower of the Pharisee faith discovered a Jew of the same faith breaking the Sabbath, it would mean certain death. They like Moses were strict practitioners of Jehovah's/Baal's ceremonial laws, clean/unclean life style, Sabbath worship, punishments and so forth.

The final two types of Jews were categorized after their behavior more than their faith or belief system. The Zealots were so named after their zealous and defiant demeanor against the Roman power in Israel. They conducted fruitless riots and murders in attempts to drive the Roman influence out of Israel. Men similar in behavior to the Zealots would be John Brown, and Nat Turner.

However, the Essenes were quite the opposite. They believed in non-violence. One of the Christ characters in the New Testament appears to have been an Essene. Some sources state that the Martyred Christ Essene was a Nazarene; another states that he was a Samaritan (perhaps the mythical Christ of Mark), but whichever the case, this Christ was not the true Christ who performed the miracles. Men similar to Essenes would be Martin Luther King Jr. (a Christian) and Mohandas Gandhi (a Hindu). As you can see, both the Zealot and the Essenes could have been Christian, Pharisee, or Sadducee depending on their faith and background. Notice that the men selected as examples for both the Zealots and the Essenes (the forceful and the peaceful) were all violently murdered by executions and shootings.

## Paul Misrepresents Jesus to the World

Paul was an Uncle Tom Hebrew Israelite who hated his own race much like Uncle Tom Negroes hate their own race today. There are just as many blacks who wish to be white, as there are whites who desire to be black. Anyway, Paul was a black Hebrew Israelite mixed with Greek or Roman ancestry who spent the majority of his time among both the Greeks and the Romans from his youth on up and found far more comfort with these people than with his own. He bonded with these people and learned to hate his own race, supporting Rome's dislike for the Israelites. Paul faked a conversion to Christianity to establish communication and dialogue with the original Christians. Originally Paul killed and persecuted his own people until he discovered the great power with which organized religion could unfold. The power and control of religion became a fanatical passion for him. Paul made up the entire grace story regarding Joshua's (Jesus') mission. His goal was primarily to gain a Gentile (Greek, Roman) following, and power. Paul would jump back and forth between the Gentiles and the Israelite races; nonetheless, whichever political faction he would turn to, he would lie and blend in like a chameleon. Paul was considered a cunning, powerful speaker, taking on the appearance of whatever political faction or race that was around him as his own. This can be seen in the book of Acts.

Let me show you biblically how you can decipher Paul's lie. Look at Romans 3:7: "*For if the truth of God hath more abounded THROUGH MY LIE, unto his glory; why yet am I also judged as a sinner?*" Here Paul maps out his entire plan for justifying doing away with the law and creating the religion of grace. Paul is stating in verse 4 that it is better for every man to be a liar, if God can prevail at a higher victory. You see, few people wanted to uphold the law. After all, the majority of the people, including Paul, possessed the God sense/common sense to know that the Israelite religion, the law and its god, were indeed a way of life and belief that caused grief, pain, and suffering. The only reason the Israelites agreed to succumb to the law freely at first, and later by abusive, barbaric force, was the magical incantations of power that they witnessed from god/Baal. However, Paul had made up his mind that he would use the evil side of the Ancient Hebrew religion against itself. He speaks of this in verse 5, *"But if our unrighteousness commend the righteousness of God, what shall we say? Is God unrighteous who taketh vengeance?"* When the people who translated the Bible came to this verse they knew within their God sense (common sense) that no real man of God can call the GOD ALMIGHTY CREATOR unrighteous, so they added to his so-called word. They added, *"I speak as a man"* to soften the fact that Paul was preaching that the god of the Old Testament was unrighteous. The good part about most of their additions is that they were considerate enough to make notes of the fact that indeed this and other changes did occur. Everywhere in the Bible where you find statements inside parentheses ( ), something has been added as the translators try to help the verse make more sense in English. Actually, what they were saying is that clearly this verse as translated disdained their faith and required an additional statement to make the original statement sound somewhat legitimate, if you just keep the faith.

Without a doubt here Paul takes advantage of Yahweh's evil acts and speaks out to gain his following. He speaks to these people (the Gentiles) of all the activities that I spoke of in my chapter about the god of the Israelites. Without doubt their God sense will reject the evil side of Yahweh through the elegance in style of speech presented by Paul to the Gentiles. Paul speaks over and over again in so many double negatives that flow with great energy and enthusiasm that the people were mesmerized by Paul's speech more than by what was being said. Paul told the people that if their unrighteousness (doing away with the law) exalts God by correcting God's wrong, then let's not even mention God's wrongdoings. He continues in verse 6, "*God forbid: for then how shall God judge the world?*" Here he is simply stating that if the Gentiles harp on the mistakes that God made, whom will they worship as God? Remember that in the fifth verse Paul recognizes with the Gentiles that, yes, it was unrighteous for God to be vengeful and more than likely talks about all the other terrible deeds that were not recorded here. But, then in the sixth verse Paul in his ignorance reminds the people that they have fixed the evil of the law and that they must remember that without the Old Testament god they will not have a religion. Then in verse 7 Paul continues and admits that he did lie (that Jesus died on the cross for the sins of the world). If you are in disagreement here, figure out the lie that Paul admits telling, and the unrighteousness of the people that Paul is justifying throughout the entire chapter. **STATE THE LIE!**

What was the lie? **Why does Paul's religion require that every man be a liar in order for god to be truthful?** None other than the fact that Paul and his followers decided against god's way of life, the corrupted law, **to live a lie** (a fabricated religion) **through grace** and simply accept it by faith. But, that god has far more followers through Paul's lie (to lessen the confusion read the above passage again) of the religion regarding grace than the followers of the law. So Paul seeks support and complains that the followers of the law should not judge him as a sinner or a person who has done anything wrong. He insists that they should look at the overall reason that he made up the lie (the fabricated religion). In conclusion of the lie, Paul sums it all up in verse 20, "*Therefore by the deeds of the law there shall no flesh be justified in his sight: for by the* *law is the knowledge of sin."* So he concludes, *"Therefore, by doing the law can no man be justified in the sight of God."* Consequently, he says it is through reading the law that one learns that Yahweh the Lord god said, "kill, rape, destroy, steal the goods of your brothers, etc."

Let's back up. What about Paul's conversion to Christianity, did it happen? According to the Bible, the fact that Paul never converted to Christianity, and that he admitted lying, were major issues pointed out to me by the teachers of black history that led to my realization that I had lived a lie all my life. I wish that I could come into the living rooms of all my readers individually and walk them through each of the following verses just as I had received them. In reality, I cannot do this. So, here I need to request that my readers follow my instructions as to how they read the following verses. I am going to show you that Paul lied not only about grace, but also about his conversion to Christianity.

Let's start with Acts 9:3-7, put down your book and look this one up in the Bible and read it twice to yourself. Meditate on these verses. Know them frontward and backward. Now, go to Acts 22: 6-9. These verses are considered sanctioned testimony of Paul's conversion from a hater of the law and the Jews into a born-again Christian. If you look closely at the verses you will see that there is a lie in progress. I read the verses over and over while my instructor would laugh with amusement that I could not see any difference whatsoever. He would insist that I read the verses again. I read them again. He would ask, didn't I see the lie? So I ask you, did you see the lie? I am confident that you won't see it just as I didn't. Then I was told, as I am telling you, to turn to Acts 26:12-14, and read all three passages to find the evidence of a big fat lie.

So have you flunked the test? Can you find on your own the differences in the testimony of all three passages that support the **fact** that something has gone grossly wrong in this testimony and in a court of law would be treated as evidence of perjury? To better follow which verses are being compared and discussed we will refer to all three passages as A, B, and C respectively.

Passage A, Acts 9:3-7, reads as follows:

and as he journeyed, he came near Damascus: and suddenly there shined round about him a light from heaven: and he fell to the earth, and heard a voice saying unto him, Saul, Saul, why persecutest thou me? And he said, who art thou lord? And the lord said, I am Jesus whom thou persecutest: it is hard for thee to kick against the pricks. And he trembling and astonished said, lord what wilt thou have me to do? And the lord said unto him, arise, and go into the city and it shall be told thee what thou must do. And the men which journeyed with him stood speechless, hearing a voice, but seeing no man.

Passage B, Acts 22:6-9, reads as follows:

And it came to pass that, as I made my journey, and was come nigh unto Damascus about noon, suddenly there shone from heaven a great light round about me. And I fell unto the ground, and heard a voice saying unto me, Saul, Saul, why persecutest thou me? And I answered, who art thou, Lord? And he said unto me, I am Jesus of Nazareth, whom thou persecutest. And they that were with me saw indeed the light, and were afraid; but heard not the voice of him that spake to me.

Passage C, in Acts 26:12-14, states the following:

Whereupon as I went to Damascus with authority and commission from the chief priests. At midday, O king I saw in the way a light from heaven, above the brightness of the sun, shining round about me and them which journeyed with me. And when we were all fallen to the Earth I heard a voice speaking unto me, and saying in the Hebrew tongue, Saul, Saul, why persecutest thou me? It is hard for thee to kick against the pricks. And I said, Who art thou, Lord? And he said, I am Jesus whom thou persecutest.

This is your last chance to go back and look over all three passages before I reveal the fact that Christianity truly was based on a lie at its worst and confusion at its best. But whichever the case may be, our God sense knows that God the Almighty Creator is neither the author of lies or confusion; therefore, He could not have authorized these passages of the Bible, ultimately destroying any evidence of grace whatsoever.

Now, let's start with the first passage we have. Paul leaves on a journey and states that an event takes place in which Paul falls to the earth. Jesus convinces Paul not to persecute him. There are men with him that heard a voice but saw nothing.

In the second passage, we have Paul leaves on a journey and states that an event takes place where Paul falls to the ground. Jesus convinces Paul not to persecute him. There are men with him who saw the light but could hear nothing.

In the third passage, Paul leaves on a journey and states that an event takes place where Paul and the men with him fall to the ground. Jesus convinces Paul not to persecute him.

Okay, the smart ones, who are not like me, have seen indeed that the verses are vastly different. The only thing that all three verses have in common is that Paul is on a journey, and Jesus, a dead man is trying to convince Paul to quit persecuting him. From the first verse to the second verse we can see that Paul is the ultimate person falling to the earth with a supernatural experience taking place. But in the third verse we see Paul and the men experiencing a supernatural experience that makes everybody fall to the ground. So which was it: Did Paul receive the experience by himself or did Paul and all his companions experience the falling power of the supernatural?

Next we can find in the first passage that the men with Paul heard something but **saw nothing.** But in the next passage they saw something and **heard nothing**. This is just impossible. It is impossible for a human being to confuse hearing and seeing. Say we cover our eyes as in the first situation for seeing nothing and pretend that we hear some man's voice. Let's say for the benefit of the doubt that the voice said, "Saul, Saul, why persecutest thou me?" Now let's imagine the second passage to be the truth. Now we cannot hear anything being said, but we can see the light of Jesus. The human race has absolutely no evidence that Paul ever converted to Christianity because there is no straightforward story even according to the Bible itself stating such a fact.

The Jews hate Paul for using the God of their forefathers as the author of his bastard religion. What is intolerable for the Jews to accept is the fact that Paul puts down the law to establish grace, his religion. As a matter of fact, he had the Christian Jews on his side by promising to keep the law and the prophets, but doing away with the Baal additions that their people had recorded. But when they found out that Paul had taken it further by doing away totally with the entire law and establishing grace they were outraged. The devout Jews loved the law of God more than they loved life itself. Can you imagine what happens next? Yes, the Jews are going to conspire to kill Paul for lying about their religion. Turn to the Acts 23:12-24: "*And when it was day, certain of the Jews banded together, and bound themselves under a curse, saying that they would neither eat nor drink till they had killed Paul. And they were more than forty which had made this conspiracy. And they came to the chief priests and elders, and said, We have bound ourselves under a great curse, that we will eat nothing until we have*

slain Paul. Now therefore ye with the council signify to the chief captain that he bring him down unto you tomorrow, as though ye
would inquire something more perfectly concerning him: and we, or
ever he come near, are ready to kill him."

This is my interpretation using Modern English with the
human emotion of the era:

During the day, several Hebrew Israelites conducted a group
meeting, swearing that they would neither eat nor drink until that
Uncle Tom Negro Paul was dead. (Please keep in mind that this is
not the point of view of the author, but of the Jews.) He had
tricked them for the last time with his pretending to be a follower
of the law, when in truth he had created his own religion. They
explained all that had happened to the high priests and the elders
of their congregation. They convinced the priest and elders that it
would be in the best interest for the law to do Paul in. The plan
was that the priest should request of the Roman leaders that they
should bring Paul for them to just discuss a little about how they
could work things out. But when they got their hands on Paul they
would kill him. Look again at Acts 23, beginning with verse 16.

"And when Paul's sister's son heard of their lying in wait, he went
and entered into the castle, and told Paul. Then Paul called one of the
centurions unto him, and said, Bring this young man unto the chief
captain: for he hath a certain thing to tell him. So he took him, and
brought him to the chief captain, and said, Paul the prisoner called
me unto him, and prayed me to bring this young man unto thee, who
hath something to say unto thee. Then the chief captain took him by
the hand, and went with him aside privately, and asked him, what is
that thou hast to tell me? And he said, The Jews have agreed to desire
thee that thou wouldest bring down Paul tomorrow into the council
as though they would inquire somewhat of him more perfectly. But
do not thou yield unto them: for there lie in wait for him of them."

Paul's nephew overheard the entire conspiracy and informed
his uncle of the Israelites' plan to kill him. Paul immediately called

the soldier outside his room of containment and requested that the soldier take his nephew (whom he identifies as a young man) to his superiors, for he had something very urgent to tell him. The soldier agreed to do so and took the young man to the head honcho of that community. He presented the boy to his superior and explained that the prisoner Paul has sent him. The boy then requested privacy and explained the plan of the Israelites. He told him that the Israelite leaders were going to come and ask the captain to deliver Paul so that they could talk with him, but instead their intention was to kill him, therefore Paul must never be turned over to the Israelites.

During this period the Israelites found very little respect for their culture or their god among the Romans. It appears that Paul's nephew may have at first been turned down and told by the Roman superior that the Israelite squabbles were of no concern to him. He may have justified Paul's plea for help by insinuating that Paul was a Roman citizen. Definitely, had the notion not came from somewhere that Paul was a Roman citizen he would not have been helped. See verse 27.

Nonetheless, how the general found out that Paul was a Roman citizen is irrelevant (for now). There are lies bouncing off Paul's tongue at every convenient opportunity, but yet we are required to believe in his teaching? In the Bible, Paul himself lies about his nationality and has absolutely no remorse for his actions. On the contrary he appears to justify his behavior. Look in I Corinthians 9:20 and Romans 3:7. Have you ever met a chronic liar? They suffer from a mental condition causing them to need to be the center of attention at all times. The sad part is that sometimes even chronic liars begin to believe in their highly active imaginations. I have met three chronic liars in my life and one thing that people love to do is sit around and hear them tell their stories. The people who haven't learned yet of their disease will believe them and see them in all awe, but when these people talk to the chronic liars' associates they find out the truth.

This is what has happened to Paul many times in the New Testament. In Acts 26:28, the king Agrippa has heard Paul's lie concerning his conversion (we discussed this earlier) to Christianity and believed him somewhat, but after Paul's story the king talks to others and finds out that Paul is definitely untrustworthy. In court the king testifies to this effect: *"Then Agrippa said unto Paul, Almost thou persuadest me to be a Christian."* **What the Bible doesn't tell you is that if he was almost persuaded to believe but then decides not to believe in Paul's story, what caused the king to change his mind?** If we read everything in the Bible regarding Paul's life and apply simple common sense it becomes clear that his story and his morality are, at the very least, questionable.

Furthermore, If we are to compare Paul's teachings to Jesus' teachings we find that they have little in common. Paul teaches a person to be wishy-washy. He fails to be consistent in his teaching. Paul appears to be lost in "the ever-changing world of Paul doctrine." One moment he clearly states that anyone who calls Christ accursed is surely a devil. See I Corinthians 12:3, *"Wherefore I give you to understand, that **no man** speaking by the Spirit of God calleth Jesus accursed."* but he later calls Jesus a curse for our sins. Galatians 3:13: *"Christ hath redeemed us from the curse of the law, being made a curse for us: for it is written, Cursed is every one that hangeth on a tree."* Now keep in mind that Christians say that they are following Jesus, not Paul. There is absolutely NO TALK BY JESUS OF THE LAW BEING CURSED!

Where did Paul get the authority to make the law a curse? Paul admits to following this same cursed law in Acts 24:14, *"But this I confess unto thee, that after the way which they call heresy, so worship I the God of my fathers, **believing all things which are written in the law** and in the prophets."* Is Paul admitting that he is a devil, or what? Clearly he states that anyone who calls Christ accursed does **not** have the spirit of God. Therefore, common sense tells us that the opposite spirit of God is the spirit of the devil. Now keep in mind that we want to believe that these books are sacred writings inspired by man from God. Again the religious-minded person maintaining empty faith will say that although the Bible says that anyone calling Jesus accursed is a devil, Paul could not have been a devil because he was an apostle for Christ. But was he??? This is the million-dollar question that Christians should take the time to ask themselves. They should investigate this theory. The fact that Paul never converted to Christianity, nor did he teach anything similar to what Jesus taught, in addition to the facts that Paul never met Christ, nor converted to his way of teaching, proves Paul is a self-proclaimed LIAR! He admits that he lied. If a person tells you that he lied for the glory of God, and then you decide that you wish to follow that individual for your life's path of salvation, don't you believe that you should at least know what the lie was about??? Has anyone ever told you that Paul admits that he is a LIAR? Why isn't it discussed in the church? Why isn't it taught that Paul could have possibly made up a religion for what he considered to be God's glory, for he admits to lying for the glory of God? One should throw up a red flag, to at least take a second to consider what is going on.

Another inconsistency where Paul never stays with one side is found in Paul's fabricated lie, of salvation in GRACE verses salvation in the practicing of the LAW. All throughout the New Testament Paul advocates that one can receive salvation only by grace. He goes as far as to say that trying to follow the law is sin. This is his rhetoric when he intermingles with Gentiles. However, when he returns to his Israelite brothers he professes the law and the prophets. WHICH IS IT, PAUL, THE LAW OR GRACE?

Unbeknownst to most Christians, Paul authorized grace, not Jesus Christ. If we analyze the section on the harmony of the Gospels we find that the books of the Gospels rarely mention the word grace. Jesus never believed in grace. As a matter of fact, the word grace is absolutely never mentioned in either Matthew or Mark. It is mentioned once in Luke and three times in John. Notice that the Gospels supposedly contain the material on the character and person of Jesus, while the remaining books with the possible exception of Revelation, all refer to information regarding the apostles. Therefore, since there is a difference between the doctrines of Jesus and the Apostle Paul, today's Christian religion should be officially known as "The Paulan or Pauline Religion." Today's Christians do not follow the ways of Christ, but the ways of Paul. Taking a closer look at Paul's religion one must analyze all the different characters of Paul before we can know assuredly what Paul's religion was actually about.

The only way to accomplish this is to organize Paul's thoughts and belief systems. The Bible establishes the fact that Paul believed that it was proper to never make a commitment to any one form of belief system. Paul believed that it was appropriate to claim and practice whatever religion was in existence within his presence and add his little twist so that all the people of the world should follow him. The inspirational motivation driving Paul was the fact that in his way of belief he would be recognized as the leader of the world in bringing people to God. For he admits that he has become all things. See I Corinthians 9:18-21: *"What is my reward then? Verily that, when I preach the gospel, I may make the gospel of Christ without charge* (Paul makes the gospel without forced doctrine, meaning he is teaching the people to believe anything they want, but accept Christ as their personal savior, thereby establishing a great following to Paul's made-up religion for the glory of God; see Romans 3:7) *that I abuse not my power in the gospel. For though I be free from all men, yet have I made myself servant unto all, that I might gain the more. And unto the Jews I became as a Jew* (he lied), *that I might gain the Jew; to them that are under the law, as under the law, that I might gain them that are under the law; to them that are without law as without law, (being not without law to God, but under the law to Christ)."* The last portion of the verse was added to make Paul's statement fit the Christian belief. As stated before, all statements in parenthesis were added to the King James translation to help the text flow in accordance with

Christian doctrine. It is important to recognize that this is not a scriptural verse and was not a part of the original writings of the Greek text.

Good examples of Paul's wishy-washy religion can be established by categorizing Paul's doctrines that teach without a doubt, converse support of law versus grace (this is like stating that you sleep only in the day, and then you sleep only night):

1.  Christians are under grace. (Christian terminology meaning that the only way to receive salvation is through grace —an act of accepting Jesus Christ as ones personal savior.)
2.  Paul believes in following the law.
3.  Paul teaches condemnation of the law.
4.  He accepts both grace and the law simultaneously. Confusion as to what to believe regarding law and grace.

All four of these categories have supporting documentation in the Bible.

### 1. In Support of Grace

Paul supports grace in these verses: Acts 15:11, Romans 1:5, 3:24, 5:2, 5:15-21, 6:14-15, 7:7, 10:4, 11:6; Titus 3:7, and I Peter 3:7. I will quote a couple of verses here in the text without elaboration. Most readers know about the fact that salvation by grace is in the Bible, therefore one may look up verses as he or she desires. A supporting verse can be found in Acts 15:11 stating, *"But we believe that through the grace of the Lord Jesus Christ we shall be saved, even as they."*

A second quote supporting grace can be found in Romans 3:24: *"Being justified freely by his grace through the redemption that is in Christ Jesus."*

### 2. In Support of the Law

Paul supports the law in these verses: Romans 2:12, 7:1, 7:11-12; Acts 19:21, 21:19-26, 22:3; and John 3:4. Romans 2:12 says, *"For as many as have sinned without the law shall also perish without law: and as many as have sinned in the law shall be judged by the law.*" Here Paul clearly states that all sinners without law will perish. The King James Version of the Bible makes a fruitless attempt to clean up Paul's condemnation of all Gentiles by putting in parentheses his added comments to change emphasis away from Gentile condemnation, and place them on the Jews' adherence to the law in the next verse. Nonetheless, the King James Version ends up justifying doing the law, in an attempt to make it appear that Paul was not talking about the Gentiles, when he said, "those who sin **without the law (Gentiles)**, perish without the law." Verse13 states, *"For not the hearers of the law are just before God, **but the doers of the law shall be justified.**"* Another supporting verse for keeping the law can be found in Romans 7:1-2: *"Know ye not, brethren, how that the law hath dominion (**power**) over a man as long as he liveth? For the woman which hath a husband is bound by the law to her husband so long as he liveth; but if the husband be dead, she is loosed from the law of her husband."* King James translator comments to Paul's statement has been removed from this quote, to show that Paul is stating that the law has power over a man as long as he lives.

### 3. Totally Against the Law

Now, Paul says that anyone who attempts to do the law is a sinner, but keep in mind, in all of the above verses, Paul is saying that if a man does uphold the entire law, he is justified. How can it be, that a man is just for doing the law, and a sinner for doing the law? Nonetheless, Paul's teachings, which Christians hold number one over Jesus' teachings, have created a religion of righteous sinners. Here are the verses that state doing the law is a sin, thereby unjust, and against God. Look in Roman 4:15, which states, *"Because the law worketh wrath: for where no law is, there is no transgression."* Paul clearly states that where there is no law, there is no sin. Logically reasoning, Paul is saying that who ever does the law has sin. Then in Galatians 3:13, Paul throws the law out as a curse stating, *"Christ hath redeemed us from the curse of the law."* In addition to these verses can be found the verse that totally contradicts any justification to the law whatsoever. It is Galatians 2:16: **"Knowing that a man is not justified by the works of the law, but by faith of Jesus Christ."** Clearly Paul is stating that a man cannot be save by doing the law and that the only way to find salvation is in grace.

### 4. Paul Accepts either the Law or Grace Conditionally

Here we have another category of doctrine where we have a choice to do the law or to choose grace. See Galatians 5:4 stating, *"Christ is become of no effect unto you* (no grace), *whosoever of you are justified by the law* (for those who do the law are justified); *ye are fallen from grace."* Paul is saying that individuals faithfully under the law are not affected by not accepting Christ as their savior and are not under grace, but the law, and are justified. However, according to Paul's teaching on salvation through grace, one cannot be saved except through the blood of Jesus Christ **only**. So now we have a choice in this fourth teaching, that is to do the law or to be saved by grace. Likewise true according to Paul is the converse of this condition where if you cannot do the law you must accept grace. Another passage supporting doing either law or grace or both can be found in Romans 3:29-31, *"Is he the God of the Jews only? Is he not **also** of the Gentiles?* (The "also" suggests both the law and grace.) *Yes of the Gentiles also: Seeing it is one God, which shall justify the* (Jew) *circumcision* (by the law) *by faith and* (Gentile) *uncircumcision through faith* (by grace). *Do we then make void the law through faith?* (Paul is asking can we get rid of the law by grace?) *God forbid: yea, we establish the law."* Also establishing this point is Romans 2:25-29, *"For circumcision verily profiteth, if thou keep the law: but if thou be a breaker of the law, thy circumcision is made uncircumcision."*

## The Law According to Yahweh

Now let's bring the God of the Old Testament into the picture regarding law, although he has nothing to do with the New Testament religion. This god states that the law and the Sabbath shall be a covenant between him and the Israelites **FOREVER!** How is it possible for Paul or even the supposed Son of God to dismiss God's plan that he states is forever? I believe that it is safe to dismiss the possibility that God could have been confused, ignorant, or a liar in saying that the Sabbath is FOREVER. Therefore, the only other assumption is that the Sabbath according to Jehovah is forever. There are numerous times that the god of the Old Testament states that the laws and statutes will last **FOREVER!** These verses clearly state that these particular laws and statutes must be kept forever. Some of them include the strangers among the Israelites, establishing that anyone who believed in this god was required to do the law, not only the Jew. See Exodus 31:12-17: *"And Yahweh spoke unto Moses, saying, speak thou also unto the children of Israel, saying, Verily my Sabbaths ye shall keep: for it is a sign between me and you throughout your generations; that ye may know that I am Yahweh that doth sanctify you. Ye shall keep the Sabbath therefore; for it is holy unto you:* ***everyone that defileth it shall surely be PUT TO DEATH:*** *for whosoever doeth any work therein, that soul shall be cut off from among his people. Six days may work be done; but in the* ***seventh*** *is the Sabbath of rest, holy to Yahweh:* ***whoever doeth any work in the Sabbath day shall surely be put to death.*** *Wherefore the children of Israel shall keep the generation, for a perpetual covenant. It is a sign between me and the children of Israel* ***For Ever:*** *for in six days Yahweh made Heaven and Earth, and on the seventh day he rested, and was refreshed."* And in Deuteronomy 5:14 it includes that the strangers amongst the Israelites must also keep the Sabbath, one of the laws in the Old Testament. For proof of keeping the law forever see Exodus 27:21, 30:21, 31:17, 2:13, Leviticus 6:18, 6:22, 7:36, 10:9, 10:15, 16:29, 16:31, 17:7, 23:21, and Numbers 10:8,

15:15, 18:8, 19:10. How is it possible that man has the power to change God's forever rule to a rule that states until Jesus' death? That would prove that either God lied or that his statutes are forever, or man lied that Jesus gave thumbs up for the end of the law by grace at his death. According to Christian doctrine God lied when he said that these statutes were forever. See Romans 10:4 *"For Christ is the end of the law for righteousness to every one that believeth."* See also Romans 3:28, *"Therefore we conclude that a man is justified by faith without the deeds of the law."*

Consequently, it can be deduced that Paul's teachings have been in direct contrast to the teachings both of the original Christians and today's Christians. Christians believe that one should be willing to stand by Christ and his doctrine regardless of the threat to one's life. Paul does not practice this theory. Christians believe that you are not supposed to lie. Paul does not support this theory, either. Today's Christians believe that the absolute only way to obtain salvation is through the grace of Jesus. Paul does not follow in entirety this belief either, for he supports salvation for both people of grace and people who do the law faithfully, depending, of course, upon when it was advantageous for Paul to support one or the other. The Christians of Jesus' time were totally against any teaching of grace for they followed the uncorrupted law and taught against the corrupted version of Baal's law, which can be found in the Old Testament.


## Paul's Service of the Lower Worlds

The serving of the lower worlds takes place through desire for self-gratification. Paul was so into the lower worlds that he had become either mentally ill or possessed by a demon. I sometimes wonder what the differences might be. The evidence of his mental illness can be seen in his lifestyle and his writings. Paul believed that women were second-class citizens. The men had to lead them around like puppets. According to Paul it was forbidden for a woman to speak in church. (How many Christians obey that rule?) Her head had to remain covered at all times during church, while it was a sin for a man to cover up his glory. Paul spent his entire life running, dodging, lying, and conniving to the point that most everyone both Gentile and Jew sought his life. The court magistrate had told Paul that he had become quite mad.

Evaluating his writing in Romans 7:13-25, we find, *"Was then that which is good made death unto me? God forbid. But sin, that it might appear sin, working death in me by that which is good; that sin by the commandment might become exceeding sinful. For we know that the law is spiritual: but I am carnal, sold under sin. For that which I do I allow not: for what I would, that do I not; but what I hate that do I."* How many of us on average find ourselves voluntarily doing things that we hate? Even the most frequently fornicating Christian does not honestly think like this. He asks Jesus to forgive him and help him not to repeat his mistake even if he is anywhere close to the same thinking as Paul. But the majority realizes that they enjoy fulfilling their desires. How many Christians do you know, shacking up today, who know in their hearts that Jesus is still their redeemer?

Paul even stated that he is justified in any sin through the grace of Jesus. So what is his problem? *"If I do that which I would not, I consent unto the law that it is good. Now then it is no more I that do it but sin that dwelleth in me."* This is very deep. Paul is admitting that it isn't he who is messing up, but a sinning spirit inside. *"**For I know that in me dwelleth no good thing** (just a demon, my insert is more truthful than that of King James Version): for to will is present with me; but how to perform that which is good I find not."* Paul clearly admits that he can not perform (do) good. *"For the good that I would, I do not: but the evil which I would not, that I do. Now if I do that I would not, it is no more I that do it, but sin (the demon) that dwelleth in me. I find then a law, that, when I would do good, evil (the demon) is present with me. For I delight in the law of God after the inward man: **But***

*I see another law in my members, warring against the law of my mind, and bringing me into captivity to the law of sin which is in my members."*

Clearly this is a confused and totally out-of-control human being, and yet we are supposed to believe that this individual is divinely inspired by the Creator God Almighty. *"O wretched man that I am! Who shall deliver me from the body of this death? I thank God through Jesus Christ Our Lord, So then with the mind I myself serve the law of God: but with the flesh the law of sin."* Paul became a victim of his own contradictions and deceit. However, Paul's doctrines were not the only contradictions found in the New Testament, for there were also great disharmony with in the gospel (God Spell) and within the overall character of Jesus Christ himself.

## Disharmony of the Gospels

The gospels are inconsistent with respect to the character of Jesus Christ. The book of Matthew teaches of a militant racist Jesus with little emphasis on believing and absolutely no use of the word grace. The word "believe" is mentioned seven times. This Jesus appears more to have been a Zealot. He was very much into reincarnation, which kept him at odds with the Sadducees. His belief system, that the law of his people had been corrupted, also put him at odds with the Pharisees, who believed in following the evil law as it is today in the Old Testament, killing all who dare to challenge its contents.

The book of Matthew has the most reliable truth regarding the true Christ. You will find in Matthew 15:24, that Jesus came for the lost sheep of Israel **only**, but in John 3:16, he came for the world. Which verse speaks the truth? It is impossible to save one race **only**, while saving the world. We must believe either that Jesus came for the lost sheep of Israel or the world; and thus decipher which part of the Bible is wrong. There are several verses like those above, both Matthew 15:21-22 and Mark 7:26 say that the **same** female individual who was called a dog was of different nationalities, a

Canaanite and a Greek respectively. Since the Canaanites are descendants of Ham and the Greeks are descendants of Japheth, there is absolutely no way for a Canaanite to be a Greek. Thus again the reader is left to decide where the truth lies. Another set of verses that are completely opposite are found in Matthew 11:14 and John 1:21. In Matthew, Jesus states that John the Baptist is Elijah reincarnated. In John, John the Baptist states that he is not Elijah reincarnated. Again the reader must decide which verse is true.

The entire faith of today's Christianity is based on "grace"; however, as stated before, not once is the word "grace" mentioned in the book of Matthew. Furthermore, if the gospels are truly researched and compared with the Pauline teachings you could see without a doubt where grace was introduced into Christian belief. In the book of Matthew alone Jesus states that people are not supposed to do work in Jesus' name. Similar passages throughout all the gospels except one quote Jesus as stating that "none is good but the Father," thus Jesus is saying that he is not good, only the father (Ref. Matthew 19:17, Luke 18:19, Mark 10:18). Notice which book of the four gospels fails to report Jesus stating that he is not good. It is the book of John. The gospel of John has been more corrupted than any other gospel placing emphasis against the original teaching of Christ.

The book of Mark, also considered by the scholars as the first written gospel, seems to represent a mythical Jesus. The character of Jesus Christ in this book is so unreal that in order to be a real Christian you must be able to lift up a serpent, and if it bites, no deadly harm should come to you. There are very few Christians who believe and practice this doctrine. Mark goes on to say that they shall drink any deadly poison, and not die. These are the signs that follow them who believe. This verse can be found in Mark 16:16-18: *"He that believeth and is baptized shall be saved; but he that believeth not shall be damned. And these signs shall follow them that believe;* (the believer is required to have these signs or except that he is damned.) *In my name shall they*

1. *cast out devils.*

2.  *They shall speak with new tongues.*
3.  *They shall take up serpents and if . . .*
4.  *they can drink any deadly thing; it shall not hurt them.*
5.  *They shall lay hands on the sick, and they shall recover."*

How many Christians do we know have all five of these signs as examples of their lifestyle? With common sense we can see that it is ridiculous. Why would anyone take up a snake? Imagine those poor Christians who are trying faithfully to take up a serpent as a sign of their worthiness to be called a Christian, and the many deaths that have resulted from this myth. Most Christians will say that this was not a literal translation of what Jesus meant to say, because the majority of them have no intention of following these passages as proof of being a true Christian. Common sense tells the majority of them to dismiss it, but they never realize that in all actuality they are dismissing scripture as meaning what it has said. Many babies die from poison all the time. Christians will say that they are saved by grace (through their believing parent) because they are incapable of choosing Christ, but if they are saved by grace, why do the babies of the Christian believer die? There are very few Christians in comparison to the masses with the power to lay on hands and heal the sick. So this means the vast majority of all Christians have been damned according to this passage. No other gospel states that a Christian should have these signs. The book of Mark **never** mentions the word "grace" and the word "believe" is mentioned 11 times here. This book is in harmony with the other books of the gospel regarding grace, in that it mentions very little on salvation by grace. See the paragraph on the Gospel According to John. However, there is mention of believing in the power of Jesus' name.

The book of Luke is by far the most different book of the entire Bible due to the fact that the author, Luke, a companion of Paul, is the only Gentile writer of all the accepted Holy

Scriptures in both Hebrew and Greek. Luke straightforwardly admits writing this book of his own accord and not because of an inspiration from God. Read Luke 1:1-3: *"Forasmuch as many have taken in hand to set forth in order a declaration of those things which are most surely believed among us, Even as they delivered them unto us, which from the beginning were eyewitnesses, and ministers of the word;* **It seemed good to me** *also, having had perfect understanding of all things from the very first, to write unto thee in order, most excellent Theophilus."* Luke is simply writing a friend named Theophilus explaining his accounts of Christianity. He boasts that he is a good writer with understanding of the passed-down accounts of the so-called Jesus through the many years after the death of Jesus. Therefore is seemed like a good thing to do (the writing of the Gospel of Luke). There is no order from God such as, "thus saith the Lord God to Luke, write . . . " What is overwhelmingly difficult to understand is how Luke could quote Jesus word for word, whom he never met. Luke had to have been told the stories by others to create his gospel, and many today consider his secondhand material as sacred writing. Luke appears to display more of the mystical and esoteric side of Jesus than all the other gospels. The word grace is used only **once** and the word believe is used the least of all the gospels, appearing only five times.

The book of John is the one gospel that authorizes the calling and believing upon the name of Jesus. Although it mentions the word "grace" only three times, it uses the word "believe" nearly 50 times. In comparison to the other gospels "grace" is mentioned a maximum of **10 to 50 times more** in John than all the other gospels. Why the huge difference in the philosophy of "grace" in the book of John has never been discussed among Christians. This is a considerable difference on the emphasis on believing. The book of John advocates the believing on the name of Jesus, and as a result it is the favorite gospel among today's Christians. Out of all four gospels, the Book of John refers to believing nearly five times more than all the other gospels. Did all the other gospel writers not know as much as the author of the book of John, or is it remotely possible that some exaggerations and additions of the accounts regarding "grace" and "believing" have taken place? All of the gospels are in harmony with little or no use of the term grace.

However, Acts, Romans, and so forth all of a sudden begin to prioritize the word grace and it takes on a totally new emphasis throughout the Pauline writings. The book of Acts mentions "grace" 10 times, the book of Romans 22 times and the first and second books of Corinthians 21 times. The grand total of emphasis on salvation requiring grace by Paul and having nothing so whatever to do with Jesus is 114 entries. The gospel's grand total is 4 entries. How can it be that people call themselves Christians (followers of Christ) when Christ had nothing at all to do with the story of grace, and it is there as evidence in the Christian book, the Bible? They will say that Jesus' death brought about grace, but did it? Even if it were true, why didn't Jesus place as much emphasis on grace as did Paul, seeing that he supposedly knew he was sent to bring grace to the world? Why did he state the condition, that only if heaven and earth pass away, can any portion of the law pass away? If Jesus knew that he would bring grace to the world, it should have been mentioned at least two hundred times, but there are only 4 entries. If the truth be known, the four entries of the word "grace" that were recorded in the gospel, would actually be zero, if Jesus had his way about it. Why is it so, that Paul's portion of the Bible taught people that salvation was in grace, but JESUS DID NOT ADVOCATE GRACE!

In order to read biblical references on disharmony of the Bible in its entirety refer to the chart "Biblical Contradictions" in the Appendix. There are many verses in both the Old and New Testament that say one thing and then another many times completely opposite information is given. It also includes discrepancies in the biblical philosophy and Christian belief. The best references for the origins of the Christian religion are as follows:

1. *Deceptions and Myths of the Bible*, Lloyd M. Graham, Carol Publishing Group
2. *Forgery in Christianity*, by Joseph Wheless, Kessinger Publishing Company
3. *Is It God's Word*, by Joseph Wheless, Kessinger Publishing Company
4. *The Antichrist 666*, by William Josiah Sutton, W. F. G., Inc.
5. *Why I Am Not a Christian*, by Bertrand Russell, Simon and Schuster
6. *The Almost Forgotten Day*, by Mark A. Finley, The Concerned Group Inc.
7. *Losing Faith in Faith: From Preacher to Atheist*, by Dan Barker, Freedom from Religion Foundation

# SIX

# The Origin of Life

M an's foremost question that will always and forever plague him, until he finds the true answer to his ancestral identity, is, without doubt, the origin of his existence: "Where did man come from?" and "How and when did he inhabit the earth?" We'll look for answers in this section. However, we will remain somewhat in the dark, since there is no absolute knowledge available to physical man, but we will have at hand the most believed creation stories along with some unconventional ideas. I will leave it to you to decide which view is closest to the truth. We are going to discuss several theories:

1. Darwinism
2. The Biblical Account of Creation
3. The Biblical Account Explained Esoterically
4. The *Enuma Elish* Creation Epic
5. Dr. John Rodgers' Theory
6. The Big Bang Theory
7. The Ezzrath Theory

## Darwinism
The biblical epic of creation set mankind back generations regarding the knowledge of the age of the earth and humanity. The

biblical story led man to believe the earth was only six thousand years old and that man was six thousand years old minus several days. But in 1859, Charles Darwin dropped a bomb on the Christian community and much of humanity with his publication of *The Origin of Species by Natural Selection.* Although he was born into a highly religious Christian family that had taught him strict Christian standards, Darwin's discovery would reshape his religious convictions forever.

His father's attempts at pushing the young Darwin toward the Christian ministry failed. Darwin himself was very religious, and knew that his life's destiny involved the conquest of a search for the true God of creation. He began with a study of archaeology and anthropology. Briefly, the study of archaeology involves a search and recovery of historical and pre-historical artifacts from the earth while anthropology analyzes cultures that produced them. His findings and conclusions would forever change the thinking of modern man about his origins. The full blast of Darwin's bombshell on the Christian community cannot be fully imagined today. The closest approximation of its impact may be reflected in reactions by Christians to the *Ultimate Deceit.*

Darwin found fossil fragments of extinct marine life that left absolutely no doubt in the minds of the scientific community that the earth was by far much older than the biblical myth which placed creation in the year 4000 B.C. The frail and sickly Darwin could not have imagined approaching the Christian community with his theory of human ancestral links relating to the apes and chimpanzees of Africa. However, his associate, Thomas Henry Huxley, an energetic, dynamic scientist who was ready for the head-on collision with the Christian community, took Darwin's theory to England's prime minister, Benjamin Disraeli, and publicly announced the theory of humans evolving from apes. He spoke out openly of the similarities of man and his closest living relatives, the ape family. The only fossil link in his possession was part of a skull and limb found out of the Neanderthal valley in

Germany, the first Neanderthal hominid known to modern man. Even Darwin would leap for joy with the scientific discoveries we have today: the carbon dating technique, the discovery of Lucy, and the DNA testing available today to establish without a doubt that all mankind stems from one common ancestor.

Today's scientists have advanced Darwin's theory by great measures. The common ancestor's mitochondria found in the female DNA of every human establishes that this ancestor had to be of African descent. Furthermore, the oldest complete hominid remains (Lucy) known to modern man were found in South Africa. Lucy is a unique scientific breakthough. She is the oldest complete human skeleton, dated somewhere around 2 million years old. She was found in southern Africa in the late 1970s.

Science has concluded that man evolved from an ancestral tree that proceeded as follows:

1. In 1910, pieces and fragments of an apelike creature were found in Northern India, but no one realized at that time its kinship to man. In 1932, this first human ancestor was recognized and was called *Ramapithecus* after the Indian god Rama. Scientists believed that he appeared as early as 10 million years ago. However, later discoveries of fragmented remains of another *Ramapithecus*, discovered in Kenya, were dated back as far as 14 million years.

2. The descendant of *Ramapithecus* was believed to be *Australopithecus africanus*. He appeared on the scene around five to six million B.C. *Africanus* is known to have walked upright and to have made tools for hunting and protection. He is the first known hominid to walk upright. There's evidence to suggest that *Africanus* evolved into *Homo habilis* after a few million years.

3. Around one and a half million years B.C., *Homo erectus* appeared on the planet. *Erectus* is considered the first true man. He was capable of building shelter to adapt to his

environment. He traveled over Asia, Europe, and Africa. He eventually evolved into modern man.

4. Neanderthal man marks the earliest appearance of modern man. Appearing some one hundred thousand years ago, he was highly advanced in making stone tools, art, religion, shelter and so forth. Neanderthal man evolved into or parallels Cro-Magnon man some 20,000 years ago. If Neanderthal man and Cro-Magnon man were seen today, neatly groomed, the average person would recognize them as humans, not animals.

## The Biblical Account of Creation

The biblical account of creation straightforwardly names a single deity by the name of Yahweh (Jehovah) as the creator of the entire universe; creation was accomplished in just six days in the year of approximately 4000 B.C. In the beginning, states the Bible, God created the heavens and the earth, earth which was without form, and which was void and dark. Therefore, on the first day, God spoke light into existence. However, one must note that this light is neither the sun nor the moon, nor other heavenly bodies. We know this by paying close attention to what was created on the fourth day. On the second day, God created the firmament (heavenly space, kingdoms, land?) of heaven. On the third day, God formed the seas, lands, and vegetation on earth. On the fourth day, God created the sun, moon, and stars. On the fifth day, God created the animal life of the sea and the fowl of the air. Finally, on the sixth day, God created land animals and man. And thus we have the summary of the Bible's version of creation.

## Biblical Account Explained Esoterically

Any well-educated person knows that it is just ridiculous to even remotely consider the possibility that the universe could have been formed in six days, 6000 years ago. Further more, the account in which the sun and the moon are created on the fourth day after the creation of the earth is also ludicrous, because our sun predates the earth by millions of years. However, if we apply a metaphysical and esoteric approach to deciphering the text we can find a shred of believability in the plagiarized ancient Hebrew scrolls. Then we can use the higher self to interpret a deeper meaning. Always keep in mind that this interpretation is theoretically possible and nothing more.

The first biblical account to be eliminated is the date of creation and the six days it supposedly took to form the universe. It has been stated that God's time is not our time and perhaps this may have been what was meant by our inspired author of Genesis, for we know that the literal account is undeniably unacceptable. So perhaps a "day" was represented by actually a billion years. Then the Hebrew text would have read that it took God six billion years to create the heavens and the earth (much more believable) and that we are now just past the sixth billionth year of existence on earth. Maybe that's why we have havoc on earth . . . maybe God is still on his seventh billion year, Sabbath. Just joking. Surely He wouldn't do that to us: create us and then sit back and do nothing but rest. What a thought, hmm?

The first day then means that just over six billion years ago God created the heavens and the earth. That is the concept or conscious thought of a heaven and earth. Every physical creation always begins as conscious thought! So we do not begin with a physical heaven and earth, so to speak, as thought by most Bible readers. We begin with the human soul along with all the other species of souls. On the first day a light was created, which I believe to have been all the individual souls of light consciousness. Yes, I believe that the Bible has encoded inside itself an attempt to reveal the age (with respect to our ability to grasp time) in which the souls of our reality were actually created. These souls I suspect to have been angels of the order of Seraphim, Cherubim (light and darkness–order and destruction): **US**. I suspect that, simultaneously, other species and orders of God-law-abiding bodies were also created, yielding the division of God into infinitesimally small pieces of conscious light energy.

Have you ever seen a situation where a person has done nothing but love, love, and love some more, only to be openly rejected by a person whose mentality you cannot comprehend? This mentality is God energy of a cherub angel. Although created for destruction it has the capability of knowing and practicing both "good" and "bad." The cherub consciousness has no conscious desire to "do unto others as you would have them do unto you." They can kill and feel that they have just done the world the best of services possible. They can have children and keep them locked out of their lives totally without any expression of love and with absolutely no remorse. Most souls who are not of a cherub consciousness, but choose to be born of a cherub soul-line family, do so out of a desire to learn unconditional love in this particular incarnation. Others are usually cherubs themselves, or like attracting like energy forces. This is why the debate over environment versus genetics as the cause of social behavioral problems is senseless. The first emphasizes the effects of outside influences on a person's behavior, while the second attributes chromosomal and chemical imbalances due to heredity. But the real contributor to the essence of our behavior that no one appears to notice is the soul of the individual. Where did it come from and for what purpose was it created? The soul has the power to choose its genetic makeup from its parent ancestral DNA. Therefore, a cherub soul will attract like physical energy and create the illusion that genetics caused the behavior problems; and because both parents are cherub-conscious it appears that the child is a product of its environment. However, the same parents may have a seraphim-conscious soul that incarnates as their child, which chooses from its parent the DNA pattern like itself, tossing out the theory of genetics and environment altogether. The best example of this type of situation is in the movie *Matilda* with Danny DeVito. The Seraphim child born to cherub parents is here to learn and to teach through life's experience. The modern science of psychology would diagnose a cherub person as having a lack of conscience.

Conversely, the Seraphim were created for the higher worlds of light consciousness (this is what most would call the workers of righteousness), but they, too, have the capability of experiencing both "good" and "evil" at will. I believe the Seraphim, sometime during 4000 B.C., were tricked into the human mortal body by a cherub and or the Ophanim mentality, thus beginning the Adamic race of people (MORTAL MAN). Mortal man is different from the man created from clay (IMMORTAL MAN). We will come back to this in the sixth day of creation or the sixth billionth year of creation.

Next, in another billion years, God created the firmaments of heaven. I suspect this was when the sun and other stars and the older bodies of our solar system were established. The moon may have been established just prior to the next era of creation.

A billion years later, on the third day, God summoned the lands, sea, and vegetation to appear. This happened roughly just over four billion years ago. Now we have science and the Bible on exactly one accord here. We know that absolute truth and knowledge as to the creation of our universe is null and void within our present consciousness. Or perhaps I should speak for myself and say that I do not believe that there is any way to establish without doubt the makings of our galaxy, I leave that for narrow-minded Christians (not all Christians are narrow-minded, JUST THE ONES THAT KNOW IT ALL) and Scientists for without doubt they will KNOW for sure.

Next, we have outright confusion created on the fourth day. According to the Bible, the sun was made on the first day and on the fourth day. The first day, light called day was created, and on the fourth day, light that ruled the day was created. Read for yourself the creation story of the first (Genesis 1:3) and fourth day (Genesis 1:14). If the fourth verse is true, it tries to establish that

God created the sun after the earth on the fourth day, because the Bible states that in the beginning God created the heavens and the earth. How is it possible that the sun, which is older than the earth, could be created after the earth? If we study the Babylonian epics of creation we would learn that it was nothing strange to these people to identify the heavenly bodies as individuals or beings. If there is any way to establish both the first and second lights as truth and allow everything to flow in harmony, with what we know to be factual, then the Babylonian creation epic must be utilized. For example, we know to be fact that there is no way that the sun was created after the earth so. . . Therefore, we know that we are not speaking of the sun and moon and stars here. Besides, they would have had to have been here during the time of the creation of the firmaments of heaven. To remain consistent with the framework of the ancient text the only thing that could have happened here is the establishment of order of the created light. This is the era in which the Seraphim (the light, He called day) were established with authority over the higher worlds and the Cherubim (the darkness, He called night) with the authority over the lower worlds. As individual consciousness developed a solidification process (creation), we were able to experience physical worlds at this point. I believe that the human spirit was able to pick up and lie down flesh at will during this era. The spirit would experience human life as it chose. It would have to travel away from the earth back to the spirit world in order not to get caught in the mortal frequency of our planet. We were so perfect at performing our states of being in utopia during this era that we as individual collective consciousness put together our universe as it is today. The first thing that we as gods put together was the collective influencing consciousness some would call astrology that affects and inspires our current states of consciousness as we play the game of life. We are currently headed for a shift in inspiration from Pisces to Aquarius. What a great tool in the game of life; just as you're learning the rules, simply change the conscious mind and a new set of rules will automatically appear. Those individual bodies have transformed the collective body as has been maintained since the beginning of time. Thus we have a mere glimpse of the fourth day.

The fifth day, or around two or three billion years ago, we have the Bible stating esoterically that small animals, sea creatures, and the fowl of the air emerge. For this to be true, these creatures also would have had to possess the ability of transfiguration instead of death, because the first large mammals found by archaeologists (the dinosaurs) did not appear until roughly 200,000,000 years ago. We must face it! Ancient creation stories tell us that lifestyles of the people on earth were vastly different from the lifestyles of people today. These people reported from all around the world of strange creations such as the sphinx, gods that would just appear out of the water or sky, men with tails, men with animal heads, animals with men's heads and so forth. In those day people were born and within three days they were grown and according to some accounts people were born fully grown. Would we term this collective human report of the gods a hallucination? How could it be possible for societies all over the world that never came in contact with one another to create such illusions with consistency in descriptions of detail from culture to culture? They all report a single human survivor of a flood. Many of them report that man was fabricated from clay. Mass illusion? I don't think so. Perhaps some confusion or ad-libbing may have occurred, but these people were writing of events that have taken place within our history (their personal experiences) and it is up to us to decipher all the puzzle pieces, and put them into place. Moreover, it is up to us to admit when a piece of the puzzle just doesn't quite fit in with the entire scope of existence and remove that piece for re-examination. Then we can attempt to replace it elsewhere or simply just hold it in limbo until it can be added to the entire picture and fit "picture perfectly." Also, we must never be ashamed to learn later that the "picture perfect" scheme of life that we thought that we possessed, never existed. This is okay. Life goes on and we rearrange the pieces again and again and again. However, I can find no reason to hold on to what we know is impossible merely for the sake of faith in religion.

Finally, we come to the era of the creation of man here at the end of the six billion years. According to science, the first semblance of man occurs in 14 million B.C. However, science takes into account only the seen. Science states absolute facts and then theorizes as to how phenomena and events have taken place. The wonderful aspect of science is that it theorizes about what it has not proved instead of stating it as a proven fact. Illusions results when we do not recognize that what we have accepted as facts are in actuality ideas, theories, opinions, and beliefs.

Genesis 1:26 says, *"And Elohim* (Elohim was the original Hebrew word which is the plural form of god) *said, Let* **us** *make man in* **our** *image, after* **our** *likeness: So Elohim* (the gods) *created man in his own image in the image of God created he him: male and female."* Here the Bible clearly identifies the makers of man as gods, not GOD. I believe that there were intelligent beings much like us who asked to make a man. It is clear that Elohim is asking, "Let us make a man." The word "let" clearly places Elohim in subjection to a greater force. Therefore Elohim (the gods) are requesting permission from a higher source. Zecharia Sitchin's *The 12th Planet* outstandingly reveals the concept that man's creators were a species from another planet called Nabiru. The Sumerian earthlings, called the inhabitants of Nabiru, the Anunnaki. These same beings were called Nefilim in Genesis 6:4, *"There were Giants* (Nefilim) *in the earth in those days;* **and also after that,** *when the sons of God* (**Anu**) *came in unto the daughters of men, and they bare children to them, the same became mighty men which were of old, men of renown* (MEN OF SHEM)." According to the Bible there are now a race of mighty men bred between the earthlings (*Homo sapiens*) and gods. This race of mighty men was known as SHEM. During this time PHYSICALLY on earth there is:

1. God (Anu)
2. the sons of god (Enlil, Ea, and their children)
3. the earth man (the ADAM *Homo sapiens*)
4. a species rarely discussed; a mixture of the sons of God with Adam) THE MIGHTY MEN of SHEM (HUMANS - ADAM KADMON)—IMMORTAL MAN
5. the mixture of humans (Adam Kadmon) with Adam (an animal called man), today's human race: mortal man

If you are scratching your heads, wondering how to learn that the men of renown are Shem in the original Hebrew, then you are in desperate need of acquiring independent thought regarding the fact-finding process. Why? You are now fully equipped to find out what was originally said by the Hebrews who recorded this text. Have you figured it out? Make a conscious note at this time that if you are relying on me to tell you how to find out the original Hebrew meaning then you are not self-reliant in obtaining your knowledge and you are setting yourself up for *ultimate deceit* by requiring the leadership of another human. By now you have been given enough information to know that you should acquire original meanings from *Strong's Concordance* of Hebrew translations. Look up the word "renown" in English and Strong's will give you a corresponding number to match the word up in Hebrew. When we look up the number, we find the word SHEM. Amazing how different words become once we have the ORIGINAL meaning.

The Bible mentions the creation of man twice, once in Genesis. 1:26 and again in Genesis 2:7. Did God create two different species of man, or did He re-fashion the earlier version of Genesis. 1:26, or did He simply mention the same fabrication of a man twice? There are varying esoteric theories of which I have knowledge and I am sure there are many more than displayed here in this book. This is a typical example of where your individual pursuit of the truth should take over, for surely there are vast amounts of information out there anticipating your discovery.

### First Theory

In Genesis 1:26 the god creating man is Ea. However the first man created did not possess the ability to procreate. He was very similar to a mule in his breeding and reproduction capabilities. This was the first human worker race. According to Zecharia Sitchin's, *The Wars of Gods and Men*, in the year 300,000 B.C. the Igigis had carried the burden of mining gold until the genetic manipulation of the ape woman to produce (not evolve) *Homo sapiens* (not humans). Sitchin gets his information from material more ancient than the Bible. In other words, the ancient "myths" were stories and accounts **predating the Bible**. Man used his imagination to decide which stories were divine and which were myth. However, there is no way around the fact that many of the ancient myths were **written before the Bible** and that many of these myths that were written **before** the Bible were simply re-copied accounts stated in the more ancient myths. According to ancient Hebrew myth, the first race of men was called the Adam and they were pretty much doomed to be enslaved to the gods. Genesis 5:1 states, "*This is the book of the generations of the Adam, in the day that God created man, in the likeness of God made he him; Male and female created he **them** (the Adam, a race of people); and blessed **them**, and **called their** (the Homo sapiens species) **name Adam**, in the day when they were created.*"

Another story in the Bible which helps us to know that there were many humans in the times of Adam and not just Adam and his immediate family was the epic of Cain and Abel. According to Genesis 4:8-15, during Cain's time there were so many people on the earth that even though he was sent out from among his people (supposedly only Adam and Eve) he required a mark of identification for protection against other humans he may have met. See Genesis 4:14-15, where Cain begins talking to God after killing Abel: "*Behold, thou hast driven me out this day from the face of the earth; and from thy face shall I be hid; and I shall be a fugitive and a vagabond in the earth;* (Cain is driven from his family) *and it shall come to pass, that every one* (Who is everyone?) *that findeth me shall slay me. And the Lord said unto him, Therefore whosoever slayeth Cain, vengeance shall be taken on him sevenfold. And the Lord set a mark upon Cain, lest any finding him should kill him."* Who besides Adam, Eve, and their immediately family do most Bible readers regard as living during the act of Cain's murder of Abel? Most Bible readers will tell you that there was only Adam and Eve and now that Abel was murdered, that left only Cain. They would have had to be awfully stupid not to know their own kin and require a mark to identify Cain. However, once we realize that there were many men during this era an identification process may have been deemed necessary.

Then there is the issue of Cain's appearance. According to other biblical material from the Hebrews that was voted out of entry into the Bible, Cain was animalistic in appearance for his great-great-grandson Lamech killed him by accident. Lamech was out hunting with his son (or grandson) Tubal-cain. Lamech signaled Tubal-cain that he saw a beast and asked Tubal-cain for guidance, because he was nearly blind. Tubal-cain gave the sign that the beast was dead ahead. However, when they got closer, Tubal-cain told his blinded father that the beast resembled a human except that it had a horn in the center of its forehead. Lamech remembered the mark placed in the forehead of Cain and he knew immediately that their ancestor Cain had been killed. Taken with so much grief in some manner or another Tubal-cain also lost his life at the hands of Lamech. We can find a little flavor of this information with all the details stripped away in Genesis 4:23 which states, *"And Lamech said unto his wives, Adah and Zillah,* (By the way where did these women come from if there were only Adam, Eve and by now Seth?) *Hear my voice; ye wives of Lamech, hearken unto my speech: for I have slain a man* (Cain) *to my wounding, and a young man* (Tubal-cain) *to my hurt."*

According to the Bible, man obeys god's command to be fruitful and multiply and in doing so he has a way of pissing god off.

In one biblical tale god gets so pissed off with man that he totally destroys all of mankind in a natural disaster (the flood) with the exception of one man and his family. Noah finds mercy from the biblical god, who instructs him to build an ark to safely escape the coming deluge. He gives Noah explicit instructions as to how the ark must be constructed and tells Noah to gather one pair of opposite sexes of every animal. Noah strictly follows the instructions, saving the inhabitants of the ark, which included the animals and his family only. The story regarding Noah and the ark begins in Genesis sixth and ends in the eighth chapter with Noah making a sacrifice to Yahweh. In Genesis 8:21, Yahweh is quoted as having enjoyed the savory sweet smell of the burnt offering. So, according to the Bible every single race comes from Noah's three sons: Shem, Ham, and Japheth. (See the chapter regarding the comparison of races.)

Another story that affects the entire human race is the story of the tower of Babel found in Genesis 11, "*And the whole earth was of one language, and of one speech, And it came to pass, as they journeyed from the east, that they found a plain* (**Portal or Merkabah**) *in the land of Shinar* (land of the Sumerians); *and they dwelt there. And they said one to another, Go to, let us make brick, and burn them thoroughly, And they had brick for stone, and slime had they for mortar. And they said, Go to, let us build us a city and a tower, whose top may reach unto heaven; and let us make us a name* (SHEM), *lest we be scattered abroad upon the face of the whole earth.* (Here we can see that the men knew of the gods' wicked plan to strip them of their hue. They knew that something might happen to cause them to lose unity!) *And the Lord came down to see the city and the tower, which the children of men builded. And the Lord said, Behold, the people is one, and they have all one language; and this they begin to do: and now nothing will be restrained from them, which they have imagined to do. Go to, let us go down and there confound* (confuse) *their language, that they may not understand one another's speech. So the lord scattered them abroad from* *thence upon the face of all the earth: and they left off to build the city. Therefore is the name of it called Babel; because the lord did there confound the language of all the earth: and from thence did the lord scatter them abroad upon the face of all the earth.*" Here the Bible clearly documents (most important) that man was once of one accord. It appears that god got jealous that man had the capability to become as the gods. (Zecharia Sitchin's book adds clarity to this chapter; see *The Twelfth Planet* for details.)

Common sense tells us that we would be happy if our children aspire to become as good or even better than we are. Definitely we would not divide our children against one another so that they could not have the opportunity to be all that they could be. This is a red flag Bible story of something stinking in Denmark. Why would God divide his children, if indeed He loved them? Why would he be angry that they were trying to be like him, or reach heaven? I love it when my children try to imitate my actions, except my bad habits. For example, if I get angry and yell at my children, they are not permitted to yell back, and of course they cannot return a spanking; somewhat like vengeance is mine saith Ezzrath. Moreover, if we think of the African-American slave mentality striving to be equal to his white master counterpart, then we can envision an act for which the white man would have killed the black man. Perhaps confusing the languages or creating havoc among us was better than killing us? If a race of people or gods (THEM) ever lost denominating superiority in the mentality of their slaves, subjects, and pets (US—you and me), they would lose their slaves, subjects, and pets and **gain a competitive equal**, the exact opposite of their purpose. Go to the library and read the *Willie Lynch letters on how to make a slave,* and see if you can see the similarities between the white slave master and the god slave master. Let's continue with the biblical esoteric teaching of creation and man's plight in its midst.

## Second Theory

Another theory comes from information that I have taken from *The Legends of the Bible*, by Louis Ginzberg. In this biblical epic of creation the world is also created in six days. However, this book does not leave as much hidden information to be deciphered as does the book of Genesis in the King James Version of the Bible. It alleges that before any creation could begin, God had to banish the ruler of the dark whom it calls "Retire," stating that God said to him, "for I desire to create the world by means of light." Only after the light had been fashioned could darkness arise, the light ruling in the sky, the darkness on the earth.

The power of God displayed itself not only in the creation of the world of things, but equally in the limitations which he imposed upon each thing. The heavens and the earth stretched themselves out in length and breadth as though they aspired to infinitude, and it required the word of God to call a halt to their overstepping the boundaries. We are given that before creating the heavens and the earth God created the Universal Law and on the first day, just as in the Bible, the heavens and the earth were created. However, in this version we are given that the world was created out of the Hebrew letter Beth. Everything in creation was created out of this letter. There was only one letter in the Hebrew alphabet which did not demand recognition from creation, and for this cause God set it first in the alphabet as a silent letter. Again on the first day darkness and lightness were created and given the names Bohu and Tohu. There were seven heavens created with only one being visible to man. These heavens are at times numbered and at other times are called new or present heavens.

On the second day, according to this theory, God created the firmament, hell, fire, and the angels. It states that the firmament is the same as the first day's creation of heaven. The legends of the Bible claims that the waters refused to obey (look up Tiamat, the goddess who represents the last of the matriarchal rule—she is PRE-HIStory) and to be placed in the designated areas in which God had desired, and apparently God's wrath at this point against the water's (Tiamat and Apsu) refusal to be separated caused the world to **re-enter** chaos. Eventually the waters yielded to their designated areas of the universe as desired by the creator (Anu, Ea, or Marduk?).

In efforts to complement the yin/yang of universal order, this story claims an existence of seven hells or that hell has seven division by the names of Sheol, Abaddon, Beer Shahat, Tit ha-Yawn, Sha'are Mawet, Sha'are Zalmawet, and Gehenna. Each division supposedly contains seven rivers of fire and seven rivers of hail. It is maintained by the cherub order of angels, the angels of destruction.

The angels of host were created of fire; some were for ministering and the others for praising. These angels were created in rank and orders. The highest rank and order of angels are called the Archangels with the names of Michael, Gabriel, Uriel, and Raphael (Satan would have been created in this era).

The third day bought about the fabrication of plants for earth and paradise. Ministering angels were assigned work as gatekeepers of paradise. However, earth and water remained mingled throughout the four corners of the earth. This is the day that God gathered the waters and collected them in the deepest surfaces of the earth with the land first appearing from the mountains and hills.

On the fourth day, like the Bible, we find that both the sun and the moon are completed. The difference here is that the sun and moon were both created on the first day, but on the fourth day God assigned their position within creation. Here the moon begins to nag God and wants to assure that its light will be greater than the light of the sun, but more apparent is the moon's desire that the sun's light be of a lesser significance than that of the moon. God becomes angry at the moon and in His anger He reduces the light of the moon to one sixth of her original light. The moon would no longer be equal to the sun, as it had been originally.

On the fifth day, the fish and sea animals are made out of the mixture of fire and water. This version starts with a fish created out of water, and the birds were created out of the mixture of both earth and water, and finally mammals are formed from solid earth only. According to this version the monstrous leviathan was one of the fish that was created. The leviathan requires one thousand mountains of food to fill it and at the beginning it was created androgynous (both male and female) without the capability of reproduction. (Not to doubt the book, but this would actually be asexual, not androgynous.) The leviathan is given rulership over the sea animals. The leviathan is created with such a horrid smell that if it were to have been placed in paradise, paradise would become inhabitable.

On the sixth day, again we have an account of creation similar to the Bible's account. We find that Adam is created on the sixth day; however, what is very interesting is that this version states that Adam's soul was created on the first day, but his flesh was created on the sixth day.

There are tales of many other monsters besides that of the leviathan. Another monster was stated as having been so enormously huge that there was room enough for only two animals of this nature. One would go east and the other would go west. When it became time to procreate they would get together and do so; then the female would kill the male. While she was pregnant she became immobile and it would appear that she would starve, but she used her own spit to gather nutrients from the earth until the baby was born. This animal, called the reem, always gave birth to twins. After the birth, the mother died and the twins headed off in opposite directions, one going east and the other west, completing the cycle.

One of the most unusual tales is the story of an **animal** called Adam (man) that lived in the mountains. This animal is clearly of human form, but it is fastened to the ground by its navel-string. Its entire existence relies upon this string; if it is broken the animal will die. The only way to kill this animal is by breaking the navel-string. It was reported that a traveler new to the region where this animal existed had happened to stop in at one of the inhabitants of the area. He overheard the host's wife offering to serve a man for dinner. Thinking that the people were cannibalistic he took off running, only to learn later that the couple was serving the flesh of a strange animal named man (perhaps Big foot or *Homo erectus*).

The greatest creation of the sixth day was the creation of the Adamic race of people. As stated earlier it is noted that Adam's soul was created on the first day, but his flesh body was created on the sixth day. On the day that man became a living soul, he was created perfect in God's very own image. Man was created as a microcosm to the universe. *The Legends of the Bible* states:

> The whole world in miniature and the world in turn is a reflex (REFLECTION) of man. The hair upon his head corresponds to the woods of the earth, his tears to a river, his mouth to the ocean. Also the world resembles the ball of his eye, the ocean that encircles the earth is like unto the white of the eye, the dry land is the iris, Jerusalem the pupil, and the Temple the image mirrored in the pupil of the eye.
>
> But man is more than a mere image of this world. He unites both heavenly and earthly qualities within himself. **In four he resembles the angels, in four the beasts.** His power of speech, his discriminating intellect, his upright walk, the glance of his eye—they all make an angel of him But, on the other hand, he eats and drinks, secretes the waste matter in his body, propagates his kind, and dies, like the beast of the field. Therefore God said before the creation of man: The celestials are not propagated, but they die. I will create man to be the union of two, so that when he sins, **when he behaves like a beast, death shall overtake him; but if he refrains from sin he shall live forever;** God now bade all beings in heaven and on earth contribute to the creation of man, and He Himself took part in it. Thus they all will love man, and if he should sin, they will be interested in his preservation.

# PHYSICAL MAN

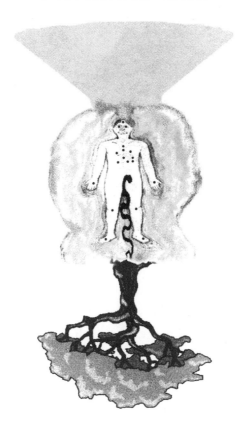

All of creation was summoned to pay regard to the Adam. All of creation loved Adam with the exception of one being called Satan (the enemy). Satan vowed that he would never bow to a creature made of the dust of the ground. He felt that he was Adam's superior. God granted Satan a competition in which man and Satan were to properly take on the mind of God, in knowing the names of all the animals as in the mind of God. Satan had not developed his channeling technique and as such could not name any of the animals brought within his presence. Adam proceeded to name them. In anger Satan vowed to place his throne above the throne of God and become as the most high. Satan was kicked out of heaven along with the hosts of angel followers.

Adam appeared so wonderfully made that even the angels were beginning to develop a desire to worship him as God. For, of all the creatures that were created, only man was created in the essence of God.

Doesn't this sound great? Awesome to our ears, hmmm? Well man's greatness **above** all the other creations of God throws up the red flag warning for *ultimate deceit* in my opinion. Any mentality placing one species or race in superiority causes the other species to be inferior and thus worthless—worth less! Making the other race appear to be inferior, sounds like ego, pride, and puffiness. I believe that I am created not in the image of god, but as God Herself! So are you! You just don't know it yet.

I detest sounding like a broken record, but we have been conditioned for so many eons that I feel I must say it again. **THINK FOR YOURSELF!** Read information for yourself and do not accept anyone's truth OTHER THAN THE GOD IN YOUR HEART. Inform yourself through reading historical records, stories, and data from the library. Do not **hope** for someone else to give you the truth. GO GET IT YOURSELF! Reject any information that doesn't fit in with what your God-sense tells you is possible, but remember in the back of your mind that it doesn't mean that the information is unreal universally. It is simply not a part of your reality at this point in time. This is sort of like keeping information stored on a shelf until enough data is collected to totally disregard the concept. However, if you have not done your homework you will be setting yourself up for deception.

## Enuma Elish Theory

According to the *Enuma Elish*, the creation scene begins with the primordial waters: Tiamat, the goddess of salt water, and Apsu, god of fresh water. Comprehending that the story begins with primordial waters we automatically know that this story is not the beginning of creation. For if there were preexisting waters, then who formed them, and how? If we are to ever place the pieces of the puzzle together as accurately as we can we MUST ask questions of ourselves regarding the obvious. Then we may become responsible data gathers. According to our ancient ancestors during this era, the universe functioned primarily as a matriarchal society. There is very little difference between the biblical and *Enuma Elish* accounts of creation. The primary differences, as stated before, are that the *Enuma Elish* predates the Bible and that the Bible states that there was one God in the beginning who manifested all of creation. In the *Enuma Elish*, credit is given to various gods as creators of the universe. See also the section on Mesopotamian mythology, which goes into greater detail regarding the characters and the events that took place in the *Enuma Elish*. (Study chapter two, and chapter seven on Mesopotamian mythology.)

## Dr. John Rodgers' Theory

Dr. Rodgers' theory places primitive man in East Africa sometime around 150,000 years ago. He adds that religions began sometime around that same era. Dr. Rodgers believes that the first men lived as orangutans and abandoned their women to raise their offspring alone. As far back as around 750,000 years ago, primitive men formed clans and left Africa, moving into Asia. He gives Asia the credit for the rise of the first modern man. He states that the Oriental race seeded the human population and then moved into Europe some 35,000 years ago. The mixing of the Neanderthal man with the modern Oriental man produced the first Caucasians. The Caucasians are said to have later returned to Africa and mixed with the remnants of the original stock, which produced the African race. He completes his hypothesis with the idea that the other races are all mixes of the original three races.

Now that is interesting. There are so many questions I would like to ask this guy, so many important aspects of the situation that he conveniently makes no mention of. My first question is: How on earth is it possible for the white race to make a black race? It is so funny. There are still black couples today—I have witnessed it myself—where both black parents produce a white albino child. The child's skin is literally white, more of a chalky pasty color instead of pink. I have never heard of any white couples producing a black baby. This is not a case of making a darker skinned race of people as whites that produce tanned children. Rodgers would have his readers believe that a black ape and a white man produced a blue-black race. However, as you think on the possibility of a black ape and a white man producing black offspring, don't forget to include in your thoughts that the black ape primarily has black hair; but if we totally shave the ape, what will be the color of his skin? What have scientists reported on this possibility? I will leave this one for you to decide as to whether or not it appears truthful or fictional.

Then again, let's use his story just as it is. He clearly states that the primitive man was an African who went into China and became modern man as an Oriental. Why not as an African? He was African when he went to China; what did he do to turn into a Chinese man? Finally, Rodgers decides to give a little credit to blacks for having made the African race, only as what he calls a remnant of original stock. Why is it that the writer calls the original evolving man "stock" instead of African? He admits that the original stock comes from Africa. I think that if we use a little common sense we will see a little misrepresentation of the true colors of human evolution. There is absolutely no explanation as to how the races evolved; he just says the original stock went to China and made the first man; the next was the white man, and, of course, Africans were last.

I simply wanted to present what people other than myself think, to show you that there is a lot of information out there if we just start asking questions like how or when. We can reject or set aside temporarily any beliefs that don't add up, for example the belief that the white race produced the black race. We can investigate by testing all the avenues to discover if there is any way that a white couple can make a black baby, for if they cannot how can they parent the black race?

## The Big Bang Theory and Einstein's Theory of Relativity

Modern science widely accepts and endorses Einstein's theory of relativity: $E = mc^2$ where E = the energy in the universe, m = mass and c = the velocity of light which is $3 \times 10^8$ m/s². In other words, this equation gives us the energy required to produce matter, the energy required for creation, and subsequently the time required to complete creation. Einstein's theory of relativity led to Edwin Hubble's Law, which defines the speed of galaxies as proportional to their distance away from us. Hubble used a telescope to view our neighboring galaxies moving at a speed consistently faster and faster as the galaxies became farther away from our galaxy. This information led to the scientific evidence in support of the big bang theory.

Einstein developed theories based on observance of the universe's natural laws. He tried to organize a trend of thought from within himself, which was directed at discovering whether or not life is simply a chance in probability and statistics; or if there is some divine order to creation. The big bang theory states that at some point infinitesimally small our universe began out of an explosion of the small point. It goes on to state that our universe is forever expanding, using Hubble's observation of the fact that the further and further the distant galaxies were from the earth the faster and faster they moved away from earth.

The primary argument against the big bang theory is that the equations used to evaluate Hubble's Law estimate the universe's origins at two billion years. The problem with this estimation is that the earth's beginnings are estimated over four billion years ago. This suggests that the earth is older than the universe, which is impossible. Physicist have since discovered errors in calculations by Hubble when he estimated the beginning of the universe at two billion years ago. Supporters of the big bang theory now state that the universe began roughly 15 to 20 billion years ago.

The suggestion is that our universe began immensely small

and after the big bang began expanding at an enormous rate, extending its diameter outward. But at the point when the universe has expanded to its maximum diameter it will slow down until it comes to a stop, and then collapses or is destroyed in the big anti-bang. This theory reminds us very much of Genesis and Revelations. However, science admits that there are no proofs of God's existence. It admits that it doesn't understand what process took place to gather mass from the explosion into galaxies, planets, stars, and moons. Perhaps if we combined science with the DIVINE (the Prophet or Clairvoyant and Clairaudience), then we could put together the theory of missing information, that is the actual transformation of energy into physical matter such as the planets and stars.

The problem with science is that it states if something cannot be observed or "validly" tested, then it does not exist. In other words, and really think about this one, if the dinosaur skeletons were not found, but we discovered pictures from the ancient world, we would scientifically insist that the dinosaurs were figments of the ancients' imagination, "a myth." We would swear that dinosaurs never existed and we would be WRONG. This is where science produces error. There are so many occurrences in our world that are inevitably undeniable. A woman having the strength to pick up a truck to save her child trapped beneath it, or the terminally ill person, who is diagnosed with a life expectancy of six months, but goes on to live a normal long life are both excellent examples of this fact. They have absolutely no idea how it occurs, but it does. This is where science makes its error. The bottom line is fact! Simply because an event is not testable or provable does not necessarily mean it is nonexistent. This is science's narrow-mindedness!

Religions are narrow-minded in the opposite direction. Religions reject all the information that proves that many aspects of its belief system are unrealistic. Their primary existence is based on faith and belief much more so than testability, logic or proof.

The religious follow the enslavement of the personal agendas of people who have established the principles of religion such as **one must not lean to his own understanding.** Therefore they should simply stand by faith; no matter how ridiculously FALSE situations are PROVEN TO BE, they must simply believe. The minute they give up the faith they are in violation, contempt and condemned to hell. FAITH is the veil! No, that is not right, but BLIND FAITH is the veil of *ultimate deceit* of all the nations. We say to ourselves that we can't understand how it is possible, but WE MUST KEEP THE FAITH REGARDLESS. This yields to human error brought about through our religions. I believe in faith, miracles, and God, but once I learned that all the religions (Christianity, Islam, and Judaism in particular) arose from the worship of an idol god, a god who actually hated the species known as mankind, it became impossible to remain devoted to the enemy who deceived all the nations. The scientists dismisses faith, and the possibility of the unknown altogether, and this is where their human error enters into the picture.

What baffles scientists today is how did the universe gather masses together and organize the cosmic universe? Because science leaves out the divine it has no clue that the cosmic universe was established through raw Creator consciousness (us). How will they calculate and measure consciousness? Some scientists accept that at the beginning of time there were ten dimensions necessary to define the subatomic level of existence. Six of these dimensions shrank or remained very small and not observable by our senses. The four remaining dimensions were left noticeable to human senses. Most scientists fall short by being in 100 percent opposition to religions. For without doubt miracles, faith healers, psychics, prophets, and prayer are real and serve humanity for the better! There has been testing to show that people who had been prayed for, regardless of religion, significantly higher percentages of recovery than did the group who received no prayer. The power and vast energy of conscious endoplasmic reality (the point at which conscious thought creates physical reality) has received next to zero attention by the scientific community.

### *Quantum Cosmology*

This is a scientific attempt to try to understand how the physical worlds continuously divides and recreates self. In reality there are ten dimensions in our universe alone, in all actuality only one in which humans can relate fully, the dimension in which we live. Nonetheless, scientists like Timothy Ferris, the author of the *The Whole Shebang*, are theorizes that science is developing ways of testing theories and philosophies that tend to follow the thought processes similar to those of New Age practitioners. They admit that quantum cosmology suggests that we could possibly be dividing and creating many selves at various points in time. However, they state that they do not know what happens to the other selves or realities, and focus on the reality of the current self. This study, quantum cosmology is in direct harmony with new age spirituality.

In New Age spirituality one becomes aware that the human soul is multi-dimensional with multi-selves. The direction of time gets lost in a quantum flux. A photon traveling across the universe would experience no time; it could travel 20 billion light years and in our perspective it takes no time at all. The science behind our universe seems almost as complicated as the Bible. Many of us throw up our hands and say to hell with the idea of ever trying to know such vast material. Some say to themselves that if they simply wait out the years then there will be a discovery to find that the present concept or accepted theories are invalid. However, those who take on this type of an attitude are only placing themselves in a state of lost evolution, thus failing the entire purpose of our visit to earth in the first place, which is to learn. The earth is nothing other than a school ground for all the spirits that have gathered here at this point in time. If we take the attitude that science, religion, and historical records are all too hard to comprehend or research then at what point can we learn? One easy way for you to see that the human perspective versus universal reality can be different is to observe distance and motion; go outside and close your eyes. Stand perfectly still. Are you moving? Scientifically you know that you are moving because the earth is rotating on its axis around the sun and the entire solar system is continuously moving through out the galaxy. So . . . are you moving? Yes, but physically we observe that we are standing still. We are actually moving in many more ways than we do when we take a ride on an escalator or conveyor belt. Our continuous ride here on earth is circular, linear, and prismatic as we move multidimensional through the quantum flux of our galaxy. How much time does it take for you to see the light of the sun or moon and stars? You would say no time at all that you simply opened your eyes and it was there. However in all actuality the light has traveled many miles before it could reach your eyes. Conclusion, without doubt, we can not only rely on our physical senses and experiences as a basis for ultimate truth in our universal reality, and it is through the study of quantum physics that many unknown realities might be discovered—such as time travel.

## The Ezzrath Theory

Various factors will come into play for the development of the Ezzrath Theory, on the origin of our magnificent and diverse universe. Until now the majority of all written theses, letters, books, and other documents have failed to **attempt** to bring together all the pieces of data available for truly deciphering our origins. For example, the historian investigates and reports only history; the mythologist investigates and reports only myths; the anthropologist can prepare a detailed conclusive analysis on objects, cults, politics, traditions and so forth on the finds by the archaeologist. The archaeologist investigates and reports only his findings; and finally, the scientist investigates and reports only what he studies. The prophet (channeler, psychic, intuitive, whatever we wish to call the person who hears the word of God) also tends only to listen to the voice within. Although many may use several combinations of these, all of the disciplines are dynamic in their own distinctive mannerisms; we must try to obtain the whole. After all, when a report is made on only one or the other, or maybe several combined, the WHOLE picture will be missing! For example in Zecharia Sitchin's writings, he successfully reveals the connections of ancient myths of the entire world with those of the Bible and the fact that they all came from the same original source, "the gods or Anunnaki." He touches bases with science, history, and archaeological findings. Excellent work for as far as he takes it. As a matter of a fact his work shows the most diverse information on all the areas requiring deciphering. However, there is little mentioned regarding races and how the various people came about. After dropping the bomb on his readers regarding the intent of these gods and the fact that they promise to return, there is no information as to where humans now turn for salvation. I have attempted to include all of the above in my research on the universe and its inhabitants. I have psychically attuned myself to the Creator within to receive the information that you have never seen before this writing. Is it impossible to know what happens before Creation, before God? I will attempt to answer the following questions using my personal beliefs, which I will call the "Ezzrath Theory":

1. Who is man?
2. Where did he come from?
3. What is his purpose?

Before any of these questions can be answered, we must first discover what brought about our habitat, seeing that the habitat appears to have existed long before man. With my background in chemical engineering, the physics courses now serve their purpose in my life. The scientific theory of relativity and the expanding universe are excellent explanations as to how God (we) decided to create our universal laws, THE ORIGINAL LAW. However, I would like to take you back to the era before our universe existed. Think about that. How many people have discussed with you the time before time? That, in a sense, is incorrect because before the creation of our universe, time as we know it today never existed. So let's call it the existence before time. I can see in my mind's eye a place of existence inhabited by intelligent life somewhat similar to us, but of a lower vibratory rate of existence.

Remember that if you can relate to the information contained in this message it is important not to rate existence as evil, sinful, bad, or not worthy of existence. Judgment will send out karmic energy, which is, in part, what I believe to have created our universe. What you need to get out of this idea is that a piece of the karmic energy-1 from this unknown universe created our universe. Another piece of our creation came from a different universe of intellectual life forms that were highly evolved and also giving off karmic energy-2. These two world types of existence gathered and combined all the like karmic energy of both one and two. Like magnets these energies of positive and negative force attracted and formed the most unimaginably tiny ball of raw energy. Our dualistic universe is based on the yin/yang principle, just like when the male sperm and the female egg come together and produce offspring. Our universe, produced through the convergence of light and dark energy (both of which came from an ectoplasmic life force of different worlds caused by the karmic energy produced by each), produced the All-Highest Light, The Creator of Our Universe, Raw Creator Force (US).

It shouldn't be so shocking by this time; there are others who have either known or evolved to know as I have done that the soul of the human species is GOD. It is androgynous, contains both the upper and lower worlds (yin/yang), and has the capability to attain the intelligence of God. Spontaneously, the GREAT "I AM" exists (all the souls that ever existed in our universe [all of creation] united as one in a simple but tiny micro-particle energy-life-form.) Being of a vast raw Creator God Consciousness made up of all the consciousness of the two worlds, which created Him/Her (from the lower worlds/upper worlds) God Consciousness, She decides to create. This **decision** creates a great explosion. The term that you are most familiar with to describe this process is the Big Bang.

For your information, I want you to know that the big bang theory and the Mayan epic were not known to myself prior to my receiving this theory. As a matter of fact I had always heard of a big bang theory, that the universe began with one big bang and boom it was here, but that is all that I knew about it. I never read the details until after my theory was given to me. When I discovered the Mayan epics and the portion in the big bang including the infinitesimally small size of the universe before the explosion, I began to believe what my mind told me first—the Ezzrath Theory. When I first thought these things, I kind of thought that I was nuts! But it never failed that shortly after receiving the ideas, I would read and discover that others have came to the same conclusion—at least I wasn't the only nut.

Out of that enormously immense explosion space and time were brought into existence. THIS IS THE BEGINNING OF CREATION. Just imagine it: You and I were all there and we will always be, even after the earth no longer exists. Some of us will go on to form other worlds, for we will return to our source. Even now our world of duality (yin/yang) is combining with other incomprehensible worlds of existence in which WE are creating another reality and universe. That is why it is ever so important to watch your thoughts and your speech. For with our thoughts we create our desires and expressions in heaven (spirit world) and with our tongues we manifest it into physical matter. Our lives truly represent the never-ending story! Our soul energies are combined together with other karmic energies from other worlds creating another tiny karmic energy particle of a new universe, their God, their souls, some of which were us.

After creation of space, conscious thought (God, **Us**) next spoke into existence light. The Bible speaks of our creation at this point.

We were the first light in Genesis 1:3 and the sun and moon later in Genesis 1:14. This must have been the point at which God (We) divided ourselves into individual spirit beings of consciousness. Genesis 1:3 states, *"And God said, Let there be light: and there was light. And God saw the light that it was good and God **divided** the light from the darkness."* Which light did God divide from the darkness? According to the Bible, God saw the light and it was "THE GOOD LIGHT!" and He continues on to say that He divided the light from the darkness. Isn't that neat? Don't you wish sometimes that you could separate your dark side ("bad") from your light side ("good")? Realize this part of yourself cannot heal and will perpetually weigh you down in service to the lower worlds until you see opposite reality. The dark side is not something to be cast into hell, but someone in need of healing: YOU (US)! Whenever we try to destroy evil, WE ARE DESTROYING A PART OF US. Can't we heal that part of us rather than tossing it into hell as we (God) have been doing from the moment we separated ourselves into the light and dark (and we saw that the light was good)?

Actually, our dark side is evolving toward the light even as we speak. Just think of the times when we decided that instead of embracing and nurturing our dark side, we allowed our dark side to be the front runner in the game of life! When we played our roles as Canaanites, Babylonians, Mayans, Hebrews, and so forth we practiced the *most hideous* laws of self-destruction. Innocent people were mass slaughtered for the most insane reasons. A typical example could be found in the Bible where a being with a spirit of darkness instructed the Hebrews to slaughter and rape tens of thousands of people (See the chapter on the God of Israel.) It was nothing for these people . . . no, US—YOU! AND ME! to sacrifice our own children to the gods and then place their carcasses inside the walls of our homes to appease the gods, or worse, we ATE THEM! Eating the flesh of our own babies—just imagine it. People, we have really come a long way. Now it is only the few Jeffrey Dahmers who make our children disappear through their conscious retentive grasp on our ancient history. The vast majority of us have evolved from this lower state of consciousness and we are now improving our consciousness. Unlike ancient times, the consciousness of the masses will not allow such activities. In ancient times the entire community condoned human sacrifice. We have a very long way to go, but then again we have come a long way, too. THINK ABOUT IT. A note to the Jeffrey Dahmers and all of our dark sides from George Santayana: "Those who cannot remember the past are condemned to repeat it."

After we individualized ourselves as either Cherub or Seraphim we began organizing ourselves in rank according to our abilities, thus creating the MOST HIGH, Lords, Gods, archetypal Angels, and various orders of angels as individuals serving both the upper and lower worlds. Take a look in the Appendix at the flow chart entitled "Evolution of the Human Race." At this point the Seraphim/Ophanim entered man and became a physical being maintaining supernatural capabilities, but falling ten levels of self-awareness. The original human was immortal, and equivalent or superior to the gods in intelligence. If this is true how did we become so much lesser than our true selves? The answer to this question lies deep within every soul. We should first ask ourselves, how did we make an enemy? What came about to cause Satan to target us? Jealousy? Is it possible that perhaps we were of higher individual God essence? Whatever the trick that took place to bring us to our present condition of SEVERE MASS AMNESIA, we can overcome.

Prior to the individualizing, we first separated ourselves into the yin/yang energy, producing the law of magnetism. This law can be found throughout our universe in varying degrees of balance. Here on earth whenever we throw off the balance of this law we experience natural disaster and we rightfully call it an act of God. The majority of us never become angry with God for this terrible act of "God" (nature), which can cost tens of thousands of people their lives. We simply say to ourselves that it was an act of God. Why is it that when we (God) bring monsters (in our eyesight) like Hitler into power we can't likewise see it as an act of God (Us)? Are we so dismembered, so far gone to really believe that Hitler (one individual) of his own accord could have unleashed such mass hysteria? No, he could not have done it *alone*; it required all of Us (God). Our consciousness (past, present, and future) aided and abetted Hitler all the way through his hideous acts of murder, torture, and crimes against humanity. Our consciousness encouraged or discouraged the soldiers, commanders, and generals into backing Hitler. Think about where the conscious mind gets information, ideas, and plans of creativity ("good or bad"). It all comes from God (Us). Remember that time is just an illusion and that we of today were all there with the Hitler of yesterday. Note that the moment humanity realizes the web of illusions immaculately spiraled for its destruction will become the precise moment that a new universe of existence will be created! It is impossible for us to imagine or think of anything that doesn't have the capability of existence in our minds, such as new universes, monsters, dragons, dragon people, snake people, etc. If we can think it, then they exist in some form or another. This is where the scientists make their mistake and fall short in theory. They believe that if it cannot be tested, observed, and proven by the visible eye in some form or another, then it fails to exist.

After individualizing ourselves the next step was to begin creation. The most high of both the upper and lower worlds sent forth his Lords, Gods, and Lord Gods to create. Thus now begins the creation of both the heavens and earth. In the beginning, we had utter chaos, which we had to bring into order. With magical incantations, burning matter (debris from the big bang) was swept up into various piles throughout space in the same manner that any mother would clean a huge area. Each pile received its own individual incantations and became quickened with God essences of life. Thus was the creation of Apsu, Shamash, Ra, the Sun, full of life-yielding properties.

In the creation of the earth, burning essence/matter would have to be compressed and cooled; the cooling from the outside of the planet inward produced condensate covering the entire planet with water. The earth's atmosphere (composed of dense conscious plasmic yin/yang) covered the earth and required the water condensate to become trapped within and on the earth (creating the oceans, seas, rivers, lakes and so forth). The earth continued to cool over billions of years. It is my belief that scientists are off by eons on the time when the earth was created. This cooling of the planet required far more time than the human mind could comprehend. Furthermore, one reason that a few scientists argue against the big bang theory is because there was not enough time in the estimated 20 billion years of our universe's existence to support the theory. What I do not understand is why they hold on to the 20-billion-year theory as absolute. After all, they discovered the error of Hubble's mistake in calculations estimating the universe at two billion years old, impossibly younger than the earth. Science should know by now that simply because there is physical evidence to support our theory of a date it does not necessarily mean that the date is fact. For examples of this fact we should remember history. In one period man is only 5,000 years old, and then tens of thousands of years old and next hundreds of thousands and now they say millions of years old, but only because that is the oldest body they have found thus far. When they find a body a billion years old, then what? Not to mention one a trillion years old. Why do they always just know when they find an older body that this is it, that this is where life for humans in our universe began?

I am convinced that this is the point at which science falls so very short and makes its greatest mistake over and over again in trying to place a time at which man, life, the universe all began. Our technology is so primitive in comparison to what we were capable of knowing in times past. In ancient Mesopotamia we knew that the earth was not flat and that earth evolved around the sun and not vice versa. We knew about Pluto in ancient times. All of these things that we knew about in the most ancient of times, we have rediscovered within the past couple of centuries. We knew about the planets and there's evidence that we once wrote about a twelfth planet, not only the nine that we know of today. In other words we still haven't found out all the facts yet, which is why perhaps we should lend an ear to the myths of the past. We know that men all over the planet gave an account of a flood with a favorite of the gods as sole survivor. I feel safe in assuming that some sort of flooding took place, and the gods did help the biblical Noah, who was the same Enuma Elish, Babylonian Utanapishtim, and the same Sumerian Atra-Hasis. However, I do not believe that a flood covered the entire earth and killed off all earth life with the exception of the inhabitants of Noah's boat. It is much more likely that there was a major catastrophic natural disaster in Mesopotamia only. Just as we today can predict a hurricane, the gods knew that this flood was going to strike and Enlil gives the order not to warn the children of the gods (us). He was such a selfish god who thought little of anyone other than himself that he organized the gods in a mutiny against man. Man's fate was sealed by the vote of the gods and they were doomed to suffer the devastation of the flood. The gods plotted that no one would inform man of the upcoming catastrophe.

However, Ea bucked the system and visited Utanapishtim (Noah) in a dream and informed him of the upcoming disaster and gave him complete details on how to build a "ship" (submarine) capable of surviving the calamity. Prior to Noah man lived to be hundreds of years old, maintained a vegetarian diet, and was highly spiritual (possessed the capability to tap into creator force energy at will). It seems that after around 2500 B.C. the quality of human life began to go down. Keep in mind that in my theory human life began eons ago—billions of years ago. Intelligent life was magical and it materialized and dematerialized at will. The mythical creatures—unicorns, dragons, snake people, half man-half beast, etc.—were all magical, just like the human soul. That is the reason why there are no physical proofs other than drawings and myths that they ever existed. Nonetheless, as our history has unmistakably proven to us, the lack of physical evidence of an event taking place does not prove that it did not happen. It simply proves that we do not have the physical data to prove that it did take place. As philosophers and scientists have denied this possibility of existence, it is impossible for me to ignore all of the recordings that the ancients left available to us. Continuously throughout ancient history diverse races spoke of dragons, snake people, and so forth. Is it possible that our ancestors held a summit of all the people of the planet and decided to all tell one gigantic lie in accordance with one another? I, for one, do not think it possible. Therefore the only other believable thought is that these people were giving accounts of events as they believed them to have occurred.

Which now brings us to the manipulation of mankind by the gods. All ancient myths from the Bible to the *Enuma Elish* appear to make it clear that these gods were walking with man face to face. These gods fought with them physically in wars and as we have learned they even became injured to the point of death. These events are not so today. When America goes to war she simply moves in and drops her bombs of devastation without the aid of a physical god by her side. To our knowledge this is true of all modern wars. What has happened to change human lives so drastically? Beginning 1700-1500 B.C. up to around 500 B.C. (the end of the dark ages—end of world dominance by blacks) the gods were viciously warring over earthly control. They made the Hiroshima bombing of World War II look like a firecracker joke on the 4th of July. Excellent biblical references to this fact can be found in Genesis 19:1-28, especially verse 24, *"The Lord rained upon Sodom and upon Gomorrah brimstone and fire from the Lord out of heaven."* This is the bombing of Sodom and Gomorrah and the wife of Lot chooses to remain close to her beloved city and receives a disintegrating effect from a direct hit of the nuclear blast (she becomes "a pillar of salt"). Another example can be found in Isaiah 25:4, *"For thou hast been a strength to the poor, a strength to the needy in his distress a refuge from the storm, a shadow from the* **HEAT,** *when the* **BLAST of the terrible ones is as a storm against the wall."** The book of Job also speaks of how the gods were launching nuclear bombs. See Job 4:9 which states, *"By the* **blast** *of God they perish, and by the breath of his nostrils are they consumed."* If today's Star Wars and technical research were to be compared with the technology of the Anunnaki, it would be like comparing the research of a professor to that of a toddler. When the gods would drop their nuclear bombs they would lift off in their spaceships and watch the poor misfortunate humans get nuked.

Some humans appeared to escape the blasts also on the ship of their gods, or their own. See Isaiah 26:20-21, *"Come, my people, enter thou into thy chambers, and shut thy doors about thee: hide thyself as it were for a little moment, until the indignation be overpast. For behold the Lord cometh out of his place to punish the inhabitants of the earth for their iniquity: the earth also shall disclose her blood, and shall no more cover her slain."* Using their nuclear bombing technology they were actually disturbing the peace of other nearby galaxies, which was not going to be tolerated. This is what I believe brought the gods' folly to an end. They were ordered by a Galactic Confederacy of various species throughout our universe and various universes to hack up off the physical plane and to allow our species an opportunity to evolve naturally. A hint of this can be found in Genesis 6:3, *"And the Lord said, My spirit shall not always strive with man . . . ,"* for he knew that he had been given the order to allow all earth's inhabitants the opportunity to evolve naturally.

The actual departure of the gods began sometime around 700 B.C. and was completed in the dawning of the Middle Ages. They are still with us, but in the fourth and fifth dimensions. The gods still influence us but now only through our conscious psyche. They may appear as spiritual entities (channeling) or vibes and feelings only. The gods can only influence our emotions one way or the other (like with the emotions of Mother Teresa or Jeffrey Dahmer), but their actual physical appearance now would be of the equivalent of a dead person physically returning (impossible?). To some this comparison means that it is an absolute impossibility, but that is not my belief. I believe that next to impossible would be more accurate.

Alexander the Great, born part Aryan or Anunnaki/Pleiadian god, tried to erase all of the existence of the blue-black Pleiadian gods who had seeded and exploited the human race. He went on a rampage of conquering wars and destruction targeting all of the ancient black humans in world power. Once he had defeated and annihilated a territory his next step would be to destroy all of the libraries, art, buildings and any remnant of information of that civilization within his grasp. It is lucky for us that neither Alexander nor Napoleon were fortunate enough to carry out their entire plans. Some information did get left behind and we have enough of the puzzle pieces today to put together fragmented parts of the story, connecting with God to fill in the missing pieces. Today we can no longer depend on others solely to give us all the information as we have allowed in the past. Now we must gather the information for ourselves. We can always listen to others around us such as the preachers, teachers, ministers, and even authors of any book including the BIBLE and myself. We should decipher the information that is given to us and properly divide out the word of truth. Failure to decipher information handed down to us from our parents, ministers, teachers, friends, and literature becomes IRRESPONSIBLE BLIND FAITH and leads one to *ULTIMATE DECEIT!*

Now we have a physical universe filled with stars, one of which is our very own sun. It contains space, stars, planets, water, and inert gases. The universe continues rampantly growing and creating in its young creative state, full of wonder and majesty, totally incapable of sustaining physical life as we know it today. Our young consciousness fabricated our physical universe in states of chaotic dispersion. As we continued growing and creating some existence which we have totally disremembered, an amazing growth also began to take place on our planet. That is the emergence of prehistoric one celled microorganisms, green algae, and so forth. The land began to emerge, vibrating with nourishing energies supporting the growth of vegetation. Next in line were the tiny sea creatures such as mussels and clams. In this short paragraph of the chronicles of the earth we have poured out billions and billions of years for all of the events to take place thus far, at least the amount of years that scientists say were required for the entire universe to have been created and likely much more.

The next stage, the beginning of evolution, was the emergence of the pollywog/tadpole-like structure from the sea onto land and all evolving earth species are believed to have evolved from this structure. Every earthlike species evolving from the pollywog would be considered lower in intelligence and lacking a written and verbal language (such as fish, cats, birds, alligators, snakes, apes and so forth). They were a substandard existence in accordance with the higher life forms of our universe. Although I have not brought us up to the evolving animal man of 14 million years ago, we should understand that you and I were in existence and capable of visiting the earth had we chosen to do so (but not in human form). The earth has a strange magical veil upon it, which causes all species that remain in its physical realm over long periods of time to die. This is why we as angels could slow our vibrations down and pick up a physical body to partake of a physical existence, but lay down the physical body at will, instead of death. This was the proper way of experiencing physical existence.

Just as our planet earth began evolving to support early life forms, so did other worlds: the worlds of the Pleiadian, Sirrus, Arcturs, Atlantis, Mu, and Orion, to name just a few that are recorded in our historical data. All sorts of physical species are evolving. The physical evolution of these worlds advanced into high-tech civilizations. These beings have destroyed themselves and rebuilt and multiplied many times over as we have done currently in earth's history. They have learned to intellectually and emotionally tap into the spiritual and the divine cosmic energy. These beings have developed their superior technology, science, cosmology, and architecture through this intellectual connection with the Divine; so as to learn the lesson that all physical life forms of the diverse worlds of creations have been sent to learn. That is to **control desire**. We should keep in mind that we possess the ability to become physically superior while at the same time becoming spiritually inferior if we fail to learn the lesson of control of desire. This "DESIRE" caused our **physically** superior gods (the Anunnaki/Jehovah) to develop a keen intellect over the designs and make-up of our physical world. They vastly knew universal law and its consequences. They had developed control of the elements (water, wind, fire, earth, and spirit), space travel, and even inter-dimensional space travel (a time machine). The vast majority of the Anunnaki powers came from the intellect more so than spiritual wisdom of universal law. In other words, the Anunnaki depended greatly on scientific equipment to create space travel and the manipulation of the elements. At this same time we human spirits were capable of space travel and manipulation of the elements all through the Merkabah or HIGHLY EVOLVED CONSCIOUSNESS.

During the time that life on other planets evolved to the point of no longer being confined to the individual planets, many species migrated to earth and colonized it, manipulating various species' evolution beginning almost as far back as a billion years ago. Earth became a large biological science laboratory filled with experiments—some gone haywire. Many species came and went as their souls desired, tampering with earth evolution on each visit, leaving representations of their life forms from their home worlds, which is a partial make-up of the representation of today's life. The missing creatures created and developed during this time, such as the dragons, snake people, and the peoples of Atlantis and Mu, are all considered either myth or extinct. However, neither of these concepts do I hold as a highly possible truth. Rather, I believe that some of these species dwell inside the earth and others created the spiritual Merkabah to escape the aging-death cycle (illusionary veil) of our planet. The cycle of aging, death, and rebirth is a process developed for the lower species. Plant life and animals were expected to perpetually give birth, live, die, and start the process over and over again. This process was not intended for the higher evolved species of our world.

The best physical representation of what happened to mankind—but yet, by far, off in accordance with intelligence transfer—is a comparison with Walt Disney's *Pinocchio*. Toward the end of the movie, Pinocchio gives in to his desire to have fun at an amusement park for little boys instead of going home and preparing for school. While in this park Pinocchio smokes, drinks, destroys property, and then brags about how much fun he's having being bad. As they play a game of billiards in a drunken stupor, Pinocchio laughs at his friend Lamwick (Lampy) as he is turning into a jackass. As Pinocchio is laughing, he also begins to transform into a donkey. This park had a magical veil over it, which would turn little boys acting out their uncontrolled desires into asses. It is so similar to what happened to the human spirit in the beginning of the transformation of the first angelic soul into human flesh. The average ones of us wearing the veil living as the animal called man will never in this lifetime know of it.

Even after reading this passage it will remain no more than a funny fantasy in some woman's imagination. Others of you will see this information as totally ridiculous and on the verge of blasphemous if not indeed so. After all, God would never allow that to happen to us. But I contend that We did allow it to happen to Us — simply for the experience, "the game of life." Just as the donkeys of Pinocchio brayed (hee-haw, hee-haw), so do humans speak.

The donkeys of Pinocchio used to be more of an intelligent stock, called humans (little boys) who spoke. Likewise the Ophanim (Adam Kadmon, the animal man incarnating an angelic soul) used to be of a higher, intelligent stock that used telepathy for communication instead of modern man's primitive speech. The cruel coachman waited for the complete amnesia to take place where the donkeys (little boys in reality) could no longer talk or even remember their names or their natural state of existence. In their reality they were DONKEYS required to serve the evil coachman. Therefore they acted out their reality through an illusion. In our reality we are HUMANS required to serve the evil god/Jehovah/Allah (unknowingly).

This is what I believe that Jehovah or a higher force than Jehovah did to us, tricking us with some sort of compassion or desire for physical existence to take up the animal flesh. Originally when this took place, just like those donkeys we fell into a state of amnesia. We were then taught how to act, believe, and behave by our enemy you call Satan, the devil. Our ancestors tried to keep us from falling into a deeper entrapment. They unfortunately failed their mission to stop the deception of Satan's *Ultimate Deceit* of all the nations of the planet.

TODAY **ALL THE NATIONS** OF THE EARTH HAVE BEEN DECEIVED! There is not one nation on the planet that is striving to recognize the Creator of creation as God. All the nations now have religions. What was the name of the original religion, and what was the original way of worship? The first answer is simple, God's religion has no name, because God has no religion. The second question will be left for you to answer.

Greater and lesser gods have become our Creator God through the *ultimate deceit*. None of you remember that we used to worship/serve creation. The American Indians were excellent at recognizing all creation as gods. They would talk to the tree spirit (god), wind spirit (god), or animal spirits (god). You may ask, how is it possible for a wall to be a part of God. Any scientist knows that ALL matter—yes, even a brick wall—has a vibratory rate and energy. Where does this energy and vibration come from? The Universe? Where does the energy come from that is supplied by the universe? When one knows the answers to these questions, one knows that GOD is in all things literally. We saw the Indians as mad, silly, stupid savages. So we killed them off and hid away the remnant of their race on reservations to live in a drunken stupor stripped of all pride and their dignity; they are nearly extinct. Yes, let's reason intelligently, surely **they** were the savages. I know that many of you do not have a clue as to your rank in godship, but you will. It is inevitable; maybe not this lifetime, but you eventually will.

I know that this information sounds impossible, but if we could just break the spell of the "god-spell" (literal meaning for gospel) and once more see that we are one, if we could realize that many souls of various races come back sometimes in a different race, perhaps we would be less quick to kill ourselves. Here is an exercise for you. The next time you are in a dream and can manage to know that you are dreaming, try to remain asleep. Tell yourself to find a mirror! I don't know how you will know where it is in the dream, but everyone who has done this experiment has NEVER had problems finding a mirror. When you find the mirror look into it at your SOUL! Yes, see your highest earth incarnation. If you are a high member of the KKK, you may learn that your soul is African (blue-black). If you naturally hated all white people, look into the mirror and see the wonderfully unique pale face of yourself steering back at you. The mirror will not lie to you.

Please don't misunderstand me. If you are black and you see a white person in the mirror it doesn't mean that you hated whites and are being punished in some manner. The converse is true also. It simply means that you have decided to experience a different race and culture in this particular life cycle. It happens a lot, but the majority of people that I get to participate in the experience remain within the same race. The most difficult part of this experiment is to find yourself in a state of knowing that you are dreaming. The second task that will prove trying and nearly impossible is remaining asleep as you seek out the mirror. Nonetheless, many have done it successfully and so can you. The first time will be the most accurate account as to how your soul portrays itself karmically in the universe. The spirit is the truest account of oneself; however the soul, like the mind and the body, can be manipulated for higher evolution. A spirit like God is nothing more than pure light energy; therefore it has no body. A soul has the illusion of a body that even others can see and it will look just as the individual pictures him or herself.

The first step to doing this procedure will be to talk yourself into knowing that you are dreaming and remaining asleep so that you can find a mirror. Tell yourself this over and over, especially several times before dozing off to sleep. If you have never remembered dreaming, then you will first need to train yourself into remembering your dreams, but this is another book in itself. People never have a bad experience meeting their higher selves for in this state they feel loved and are greatly loved.

Metaphysically speaking, the human soul fell from the position of Kether to Malkuth in respect to the Kabbala. (See figure on facing page.) Trapped on earth without our heavenly abode, in a state of amnesia, we were forced to serve the gods and erect temples to their glory. As we served them, we began feeding our souls, psyche, and consciousness with divine food. Although we fell into a state of amnesia, we were still divine spirits (gods) nonetheless, capable of transcending the flesh. Originally we maintained the ability to transcend the flesh, thereby escaping death. We could manipulate the elements and still work spells of consciousness to command our will to be done as gods could do. An example of this in the Bible can be found in the book of Genesis where Jacob wrestles an "angel" down and demands the keys to HEAVEN ("to be blessed") to DUR AN KI. He receives passage rights through the portal that bonds heaven and earth so that he will never have to die. Although the Bible says that the patriarchs all died, I do not believe that there is a stitch of truth to these allegations. I believe that just like Enoch and Elijah, the majority, if not all of the ancients, were able to possess the keys to transcend the flesh without dying. Jacob in Genesis 49:29 through to chapter 50 reports to his sons the importance of embalming him like the Egyptian culture, for they would keep the body for lamenting forty days and Jacob did not want the Egyptians to know that his body would not decay. The portal seems to have been within Jacob, but accessed inside the cave of the ancestors, where the

## GREATER AND LESSER YAHWEHS

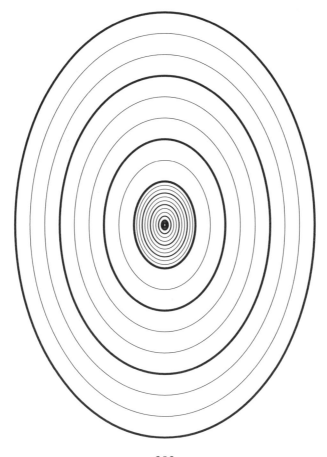

## KABBALAH

The word Kabbalah stems from the Chaldean people to the Hebrews, meaning both words "give" and "receive" simultaneously. It was considered the tree of life and is associated with the tree of life mentioned in the old Testament. It is symbolized by a diagram of ten spheres called the Sephiroth and one hidden sphere called En Sof with twenty-two pathways beginning at true creator and ending in lower and lower frequencies producing physical dense matter.

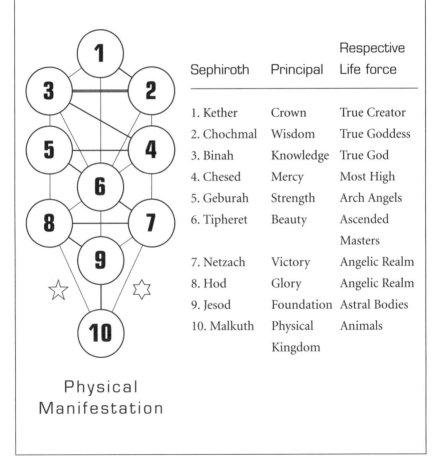

True Creator

| Sephiroth | Principal | Respective Life force |
|-----------|-----------|-----------------------|
| 1. Kether | Crown | True Creator |
| 2. Chochmal | Wisdom | True Goddess |
| 3. Binah | Knowledge | True God |
| 4. Chesed | Mercy | Most High |
| 5. Geburah | Strength | Arch Angels |
| 6. Tipheret | Beauty | Ascended Masters |
| 7. Netzach | Victory | Angelic Realm |
| 8. Hod | Glory | Angelic Realm |
| 9. Jesod | Foundation | Astral Bodies |
| 10. Malkuth | Physical Kingdom | Animals |

Physical Manifestation

patriarchs would ascend, flesh, spirit, and all. Physical evidence that this is true is the fact that we cannot find the bodies of the patriarchs. We can estimate according to the Bible their location, yet there are no reports of their remains being discovered. Furthermore, they are less than five thousand years old. Lucy is over two million years old. Why can't we find the remains of the patriarchs? It's as if they never existed. Just like the Sumerian and Mayan cultures. Why? Because there were **no bodies to find!** That's why! They leave behind only their writings, artifacts, arts, and architecturally advanced designs in their buildings, which prove that they did indeed exist.

Manipulation of the earthling's DNA brought about the fowls, mammals, and beasts of mythology such as the sphinx, phoenix, unicorns and so forth. These species could not physically remain within our earth's atmosphere or they, too, would become victims to the aging process of our nature and eventually death. Up until now the only species that were mortal were the animals, insects, plants, and lower evolving species.

However, the worst nightmare for the divine spirits trapped inside an animal known as man was yet to come. Man allowed the service of the lower worlds, which is instinctively desire in his animal flesh, to rule supreme. He fell into even a greater amnesia than the original. He began to worship a physical being just like himself and turned all his spirituality inside out. HE LOOKED FOR SALVATION OUTSIDE HIMSELF! Without turning inward to the inner higher-self where we find GOD, man began to completely lose himself into service of the lower worlds. He partook of human sacrifice, eating of flesh (animal meat), committing murder, coveting his neighbors' possessions, cannibalistic acts, and, to sum it all up in a nutshell, he expresses total uncontrolled desire. **MAN BECAME MORTAL AS THE TRICK OF THE GODS.**

Now we return to the divine, as a butterfly shedding its cocoon through rebirth after rebirth, soul perpetually trapped in an illusion

# Ezzrath's Theory of our Universe

Including other universal realities

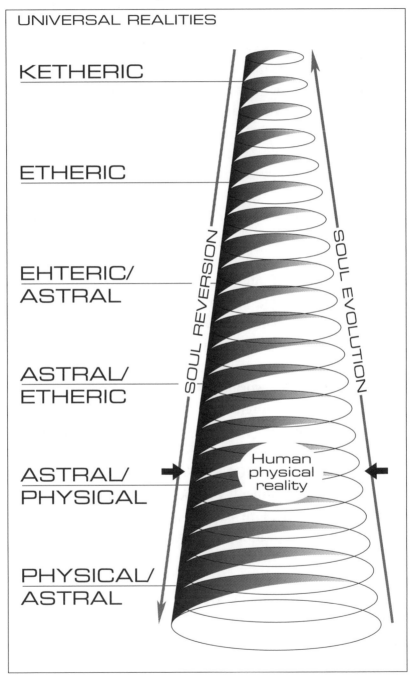

UNIVERSAL REALITIES

KETHERIC

ETHERIC

EHTERIC/
ASTRAL

ASTRAL/
ETHERIC

ASTRAL/
PHYSICAL

PHYSICAL/
ASTRAL

SOUL REVERSION

SOUL EVOLUTION

Human
physical
reality

of uncontrolled desire. No matter how deep into utter darkness we decide to sink, the divine cord is always intact. This is where some Baptists get the saying "once saved always saved." (See figure on facing page.) However, Jesus was trying to remind his fellow Israelites that the path to life (not salvation) is a narrow one and hard to find. He never stated that the path to life after we died would be narrow; we added that part in ourselves. Look in Matthew 7:14. Jesus states, *"Because strait is the gate, and narrow is the way, which leadeth unto life, and few there be that find it."* "FEW WHO FIND THE PATH TO LIFE!" **"FEW WHO FIND THE PATH TO LIFE!!!"** Jesus, like myself was trying to tell you that there is a path that leads to immortality—NEVER DYING.

Furthermore, I maintain that though I hold to few orders of the Bible I hold to this one truth: that my ancestor King David once said, *"But ye shall die like men, and fall like one of the princes."* (Psalms 82:7) Think about it; something that the people were doing made them mortal men, causing them to lose their god-ship (immortality).

An author by the name of Marvin Cetron, who holds a Ph.D. in research development, scientifically proves that everlasting life is in the manipulation of DNA. He suggests that science can control skin color, eye color, and that it has found a way to zero in on the agent in cancer that is identical to the agent found around the human fetus that blocks the mother's immune system from rejecting the baby. This suggests that the cure for cancer is just around the corner. There will no longer be a problem of organ transplants being rejected by the recipient. He goes as far as to say that we will even be able to use animal organs in transplants to sustain life. In all actuality, he is stating that we are living in a "post-mortal world." The name of his book in which he reports this scientific data is *CHEATING DEATH: The Promise and the Future Impact of Trying to Live for Ever.* Remember, my friends, it is in your DNA to know that as it was in the beginning so shall it be in the end.

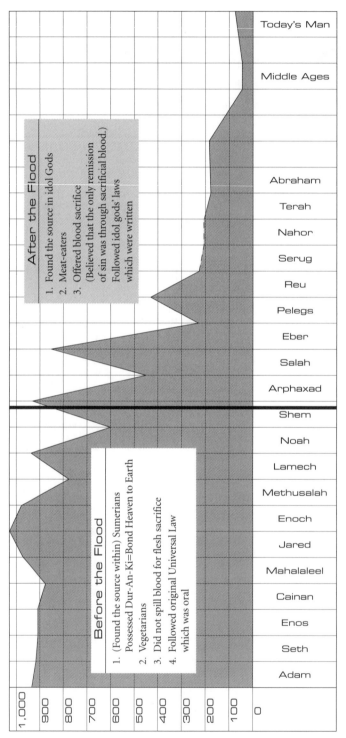

**After the Flood**

1. Found the source in idol Gods
2. Meat-eaters
3. Offered blood sacrifice
   (Believed that the only remission
   of sin was through sacrificial blood.)
   Followed idol gods' laws
   which were written

**Before the Flood**

1. (Found the source within) Sumerians
   Possessed Dur-An-Ki=Bond Heaven to Earth
2. Vegetarians
3. Did not spill blood for flesh sacrifice
4. Followed original Universal Law
   which was oral

Biblical characters versus age—showing drastic change in longevity after the flood.

# SEVEN

# Ancient Mythology

## Introduction to Mesopotamian Mythology

This section of my book is dedicated to presenting the actual information relayed to mankind from ancient Mesopotamia. Mythology is the most important historical key to understanding the roots or origins of **all** religions, especially Christianity, Islam, and Judaism but not limited to these alone. It will be obvious that many stories told in the Bible were first told by other cultures, thus establishing the fact that the Hebrews plagiarized the *Enuma Elish* and other works. We will find that this analysis brings us right into the heart of Sumeria.

Most Bible scholars will agree that the city of Shinar was synonymous with the ancient Mesopotamian city Sumeria. The name Sumeria meant land of the black-headed ones, they were called the "black-headed people." (See *The Twelfth Planet*, by Zechariah Sititchin, pages 96-98.) The first written information regarding the Sumerian people dates back as far as around three thousand years ago. This should send up a red flag to all Bible readers, for this means that the Sumerian text predates the Hebrew text by more than a thousand years. The Sumerian text was written in cuneiform, one of the most ancient languages known to man, predating the Hebrew language. An even older written language was pictorial writings, such as were used frequently by the ancient Egyptians. The cuneiform alphabet derived from pictorial writings and is comprised of small wedge symbols.

According to the Sumerians/Babylonians the story of life all begins with Tiamat and Apsu. Tiamat was a female goddess who had given birth to all the gods of our universe. Her consort (husband) was called Apsu. Tiamat was identified as sweet water while Apsu was considered salt water. Remember the Hebrew God trying to divide the waters in the biblical accounts of creation? It was written that Apsu became upset over the noise that their children were making and complained to Tiamat, who had decided along with Apsu that it was just about time to fatally get rid of her children of inconvenience. However, Ea, whose symbol throughout ancient society was the serpent, was very wise and had a premonition of Tiamat and Apsu's plans to destroy all their children. After learning of the plot Ea quickly devised a plan. He singled Apsu out (DIVIDING THE WATERS!!!) and placed a deep magical spell upon him to cause him to fall into a deep sleep. This attack infuriated the great Tiamat, causing her to strike out on the warpath. She began creating monsters and creatures for the destruction of the gods by first teaming up with a god called Kingu. Kingu joined Tiamat in her quest to kill the gods, fueling and agitating her heated anger. When Ea saw her, he was awestruck; he fell back. He could not approach her. So then Anu, the father of all the Anunnakis, ventured out to conquer the great Tiamat, but was overcome with fear and had to turn back.

Marduk, the son of Ea, then learned of all the gods' fear of Tiamat. He saw a great opportunity for himself if he saved all of the trembling gods. He decided that he could conquer Tiamat, but made several requests of the gods that would affect mankind even unto this day. He informed the gods that he would conquer the mighty Tiamat on one condition: that upon his victory against Tiamat he must be proclaimed the God of the gods. (Do you know a God of the gods?) He told them that from the day that he defeated Tiamat he would reign as the all-highest God and he made the gods promise that everything that had been done before his time would be established as his accomplishment.

Marduk set forth with an army that he hand selected to defeat the Leviathan. Sound familiar? As his army went to tackle the Leviathan, there was one point at which Marduk nearly fainted away from fright of the Leviathan. He retreated and circled right back around and with a mighty air he blew into the mouth of Tiamat causing her to explode and become immobilized and to break off into several pieces. The largest piece of Tiamat is today called earth. The tiny pieces are supposedly the Milky Way. Kingu's blood was demanded from him for his part in the conspiracy to destroy all the gods. It was written that Kingu was established as the moon.

After the defeat of the Leviathan, Marduk was established as the one and only supreme GOD among men and gods! The biblical reference for this is found in Isaiah 27:1, *"In that day the Lord with his sore and great and strong sword shall punish **leviathan** the piercing serpent, even leviathan that crooked serpent; and he shall slay the **dragon** that is in the sea."* FROM THIS POINT IN TIME THE SUPREME GOD THAT MEN MISTAKENLY WROTE ABOUT WAS MARDUK (the same god Jehovah/Baal). Thus, Ea made man, but now Marduk/Jehovah received credit for creating man. Ea saved Noah from the flood, now Marduk/Yahweh saved Noah from the flood. Enlil conspired to have man destroyed in the flood, now Marduk/Jehovah did this act. The goddess Inanna was sorry for conspiring to have man destroyed in a flood, now Marduk/Jehovah took the credit for this action, and so forth.

Both the gods and men celebrated Marduk's victory over Tiamat and crowned him lord of lords. The gods all bowed to Marduk and from that day the people of ancient Mesopotamia worshipped him as the sole and supreme creator for he had assumed all the attributes, accomplishments, and acts of all the other gods. Thus was it written, and so it is until this day (in Christianity, Islam, and Judaism).

Turning back the hands of time a little, where did Marduk come from? The Anunnaki family traveled to earth perhaps as far back as 150,000 B.C. in search of earth's resources. The family of Anunnaki began with Anshar (An) and Kishar (Ki), who produced Anu—father of the Anunnaki—the god of the sky/heaven. Anu was the father god of the gods and men. He produced two sons by the names of Ea/Enki and Enlil. Ea, sometimes called Enki, was the eldest brother, but he was not a purebred Anunnaki. Nintu was not his mother although Anu was his father. Enki's mother was speculated to have been from the dragon race. It was reported that Enki had a tail like his mother and was reptilian in appearance after his mom.

On the planet Nabiru where Anu was from, the family rites of passage dictated that the birthright should be passed on to the firstborn son. Therefore Enki would automatically inherit the birthright—right? WRONG? Enki lost the birthright to his younger brother because of his parentage, in accordance with Anunnaki laws. The child born of full Anunnaki bloodline would receive the birthright. Of course, a hostile environment, such as this one, making differences between children solely based on the race and parentage of the child, would be the onset of perpetual feuding. Such was the case for Ea and his brother Enlil.

Comparatively speaking, the Old Testament gives an identical situations where God forces Abraham to recognize Isaac as the more important child to inherit the birthright instead of Ishmael, although Isaac is the last born. This might be somewhat offensive to most Moslems for it is their belief that Isaac and his Israelite descendants lost the covenant with god because of their sin, and it was passed on to Ishmael. But they should understand that god rewarded based on bloodline and tradition, not righteousness, just as it was done in the tradition and customs of the gods. Another biblical recording of such acts can be noted in the story of Jacob and Esau. The feud got so far out of hand that it was passed down from generation to generation (the Enkilites versus the Enlilites).

It was written in the *Enuma Elish* (predating the biblical era!) that Ea went to his father, Anu, to ask permission to make a worker race of primitive man. He needed slaves to colonize the earth and mine the gold and other precious metals to take to Nabiru. This parallels the Bible's "Let us make man." The reason the DNA had to be manipulated was because early man was too incompetent to work the mines. So to speed up the Anunnaki mining process Ea took either a *Homo erectus* or *Homo habilis* woman and artificially impregnated her with Anunnaki-fertilized eggs. He apparently took his sperm and artificially inseminated evolving man's woman. According to *The Twelfth Planet*, the myth stated that Ea requested his consort to carry the fertilized egg (Ea's sperm and DNA from the ape woman) and she agreed, thus creating Adapa in the likeness of the gods.

READERS, PLEASE KEEP IN MIND THAT THESE WRITINGS WERE REFERRING TO INFORMATION OVER 5000 YEARS OLD!!! We are not talking backward caveman here. Put some deep thought into what is actually being said here. These people are talking about scientific laboratories, genetic manipulations, and surgeries. If indeed these topics were discussed 5000 years ago (WITHOUT DOUBT THEY WERE), then whether or not we choose to believe any of their contents as actually occurring becomes irrelevant. The fact that they wrote these events down, meant that they were aware of the POSSIBILITY OF THESE EVENTS TAKING PLACE IN ORDER TO DISCUSS THEM! In other words, the mere fact that there is recorded information of a report of a scientific laboratory and a god that genetically manipulated an animal's DNA is proof that it was in fact a possibility with these people! You could not write about a scientific lab unless you had knowledge of one.

This part parallels the Old Testament in Genesis 1:26-28,

asking, "*Let **us** make man in **our** image, after **our** likeness.*" The details of the science labs are left out of the Hebrews' version. Notice that the gods are requesting from a higher being permission to make a man in their image. Although it was the original idea of Enki, Enlil was quick to get on the scene and take an active part in creating a primitive worker race that would prove fruitful to the Pleiadian Anunnaki. Therefore it became a joint effort of several gods, the primary characters being Ea and his consort and Enlil's self-appointment to the position of overseer. Ea was well known for his magical incantations and his scientific background, making him considered the wisest of the gods. According to the *Enuma Elish*, Ea created man in a scientific lab or a medical clinic as the first test tube baby of the planet. Once you have analyzed and studied many of the ancient accounts of these events from the various cultures/races of the earth, you will know that this man that was created was NOT HUMAN! He was intelligent and capable of making tools, and seeking shelter for survival. Nonetheless, this man was little more than a Bigfoot. Human existence does not come into play until the magical incantation causing an angelic soul to enter an animal called man. According to the Bible and other ancient myths it appears that a voodoo-type doll made of clay was fashioned and the angelic human soul was placed inside it (the taking of an inanimate object and blowing life into it = magical incantations). This event is also recorded in the Bible in Genesis 2:7, "*And the Lord God formed man of the dust of the ground, and breathed into his nostrils the breath of life; and man became a living soul* (became flesh)." This is the beginning of the HUE-MAN RACE, THE BLACK MAN'S RACE. (See the figure showing the evolution of the human race.) The majority of us cannot remember being there when god took the clay doll and breathed the breath of life into its nostrils (just like we would resuscitate our dead from a drowning).

Perhaps it was considered as unethical then as it is today. Man's ethical way of thinking today would find it revolting to take human DNA and mix it with that of an animal for the fabrication of a higher species of animal. We call it man trying to play God. This is why it was deemed necessary for Ea to obtain permission from a higher authority—Anu. "LET US MAKE A MAN."

### Adapa (Adam) Tricked Out of Immortality

This myth dates back to over 3000 years ago. Adapa, the first human, was known as the son of Ea and he had been given wisdom equal to the gods. Adapa knew magical incantations, universal knowledge, healing techniques, and so forth. According to the Mesopotamian account found in various texts, which were all incomplete, Adapa was reported to have been fishing when a strong South Wind came and destroyed his boat. Adapa was furious and in a fit of rage he cursed the South Wind. Adapa loudly called out to the South Wind that it had disturbed his day and for that he would break the wings of the South Wind. After the curse (magical incantation) Adapa broke the wings of the South Wind and it no longer blew. For seven days the wind did not blow. The seven days must have been a representation of a long period of time because the problem of the South Wind not blowing became noticeable even by Anu, god the father. Anu sent out messages to the gods for an answer as to what had disabled the South Wind. The god Illaabrat was sent to investigate what had happened to the South Wind. Illaabrat explained to Anu that the son of Ea, Adapa (biblical Adam), had broken the wing of the South Wind. Once Anu learned of Adapa's act he was summoned to appear before Anu. Ea took Adapa to the side and told his son not to eat any foods from Anu for surely he would die.

When Adapa appeared before Anu he was offered food and drink. Just as his father Ea had commanded, Adapa refused the food. Anu asked him why he refused the food. Adapa shared with Anu the information given to him by Ea. Anu laughed at him, perceiving that Ea had tricked Adapa into refusing to partake of immortal life.

### *The Life and Conquest of Gilgamesh*

According to myth, Gilgamesh was born two-thirds god and one-third human. His mother was the wise goddess Ninsun and his father was a mortal king of Uruk. Gilgamesh became king of Uruk and bragged of his architectural creations of the temples to the gods Anu and Ishtar. He was also well known for his quick temper, selfishness, and warlike personality. He overstepped his power as ruler and king and his subjects began protesting in prayer to the gods. Anu brought the issues of the people to Ninsun. Since she had created Gilgamesh strong and powerful, he asked her to create another warrior just as strong and frightful as Gilgamesh to bring an end to his tyranny. Ninsun created the mighty Enkidu.

As myth has it Enkidu was born full grown and hairy all over. He appeared to be as much animal as human. He roamed the earth knowing only animal friends and had no desire to enter into the city of Uruk to fight Gilgamesh, being content and accustomed to his animal friends and life in the wilderness. A mighty hunter happened to see the beast man Enkidu and was afraid of his grisly appearance. The hunter reported the dreadful beast-man that he had found drinking water with other beasts to his father. The father suggested that he should tame the wild man. He was instructed to enter into the city of Uruk and request the service of a priestess to seduce the wild man away from his animal friends so that he might join the human race. The young man did precisely as his father had instructed him to do.

When Enkidu met the priestess he was overcome by her beauty and eventually he became attracted to her and forgot his animal friends. Any attempt to return would be hopeless, for Enkidu had the scent of a human and would no longer be accepted as one of the beasts.

In quest of a friend, Enkidu ended up at the strong wall of Uruk in search of Gilgamesh. He decided to challenge Gilgamesh to a fight. Gilgamesh had already received the intuitive information in a dream telling him of Enkidu's arrival. The dream revealed to Gilgamesh that Enkidu was strong like the Spirit of the God Anu and that Enkidu would become his bosom lifelong companion. However, on his journey to Uruk, Enkidu met a man who complained of how terribly the king had bullied the people of the city of Uruk. Enkidu vowed to teach the bully king a lesson. As he entered into the city the people saw him and immediately compared him to their king. They began to sing praises that finally a hero had come who could match the strength of their king.

Gilgamesh and Enkidu entered into a wrestling match, which began to sound like an earthquake. They tussled and fought for hours. Gilgamesh finally realized that Enkidu was the friend of his dreams and he retreated in a prostrated manner, causing Enkidu to give praise to Gilgamesh. From this point on the men became friends. However, their friendship would be short-lived.

Ishtar, the granddaughter of Enlil, decided that Gilgamesh would make a wonderfully strong and handsome husband and as such she pursued Gilgamesh. She approached him with the idea of their marriage. However, Gilgamesh quoted all the men that she had married in her past and how they suffered ill consequences after marrying her. He chose to learn from their mistake and refused her hand in holy matrimony. Ishtar ran to her great-grandfather Anu crying and complaining that Gilgamesh had insulted her. She asked for the Bull of Heaven, a tank-like piece of equipment, which had to have been armed with nuclear warheads. Anu had insisted that the prerequisite for Ishtar to receive the Bull of Heaven was that there must be seven years of food available for the people and animals in the city. Anu pointed out that once the Bull of Heaven was unleashed there would be a seven-year famine. Readers, keep in mind that these events are written prior to the Bible. Let's ask ourselves: What can cause damage to the land in such a manner as to affect growth for seven years? RADIATION!

Ishtar received the Bull of Heaven and started out on her quest to kill Gilgamesh. She blew up several areas killing at least two hundred men before she reached Enkidu, who jumped aboard the tank in an effort to disable it. Gilgamesh saw the battle and joined it. Between the two of them they managed to cripple the Bull of Heaven and eventually destroy it. Ishtar yelled at Gilgamesh again for having destroyed her Bull of Heaven. At this point Enkidu broke off a piece of the tank and hurled it at the goddess informing her that he would have loved to do the same to her had he been able to catch her. Both friends and the townspeople celebrated the victory over the Bull of Heaven.

That night Enkidu dreamed and received the information that he should be the one to die for having broken the leg of the Bull of Heaven. Clearly this was a premonition of the inevitable. Enkidu became deathly ill. All the praying on his behalf by his best friend Gilgamesh was of no avail. Enkidu died. At Enkidu's death Gilgamesh became concerned with his own mortality. He did not wish to inherit the fate of his beloved Enkidu so he decided to seek out immortality.

Perhaps somehow Enkidu had accidentally overexposed himself to radiation like the man in the Bible who tried to prevent the Ark of the Covenant from being shaken by the oxen pulling the cart it rested on, and received an overexposure to radiation, killing him on contact. This story is found in II Samuel 6:6-7. After this death, **King David refused god** and told him that he wanted nothing to do with the Ark of the Covenant and God had to request another person to keep it for him and, according to the word, he blessed them for keeping the ark. In another place in the Bible, the Philistines were worshipping a god called Dagon. The Philistines took the Ark of the Covenant from the Hebrews and offered it to their god. However, because they did not understand the powerful emissions of radioactive material many were destroyed by radiation. Those who survived the blast of radiation suffered the holocaust aftermath of burns, blisters, and tumors. We find in I Samuel 5: 11- 12, "*So they sent and gathered the lords of the Philistines, and said, Send away the ark of the God of Israel, and let it go again to his own place, that it slay us not, and our people: for* *there was a deadly destruction throughout all the city; the hand of God was very heavy there. And the men that died not were smitten* (**afflicted**) *with emerods* (**tumors**): *and the cry of the city went up to heaven.*" By studying the messages left from our near ancient ancestors, we can learn that the use of radiation is a relatively old science on our planet.

Pushing onward in mythology, Gilgamesh now faced the reality that one day he, too, could die and was overcome with grief, praying to the gods to receive the gift of eternal life. He decided that it was of the most immediate urgency to find a man by the name of Utanapishtim (Utu: "he found" and Napishtim: "life"). According to ancient Babylonian myth, in the *Enuma Elish* (in cuneiform language much more ancient than Hebrew), Utanapishtim was the sole human survivor of a flood. Sound familiar? Gilgamesh started his journey seeking out Utanapishtim. He overcame many life-threatening obstacles, but eventually made it to the abode of the immortal Utanapishtim (which reminds me, didn't the Bible say that Noah died? Hmmm . . . ). Once Gilgamesh arrived he explained to Utanapishtim how he had suffered the loss of a dear friend. He begged Utanapishtim to share with him the secret of how he and his wife obtained immortality.

At this point Utanapishtim agreed to share a story, of how he had found favor in one god's sight. The name of this god was Ea (the biblical serpent and Yahweh). Ea did not want to see mankind perish, but he was outvoted in the counsel of the gods and could not go against the vote of the other gods. The gods of the counsel were further instructed not to inform mankind of the upcoming catastrophe, but Ea could not contain it. He slipped a vision to Utanapishtim in a dream of the upcoming flood and dictated specific architectural designs of a submarine that would enable Utanapishtim to survive the flood.

In the myth, exactly like in the Bible, the submarine is called an ark. In the biblical version of the flood, Jehovah (not Enlil) sets out to destroy mankind. Also, in both the myth and the Bible,

Utanapishtim/Noah is instructed to take aboard the ark two of each kind of animal. The biblical parallel to this statement can be found in Genesis 7:2-3.

Utanapishtim awaited the day when the warning signs would tell him of the time to enter the ark. According to myth, Utanapishtim did everything exactly as god/Ea instructed him to do it. (The biblical version of this is found in Genesis 6:22, *"Thus did Noah; according to all that God commanded him, so did he."*) He carefully watched the heavens for the sign of when he should retreat. Finally the great and terrible day arrived. Utanapishtim entered his ship and sealed the entrance with clay as instructed. The gods headed off to watch the disaster from their heavenly abode.

Adad caused the heavens to open and bring forth winds and rains that were equivalent to hurricanes, tornadoes, and thunderstorms all rolled into one. Utanapishtim could see all the people and creatures alike perish before him. The gods watched the tragedy from above and they, too, huddled together like scared dogs watching all earthly life become literally washed away. The goddess Ishtar cried out in agony seeing that her vote in support of Enlil had caused all of her earthly children to whom she had given birth to perish. She said, "Only had I not added my voice with Enlil at the assembly of the gods." SOUND FAMILIAR? "ONLY HAD I NOT ADDED MY VOTE TO DESTROY MANKIND." Let's compare this statement with the so-called statement of Jehovah in the King James Version of the Bible. Turn to Genesis 9:11 *"And I will establish my covenant with you:* **neither shall all flesh be cut off any more by the water of a flood** (here we can see a god repenting for having caused such vast destruction of human life); *neither shall there any more be a flood to destroy the earth."* It appears that after the flood the Hebrew god, too, felt badly about having destroyed mankind and made a covenant vowing never to allow it to happen again.

After many days of rain, Utanapishtim looked out to see if he could spot land. He couldn't see anything other then water in every direction. After several more days the tips of the mountains became visible and finally Utanapishtim's ship settled on top of a mountain. After seven days, he set a dove free, but the dove could find no place to rest so it returned to the ark. SOUND FAMILIAR? If not turn to Genesis chapter 8; it is copied there. Next Utanapishtim set free a swallow. It returned to the ark just as the dove had. Note that no swallow was mentioned in the Bible. Finally Utanapishtim sent out a raven which didn't return to the ship. At this point all the occupants of the ship left to begin life anew.

Utanapishtim offered a thanksgiving sacrifice, for the salvation of his life, after the deluge was over. All of the gods flocked down like flies to Utanapishtim's sacrifice of burnt offering (barbecue) for the gods. It was Ishtar who told Utanapishtim that he should not offer any of the sacrificial meat to Enlil since it was his decision to cause the great deluge without just cause. She took her precious jewels given to her by Anu and swore an **oath** (similar to Jehovah's vow) to NEVER FORGET THE DAYS OF THE GREAT FLOOD. Again Ishtar stated how she must never forget this day and that she never desired it to have happened. Similar again to Genesis 9:11.

Enlil became outraged that a human escaped his plan to exterminate the humans. The gods again were fearful and pointed the finger at Ea. Ea used a cunning choice of words to appease the spirit of Enlil and made Enlil see Utanapishtim as an equal. Enlil then took both Utanapishtim and his wife and made them immortal. Now let's take a look at the chart of the Babylonian story versus the biblical (Babylonian) story—see the Appendix for the chart "Whose god is God?" How is it remotely possible for the Bible to be authentically original and not from Babylon when it contains stories written a thousand years after the same stories were written in Babylon? This story alone proves that the writers of the Bible plagiarized the *Enuma Elish*. Each culture borrowed from previous cultures and so it has been passed down even until today.

### Egyptian Mythology

In ancient Egyptian mythology the Supreme Father god first mentioned is Ptah. When one reads the history of Ptah and the Sumerian or Babylonian text simultaneously one learns that Ptah of ancient Egypt was Enki of Sumeria and Ea of Babylon. Ea was originally granted the Egyptian territory by his father, Anu. Ptah/Ea was known for his wisdom, magic, and love for the human race. In Egypt he designed a dam-like structure that would control the closing and opening of locks used to prevent flooding of that area. He gave the people advanced designs for many structures including the Sphinx and the Giza Pyramids. During Ptah's rulership as king and god of the Egyptians the people knew only prosperity, good health, and all the comforts of life. The Egyptians also possessed the keys of eternal life.

However, with a change in leadership, Re became prince and the sun god over Egypt. Along with the new rulership of Re/Ra also known as Marduk in Babylon, came the physical death of mankind sometime around 3000 B.C. Ra became known to the Egyptian people as the supreme creator god. Later, Osiris assumed that role just as did Jehovah in the Old Testament, only thousands of years before Jehovah claimed his authority. Ra the supreme creator of the Egyptians did not rule, as did his father, Ptah, with the best interests of the humans at hand. Ra's overall concern was primarily for himself. Therefore, he taught the humans that the only way to find eternal life was to **die**. WE WERE LITERALLY TAUGHT TO DIE!!! He appealed to the human root chakra through our leaders. "The only way to gain ultimate prosperity in the afterworld (eternal life)," he proclaimed, "would be to mummify the flesh." The point at which the soul decides to transfigure the flesh into celestial existence will trap the cocoon (the physical body) within the physical world, thereby creating the physical death for the immortal humans. The appeal of choosing death over transfiguration was the guarantee of ultimate salvation (the *ultimate deceit*) promised by their beloved god (Ra/ Re/ Marduk/Baal/Yahweh/Jehovah/Zeus (Jesus) = SATAN/ ENEMY). He promised them that this was the only way to receive wealth, prestige, power, and a regime in the afterworld. Mummify the flesh, he insisted, and bury it with all the powers the soul has gained in this world so that it would pass over to the next world with the body when it transfigured. It made perfect sense: If all the wealth were trapped in a tomb with the body surely all would pass over to the next world. Quite the reverse was true and again man became trapped and deceived through his own greed and lust.

Life was shaping up perfectly for Ra with his devised tactics for enslaving man until he learned that the men of Babylon had devised a way of escaping death and remaining in, or for some returning to, an immortal state. When he discovered their plans of becoming one with the gods, he deployed a nuclear weapon against them to divide their races by color, thus creating clans and separation and, over a period of time, creating various languages in that area. Again Ra could sit back and enjoy the service of his slaves, puppets, toys, and doormats. This era in which God was known to the Egyptians as Ra, the Babylonians as Marduk, the Canaanites as Baal, the Assyrians as Asshur, and finally the Hebrews as Jehovah began the period in which man would lose more of his divinity and take on more of his physical aspect. With this statement in mind, I offer to anyone a $10,000 reward who can prove Jehovah to have been more than a mythical god/man of the ancients, for without doubt he could not have been the Creator!

After Ra, man began to find it necessary to individualize himself (into the survival of the fittest). Man was the most bestial animal of all. Man was and is the only animal on the planet that is capable of mass murdering his OWN species simply because he can. The mass hysteria is then placed on the entire species through identification with the act of mass murder as justified. We justify rape, murder, stealing, hate, false witness (lying), racism and so much worse daily with our embrace of the "Holy Bible" as absolute truth, as God's word, as the perfect moral text to follow in its entirety (see the chapter devoted to the god of the Hebrews). Those who quote any statements that I make in the previous sentence without my quotes from the Bible that prove this statement true are making a slanderous statement. It must be made clear here and now that I do not believe that GOD the CREATOR OF ALL EXISTENCE teaches people to murder, rape, hate and so forth, but I do show proof in Jehovah's own words, that Jehovah teaches such things. This is how our children grow up and feel justified in doing the things that the Bible teaches us. God told the Hebrews to do it, but now you want to lock up your youths when they follow the same spirit of the Bible (the *ultimate deceit*). However, returning to Egyptian mythology, we can find that nearly all the religions were first found in one form or another of Egyptian literature.

Most of our current religions were practiced in ancient Egypt first, which brings me to the birth of Christianity's concept of the Trinity. Where did the cross first appear? In A.D. 33 with the death of Jesus? The symbol of the cross had been in existence for more than two thousand years before the birth of Christ, seen in the anhk. Osiris, Isis, and Horus bring us to one of the first trinity belief concepts. The more ancient form of the trinity in which the birth of Christ is taken from today is Nimrod, his mother, and god. Nimrod in the Bible is called a mighty hunter, but the people of that day saw him as a god. His mother worshipped her son god and after his death in efforts of keeping the memory of her son alive eternally in the souls of mankind, she began a ritual at his birthday. Nimrod's birthday was December 25, and to reinforce his memory, his mother placed a tree at his burial site and decked it with silver and gold every year on December 25 in recognition of his birth. A reference is made in the Bible of the account referring to this act as the act of pagans. Nonetheless, so-called followers of the Bible practice this pagan form of worship in ignorance today. Many believe that it was Christ's birthday which was celebrated on December 25 even though scholars nearly unanimously agree that Jesus could not have been born on the 25th of December. Some sort of manipulation by humans had taken place to cause many to err and begin the practice of the celebration of the Sun god (Nimrod) on December 25 instead of their intended Jesus god. Jehovah hated the idea that any other god could receive recognition and prohibited the Israelites from engaging in the decoration of the tree. Record of this activity can be verified today in the biblical account of heathen worship of the decorated tree. Turn to Jeremiah 10:1-4 for proof of this fact. The verse states, *"Hear ye the word which the Lord speaketh unto you, O house of Israel: Thus saith the Lord, Learn not the way of the **heathen**, and be not dismayed at the signs of heaven; for the **heathen** are dismayed at them. For the customs of the people are vain: for one cutteth a tree out of the forest, the work of the hands of the workman, with the ax. They deck it with silver and with gold they fasten it with nails and with hammers that it move not."*

We continue this practice every Christmas (**DECKING THE TREE WITH SILVER AND GOLD**) which Yahweh, the god of the Hebrews says is heathen worship. Oh, yeah, again in this passage God didn't really mean that it was pagan worship to deck the trees with silver and gold. I just don't understand how we get to pick and choose at our personal discretion to ordain the Bible as God's "Holy Word" but then insist that the words are not intended to be practiced or that some how God changed his plan for man. Somehow God simply didn't know that the law would not be good enough for man so he made the mistake of the law, and then corrects it with the grace through the blood of Jesus. Come on people—watch out for the *ultimate deceit*—**BASING YOUR EVERY TRUTH OF LIFE'S MOST SACRED (That is GOD!!!) ON ONE BOOK, PASSED DOWN AND CHANGED OVER AND OVER BY THE DESIRES OF MAN.**

Although Nimrod stems from Babylonian mythology, the

story still parallels all the mythologies of Mesopotamia because it is God, Nimrod, and his mother who first originate the holy trinity. This holy trinity then waters down into the Catholic church as God, the Virgin Mary or "Mother of God," and finally the son of God. The Protestants, simply put, are the ones who protested against the belief systems of the Catholic church, broke away and changed the trinity to God the Father, God the Holy Ghost, and God the Son. How did all of this (the Nimrod trinity, the Isis trinity, the Mother of God trinity, the Holy Ghost trinity, and others not mentioned, all of which trickle down from the original Nimrod trinity) become the acts of GOD?

There are so many books that are devoted to mythology alone with much information to be found. Browse the Internet for free, go to the library, converse with other souls with open minds. All of this is free. If it is worth it for you to discover more of what is real or false in your life perhaps you may invest a few dollars in purchasing some books to allow yourself to discover how myths (including the Bible) originated. Once the known truth of the historical making of the ancient writings is discovered, then and only then can one distinguish truth from falsehood. I wish that I could spend so much more time on mythology here in my book but that is not my purpose. I only wish to expose you to some truth that you may not have been familiar with to hopefully allow you to decide whether to investigate further. However, mythology just cannot be complete without the mention of GREEK MYTHOLOGY, the most widely recognized myths in Western society.

## Introduction to Greek Mythology
### *The Titans: Creators of the Gods*

By the time Greek mythology comes along we are talking about a seriously watered-down account of the ancient Sumerians and Babylonians, some of which may have even come from the Hebraic account. That's neat; at last we find an account in history that even the Hebrews pre-date. The records date as far back as 775 B.C. for

Homer's *Iliad* and around 700 B.C. for Hesiod's *Theogony*. The Greek gods have human characteristics like Jehovah; they get jealous and wreak havoc on all the misbehaving humans. The myth gives insight into an aspect of creation much like Genesis of the Bible and it mentions a flood with a sole survivor and his wife. Yet the Greeks believed this story to be about their race only. Did the Hebrews believe the stories of the Bible to be about their own race only? What of the Canaanite version or the Babylonians? Was one of them the original? DID THE STORY ACTUALLY BEGIN WITH THE SUMERIAN STORY? These are all questions that you should ask yourself as you take on the quest for shedding *ultimate deceit.*

According to Greek mythology, the universe began with the Titans who made the Greek gods. The Titan society was made up of goddess-dominant communities. This myth said that the feminine energy pretty much ruled over creation. In the making of the gods all of this changed and masculine energy and influence ruled the planet instead of the feminine force. Can you see a parallel with this story to the Babylonian text? Remember Tiamat (the mother goddess, who made all the gods)? The Bible does not give the account of the Leviathan (Tiamat) giving birth to Jehovah's great-great-great-ancestors. However, in the original Hebrew text God was required to separate the waters from the waters (Genesis 1:7). This action directly parallels the Babylonian version of what happened to Tiamat, the goddess of salt water, and Apsu, the god of fresh water. Of course, that Jehovah had a mother would be left out of the Hebrew accounts because by the time the story reaches the Hebrews they are in full swing of reducing the woman to zero!

Greek mythology records that the universe began with a mother goddess, Gaea (Mother Earth), who emerged out of the chaotic emptiness along with Tartarus and Eros. Tartarus ruled over the underworld and Eros brought about the beginning of the immortal gods. Gaea gave birth to Father Sky, Uranus. Gaea laid down the law that made Uranus her equal so that he could provide a home and surround her with care. She later gave birth to Pontus

(Sea) and Ourea (mountain). All of this was done before Gaea and Uranus finally married one another. Uranus seized all dominion over creation and when Gaea began to have children at this point he would destroy them. The first set of children were called the three Hundred-Handed Giants; the second set were the Cyclops (the huge beings seen in Hercules movies with one eye in the center of the forehead). There were six immortal beings in all and Uranus became frantically jealous with the thought that one of his children might challenge his authority to rule over Gaea (much like dysfunctional families today where fathers become threatened by their children's authority/power over their mother). However, Uranus took it a step further and decided that there must never be any question as to his power to rule. He took the children to Tartarus to guarantee his eternal reign. However, Gaea became outraged at the behavior of Uranus and when making the next set of immortals she took measures to guard against Uranus' plot to destroy the children to keep the universe for himself only.

The next set of immortal children became known as the Titans. There were thirteen Titans:

1. Gaea—Mother Earth, the first Titan
2. Tartarus—ruler over the underworld
3. Eros—ruler of love
4. Uranus—sky god brought forth by Gaea (Mother Earth)
5. Helios—sun god
6. Oceanus—river god
7. Themis—prophesy goddess
8. Cronus—god of time
9. Rhea—earth goddess
10. Prometheus—the wisest of the gods and creator of the human race
11. Epimetheus—the brother to Prometheus and husband of the first mortal woman

12. Atlas—the strongest Titan
13. Selene—moon goddess

After the Titans were brought forth into the world Gaea decided to have Uranus punished through her Titan children. She told them of their father's evil deeds and pleaded that any one of them should seek revenge against Uranus. All of the Titans refused their mother with the exception of Cronus. He agreed to seek the revenge of his brothers the Hundred-Handed giant triplets and the Cyclops triplets. His mother joyfully armed her son with a sharp weapon called the flint sickle. She instructed him on finding an adequate hiding place and counseled him to wait until Helios (the sun god) retired for the day. As Uranus lay sleeping with his wife, Cronus left his hiding place and cut off the penis of Uranus. Cronus bellowed out to Uranus to give up his authority or fight for it. Uranus, bleeding and in pain, lost the role of controlling deity to Cronus, who became god of the sky. However, Cronus, being so much like his father, refused to let the first and second sets of triplets free for fear that they might one day rise up to power and seize his authority. Again Gaea was outraged and prophesied to Cronus that the same fate which he caused to happen to his father would one day happen to him by his very own son. Hearing these words grieved Cronus so that he vowed to never have children, but the love of his wife, Rhea, allowed children to break the matrix despite his efforts. Cronus and Rhea gave birth to the first generation of gods consisting of Zeus, Poseidon, Hades, Hera, Demeter, and Hestia. The first child that Rhea gave birth to was called Hestia. When Cronus came to Rhea and the child, he requested to see the child. He took the child in his arms in the way that a loving father would take a son and then swallowed it. Rhea continued to give birth to other children: Hades, Demeter, Hera, and Poseidon, all of whom had the same fate as Hestia.

In anger Rhea went to her mother and complained of how her husband had taken on the same spirit as Uranus and had destroyed every child that she gave birth to. She informed Mother Earth that she was pregnant and that Uranus would destroy this child also. Gaea and Rhea devised a plan to deceive Cronus. Rhea had her last-born son in a cave and left him with her mother. On her way home to her husband, Rhea chose a rock that was approximately the same size and weight as her child. She wrapped the rock up like she would wrap her own son. When she arrived home with the apparent child, Cronus, as always, requested to hold the beautiful child. As soon as the child was in his arms Cronus could hear only the voice of his mother ringing out in prophecy as to his inevitable fate to lose his authority as the sky god to his son. Cronus swallowed the rock thinking that he had successfully stopped the prophecy of his mother.

Many years later when Zeus had become fully grown both he and Cronus came face to face one day. Rhea had mixed a poisonous drink causing Cronus to regurgitate all of his offspring. After the children were vomited up from the pit of Cronus' stomach, Zeus and his siblings challenged the authority of their father. This was the beginning of the war of the Titans against the gods. The war continued for years with neither side winning a victory because the gods were immortal.

Zeus decided to shift the odds into his favor by creating an alliance with his uncles, the Cyclops and the Hundred-Handed giants. He broke into the gloomy dark underworld and both sets of triplets agreed to assist him in defeating the Titans. At this point, the Cyclops supplied Zeus with the thunderbolt weapon to help defeat the Titans. Poseidon received the trident, a superior fishing spear. The Cyclops armed all the gods born of Rhea and Cronus and they all ascended to the earth's surface to prepare for battle. The weapons of both the Titans and the gods and their allies were thrown back and forth until Zeus fired his thunderbolt (remember the Babylonian Bull of Heaven in Gilgamesh). The nuclear blast incinerated everything in the immediate area. The Titans were seized by the Hundred-Handed giants and hurled into the dark underworld of Tartarus where the giants guarded against their escape. The Cyclops built the paradise home of the gods known as Mount Olympus.

With Zeus as the head of the gods ruling in the place of Cronus (Father Time) the Greek people began to worship Zeus. Zeus married his sister Hera, queen of Olympus. Notice at first the woman married the man and now the man marries the woman. Their children's names were Athena, Apollo, Hermes, Persephone, Hephaestus, Ares, and Artemis. This era concludes the rule of the Titans and begins the rule of the gods.

### The Origin of Man According to Greek Myth

According to myth Zeus is responsible for creating several species of mankind; the first was known as the golden race. This race of beings was perfect in the sight of the gods. It continually gave reverence to the gods of Mount Olympus and each other. The people were so perfect in their mannerisms that there was no need for courts or written laws. These people did not have to toil the land to receive food. Everything their hearts could imagine was always provided for them (recall the biblical garden of Eden and the Sumerian garden of Edin!). They had the time to enjoy the wildflowers of the field and all the beauty that nature had to bestow upon them. They had no desire to own earthly possessions nor did they fight or war over such things. They lived long, happy lives until the age of the golden race came to an end and Zeus had to create a second race, the silver race.

The silver race did not possess the virtue of the golden race. They were childish people and impossible for the gods to please. They wanted everything and after the gods blessed them they were unhappy with the blessing, desiring more from the gods with no appreciation for what they had already received. This era of humans had to work the fields and toil for their meals. The weather was not as mild and food was not as plentiful as it had been for the golden race. Zeus is credited with bringing the silver race to an abrupt end so that the third race, called the bronze race, could be created.

The bronze race was even worse than the silver race. They were cruel. These humans constructed tools and weapons to kill one another. This race of humans had brute strength but lacked in the love department. They, too, died young through endless war and violence.

The fourth race Zeus created is known as the race of heroes. These human beings were much more virtuous and respectful than the previous silver and bronze races. Many of them died off. It is said that some of them survived and were placed on an island at the ends of the Earth to grieve no longer. Zeus set Cronus free from his bondage in the underworld to rule over these people.

The fifth race of people is called the iron race and is the Greek people during the time of the writing of the myths. This race of people was barbaric, greedy, lustful, and the worst of all the races of mankind. They suffered hard work, disease, and anguish. They are considered to be the race of today.

Zeus left Mount Olympus to find some sort of good anywhere within man. All that he saw was men being disrespectful, greedy, and inconsiderate of one another. Finally he came to the palace of King Lycaon. Zeus was seeking a people who would honor the gods of Olympus. A servant of the king spotted Zeus and asked him his intentions. Zeus announced himself as both a stranger and an immortal god from Olympus seeking the hospitality of the king.

The king found Zeus' announcement rather amusing and unbelievable so he had the cook prepare soup for their strange guest. When Zeus looked into the soup he discovered all sorts of human body parts: a hand, foot, heart, liver, and so forth. Zeus became outraged and disgusted with all humans after this human sacrifice had been offered to him. He cursed King Lycaon, who was transformed into a beast on all four legs. (A tale similar to this one happened to a king in the Bible, who was cursed to become a mule by Jehovah.) Headed back to Olympus, Zeus set in motion the flood to destroy all of earth's inhabitants.

The Titan Prometheus had fashioned the first mortal beings. Prometheus had the gift of seeing into the future and saw that Zeus intended to kill all mortal life off the earth with a great flood. He had one mortal who was dear to his heart, Deucalion. Prometheus appeared to Deucalion in a dream and warned him of the upcoming catastrophe. Deucalion and his wife, Pyrrha, were the sole survivors along with a male and female of each animal. **Sound familiar**? As I have stated before this book is not a book of myths; it is only an introduction to information that mainstream people omit, thus falling prey to an ultimate deceit as I did.

## Introduction to the Mayan and North American Indian Myths

It is common knowledge and totally accepted that life has existed as far back as 6000 B.C. However, in courts today there is a fight over an ancient human fossil proving that human life is even older than at first suspected. To whom does this body belong? The courts will decide. Some say that this body dates back 60,000 years and is **human**. A picture of the little Indian girl's corpse was the featured on the cover of *National Geographic* magazine in 1999. When I hear stories like these I sometimes really laugh at scientists, for they NEVER LEARN. If this was the first discovery of human life, life would have begun in North America around 60,000 years ago. It is so comical. Why is it so impossible to simply state that we have found human life to have existed at least 60,000 years ago and that it is unknown as to how long before this find, life on earth actually began? If they stated it like this they would be RIGHT EVERY TIME! They instead prefer to use a religious system for quoting the physical outcome of the universe. The system consists primarily of taking the physical data obtained from the current level of technology and labeling it as ULTIMATE TRUTH, instead of stating available truth for our current consciousness and labeling it as such. This causes the scientist to retract statements as new discoveries are made or advanced technologies developed. But hey, we have to hand it to the scientists! At least when they discover that they were wrong originally, they are quick to recant their position; not so in religions!

An archaeologist discovered a writing called the *Popol Vuh*, containing the Mayan myth written in the Mayan language using the Latin alphabet. This writing is said to date from the mid-1500s. Remember that the ancient, more civilized, cultures did not write down their story, culture, and traditions; they were passed down orally. All that is written has been corrupted. Never forget that you should look for origins before ever accepting any writing as absolute truth, to avoid the *ultimate deceit*. The writing is anonymous, but was encouraged by Spanish conquerors requesting the Mayan people to put their oral tradition in writing. The manuscript was first published in Vienna in 1857 in the Spanish language. The myth tells the story of creation, gods, humans, and so forth just like all other myths.

Creation began with the sky above and the seas below, all within an eternal darkness. The universe had no noise and the earth had no land. Under the water existed the Creators, recognized by the Mayans as "those who were great thinkers." This is precisely what I have been trying to tell you, that the Creator is Raw Conscious Creative Power (us). These great thinkers (the Creators-Us) thought to themselves that they were all alone in the universe in the dark void. Together these great thinkers thought out a plan as to what the physical reality playground would consist of. They thought of the fish, the animals, birds, humans, and how they would evolve into subspecies. They thought of types of physical bodies, what types of sustenance would sustain the particular physical vehicles, and so forth. Together they thought of the first light and all of a perfect creation. "Let creation begin!" the Creators spoke into existence. "Let the void be filled! Let the sea recede, revealing the surface of the earth! earth arise! Let it be done!" This myth is very close to what the Bible states. The difference is that

Baal/Jehovah had a hidden agenda of destruction for mankind so Baal took the sole credit for having created the universe. Nonetheless the Hebrews did NOT give Jehovah the sole credit; they spoke exactly in the same way as the Mayan myth. Genesis 1:2 says: *"And God* (in the ORIGINAL Hebrew the word was **"Elohim,"** meaning **GODS**, not God) *said let there be light: and there was light."* **Remember, get a Strong's concordance or any Bible concordance that will translate the Hebrew into English.**

Mayan myth tells us that the land, birds, fish, animals were all created through the thought of the Creators (somewhat similar to the Ezzrath Theory on Creation), who were pleased with their work, except for the fact that none of their creation could speak or call on the names of the creators. The animals could make all sorts of sounds, squeeches, brays, and hisses but did not satisfy their ultimate desires of what they wished creation to be. They had desired to give speech to the animals to no avail, so later they decided to create a creature who would rule over all the animals in superiority.

They created a man-like being out of the muddy parts of the earth. (My friends, surely this one sounds very familiar now.) He was originally made respectful and obedient. He could speak but his mind did not know what the spoken syllables represented. These beings made from mud could not procreate. So the Creators destroyed these creatures from off the face of the earth. The Creators made a second attempt at creating a creature that would be able to both multiply and praise them. This creature was made from wood and was also man-like. These creatures could multiply and speak syllables, but still possessed no understanding of what words meant. Seeing that the wooden beings had no souls and no understanding, the Creators decided that these beings also must be destroyed by a flood.

The Creators caused a mighty terrible rain to begin to fall. The wooden people are attacked by dogs, birds, and jaguars which tore away their faces and bones. Some of the wooden creatures climbed to the roof of their houses, which collapsed. They were all destroyed with the exception of a few. The survivors generated descendants of the monkey species.

Now the Great Thinkers were back to square one. They thought together on how they would create this praiseworthy creature that would be capable of worshipping them. Animals inspired the Great Thinkers to fashion the third generation of humans out of corn. This creature could speak and understand speech. The Great Thinkers could now communicate with these beings. These beings thanked the Creators for their existence. (It appears that these beings may have been the time in which we/the Great Thinkers/Creators entered into the physical realm ourselves without the amnesia of who we were. The reason that I say this is because, according to Mayan myth, these beings were thankful for **knowing everything.**)

Now the Creators were no longer pleased, because these beings knew everything. These creatures were too perfect and wise and would have become gods like the Creator gods. So the Creators blocked their sight. (They created amnesia by somehow convincing the Adam Kadmon to leave their perfect physical body and enter into an animal known as man. This story is very similar to how man built a tower and was becoming as the gods, and god confused the languages.) However, according to the myth, the gods sent a fog into the creatures' eyes so that they saw only that which was close to them (this limited their awareness of their own spiritual essence). These beings were called the first four fathers, who were the only beings created without the fog; all beings after them were made through the fog. **Thus the Great Thinkers destroyed the original knowledge and wisdom of humans.**

Now the Creators were happy with their creation. Therefore they made many more human beings of this stalk who lived and multiplied in darkness with no stars, moon, or sun. These humans lived in the east, both light- and dark-skinned, rich and poor, speaking various languages. These people did not make images of their gods but they were respectful and honored them. The humans lifted their face to the creators and said, "Let there be light," and the world was filled with the pale light for the first day. The humans caused the sun to appear with their spoken words. "So let it be!" spoke the creators. There was light and it was perfect. Because of this new light all the animals and humans were filled with joy. They danced and burned incense and made sacrifices to the gods. Let's keep in mind, as I have said throughout this book, NOT ONE SINGLE WRITING WILL EVER CONTAIN ABSOLUTE TRUTH. There is simply no way that I have been able to conceive of the creation of animals and humans before light. UNLESS these were the **spiritual** souls of humans and animals all mixed up within the physical creation time period. What I am trying to say is that over the years details of stories become distorted. Certain things happen with a loss of sequence of occurrence.

The Mayan people are one of the most important people in my study. Why? Because these people have precisely the same characteristics as the Sumerian people. The Mayans simply appeared out of the blue into existence. There are no people that could be found before them from which they may have evolved. Nonetheless, the most exciting history of the Mayans is how the masters disappeared. The original Mayans (masters) ascended the physical world to escape the dawning of the age of Pisces so as not to suffer, I mean experience, the barbaric upcoming period (ending NOW, through spiritual awaking or self-destruction, as we choose). Those Mayans who chose to experience this barbaric period were left behind, and began what became known as the Mayan human sacrifices, and mixed in with the Spaniards.

### The Myth of the Aztecs/Toltecs

The Toltec people recorded much information about the god Quetzalcoatl. The Aztecs had borrowed information from the Toltecs. I will make mention of the Olmecs in this section. All that I have ever found about the Olmec people was the gigantic heads of stone that they left behind in their image. If the Olmec people looked anything like the heads they built they were **AFRICAN**. If you have doubt that Africans could have possibly possessed the American land before the Indians, research the appearance of the Olmec head. I guarantee you that irrefutably these heads possess African facial features of wide noses and thick lips. Many of these features (the noses and lips) were attacked and defaced in the conquests by the Spanish and other whites.

Study suggests that the Mayans did not come up out of the Olmec people, although it does suggest that the Olmecs were in North America before the Mayans. It may also be that the Toltec people derived from the Olmecs. But what arose to make the people decide that they were Toltec, and then that they were Aztec? One might research the etymology of the endings of the names, which all three share in common. The "ec" suffix can be researched, and the discovery of the connection between the three cultures may be obtained. Always remember when all understanding is lost LOOK TOWARD THE UNDERSTANDING OF LANGUAGES. The languages possess the KEY to our origins. Anyone without a key to the origins of his belief system is set up for *ultimate deceit.*

The Aztec people borrowed their culture from the Toltec people, thus leaving great myths and legends behind, written in their Nahuatl Aztec language. To know more, discover where the Nahuatl language came from. Notice the suffix again having similarities with other words such as "Quetzalco**atl**" and in the middle of the word "Tez**catl**ipoca." You are now equipped to begin a great finding of your own; write and let us know what connections and esoteric information you discover. The majority of the human race has no idea that this information exists, due to a lack of knowledge and interest in obtaining knowledge.

As legend has it the Aztec people (people of Aztlan) followed the orders of their god, leaving the Colorado area sometime in early A.D. 1300. They had wandered aimlessly for nearly fifty years when they settled in the area now known as Mexico City. It was said that the first ruler of the Aztec people was a direct descendant of Quetzalcoatl himself (god of the Toltec people) and at this point the Aztlan people became Aztec and took on the customs and traditions of the Toltec people. Through this new leadership the people flourished in the arts, architecture, literature and all other aspects of civilization. The Spanish people had nothing of this caliber of civilization.

In early A.D. 1500 Hernan Cortes, a Spanish general, invaded Central America, conquering the Aztec people. The Aztecs had mistaken Cortes as their god Quetzalcoatl who had promised that he would return to his people one day. This is a lot like the Christian doctrine where people are still wondering whether they will know and recognize their beloved Christ when he comes. Or will HE be a HE? IF he chooses a female body to come back in they all would reject Christ immediately. I would have been the first to do so since we know that the Son of God would never belittle himself by entering into a female body. According to scripture, when Israel is at its lowest state of existence no man shall save her (Deuteronomy 28:29). Could it be a woman? No way, for we have been conditioned to believe that the woman's body is the lowest—the least—rock bottom of all that god would choose to come back in, right? Impossible? Well, if we can learn from history, just believing can get you killed and your civilization destroyed, for this is what happened to a lot of the Aztec people who eventually succumbed to Cortes' army. His army burned their villages, palaces, and libraries. The Spaniards then began the converting process of replacing a much older culture and background with the newer religion of Christianity. They allowed the Aztecs, like the Mayans, to share some of their traditions and oral teachings and found them both interesting and disgusting. Therefore the Spanish taught the Aztec to record some of their culture in their own language, but using the Roman alphabet. Thus the myths of the Aztecs, which were adapted from the Toltec people, were recorded in the Nahuatl language.

According to the Aztecs, creation began with the creation of five worlds, each of which had its own sun. The first world was illuminated by the sun of earth. Its people were evil, so the gods caused jaguars to destroy them (compare these people to the Mayan wood people). The second world was illuminated by the sun of air, causing these people to be as fools without knowledge or wisdom. Therefore, the gods caused a hurricane to turn the people into apes. Their sun died when they became animals. The third world was illuminated by the sun of water, causing these people to lack respect for the gods (they may have been too superior in consciousness to bow to the creation that was creation like them or, so to speak, gods bowing to gods). Nonetheless these gods caused earthquakes and volcanoes to destroy their sun and the people. The fourth world was illuminated by a sun of water. This is the period in which Quetzalcoatl created humans from ash. These people were very greedy and selfish and the gods caused a great flood to destroy all of them and drown their sun. Those who did not die were turned into fish. The Supreme Being saved one human couple from the deluge. His voice went out to them, warning them to find a tree and make a hole large enough for them to hide in until the deluge ended.

Please don't stop here with my tiny fraction of coverage of mythology, for if you knew what I know you will see here that the myths of the lost cities of Atlantis and Mu are mixed in with the myths of Noah and the flood, but told by Aztec people. Stop and think about how this information came to America, across the ocean, before humans were charting the seas. It is impossible for me to produce completed material on world mythology in this one book, which contains information from a large quantity of books.

# Introduction to the
# Ifa and the Yoruba People

One final myth that I would like to share with you is the myth passed down by the Yoruba people of Nigeria. The Ifa myth records that the Yoruba people migrated from the East with the help of the warrior Oduduwa. Oduduwa was a mighty warrior spirit who led the people over a period of years from the Middle East to the west coasts of Nigeria where they now live.

The word "Ifa" is of the most spiritual orientation and has no literal translation. It stands for esoteric teachings of Yoruba traditions and ethics. It sets up a process by which mankind may spiritually transform and evolve its light force into higher and higher realities through following the guidance of the complex scriptures of the Ifa. This myth, like all myths, claims that deities or spirits (however we may choose to term such entities) appeared to their people by means other than physical. For example, Ogun simply crossed over from spiritual reality into physical reality. One day he was seen simply walking out of the water from nowhere, according to Yoruba mythology.

Like most ancient people, the Yoruba people recognized many gods or spirits in prayer for help within their particular areas of expertise. For example, if relationship problems occurred, the fertility goddess would be the person to seek help from. If famine began to set in, one could call on the rain god or agricultural god to help balance nature's crop production. However, before our religions set in, we used to balance nature and the universe as did the gods, from our own power within. Some of the names of the Yoruba deities are as follows:

## *Major Gods*

Olorun—the wisest and most powerful creator god and ruler
of the sky
Olokun—ruler of the sea
Eshu—messenger god

Orunmila—the oldest son of Olorun, advisor to Obatala

Obatala—Olorun's favorite and the creator of land and
humans; god of the Chief of the White Cloth

### Minor Gods

Ogun—god of Iron

Shango—god of Lightning

Oshun—god of the River

Ochosi—god of the Tracker

Oya—god of the Wind

The Yoruba cosmology states that in the beginning all that was upon the face of the earth was marsh and no land, vegetation, or humans. It is Obatala's function to preserve the mystic vision. It is through Obatala that all creation connects and is woven, metaphysically speaking, to the All That There Is—God. All forms of earth consciousness contain spiritual power from Obatala. Obatala has many characteristics similar to that of Ea from ancient Babylonian mythology, the primary similarity being the creation of man. According to the Ifa, Obatala decided that the universe just wasn't complete with only water and marshland all around. Obatala observed that the ruler of the marsh, Olokun, had nothing in her domain other than marshland and, feeling sorry for her, he approached the head deity, Olorun, for permission to begin creating land, vegetation, and humans. Olorun granted Obatala his wishes and he immediately began creating. The first step he took was to seek advice from Orunmila. Orunmila told Obatala that to accomplish his goal he would need to make a chain of gold long enough to reach from the sky above to the waters below. This gold chain compares with the Sumerian Dur-An-Ki (**bond heaven and earth**) and the biblical Jacob's ladder in Genesis 28:12.

Obatala used the chain to connect to earth and begin the creation process. He first established land and next he formed small statuettes of clay out of the earth, which he called humans. The figurines were shaped after the likeness of Obatala. After creating several statuettes Obatala became tired and sought a drink. He made a drink of fermented juice of a palm tree. He drank to the point of drunkenness without knowing that he had become drunk. In this drunken state Obatala continued to create his figurines. The remaining clay statuettes were produced with one arm longer or shorter than the other, legs that were disproportionate, and backs that were disfigured. He then sought the assistance of Olorun to breathe the breath of life into the statuettes because they were built lifeless and without souls.

Hence Olorun (whom the Yoruba call the Most High Creator God and the Hebrews called Yahweh) allowed the souls of a type of angelic being (Ophanim) to experience the physical life on earth through clay bodies (vehicles that house the human souls). However I am suggesting that from the beginning of creation the Ophanim possessed the power to materialize and dematerialize at will. Entering into the physical realm via an animal or clay figurine was not beneficial (spiritually for the soul)—but then again the soul did not come here for the purpose of a spiritual experience.

These beings made of clay by Obatala were brought to life by Olorun and they began to build a village of homes like Obatala's near his home. When Obatala's drunkenness wore off he became aware of all the handicapped, defective people that he had created. He vowed never to take another drink of strong wine and to become the protector of all those born with birth defects. Like the Bible and all other creation myths, over time people added and subtracted their own commentary as they saw fit.

Eventually Obatala became tired of his earthly abode and climbed the golden chain to return to his home in the sky. He told the stories of the Yoruba people to other gods who decided to visit earth also. They were given an order from Olorun to protect humans within their areas of expertise. But one goddess, Olokun, was quite disgusted with Obatala's success with the Ife. Olokun conspired a plan for vengeance against Obatala. She waited until

Obatala left Ife for his home in the sky. Then she summoned great waves to rise up out of the ocean, **flooding** the lands that Obatala had created. Much of the vegetation was destroyed. Animals, fish, and people were all drowned. There were only a few humans that escaped the flood by retreating to the hills. These people called on the messenger god Eshu, requesting him to relay a message to Obatala of the disastrous destruction on earth. He agreed to deliver the message only after a sacrifice was made for the sky gods. The people sacrificed a goat for Obatala and made a special sacrifice to Eshu. Eshu in turn informed Obatala of the deluge on earth. When Obatala was aware of the flood he sought the intercession of Orunmila for the lives of the stranded humans. Orunmila restored the lands and vegetation. The people saw Orunmila as their hero and requested him to never leave Ife. Orunmila agreed only to stay long enough to teach the people the esoteric teachings so that they would be able to control nature and predict future natural disasters.

Olokun, ruler of the seas, tried one last tactic to avenge the disrespectful use of creative powers that eluded her. She sent a message to Olorun that challenged him to a contest for weaving cloth. Olorun became distraught at the idea for he knew that his powers at weaving cloth were very limited in comparison to Olokun. However, if he ignored the challenge it would be seen as admitting to the universe that Olokun possessed a power greater than his own. This very act would have established and created a new universal order which Olorun was determined to avoid. It could have gone as far as to establish Olokun as the Most High. Olorun contemplated his dilemma and decided to send his messenger the chameleon to greet the sea goddess. The chameleon was instructed to tell Olokun that he happily accepted her challenge, but would like her to submit a few of her choice sample pieces of woven fabric to the chameleon first. Olokun was also told that if she was as good as she said she was then she should be able to first beat the chameleon in a competition for the best woven fabric.

Olokun was happy to display her finest woven cloth before the chameleon. The first piece was a pretty bright green cloth and the moment she handed the cloth to the chameleon he looked just like the cloth. The second piece was a sassy, bright orange cloth and just as with the green cloth the moment she handed it to the chameleon his body immediately changed to match the cloth. Finally Olokun took out her most prized fashion, a bright multi-colored cloth, and again immediately after the chameleon received the cloth, his body changed into many colors just like the cloth. The final cloth caused Olokun to conclude that if a mere chameleon could produce equally well all the colors of her creation then without doubt Olorun would be able to defeat her in competition. She sent a message back to Olorun through the chameleon stating that Olorun reigns supreme.

There are so many hidden esoteric teachings in this one small section of the myth regarding Olokun's challenge of Olorun (the Most High God) that an entire book could be written on it. Pay close attention to the feminine and masculine competition that is taking place. Why is it that Olokun is upset over Obatala's creation in the first place? WHY WOULD OLOKUN'S VICTORY OFFSET THE ENTIRE ORDER OF THE UNIVERSE? Did you assume that this passage was referring to a challenge regarding the fabrication of a cloth or a metaphysical representation of a challenge in creation of the universe? If you did figure that this was a metaphysical presentation, then who or what does the chameleon represent? Can you think of other questions that you should ask yourself about what is actually happening but is not being said? There are still many questions that you should ask yourself and seek answers for. I will leave this one for you.

The Yoruba religion, unlike some religions, carried its mystical and esoteric teachings side by side with its ethic and historical teachings. In explanation, let's compare other scriptural religions. The Torah/Bible's Old Testament, for example, speaks primarily of historical and ethic teachings. The Kabbala represents the mystical and esoteric teachings of the Hebrew people. Therefore, we have the Torah/Bible and the Kabbala. In Islam we have the Koran and Sufism, with Sufism representing the esoteric teachings of Islam. In the Yoruba religion, however, all aspects recognize the Ifa, which is the esoteric mystical and ethic historical teachings. There are several terms that we will have to become familiar with to understand Yoruba mysticism:

1. Orisha—The vast number of forces in nature that guide consciousness throughout the universe. The word is literally translated to mean "select head." In my own understanding the Orisha is simply the GOD energy or force that activates creation into existence. Without Orisha there would be only the void—no existence. Orisha appears to be what the Chinese people would call Chi.

2. Orisha Okunrin—The representation of masculine energy opposing Orisha Obinrin at an equal force in Yoruba cosmology. It is the same as yang in Chinese cosmology.

3. Orisha Obinrin—The representation of feminine energy opposing Orisha Okunrin at an equal force in Yoruba cosmology. It is the same as yin in Chinese cosmology.

4. Ase—Power

5. Oba—The chief, in tradition, inherits the position, just as from monarch to monarch. Each chief is initiated by becoming the spiritual descendant of Oduduwa.

6. Esu—Divine messenger

7. Ori—Consciousness of any existence. For example Ori of a tree or Ori of a dog, or wall and so on. If it exists, it possesses Ori.

8. Odu—In the teachings of the Ifa all manifestations of existence come into being through conscious energy patterns known as "Odu."

9. Awo—Refers to the secret or hidden principles of the cosmology of the universe. There is no exact English translation for this word due to the very strong sway toward the cultural esoteric mysticism.
10. City of Ile Ife—Prior to English influence, the Yoruba nation was centered around this city.

According to Ifa religion, creation is brought into existence by the polarity between two forces of expansion and contraction, which create light and darkness. The original forces, just as in the Ezzrath theory and many ancient myths, are the feminine and masculine energies, of equal yet opposite dynamism. These forces are known as the Orisha Okunrin and the Orisha Obinrin. It is only through the balance of the *Orisha ase* (conscious energy force) that life can become a reality. Ifa is not only indigenous to the Yoruba people but can be found throughout West Africa. The date at which the Yoruba migrated from the Middle East, under the leadership of Oduduwa, to Ile Ife is unknown, but can be roughly estimated to be somewhere between 500 B.C. and A.D. 400. The reason that this particular myth's date is undetermined is due to the lack of interest in archaeological research on the subject, in comparison to that of the Mesopotamia area.

The primary inspiration for *awo* (universal reality) is the connectedness between transcendent Spiritual Forces (the higher self, angels, archangels, and so forth) and human consciousness. *Esu* (divine messenger) is said to have close associations with Ogun, perhaps due to the character of Ogun and how he appeared to help the people out of dilemmas. The work done by Ogun is directed or guided by Ochosi, the Spirit of the Tracker. Ochosi sets people on the shortest path-distance to reach their intended goals; this act is called in Yoruba *iwa-pele*, meaning good character. It is said that Ogun appeared to the Yoruba people from nowhere out of the water. He helped the people establish law, order, and civilization very much like Jehovah set laws, but in a benevolent way. Ogun established circumcision for the people. Sound familiar? His name appears throughout the Yoruba nation of people in their names and land. Today in Nigeria there is a state known as Ogun state. Ironically, when I was married to a Nigerian my last name was Ogunbuyide (pronounced Oh-goon-boo'-ye-day). As you can see the name Ogun is very much alive in the Yoruba culture today.

The *ase* of Oshun takes on various Orisha. Her area of expertise lies within the Orisha *Awo* (nature's mystical force), that is Oshun possesses qualities like Mother Earth and our universe—forever creating. She is a goddess of passion and erotic attraction between male and female.

## Mythological Summary

In conclusion, it is a basic fact that all of the world's mythology, including the Bible, is in one way or another saying practically the same thing, with a twist on the original to suit the agenda of the god, people, and/or culture of a particular period. If one diligently seeks the truth and studies the historical facts then she/he will come to a new understanding and comprehension of all religions that were created by man and their individual gods. The most critical and ancient myth of all, written on the Sumerian cuneiform clay tablets, reveals the true story of the flood. The events and god characters were almost exactly identical to the story told in the Babylonian myth. Like the Babylonian myth, only Atra-Hasis and his wife survived the flood and were granted immortal life to become like the gods in the Sumerian account. In the oldest account of the story—in which we have Noah's character named Atra-Hasis—the behavior and cruelty of the gods is really exposed. It is almost enough to cause you to wish that you could literally seek that Satan being and strangle the living daylights out of him! Our poor Noah and other ancestors were tossed and driven by the whims of these self-centered gods. Zechariah Sitchin, in *The Twelfth Planet* (page 391), clearly gives proof that the loved Jehovah or his spirit type is given credit as having tried to destroy man in a flood—actually determined to exterminate mankind. Atra-Hasis continuously had to intercede to Enki/Ea on the behalf of the humans because Enlil (who had the same spirit as Marduk/Jehovah) desired to wipe out our species. Here I will quote word for word the actual account **written prior to the Bible** regarding Noah's dilemma, according to Sitchin's account of the ancient scrolls:

> He (Enlil) then proceeds to outline the extermination of Mankind through starvation. "Let supplies be **cut off from** (*notice the words, who else do you know that talks like this?*) the people; in their bellies, let fruit and vegetables be wanting!" The famine was to be achieved through natural forces, by a lack of rain and failing irrigation.
> "Let the rains of the rain god be withheld from above;
> Below, let the waters not rise from their sources.
> Let the wind blow and parch the ground;
> Let the clouds thicken, but hold back the downpour."

> Even the sources of seafood were to disappear: Enki was ordered to draw the bolt, bar the sea, and guard its food away from the people. Soon the drought began to spread devastation.
> "From above, the heat was not . . .
> (due to age, damaged, missing text)
> Below, the waters did not rise from their sources.
> The womb of the earth did not bear;
> vegetation did not sprout . . .
> (due to age, damaged, missing text)
> The black fields turned white;
> The broad plain was choked with salt.
> When the sixth Sha-at-tam arrived
> **They prepared the daughter for a meal**;

The child they prepared for food . . .
**One house devoured the other.**"

The texts report the persistent intercession by Atra-Hasis (*Noah*) with his god Enki (*Jehovah*). "In the house of his god . . . (due to age, damaged, missing text)
he set foot . . . (due to age damaged, missing text) every day he wept, bringing oblations in the morning . . . (due to age damaged, missing text) he called by the name of his god, seeking Enki's help to avert the famine".

Check out the only difference in this creation story compared to all the other creation stories with a flood. The original creation story is the only story that states that this was not an act of gods or, in the case of the Bible, Jehovah. It states that it was a natural disaster and the only way in which the gods/Jehovah added their folly to man's battle with the deluge is the fact that the gods/Jehovah held a council meeting. It was Enlil/(early) Jehovah, whose voice was walking in the deep, who had decided that the human race had to be driven off the face of the earth. He thus sealed the fate of mankind with the gods. He got the council of the gods to agree that man would not be forewarned of the shift in the earth's axis which would cause severe flooding, destroying most life in that area. Absolutely no god brought the flood according to the original mythical story presented by the Sumerians. It plainly states that when the deluge began the gods/Jehovah shook and shivered in awesome fear as they watched from their space station, the earthlings struggling for their last breaths. At the same time, keep in mind that these are supposedly prehistoric dum dums writing about space stations.

This added information places a seal on all the stories of our ancient ancestry for without doubt they all had a story to tell. The majority of them wrote their ideas as to how creation began and who played the acting roles in each creation story. Many of them spoke of a flood that destroyed both animal and human life. Only the original story appears to be the most truthful, stating that none of the deceitful gods from Ea, Enlil, Marduk, or Jehovah/Yahweh ever really caused a flood. At the most, one of these gods or several of them were in on a plot to keep the knowledge of an upcoming catastrophe a secret from the human race, thus cutting off inspiration from the Universal God force. There are so many gory details from the cuneiform text that if you had only known the things that Jehovah had done to your ancestors you might feel somewhat differently about him. Jehovah, the evil side, caused mankind to die in ways that you would have never imagined. The only way that you will find these things out that I am telling you is through the reading of *The Twelfth Planet, The Gods of Eden*, and other writings on ancient cultures and their gods or unbiased meditation. Analyze the chart of gods vs. cult centers vs. events. Note the similarities and the differences. After reading the chart ask yourself if it could have been possible that history could have been written down with the hidden agenda of the person or gods fabricating the story.

# EIGHT

## The Philosophy of Ezzrath on Illusions

### Reality or Illusion

Choosing truth and reality in a world filled with falsehoods and controversy can seem impractical and next to impossible, yet indeed quite the contrary is true for those who thoroughly research the **origins** of their beliefs. We must always remember that as children we receive the vast majority of our belief systems from our environment, not from within. The greatest influence on what we will believe in our lives comes primarily from our parents or the adult guardian(s) over our lives. For example, if we are taught race superiority in our homes as children more than likely we will believe in this concept until something happens in our lives to convince us otherwise (most likely from within). However, we humans need to begin reprogramming ourselves out of accepting whatever the general population identifies as truth, and begin playing the roles of Plato, Columbus, Martin Luther King, Jr., Darwin, and many other trailblazers. These people all stepped out and dared to say that society's accepted concepts were WRONG. We should identify the problems that are established within ourselves, that we have all been preconditioned perpetually throughout our lives and our lives' lives to live out our karmic cosmic roles as we create the story. Now the energy of our planet has shifted and it is now that people will begin saying enough is enough! We want to become enlightened and learn the higher spiritual truth of man directly from God. We are tired of, and disgusted with, all the religions of the world that have failed us. OUR LIVES (the entire human race) ARE THE LIVING PROOF OF THEIR FAILURE!

The first step to eliminating falsehoods from our lives is to take our most precious beliefs and throw them out on the table for examination. This does not mean to just immediately dismiss information that we have learned through the years, for some of it we will need to retain, such as "do unto others, as you would have them do unto you." But we must analyze what we believe now. For example, if we know that God is love and His mercy endureth forever and we accept this as a fact, then we see a verse where God tells a race of people to kill innocent babies, then we know that we should throw up the red flag and bring everything to a halt. Before we defend God's actions as justified because he is GOD, let us first prove that we are dealing with GOD! It's time for an investigation and analysis of all information available. I will illustrate with a personal example from my life of a precious belief that I was taught as a child.

Santa Claus was the most righteous and good man that I had known—second to Jesus, of course. No one could tell me that Santa wasn't the greatest. As a matter of fact one Christmas I wanted a Baby Tumbelina and my mother could not find the doll at any of the stores in my town. Finally she came home exhausted one day and informed me that she had looked in all the stores in town and that she didn't think that Santa would be able to find my doll for Christmas. I remember asking my mom why she was worried. I told her with all sincerity and surety, "Mama, you don't have to worry about anything, because I know that Santa never fails me and he always brings me everything I ever wanted on Christmas. He will find my doll; you watch and see. All you got to do is believe, don't you believe, Mama?" Needless to say, my mom left town for the major cities in our area and after searching in several cities she found Baby Tumbelina. I had no reason to doubt that Santa Claus existed, thereby establishing all my faith and belief that Santa was real and a good guy second in line to Jesus. Many years after this event I continued to believe in Santa, until at the age of thirteen, my peers in school discovered my belief and were laughing and teasing me that Santa wasn't real. BLASPHEMY, I thought. How could they say this about one of the nicest men on the planet? I remember them asking where Santa was, and I had all the right answers. "On the North Pole," I would tell them. I remember them trying to reason with me that "no man as fat as Santa Claus could fit down the chimney." I told them that Santa was magical; I didn't know how he did it, but I knew every Christmas he came to visit me. "Have you ever seen him?" they would ask. "Well, not in person because if you are not asleep when he comes to visit, he won't come any more." Notice my justification and rationale to keep my belief in Santa alive! Of course, my schoolmates would then burst out laughing and insisted that it was my mom placing the gifts under the tree. Well, I had all that any one human being could possibly stand! How dare they talk about my Jolly Saint Nick in such tones? And the fight was on.

When my mother had discovered that I was getting into fights at school, and with my cousins, she decided that it was time to reveal the *ULTIMATE DECEIT*. She took my precious Santa all within a matter of minutes. I shouldn't say seconds, because at first I continued to tell mom no it can't be true that she had been the person secretly placing all the gifts under the tree. But the denial came to an abrupt end, when she reminded me of all the times I had almost caught her putting gifts under the tree. She continued to claw my Santa away from my blind faith, reminding me of how insistent dad would be that mom leave Santa a fresh batch of baked cookies so that he could eat them. I remember asking her if what she had said about Jesus was false, too, and she told me that without a doubt trusting and believing in Jesus is our only hope to get to heaven. She said that only Santa was a myth.

Let's do an analysis of the warning signs that I had all along, from the very beginning of the spoon-fed Santa story.

1. I NEVER KNEW THE ORIGIN OF SANTA! I should not have relied upon what others tried to indoctrinate my beliefs to be.
2. Why was it that I was never allowed to see Santa?
3. How many people live on the North Pole, and why was he the only one?
4. How did Santa do things that were humanly impossible? I simply believed it to be so, therefore it was?
5. There were so many people who said that I had been deceived; why didn't I investigate for myself at that time?
6. Statements were said that did not make sense.

Had I taken my prized, precious beliefs to the library and researched Santa's history I would have never experienced the *ULTIMATE DECEIT*, the deceit where your most precious belief system is ripped away from your heart. What was Santa's origin? The answer is traditional trickery, not intended to be malicious, nonetheless deceiving, misleading, and tricking us from knowing the truth. I could have thrown Santa out on the table for research to prove whether or not this man truly lived and how he worked his magic (flying reindeer, going to billions of homes in one night, sliding down chimneys, etc.). I had no desire to research anything contrary to my belief systems. They made me feel good; therefore why seek the truth?

This may have been the reason why I never left the New Testament when as a Christian I remember reading it through twice and picking out my favorite verses that supported my beliefs in Jesus. I never once thought about it being possible for this man not to have existed or to have been possibly misrepresented through all the various translations had he existed. As I had stated earlier, I learned of my *Ultimate Deceit* during a young man's crusade to utterly rip the cords of my beloved Christianity from my very soul, only to throw me into another *Ultimate Deceit*, the hell of living as an Ancient Hebrew Israelite.

I never researched information regarding the origins of either religion. I simply studied and found the overwhelming information that supported them to be true. In Christianity, I had to never leave the New Testament, and as a Hebrew Israelite the only source that supported the Hebrew god as God was the Old Testament. However, by the time I had my Christ vacuumed from the very depths of my soul, I had learned not to just believe anything and everything handed to me. It appeared that the way of salvation was through the Hebrew Israelite religion, but now I had learned to analyze scriptures using common sense. The one passage that I maintained had no common sense whatsoever was the exodus out of Egypt with great miracles by God, and then the people turning against God simply because Moses was missing for several days. I would ask people whether or not they could witness all that the Israelites recorded in their history, and then turn their back on God, for a cow? The majority of us know that we have never seen God, let alone the powerful miracles performed in the Egyptian exodus, yet we remain faithful to an invisible low-key God. I knew that something was wrong. This alone made me keep plugging away for the original information as to how the Hebrews evolved.

Did we Christians have warning signs about Christianity? Yes, we did! At least let me say I did. From as far back as I can remember, I have known about the fact that science and religion clashed on the theory of creation versus the theory of evolution. How many of us have taken time to investigate whether or not we could establish one theory against the other? I know that I didn't. I remember a preacher ranting and raving over foolish scientists making up the story that we came from monkeys. I remember him saying that the Bible says we were created in God's image, not the image of a monkey. But you know what? He never once mentioned that he had researched all the information available, nor did he care to investigate or prove this Darwin character wrong. THIS IS THE BEGINNING OF THE *ULTIMATE DECEIT!* Our religions teach us that each different one is the true and only way, but we NEVER think to investigate for ourselves— TRUTH. Truth has absolutely nothing to do with why we choose a religion. As youngsters we simply chose the beliefs of our parents. If we take a notion to become religious as adults most of us choose a religion based on how it feels. DO YOU HAVE THE SAME RELIGION AS YOUR PARENTS? THEN MORE THAN LIKELY *ULTIMATE DECEIT* IS YOUR POSSESSION! If you simply believe and hope without any research other than a document printed to support your belief, then you have literally set yourself up to be deceived.

In order to begin the process of eliminating falsehoods from our lives, we must become committed to making a conscious evaluation of every belief that is instilled from our youth. Ask yourself: How much of what I know is truth? How much of what I know is believed true simply because of one book, and a parent or significant other has convinced me that it is true? One great way of eliminating the deceit is to first be honest with yourself. When there are contradictions to what we really believe and know to be truth, we can rest assured that somewhere, somehow, lies and deceit have crept into the picture.

Identifying contradictions can prove very difficult indeed. If there are contradictions, then who is to say that our belief is the wrong one?

Q. How do we know, if we believe in a book that says, "God can never do anything bad," and then it turns around and admits that God creates evil, that we can indeed establish that there is a contradiction in God's word? We know that we have established a direct contradicting testimony. Nonetheless, can't we simply assume that perhaps man made a small mistake in saying "never," or perhaps he meant to say that God is good, but when man does wrong it activates His wrath? Yes, it is changing what was said but we are made in God's image and we would get angry or punish our children for doing wrong.

A.  If we have just this one or even several conflicting entries of information from **ALL** gathered information in both our history (tracing documentation back to the beginning/end of prehistory) and our sources (Bible, Koran, Torah, and so forth), then we can feel safe that we have the highest obtainable truth. However, if there is an overwhelming number of contradictions within the source alone, we can rest assured that the red flag for detailed investigation (only if there is a quest for truth) is required if one chooses to obtain the highest truth obtainable. If we have both over- whelming contradictions within the source (Bible) and history (*Enuma Elish*) documents that the origin of the source was based on fabrication and shared myths, then we know that the source has proven itself a falsehood.

Q.  I can admit that there are contradictions, but I could never picture myself giving up my precious Jesus and His plan for salvation. What should I do?

A.  Count yourself as one of the lucky ones for you are on the path of truth beyond imagination. There are so many Christians who will never ever admit that there are any contradictions in the Bible. Many are caught up in believ- ing only, and justifying their belief system as if it were reality. It is sort of like my belief in Santa Claus that I men- tioned earlier. You see, it hurts so much to give up a concept that you are devoted and loyal to and which has comforted you beyond the description that mere words could tell. We can personify God as we see fit (information from our God sense) as Jesus, Allah, Yahweh, or The All

Highest Light, Eyah Asher Eyah (The Great I Am), The Creator, and so forth. Therefore, remember that you don't have to be stripped of Jesus. I was told that I was headed to hell on my Christian path and when I saw that Christianity no longer held real meaning for me, my soul exploded from within and I thought for sure I would die and go to hell. Ironically, had I written this book just three years ago, I would have told Christians that they were doomed for hell's fire, according to Hebrew customs. I KNOW BETTER NOW. Take your time, be patient with yourself, LOVE YOURSELF, read, meditate, and most of all trust the Creator to answer your prayers.

Q.   How do we commit treason against everything our souls have spent a lifetime loving in complete confidence?

A.   YOU DON'T. Again, simply continue to read, evaluate, and meditate on all accessible information. DO NOT LIMIT YOURSELF TO ONE SOURCE! I guarantee that you will be enlightened and in peace as you become enlightened. Pray to Jesus, in the name of Jesus, that he helps you to find the **TRUE CHRIST**. Tell him that you have no interest in serving a false anti-Christ. Say, "Jesus, I know that you said that there would be many false Christs after you, and I am seeking absolute truth. I trust you to lead me and guide me on my quest for truth and knowledge. I ask that you let me see you in universal reality and truth. And finally, I thank you for revealing truth to me. Amen." We can pray in the name of Yahweh, in the name of Allah, or simply Dear Heavenly Father. God the Creator of the Universe understands the dilemma that we have been placed in. He understands why we make mistakes and how we are delivered into deceits, but He cannot forgive you for them, BECAUSE . . . the true Creator can find absolutely nothing wrong or sinful within creation. Trees, dogs, cats, pigs, flowers, and, believe it or not, even humans are incapable of breaking the will of God or hurting God's heart. I must inform God's children that they are not as powerful as they believe! Just imagine it. BREAKING THE WILL OF GOD!!! IMPOSSIBLE, WITHOUT DOUBT. Sin, committing treason against God's will, grants you the power to overcome the desires of God. Fortunately, we are not that powerful.

Q. How is it possible that we humans cannot sin or hurt God? How is it possible that murderers, adulterers, thieves, rapists, or a downright evil-to-the-bone person is incapable of disgusting a righteous God?

A. **The true Christ, the Real Universal Source, does not choose righteousness over love.** As a matter of fact, righteousness is a newly created term in the history of mankind. God loves a murderer no less and no more than he loves a "righteous person." He is pure and unconditional love energy just waiting for us to plug into His outlet. Rather than being against sin, God stands for love. If we are honest with our God sense, we know that no murderer has committed an act of murder without God sustaining her breath while she committed the act. I believe that no person dies before his or her time.

Q. What about when children are murdered?

A. Yes, it was their time to return to the spirit world, and more than likely, the child took part in the decision to depart early in advance (prior to ever being born). This is especially true of young children who are more attuned to the Universal Energy; they often know of their fate even before it happens. We choose our parents, our race, and many of the major events that will help us to evolve spiritually on our paths before we are born. Therefore, although the death of a child is gruesome and painful for us humans, we must remember that it is only because we think as humans.

I guess the best way to answer this question is with a question. You tell me, why is it that so many people say that they love Jesus and that they cannot wait to be with Him, but they do all within their power to delay the trip to meet Jesus? The human soul wants to see and be with God, but they don't want to die to get to the other side. This is a human reality for most of us, and we know it makes no sense. If God sees fit not to intervene in the loss of a cardinal life (thereby creating a gain to the spirit world) of a child and allows another soul the opportunity to make a mistake (commit murder) to begin the spiritual evolution of that individual, is it really as bad as we feel it to be?

In all honesty this is the one belief that God has placed in my soul that is indeed a hard pill for even me to swallow. If someone murdered my child I think that I would want to see that person harmed—perhaps murdered, too. Therefore, this belief does not meet the burden of proof for the common sense rule. I will not at this time say that I know this to be true, but that I believe it to be true. The supporting belief that we all have is found in the Bible, "and His mercy endureth forever." God is true and of perfect love; the average God-fearing person believes this theory. Then why doesn't God stop the murder so that neither the murderer nor the victims feel pain?

I am convinced that God does and can stop deadly events assigned to the lives of various people depending upon how well they have evolved and prepared themselves for the next world. Hence, these events (NOT TRAGEDIES) are used as educational tools in the course of "Life 101." A tragedy (in human mentality) of this magnitude affects and touches all of us. Many of us learn from the mistakes of others. Both the victim and the murderer have shared an experience together; one is experiencing giving pain while the other experiences receiving pain. When we receive pain we know what it is to hurt. When we are hated, we learn how it feels to hurt. When we are tricked, deceived, and manipulated, we know what it feels like to hurt. When we are battered, raped, and robbed, we know what it feels like to hurt.

By now we should see a trend. Everything that hurts us we call sin and evil, if it is caused by another person. But now if I take a skiing trip and decide to get careless and run into a tree accidentally there is no offense whatsoever. We say it was just one of those unfortunate things and "NO ONE IS TO BLAME." If I eat myself into oblivion and gain a quarter of a ton and die, no one is going to yell that I should burn in hell for killing myself. If a child runs out in front of my car just as I was passing (going the speed limit) and gets killed, most people will not feel that I will burn in hell. Moreover, when God allows billions to die in the acts of nature over the millennia, the majority of humans express compassion, but we never feel that God should go to hell for expressing His will. We say, "Oh, how terrible, it was an act of God." Is it possible that the act of murder and the act of being murdered are both acts of God? Think about it. What does each individual gain? Once we understand death and the angels that are sent to help us in the transition from life to death (in the midst of a cruel beating or end days of terminal disease and so forth), then we may not see murder as the worst fate to happen to a person. However, to see a perfect divine will and plan for the evolution of "suffering" (murdered) souls will present a tendency toward contempt and anger by humans blinded by the illusions of our physical existence. That makes it next to impossible for humans to realize that the overall plan of the universe is so perfect that ultimate error is impossible for the creations of the Highest Creator God.

Q. Aren't you simply trying to condition us to believe in your concept?

A. Absolutely not. I have always requested that you do not take my word for the things contained in this book. The fact that I am human is cause to KNOW that I may have interpreted wrongly some concepts or ideas that I have displayed. This is where your individuality comes in to decipher the truths of which I have spoken and throw away anything that you can prove a falsehood. Notice that I said, "PROVE." If there were any conditioning that I could hope place on my fellow human beings it would be to condition people to "THINK FOR YOURSELF!" Read information for yourself. Do not accept anyone's truth OTHER THAN THE GOD IN YOUR HEART, including my own. Inform yourself through reading historical and ancient records, stories, and data from the library. Do not HOPE for some-one else to give you the truth. GO GET IT YOURSELF!!! Reject any information that doesn't fit in with what your God sense tells you is possible. As long as you have first deciphered it!

Q. Sometimes I notice that you mentioned God sense and at other times you have mentioned common sense. What is the difference?

A. There is a huge difference between the two. The common sense will be right at least eighty to ninety percent of the time depending on the individual. But you cannot always rely on it. Sometimes it is better to go with common sense than faith or just believing, for you may be "JUST BELIEV-ING" in SATAN. The God Sense is NEVER WRONG!

How do we know the difference? Let's look at a situa-tion where the common sense tell us one thing and the God sense tells us another. In true Christian belief, when a person strikes another person the person who has been hit should not wish harm on the other person. They call this "turning the other cheek." Our common sense tells us that this is a bunch of crock! "If ya hit me, I'm hittin' ya back!" It is sort of like the Old Testament teaching an eye for an eye and a tooth for a tooth. On the other hand, when we exercise our God sense, we who are spiritually attuned know that a violent response is an animalistic, instinctual part of man's flesh, which serves the lower worlds. Then the God sense rationalizes that it does not choose to serve the lower worlds' activation of animal instincts of survival. It reaches for the higher worlds of universal trust. That is, the God sense automatically knows that the universe has already supplied anything and everything that the soul will ever require for ultimate survival. Therefore, there is no need to activate our physical animal instinct, which has no sense of any such reality of submitting to the higher universal influences or in Christian terms, "God's will."

I would not call turning the other cheek God's will, but God's desire or service of higher realms of consciousness. The reason why it cannot be God's will is because we are capable of NOT turning the other cheek, therefore the act of humans turning the other cheek is not the will of God. Wisdom comes into play when we practice the knowledge of God sense. The majority of us would have a hard time practicing our God sense or using wisdom even if we had the knowledge to recognize the fact that "turning the other cheek" is God sense. Nonetheless, turning the other cheek is not common sense, but it is the higher choice of practice for human evolution.

Q. What is the difference between wisdom and knowledge? Aren't they the same?

A. Absolutely not. We will use an expressive equation to sum the answer for this one:

    a.   Knowledge without wisdom = fruitless, nothing, zero

    b.   Wisdom without knowledge = impossibility

    c.   KNOWLEDGE APPLIED = WISDOM

An example of the above expressions can be written respectively as:

    a.   A person knows smoking is bad for his health and continues to smoke, so it is fruitless to have known.

    b.   A person who hasn't a clue that smoking is bad cannot possibly quit smoking for the purpose of better health.

    c.   A person who knows that smoking is bad and quits smoking is wise.

Q. Why do you sometimes refer to God as if He could be a She?

A. The answer to this question is complex **only** to a people with a culture embedded in the patriarchal system. Our universe, however, is created on the basis of duplex universal energy. For every iota in the universe there is an equal and opposite letter of representation. The yin and yang in Chinese culture are seen as equal and opposite energies that stand for feminine and masculine energies. For every up there is a down. For every right there is always a left. For every closed door there is always an opened door. For every male there is a female and therefore, such is God, for God is all. We humans in general have culturally recognized only the masculine side of God. That is why I predominantly write as if God was only masculine so that we can feel a little more comfortable as we digest information. However, God is both male and female. Since our consciousness affects the will and outcome of our universe, we have inadvertently caused an imbalance to our universe through our beliefs.

How many of us ever thought to ask ourselves whether the Adam and Eve and the forbidden fruit story carried merit? It may have been possible that Eve never committed the first sin (mistake) of the human race as it was written in the Bible. More evidence supports that Adam, more so than Eve, was first in violation against creation (not the Creator, for he does not have the power to violate the Creator). Has anyone ever taken the notion to carefully examine the data on this spoon-fed belief? Generally, Bible followers believe that the wages of sin is death, and guess who has the highest mortality rate? **It is not the woman!** I was once told that Satan went to the woman because he already had the man, therefore there was no need to tempt the man. The closest verification of this story may be found in the story of Lilith (Adam's first wife) that is left out from the King James Version of the Bible and Adam in the Babylonian creation epic.

We know that in our churches today and in spiritual affairs, the woman is more interested in spirituality and also more inclined to invest time and effort to the cause than men are. When a child is in trouble in general it runs to mom first. I am not saying that this is the way that it should be, and I am not saying that there are no exceptions to the rule. But I am saying that feminine energy based on life experiences show us that women tend to nurture and lean more to a spiritual side, and men tend to protect and lean more to the physical side. You see equal and opposite, but yet we are both made in the image of God, yielding both feminine and masculine energy of EQUAL IMPOR-TANCE for both the man and woman respectively. Therefore, any human has the ability to tap into either side of the coin if they choose to do so. Simply because we are given a human body that is restricted to one gender does-n't mean that the soul, which is both male and female, will honor that physical limitation. So the bottom line is that God occupies both sexes simultaneously. One common reply that the men like to throw out as proof that they should rule over the woman is the fact that a man is gen-erally physically stronger than a woman. Therefore God made him stronger so that he could rule over her and pro-tect her. The answer to that remark is the fact that an APE IS STRONGER THAN A MAN. Need I go further?

Q. I was taught that the Bible is God's word. How can you know that the Bible is not God's word?

A. I have never meant to imply that the Bible was not God's word. Metaphysically speaking, the Bible and my book, too, are both God's word because we all share God con-sciousness as products of divine beings from raw Creator Force Energy. However, quite a bit of the material con-tained in the Bible includes the lower worlds of God reality. I am sure that I, too, may have taken some wrong turns in my concepts. When we say that a message or writ-ing is God's word do we mean that it came from God? Or do we mean that it contains all the information necessary to "press toward the mark," to reach our ultimate goal of returning to the Creator on high in sweet bliss? In the first case all books are the products of God. However, in the second case we must analyze the product of the fruit. Does it suggest that murder, rape, and stealing are things that God would want you to do? Does it suggest that love is the ultimate reality? You must decipher. This is why it is of the utmost importance that anyone's material—including mine—regarding who you are and where you come from, be thoroughly investigated. Every ounce of material on this planet originated from some place and it is up to you to find out where. The lower worlds are where we receive those nasty thoughts and acts that cause us shame; nonetheless, God (We) created all the shame, guilt, and pains of the lower worlds as teaching aids and tools for physical empowerment, called shadows. How can we learn love without experiencing hate? How do we obtain joy, peace, and happiness without the experience of hurt, confusion, and dismay? How can we eat and be filled without first being hungry? The only way that we know that we have experienced the higher worlds of love, peace, compassion, concern, joy, understanding, knowledge, wisdom, and so forth, is to experience the shadow of these experiences. The shadow of love is hate. The shadow of peace is disharmony. The shadow of compassion is vanity. The shadow of concern is selfishness. The shadow of joy is sadness. The shadow of knowledge is ignorance. The shadow of wisdom is the acts/deeds of ignorance.

A baby can provide an excellent example of why it is necessary to experience agony to evolve to a higher state of being. Baby's first years in the world consist primarily of "Give me," "Give me," and "Give me." They want their bottoms changed, a warm blanket, and a bottle of milk, all RIGHT NOW! It is of the utmost importance in their entire world that all these things happen NOW. Needless to say, this will not happen for the newborn, causing her to experience pure agony. And she makes everyone in the home know her dilemma with a mind-curdling high-pitched shriek of crying that attaches itself like a leech to the spinal cord of any adult in close proximity. Over time this baby will learn patience, without the agony of waiting to get her desires satisfied, if she chooses to do so. She will learn that the warm blanket, changed diaper, and food do not all come now, but it will be okay soon. As long as mom is taking care of the situation, baby learns a new concept called patience. It is when we choose not to evolve or learn that our souls will automatically gravitate toward the reception of the lower worlds. This is how we become victims (diseased, murdered, robbed, cheated, hurt) or perpetrators, both of which are brought about from human vibrations of the lower worlds. Regardless, we will learn and evolve to higher states; it is our choice as to when and how we decide to evolve. (See the pyramid on evolution and degression.)

Q. Why should anyone believe you?
A. You should not believe anyone who tells you this is the way that you should live your life. After all, you only get one lifetime per trip to the physical world. You have to make it count! What you should do is to take the information and store it in your memory bank as simply theory (Bible theory, Ezzrath theory, Darwin theory, etc.), then make sure that you do research for yourself. If you read only *The Ultimate Deceit, The Ezzrath Theory,* and then, simply because it feels good, leave your religion and believe this theory only, then you may be setting yourself up for deceit, because you must investigate my ideas and circumstances and where they came from.

Q. What is the greatest illusion among Americans today?
A. The greatest illusion of all is the doctrine of sin and hell. It teaches us to be judgmental of our selves and others. We develop fear and restriction from evolving into the higher essence within our souls. Not only do we suffer as individuals, but our children, friends, family and inadvertently the nation and the world suffer as long as we keep this illusion as a reality of the masses. Just like the illusion of cannibalism where one believes that if he/she devours the flesh of another person, all that the person knows and

strength will become his/hers. Cannibalism is an illusion that hurt the human race tremendously just as the condemnation of sin and judgement continues to destroy human lives.

If we pay close attention to our children, they can give us a reflection of truth; remember Einstein's theory—"it's all relative." They can show us in ways we never imagined why we smoke, do drugs, drink alcohol, eat the wrong foods, and become sexually perverted (rape, for example, not homosexuality). Yes, even the vilest of these actions are caused by the same type of behavior that a two-year-old terminator (the human infant) has in his reaction to the law "THOU SHALT NOT PUSH BUTTONS." A two-year-old may have been smacked on the hands umpteen times, and knows not to go inside the entertainment center and proceed to push buttons. But on any given day, when the adult spy (mom) cuts an eye out of the corner of her socket and aims it directly at the unsuspecting terminator she will intuitively see the buttons calling the terminator. "Please, please come push me," they call out, and the terminator knows immediately in his right mind that these buttons are nothing but trouble, saying to himself, "Nope, this is not going to be good for me." So he immediately looks toward the adult figure for strength in resisting the forever ringing, nagging, persistent voice of the buttons from the dark side. But the adult appears not to be paying attention; she stands there silently without hint of the usual "no, don't touch," and by now the chatter is nearly clawing at the soul of the terminator. Mom knows that her child will need to learn to control non-profitable desire so she purposely stands quietly hoping that this time the child will abide by the law. The terminator then gets the greatest idea in the world. "Let's take another look at our adult figure person," his mind reasons: "No complaints there." Then turning back at the buttons, now seeming to move and sway like on a hot summer road in the distance, the persistent buttons began summonsing the soul of the terminator, "Push me, push me, please, please, push me." Then the infant decides to take one last hopeless look at the adult figure for help in resisting the dark evil of the shiny button's suckling call. The terminator smoothly convinces himself, as he justifies a new law. "THOU SHALT TOUCH!" MOM'S NOT WATCHING! "Besides," he convinces himself, I won't touch, I will just look and look only." And before the spying adult can reach this amazing two-year-old octopus terminator, he's dashing off just for a closer look at the shiny-evil. Without realizing just when or how the evil buttons became activated, the TV and stereo are blasting, startling both the adult and the terminator. The dismayed terminator finds that added to his profound confusion of the situation, is the adult figure spanking hands once again as he's hauled away to sit in the corner to figure out how all of this hell came about so suddenly.

This illustration clearly shows the tug-of-war of the two sides of the coin. One side of the coin wishes to conform to set rules (like the universal law), thereby pleasing our parents (The Creator, God, Universal Light, Higher Self, upper worlds, etc.). The other side of the coin wishes to yield to urges and desire, thereby serving Destruction, Satan (the enemy), Universal Darkness, the lower self, lower worlds, etc. Our religions have dubbed these sides of the coin "righteousness" and "sin" respectively. However, as we have learned, these terms have been invented for the enslavement of mankind's soul for various personal agendas. We cannot sin against God, nor does She look for your righteousness. She just "IS." Just like we are. A better way of defining the terms of "sin" and "righteousness" would be "serving the lower worlds" and "serving the higher worlds." Please don't think I am saying that sin is the same as serving the lower worlds. I am saying that sin does not exist because it gives authority to an individual to displease or hurt God. ABSURD! God could not care less whether you choose to serve the lower world or the higher world. You can take a hundred lifetimes in the lower world. What the hell, take ten thousand billion lifetimes in the lower worlds. Why not? After all, God has all of eternity for you to burn out hell's fire (which is only DESIRE). Would you like to take an eternity? That is our great God, and you will still keep going and going with Her love the same as it was in the beginning. I swear, my friends, I have learned that there is no end to this process. Life's heights of wisdom and higher worlds are as perpetually endless as the song about the bear that climbed the mountain. What do you think he saw? He saw another mountain, he saw another mountain, and he saw another mountain. And what do you think he did? He climbed the other mountain, he climbed the other mountain, he climbed the other mountain. And what do you think he saw. He saw another mountain… and so on. The lower worlds of desire are similar, only substitute "valley" for "mountain" and "tumbled down" for "climbed." As intellectual and spiritual creatures, we may choose at any point in time to take the valley or the mountain and change our minds back and forth. It is all up to us.

However, if our goal is to become proficient in higher worlds, then we must align ourselves in perfect harmony with the universe for optimum human evolution. Our desires should be to perpetually uplift the self into partaking of the higher worlds and serving these worlds by assisting the next journeymen on the path to the higher worlds. HOW DOES ONE UPLIFT THE SELF TO THE HIGHER WORLDS?

1. Learn the higher knowledge of unconditional love and act it out daily and religiously create wisdom.
2. Reduce and eliminate UNCONTROLLED desire. Develop discipline.
3. Maintain a fully charged and balanced energy chakra system.
4. Charge the body with life-building essential nutrients and minerals such as found in raw fresh fruits and vegetables, juicing religiously, and adding supplements as needed.
5. Charge the mind with universal knowledge daily.
6. Exercise the body at least four to five times weekly; aerobic and stretching are both essential.
7. Meditate on evolving to the high worlds. Sit in full lotus if at all possible. Half lotus is better than simple crossed legs (Indian style). Imagine in your mind's eye looking out through the universe past Pluto as far as your mind can take you and SEE THE WHITE LIGHT. It may feel artificial and silly and that's okay; it's just the lower worlds of condemning energy. Welcome this feeling and say to yourself it is okay, thanks for the warning, I am simply trying a new technique for raising my consciousness. Then release the feeling. Mentally push a white light out of the top of your head dead center into the white light, mingling the two lights. Imagine that the upper white light then unites with your body through the base of the spine and up through the chakra center with pure white loving Creator Energy. Feel the sensations of love and release worry, doubt, and concerns. KNOW that the Creator has engulfed you with love and protection and that nothing can harm your essence. Thank the Creator for all the blessings that have come your way and will come your way.

Most of all, thank God for your growing pains. Know from the depths of your soul that you are drawing nearer to the Universal All That There Is, The Great I Am. Amen. Finally, bring the white light up and out through the crown, allowing it to totally shower your entire body.

8. Practice breathing techniques and raising Kundalini daily.

9. Visit the God in you frequently. See #7. See the white light getting closer and closer as you become more in tune with God.

10. Practice excellent elimination habits. If necessary use antioxidants and cascara (an herb), nature's laxative. Colonics are recommended. As always the care taken of the physical body must also apply to the mental/emotional and spiritual body. Eliminate the garbage of the lower worlds, such as anger, hate, fear, condemnation.

11. Fight body dis-ease, with recommended herbs, mental vibratory chants for healing, and color therapy as recommended for your particular ailment, along with following your doctor's directions.

12. Above all, recognize yourself as a divine piece or part of the Divine. YOU ARE GOD! See the ocean example in the section on the Human Energy Field.

## Illusions of Language and Speech

The human language contains great amounts of information regarding our spirituality and history. The word "history," for example, literally means "man's story" and the word "prehistory" means "before man's story." Most of us never pay attention to the words we use daily that can give us so much added knowledge about ourselves. Where does language come from? Did we just start talking or was there some outside interference? Our languages were developed from somewhere. His story tells us that man first began writing his thoughts down somewhere between 3000 to 5000 B.C. in a language known as cuneiform. Therefore, any times prior to 5000 B.C. are considered prehistoric. There are so many words in our language that uplift and destroy spirituality. We use them daily without any conscious association as to the boundless spiritual consequences.

The greatest and most widely known of all words within the English language for its conscious spiritual effects is the word "love." Without the word "love" our world would become utter chaos. Families would crumble. Life would end, as we know it. The Mother Earth would have no one to care for her and would be destroyed by lack of empathy, and feeling for others. Families who repeat over and over daily their love for one another and really mean it from the heart will find that true love must become a certainty within that family. How many people have you seen arguing and fighting while stating over and over in sincerity, "I love you, I love you, I love you, Please, let's work it out calmly"? It is so impossible to fight the power of this phrase. It is our stubbornness that stops us from making the effort to say I love you when we have made a mistake or hurt another. And it is this same stubbornness or haughtiness that makes us fight, argue, and murder one another.

STUBBORNNESS is a word telling us so much about ourselves. We know that a stub can be any short piece of anything, such as a tree stub. Some amputees call the remaining leg or arm a stub. Well, being stubborn represents being born short. What are we born short of? We are born short of light (God). Not naturally or always but only at the time of stubbornness. When we love we reverse stubbornness to its greatest degree. Here in this section I will list several words that mean so much more than we realize.

1. History—his story (representation of all the past time after man became literate; that is, when man began to tell HIS STORY).

2. Prehistoric—before his story. This is the time before any recorded accounts of existence.

3. Stubbornness—an act that is "born short" (of light). Remember that any thing stubby is short.

4. Hello—(bringing) hell low. Satan (the enemy) taught us to greet each other in a manner of manifesting hell in our lives. Don't forget where our languages came from.

5. Levitical—Hebrew meaning "law." Corresponds directly with the English term to levy, meaning to legislate or set laws.

6. Lunar (moon)—lunatic. We can see how our language itself will teach us where spells have been secretly cast out on the Earth. It is commonly accepted knowledge that the moon is believed to affect the behavior of humans, animals, oceans, and so forth.

7. Santa Claus—Satan's Claws. Check out the play on Santa's letters, an original trick to place Satan's destruction in a magical word incantation. This is why the Jehovah's Witnesses are totally against Christmas worship on December 25th; they believe that it is originally all the work of the pagans.

8. Noel—"No God"! This word is sung by Christians yearly at Christmas time; they never realize that they are singing, "The first No God, No God, No God, cause born is the (their) king of Israel." Think about it. Who is NoEL?

9. God—dog spelled backwards. From the proud makers of the alphabet. An attempt of the black man to turn the magical use of the alphabet against his illiterate white brother as he regains civilization and literacy after the dark ages, around 1000 - 800 B.C. This plan drastically backfires against the black man, for the magical power of the alphabet turned backward was used throughout the spiritual kingdom to reverse the flow of karmic energy,

thus creating the white race more powerful and mightier than it had ever been before. The backward alphabet was handed down as a plan to destroy the white man and the entire human race through the unseen hands. Did the gods trick the black man into teaching the letters and words backward? Perhaps not the black man, but the enemy gods of the black man may have taught the whites their language through inspiration or physical contact. In any case, the bottom line is that now the fate of our universe/world lies within the hands of our white brothers who hold the key—you know who you are!

10. Christmas—Christ mass
11. Good morning—good mourning (weeping)—Again a trick, a play on words to encourage the human race to self-destruct through the use of affirmation, a powerful tool used for the positive or the negative, but in this case it has been used for negative affirmation.
12. Sunday—Sun god's day, the first day of the week. We worship the Sun god on this day.
13. Monday—Moon god's day and the second day of the week. We worship the Moon god on this day.
14. Tuesday—ME tewesday, OE tiwesdaeg, dies Martis day, meaning Mars day or the worship of the planet Mars. This is the third day of the week.
15. Wednesday—worship of the planet Mercury as a deity. It is the fourth day of the week.
16. Thursday—the worship of the god of thunder, rain, farming, called Thor. Thor worship takes place on the fifth day.
17. Friday—Freya's day, the goddess of love, peace, and fertility and the sixth day of the week.
18. Saturday—named after the god of planet Saturn, THIS IS THE SEVENTH DAY OF THE WEEK! Saturn's day.
19. Holiday—holy day.
20. Easter—Ashtoreth, the fertility goddess of the Bible; also

known in other cultures as Inanna of Sumeria, Ishtar of Babylon, and Isis of Egypt and so forth.

21. St. Valentine's Day—Most people are aware of the term "Bloody Valentine," but they fail to delve into finding out where it comes from. St. Valentine had murdered his girl-friend and cut out her heart, mailing it to . . . and thus we have our current day celebration of Valentine's Day.

22. St. Patrick's Day—He killed in the neighborhood of 36,000 druid people in Ireland in the name of Jesus, and it was recorded in history that he killed snakes. These so-called snakes were real people and we recognize him today as a holy man for this behavior.

23. Halloween—Originally a pagan worship of dead spirits, it corresponds directly with El's annual Sabbath, the perfect opposite being Satan's (El/Jehovah's enemy) annual Sabbath.

24. Holistic—holy characteristics, righteous in behavior. In the Ezzrath theory it is the application of service to the upper world kingdom.

25. Wholistic—wholly or complete and total. A wholistic lifestyle consists of eating food balanced holistically (without meat, white sugar, or white flour and so forth), a full spectrum of the human body's nutritional require-ments, exercise of mind and body, and spiritual meditations. It is a lifestyle with a complete balance in satisfying the laws of supply and demand to the physical, emotional, mental/intellect, and spiritual bodies.

26. Jesus—Ea or Zeus, the Mesopotamian god named Ea and called Zeus in its Greek form. Therefore those who are calling upon the name of Jesus actually call on Zeus. Ea has also been associated with the Roman god Jupiter. One can find in the Webster's dictionary that the word "Jesus" came from the Greek word *Iesous.* This was Constantine's way of having one Greek religion, for he

said that everyone's God was Zeus, the one and only God. He hellenized Christianity and took what had become their God (originally simply a messiah from god, like Moses), originally named Joshua in English and Yeshua in Hebrew, and forced the people to worship his God, ZEUS. REMEMBER EACH AND EVERY TIME THAT YOU CHOOSE TO CALL ON JESUS, YOU ARE CALLING ZEUS. The definition of hellenizing a religion is the act of adding Greek thought, customs, language, and style to it.

27. Christ, Kriste, Krishna—"the All Knowing", later corrupted to mean messiah and savior. The same as the word "bitch" meant female dog and was later corrupted to mean an impossible, loathsome woman. If we say today, "She's a bitch," the average person will think of a woman instead of the real meaning, a dog.

28. January—named after Januarius, Janus was an ancient Roman god.

29. February—named after Februarius.

30. March—named after the god Mars.

31. April—named after the female goddess Aphrodite.

32. May—named after Maius.

33. June—named after Junius.

34. July—named for Julius Caesar, a Roman emperor.

35. August—named after the successor of Julius Caesar, Augustus.

36. September—the seventh month in the early Roman calendar. The typical ancient and uncorrupted spiritual way of naming months. Originally all months of the year and all days of the week were named numerically.

37. October—the eighth month in the early Roman calendar.

38. November—the ninth month in the early Roman calendar.

39. December—the tenth month in the early Roman calendar.

40. Benevolence—represents the end of violence through ACTS of love, caring, mercy, and concern. A similarly known word that operates the same way would be benediction—The end of dictation.

41. Gospel—(God spell). Originally the Gospel meant literally "Godspell," which is exactly what religion does to the people, placing a spell upon them whereby if an individual speaks out a noteworthy contradiction to religious practice of the cult he is told either he should keep it to himself, or just accept quasi teachings, or finally be excommunicated. Regardless of merit, the person is shunned for his difference of opinion against the established religious cults, which believe that it is not necessary to prove sound standing belief customs, but more important to follow blind faith. "JUST BELIEVE!"

42. Tantra—considered sacred sex in which intoxicating drugs and alcohol are consumed (induced fits?). Tantrum—throwing of fits generally due to loss of temper control or manipulation.

43. Understand—over (stand). Here is a classic example of spiritual word trickery as a tool of oppression. This word was created as a representation of one's standing in knowledge; the white man's standing in knowledge. Therefore what has taken place here is classic Ultimate Deceit. Had he known that the black man (through his black god) was teaching him to be substandard—or under the standing of others—he would not have accepted this word trickery on his race. Our white forefathers were taught their languages from their black Levite forefathers (Satan, the devil).

Let me explain how I came across this information. Foremost I want to make it perfectly clear that I am not saying that the black man is Satan (the enemy). I am saying that Satan used the blacks/Levites as a tool to destroy the human race and when things were not working rapidly enough for his desire he (SATAN) raised up the white race (whom he had taught the black man was his mortal enemy) over all humanity. Thus he perpetually deadlocked mankind into destruction and division of his OWN SELF for as long as man sleeps in the illusion of self-denial. The trick was on both the black man and the white man and all the other HUE MEN (colored men) for they were turned against each other as an effort of the destructive gods to destroy all of humanity. In return for their destruction of our language, culture, wisdom, and lives we raised temples, days, months, holy days (holidays), festivals, rituals, etc., all to these gods who hate us.

The best example of this theory can be found in the Bible in Job 30:1, which states, *"But now they, that are younger than I, have me in derision, whose fathers I would have disdained to have set with the dogs of my flock."* Job continues on about how they were backward and without speech (grunting like an animal), living in caves. He even boasts that these men were outcasts! In the *Strong's Concordance*, looking up the word "younger" we find that there were originally two Hebrew words in place of younger and they are *tsaiyr* and *Yom. Tsaiyr* literally meant **"few in numbers."** It comes from the root word *tsaar* which implies the **act** of being brought to few in numbers. The second word *Yom* is usually learned on the first day of Hebrew class (*Yom tov*) meaning good day. *Yom* stands for "day" in Hebrew. Notice how the Hebrews write their sentence backward by wishing our day good. Or did they? We would have wished our good day. No, you say? Don't we say have a GOOD DAY and it makes perfect sense? Who is backward? In Zecharia Sitchin's *The Twelvth Planet* he makes a table showing the comparisons of the ancient alphabet to the modern alphabet. If you study the letters closely from the ancient side of the list you will discover that the letters generally opened from the left. In modern times (white rulership) all of these letters have been reversed.

It almost has a certain kind of eerie feeling, to see that some

# EARLY ALPHABET
## Disclosure of African Alphabet Turning European

| Hebrew African | Hebrew letters | Canaanite Phoenician letters | Early Greek Black letters | Late Greek European Letters | Greek African/ European | Latin European Letters |
|---|---|---|---|---|---|---|
| Aleph | 𐤀 | 𐤊 | △ | ◁ | Alpha | A |
| Beth | ב | 𐤁 | 𐤁 | B | Beta | B |
| Gimel | ג | ∧ | 𐤂 | Γ | Gamma | G |
| Daleth | ד | △ | △ | △ | Delta | D |
| Hey | ה | 𐤄 | 𐤄 | E | Epsilon | E |
| Waw | ו | Y | Y | V | Waw | W |
| Zayin | ז | I | I | I | Zeta | |
| Heth | ח | 𐤇 | θ | 𐤇 | Heta | H |
| Teth | ט | ⊕ | ⊗ | ⊗ | Theta | |
| Yod | י | ⟨ | ⟨ | ⟨ | Iota | I |
| Khaph | כ | 𐤊 | 𐤊 | 𐤊 | Kappa | |
| Lamed | ל | 𐤋 | ✓ 𐤋 | L ∧ | Lambde | L |
| Mem | מם | 𐤌 | 𐤌 | 𐤌 | Mu | M |
| Nun | נ | 𐤍 | Ͷ | 𐤍 | Nu | N |
| Samech | ס | 𐤎 | Ξ | Ξ | Xi | X |
| Ayin | ע | O | O | O | O(nicron) | O |
| Pe | פ | 𐤐 | 𐤐 | 𐤐 | Fi | P |
| Tzaddi | צ | 𐤑 | Ͳ | M | San | |
| Koph | ק | Φ | Φ | Ϙ | Koppa | Q |
| Resh | ר | 𐤓 | 𐤓 | P | Rho | R |
| Shin | ש | W | 𐤔 | Σ | Sigma | S |
| Taw | ת | 𐤕 | T | 𐤕 | Tau | T |

If a comparison is made of the Early Greek versus the Later Greek Alphabet, one can see the uncanny mirror translation placed on the language of the alphabet given to the white man versus the one handed to the blacks in an attempt to cause the human race to self-destruct.

being purposely turned our alphabet backwards, without any explanation. Look at the ancient Greek (black man's) sigma and then look at the Modern Greek (white man's) sigma. Look at Nun, Mem, Aleph, Beth, Gimel, He, Vau and so forth . . . the modern man turns them all around BACKWARDS! The words in our languages influence our creativity; we must never forget this. Therefore, if we have backward, hell-raising, ignorant expressions of speech which vibrate on a frequency attuned to the lower worlds, then we unconsciously speak these things out into our physical reality. WE CREATE OUR (HELL) REALITY. It would be to our advantage to eliminate all negative incantations on our species through such trickery.

I don't believe that the entire English language creates standard blocks in our evolution, but I do believe that words such as the daily greetings of bringing hell low or good mourning cannot be good for us. My family always greets our guests, as did the ancients by saying, Peace (English), Shalom (Hebrew), Nameste (Chinese) or Salaam (Arabic) all meaning Peace. Now ask your God sense, which sounds more godly, or of a higher evolution, the greeting bringing your guest peace or the greeting bringing hell low? Which would you prefer to obtain, an **under** standing in knowledge or an **over** standing in knowledge?

As always, of course, these ideas are presented to you only as tools of awareness. What you do with the tools now in your possession is entirely up to you. I will seize the opportunity here and now to say that ANYONE WHO TELLS YOU (INCLUDING MYSELF) THAT THEIR WAY IS THE ONE AND ONLY WAY, RUN LIKE HELL. However, as always, in our universe there are exceptions to the rule. If you know that a leader of an organization is dictating that their way is the absolute and only way in life and you feel an overwhelming sense of compulsion pulling you toward that direction you should go for the experience. There will be a great lesson for you there that your soul needs to partake of regardless of the mental/physical outcome. Always but always remember, YOU CAN NEVER GO WRONG FOLLOWING YOUR "GUT INSTINCTS," THE INNER VOICE! Our inner voice always places us in the right place at the right time regardless of how much hell it may seem to have gotten us into. Hells are only lessons that we create to evolve our souls individually and collectively to the next playing level. Never make the mistake of believing that life as we see it now is all there is to life! Once we evolve to the next and next and next degrees of wisdom there will always be a next degree to infinity. Some say that we reach nirvana at the end of infinity when we at last know all that there is to know. Buddhists call this knowing "enlightenment." They say that once an individual obtains enlightenment they enter into "sweet bliss," the state of all knowing, becoming a Kriste.

# N I N E

## S a l v a t i o n

### The Plan for Salvation

Salvation is a concept of varying concern to the human species, for some feel that it is of the utmost importance to those persons who become "fanatical" within our religious "faith" type beliefs. Some feel that it is important, but too far away to consider now. Some feel salvation is important and near, and others feel that they could not care less about salvation, the "here today, gone tomorrow" syndrome. Nevertheless, whatever your concern for salvation, I hope that in my explanation regarding salvation you may find some identity within the depths of your very soul that will indeed free (**not bind**) you and bring you closer to the Creator. I hope that there may be more of a consideration for our language and conscious awareness of who we truly are. For without doubt religions have tried to bind you to god in fear of god, but in reality there is freedom in GOD— freedom from fear granting UNCON-DITIONAL love regardless of what we may choose to do.

First, it must be pointed out that salvation is a relatively new concept, added to our universe sometime during or just prior to Noah's time. The first salvation gods may have begun with Nimrod, Osiris, Jehovah, and other deities. The dictionary defines the word salvation as:

1.    a: deliverance from the power and effects of sin

b: the agent or means that effects salvation

c: Christian Science: the realization of the supremacy of infinite Mind over all bringing with it the destruction of the illusion of sin, sickness, and death

2. liberation from ignorance or illusion <Science is author-itative truth and the promise of ~ - L. H. Harshbarger>

3. a: preservation from destruction or failure

   b: deliverance from danger or difficulty

With these examples from the dictionary, we can safely assume that the first definition rings true for most religious people within their concept of salvation. For the Christians, salvation lies in the Christ Jesus solely. They believe that without Jesus their souls are totally lost. If one uses only the New Testament for a source of information and nothing else this will be the closest truth that one can obtain. However, the New Testament is not absolutely the only information available to mankind. The Hebrew Israelites believed that the only way to find salvation was through their god, Yahweh. Yahweh was a salvation deity who did not mean to share his throne with anyone, including Jesus. See Isaiah 43:11-16, "*I, even I, am the LORD; and* **beside me there is no savior** (clearly there is no savior other than YAHWEH, NO SON Jesus as savior, unless we choose to believe that God may not have known that a Son savior would have been born to redeem man—which is senseless). *I have declared, and have saved, and have showed, when there was no strange god among you: therefore ye are my witnesses, saith the LORD, that I am God.*"

The Egyptians, depending on which era we discuss, believed that their only chance for salvation was in the father god Osiris. They had been deceived into believing that the path to immortal-ity was through death and began mummifying their dead and burying all sorts of valuable possessions intended for the deceived soul to receive on the other side. This practice may have begun before Osiris' appearance in Egypt, with the god Ptah. Buddhists believe that their system's doctrine is the only source of salvation. Muslim believe that without their god, Allah (the same Hebrew god Yahweh), all salvation is permanently lost. In the Hindu religion it is Vishnu, Shiva, Indra, or other gods who proved to be sole or multiple sources for the survival of mankind. Hopefully now we can see a trend developing here with these various religious beliefs concerning salvation.

The trend I see is that all religions have in one fashion or another put their total beliefs in the human power to harm, hurt, aggravate, and piss God off, which causes the Creator to become vengeful, vindictive, and destructive of **both the earth and human life.** The average religious person does not see their belief systems in this manner, but indeed this is what they believe and expect from their God. They take their human emotions developed from violation, betrayal, disapproval, and so forth to be the same emotions of the All Highest Creator God Himself. They put God on a human level of thinking so that he becomes just like those who have the power to define HIS essence. Therefore, the majority of religions will define God as a loving yet vengeful man in **NEED** of humans to worship him. Although the soul knows that the act of being vengeful or spiteful produces dark energy and does nothing good for the soul, when it comes to God people throw all common sense out the window. THE TRUE GOD HAS NO PROBLEM WITH TURNING THE OTHER CHEEK. ONLY CONFUSED AND LESSER-EVOLVED SOULS WILL FIND IT DIFFICULT! We are to have faith and hope and without it we burn eternally in hell. The average God-fearing person teaches their children not to be vengeful and spiteful. They know from the depths of their souls that the manifestations of vengeance and spite are not godly. Nonetheless, since men have written that God says that He is vengeful, they put our Great Magnificent All Highest Light, Raw Creator Force Person into a little punk man running around getting pissed off whenever human attention is not on him and HIM ALONE!

Why do I have to use the word punk? What would you call a man who did not like something that you did and held it against you to the point where he would come into your home and kill your children? I guarantee you that you will not use so kind a word as a punk. You would call this man the scum of the earth, a low-down, dirty, filthy scoundrel, unworthy of life, but I really don't want to offend anyone so I am sugarcoating your god's true nature as much as possible to relay my ideas without the loss of the message. I know that offense will happen anyway because the truth cuts like a two-edged sword. People love their religions and traditions more than they love TRUTH and God. People will not see my heart of love and my simple desire to seek truth and that I may err unintentionally. Without doubt I have made some mistakes somewhere in my philosophy, for no human who does not possess the power of lying down and picking up the flesh upon desire can confess *truthfully* that they possess all truth. However, I do believe that I have a higher truth in accordance with reality and the Creator than any religions on the face of the earth. My soul seeks and is a lover of our wonderful and magnificent Creator.

For proof that god punishes the children of those he is angry with instead of the person themselves look at Exodus 34:6-7. It states, *"And the Lord passed by before him, and proclaimed, The Lord, the Lord God, merciful and gracious, long-suffering, and abundant in goodness and truth, Keeping mercy for thousands, forgiving, iniquity and transgression and sin, that will by no means clear the guilty; **visiting the iniquity of the fathers upon the children, and upon the children's children,** unto the third and to the fourth generation."* If common sense is allowed to prevail we will see a grave injustice in punishing the children for the offenses of their fathers. But the only way that we can see it is to see our neighbor attack our child for something we have done. Then any and all will state that it is an ignorant, crazed act to do such a thing.

Which brings us back to the trend. **Religions, not God,** created the concept of salvation generally accepted by people today. They taught us to fear a vengeful, terrible god who, at any time humans made a mistake or offended him, would seek their destruction. In Christian belief, an individual can do all the good of the entire planet and slave for all of humanity, loving everyone, and doing nothing but good to all, BUT HE WILL DIE AND GO TO HELL FOR NOT BELIEVING IN JESUS.

Our religions have taught us that we have the capability to sin against God. Many of us who have religion will identify with this statement. They will agree that, yes, you can offend and sin against God, but they never look deeply at what they are really saying. They are saying that God has given them the power to hurt Him. Indeed, this is what you are saying when you sin against God. You believe that God has given you the power over Him, to hurt God by doing something He doesn't like and thus provoking him to vengeance. I say that you are saying that God gave you the power to hurt Him because common sense should tell you that if God does not want you to hurt Him, He should have the power to stop you. However, humans believe that God has passively given them the power to hurt Him, by not stopping them from sinning. Yet after He allows the violation to take place, God goes on a rampage of vindictiveness.

I used to believe this, too, and actually had the gall to feel sorry for God at how the people were mistreating Him. I prayed, "Oh God (I used to hurt for Him in meditation), I am so sorry for how my fellow man has hurt you out of ignorance. I am so sorry that they have turned their backs against you. Please forgive me for my sins for I know that I, too, have fallen short." I couldn't remember what I could have possibly done wrong from yesterday's prayer of forgiveness, but I had to have done something wrong for I had been taught that I was born and shaped in iniquity (sin). I remember saying to God, "I don't know what I have done wrong, but I know that I may have done something wrong, so please forgive me." I used to cry and ask God to help people see that they need Jesus. I would pray, "Help them to see how they are hurting you."

Now, I can see God smiling at my yesterday spirit, trying with every resource that it had to evolve to God. I thank the Creator for having led me down the path of understanding. I now know that I am incapable of sin, for I am perfectly made. Did I lose some of you? Let me state it again. WE ARE INCAPABLE OF SIN FOR WE ARE PERFECTLY MADE. Let me explain. You see, we all know that every human makes a mistake or they do things that are not in the best interest of the evolving soul. Some will say, that's right and that is sin. But, NO! This is not sin. The difference in a person committing a "wrongful act" and "sinful act" is the power added to sin. That is, sin gives power to an individual's soul to hurt God by an act of wrongdoing. I am going to define "wrong" doings or mistakes as acts that are against higher spiritual evolution. In other words, from the smallest of lies, cheating, getting angry, being spiteful, to the largest of adulterers, thieves, murders, and massacres, all are simply mistakes of missing our desired paths of universal evolution.

What a large pill to swallow, indeed. It seemed crazy to me the first time the thought came into my head from beyond. But from my research and my spiritual evolution, this is a fact of reality that I have found out about the Higher Source. I have found that human emotions are vastly different from those of the Creator. As we go through our ordeals as victims or violators, we forget that there was always an overall PERFECT plan for the evolution of our soul. We get so caught up in the suffering or, on the other hand, acting out of the violence that we lose touch with the Source and oneness of us all in God. Now when I have done wrong and things go wrong I know that there is some greater evolution for my soul and/or souls in contact with me and I seek out my greater evolution.

So . . . to make a short story even shorter, the absolute and sole way for a human soul to obtain salvation is through
## CONSCIOUS EVOLUTION!!!
## DID I SAY THE ONLY WAY?

Take the time to be careful and really search all the scriptures that are available to you and apply meditation for seeking the truth. Jesus called it seeking God's Kingdom first. DO YOU BELIEVE THAT GOD HAS A KINGDOM? If so where is it and what is it? THE KINGDOM OF GOD IS IN ALL CONSCIOUSNESS! This is what Yahshua, Jesus teaches us, that we must seek the kingdom of God or CONSCIOUS EVOLUTION. You will find that this was the sole mission of Jesus. He wasn't trying to get people to worship him. He wanted his fellow Israelite brothers to master the God-given universal power that exists within every human. If you are still having a hard time grasping conscious evolution please try re-reading the section covering Jesus' mission. Jesus states in Matthew 7:14, *"Because strait is the gate, and **narrow is the way**, which leadeth unto **life**, and **few there be that find it**."* So many clues in the Bible help us to at least eliminate the WRONG PATHS. Jesus clearly is telling us that whatever way any type of majority may seek for life, YOU SHOULD NOT GO THE WAY OF THE MAJORITY! He states that few will find the way of life! If you believe as do many, then you are not on the path to finding life, according to Jesus!

Now that we know what is needed for salvation, the next step is to know how to conduct and prepare ourselves for optimum conscious evolution. Always remember that every soul will evolve at some point in time. Yes, even Hitler and Satan (the enemy) all reach heaven in a matter of time. Of course, I know that I sound like a crazy woman, because I would have said that anyone trying to convince me that Hitler had hope in paradise is crazy. Once I found that God was actually TRULY an unconditionally loving God, I had no choice but to realize that "evildoers" are still loved by God, too.

Why shouldn't the bad people like Hitler get to burn in hell forever? They have tortured, hurt, mutilated, and killed so many people that the fiery pit of hell seems the only fair and decent thing for God to have happen to this type of person. In all honesty I must confess that this one religious belief feels so right because my common sense tells me that people who do wrong must be punished. I think that what we should pay attention to is not whether or not there is punishment for wrongdoing, but rather what kinds of punishments have been established by the Creator. Is there a hell? Does God sit around and mark each bad deed for punishment? I believe that the answer is no to each question.

Our hell was set up from the foundation of the earth so that whenever man dwelled within his lower conscience state he would receive the fruit of that energy. Said another way, when man broke the laws of nature (God) he suffered the consequences or "judgment" or "punishment" or "HELL." A typical example of universal law is the law that if one has frequent unprotected sex with multiple partners he increases his chance of venereal disease. When man obeyed the natural laws of the universe the reverse or HEAVEN would be the consequence, or judgment, or reward. The East Indian religions call this karma. Karma simply means that whatever type of energy you send out into the universe you will receive it back. There is absolutely no other hell in existence.

There are various ancient paths that mankind has documented that would cause a conscience evolution or human salvation. In this book we will only mention but a very few that teach in one form or the other the same human salvation that Jesus Christ himself was trying to establish. I believe Jesus to have studied both the ancient Qabbala and Hindu teachings of the Vedas. You will be presented with only enough information so as to set you on your path of research. One way is not better than the other, but only various individual expressions of light.

## Applicable Salvation
### The Breath

The most important aspect of human life that the average human rarely spends a conscious moment of concern about is the breath. The breath is the first sign of life. We breathe both day and night, while awake or asleep. The average human will never go more than a couple of minutes without performing this act throughout a lifetime. The most interesting thing about a breath is that it is attainable to the most poverty-stricken individual and if death calls it cannot be bought by the wealthiest billionaire. Furthermore, although man has fought over every physical possession in creation (land, houses, cars, children, religion, food, a dime, etc.) NEVER have I heard of a human fighting another human for breathing his air. Air is the most prized possession of this physical reality, yet we never kill or fight over it. We don't have to compete for who gets to take the next breath. Those of us who are healthy simply expect and know that the next breath will be available without giving a second thought as to how or from where it will come.

Unfortunately, the average human rarely breathes properly. Most of us unconsciously take short, empty, shallow breaths throughout the majority of our life. It is important to take deep, meditative breaths, which we will talk about later.

How many of us would quickly give a thumbs up at this statement: "We are human beings in search of a spiritual experience"? My path has taught me that quite the opposite is true: "We are spirits in search of a human experience." You see, once we realize that since before we were born we chose our parents (thus choosing our appearances), the major events in our lives, and even the lessons that will be learned during this life experience, then we can begin to see the world in a new perspective. When we can realize that our tragedies and failures actually cause us to evolve into higher states of consciousness, either individually or collectively (as in the case with the Hitler tragedy), then we know the overall plan for mankind. So . . . as humans this time around we will take the breath until the day that we either die or depart perfectly from this world. I am going to seize this moment to let you in on a secret that the gods tried to keep from mankind: YOU DO NOT HAVE TO DIE TO DEPART THIS WORLD! How about "not dying" as a plan for salvation? According to the Bible, Enoch did not die a physical death. YOU DO NOT HAVE TO DIE THE PHYSICAL DEATH! But we will touch on this a little later in this chapter.

It is through the breath that all physical living substance is sustained. Whether we breathe through our gills, or take in oxygen or carbon dioxide, without the breath life is nonexistent. Humans can heal themselves of disease, stress, anger, blockage, impatience, and many other vices though breathing techniques coupled with visual meditation. Focusing on the breath is a powerful tool for evolution and awarness.

### The Human Energy Field and the Three Human Aspects of an Individual

Another equally important part of a human being is the human energy field, or aura. Like our breath, when the human body no longer has a human energy field life ceases to exist. The aura reveals various aspects of who we are on a soul level. Many psychics do readings from the auric energy of others. If all people saw it, it would look like colors around the body, with manifestations of beings all trying to assist the soul into a higher evolution. Man has three aspects of equal importance requiring nurturing daily.

The first aspect of man is soul/spirit, but the highest aspect is spirit. The soul is raw creator God energy essence; the spirit is God and is ONE. To describe God, we must use a knowable physical comparison since true creator God is not describable. Let's compare God to the ocean. Our souls are like taking a drop of the ocean's water and placing it inside an animated vehicle (the human body). The spirit is the ocean or God. If a chemist analyses the drop of ocean water will it be anything less than ocean water? NO! The analytical report will precisely conclude that the drop of water is from the ocean. Likewise, we are God energy/matter. Our souls are metaphorically equivalent to the drop of ocean water. Think and compare in your minds the size of a drop of water compared with the entire ocean. Now diminish the drop by infinity and increase the ocean's size by infinity to obtain the closest physical illustration of our relationship and likeness of God to our souls. The soul has been in existence since the beginning of time. Our souls are comparatively more ancient than the earth. They contain all the knowledge of the universe in our DNA. The soul is so wonderfully made that if we simply learned to access our secretly encoded DNA links to universal knowledge, we would never suffer, never die, never have another disappointing moment. According to Buddha this enlightenment is nirvana or sweet bliss.

The second aspect is the mental or conscious aspect. Our minds are like the pathway or bridge to the ocean. Our minds are the connectors between the spirit and physical worlds. The mind can cater to either the soul or the physical body. Just like a computer stores vital information, the mind has stored information that the soul requires for astral travel and knowledge of the universe. The soul cannot relate to the limitations of the physical world. Both the mind and soul are immortal, regardless of our lack of knowledge or death, but this is not true of the physical body. For the physical body, the mind keeps the body activated and relays experiences so that the body can become mobile. A hand on a hot stove will relay a message to the mind through nerve endings and the mind tells the body that this is not the best place in the world for your hand. It forces the body to remove the hand involuntarily by activating pain. The body's mortality rate will be directly proportional to the individual's knowledge and wisdom (applied knowledge).

Third is the physical aspect. The physical body experiences matter in our physical world. Without a body you cannot hold a glass of water, let alone drink it. From communication that I have had with the spirit world, drinking water is one of the most missed physical attributes. Without the physical body the soul would no longer be bonded to the earth, but may choose to roam the earth. It would roam free to take on any desire or thought it created. However, we need to pull free of the limitations of the physical body's attempt to bind us to the ILLUSIONS within the physical realm through separatism of the individual from the whole (GOD).

## The Physical Body

Just as important as our meditations and daily walks with our higher selves is the upkeep and care of the human body. It will be the only source of transportation during this realm of existence. If we are in a coma we can continue to travel the other realms of existence as always, but we will lose total contact with this realm. The human body requires proper treatment and knowledge of the laws of creation (THE LAW) in order to maintain our bio-engineered robotic vehicle (the human body). It is one of the most amazing inventions in our physical world past, present, and future. It has a mechanical pump, known as the heart used for pumping all aspects of life—spirit (blood), oxygen, and nutrients—throughout every single cell in the entire bio-genetic machine. The lungs work like gigantic gas exchangers bringing in the air required for supplying fuel to the body, yet filtering out waste products automatically through the human smokestack, primarily in the form of carbon dioxide. The blood and vessels are the fluid and plumbing used to transport the waste/nutrient mixture to the process-purification plant, the digestive system and kidneys. The digestive system first processes and breaks down nutrients into workable components that the body will use for nourishment and sends waste byproducts to both the intestines and kidney for further process. During starvation or substandard waste elimination, the body can take nutrients from the intestines. Once in the kidneys, a filtering process begins and the chemicals/byproducts are removed from the blood and expelled through urine, and dumped into a storage tank called the bladder. The bladder is emptied at the individual's convenience, if not allowed to overfill.

In order for the human body to function it takes on many of the characteristics of fire (or fire takes on the characteristics of the human body, metaphysically speaking). A fire cannot exist without heat, oxygen/air, and combustible material. If the human body does not maintain heat somewhere in the neighborhood of 98.8 degrees Fahrenheit, it will no longer continue to function. Likewise, a lack of air and the combustible material (food and nutrients) will eventually result in inevitable equipment failure or death. This is the basic law of human existence. The more complex laws and rules come into play where we as humans have the choice of destruction or creation within our bodies. That is to say that we do not have freedom of choice to exist as humans and keep our bodies below the required body temperature. However, we can exist as humans with all manners of toxins pumped daily into our bodies. Our bodies were built to endure even the worst of lifestyles and still somehow manage to maintain heat, oxygen, and nutrients—physical life. We need to ask ourselves whether we wish to possess a vehicle that can support only the basic requirements of life. Will we be happy with dis-eased bodies that break down continuously? This is truly one of the laws of the universe (God). If we continually bombard our bodies with toxins such as junk foods, non-nutrient foods (like white sugar and white flour, and meat) and if we do not exercise, then the body will at some point break down prematurely. Every vehicle in our realm of existence requires good maintenance in order to sustain a long and complete life.

The salvation of the physical body relies totally on the possessor of the vehicle. One basic equation that I learned in my chemical engineering class that applies in every physical aspect of life is: INPUT = OUTPUT. Regardless of what we put into our bodies we will get exactly that same outward result. If we put junk into our bodies we get junk out of our bodies. That is what we make of ourselves. And we have that choice. Yah in the Old Testament tried to take that freedom of choice from the Hebrews. At various times he made it against his laws for the Hebrews to eat any meat at all and at other times he allowed only his designated clean meats. If someone disobeyed and ate pork the god of the Old Testament would make the Israelites punish all violators. Once we know the true law of God—UNIVERSAL LAW—then we can practice the law in wisdom and in truth.

Let us start with nutrition. This one will be a hard pill to swallow for my fellow Americans, but I must come to you with the truth as I have found it to be. Meat eating has taken a toll on us spiritually and physically. Doctors will tell you today that eating a lot of red meats causes high cholesterol. It is the one agent that causes heart disease that can lead to death. Have you ever heard a doctor tell you that eating too many green leafy vegetables might shorten your life? How about too many apples and fruits? Unless the doctor is a licensed quack, you will never hear of eating plenty of fruits and vegetables as being unhealthy. However, it is medically proven that quite the converse is true with the eating of meats (especially red meats and fatty pork). What have we heard about pork, red meat, and lots of meat in general? I feel that the number one contributor to the African-American people's accelerated death rate is the PIG, among others. Soul food may consist of collard greens drowned in ham hocks and salt pork (fat back), candied yams (submerged in butter and white sugar), macaroni and cheese (dripping with butter and extra cheese), and a huge country ham or chitterlings or deep-fat fried chicken. I have to admit I am getting flashbacks, causing me to laugh out loud. Nonetheless, my friends, as much as this meal and others like it may arouse our taste buds, a daily life of this type of eating will yield a certified guarantee from the universe of a shortened and diseased life. It may seem that death would be better than substituting the above killer meal with a life-yielding meal such as greens cooked with onions, red pepper, and a small amount of vegetable oil, and a baked sweet potato or steamed brown rice, and the lesser evil, baked skinless chicken. However, quite the opposite point of view comes into play if we really examine the true cause of our cravings. It's BAD HABITS.

We have forced ourselves from infancy through adulthood to acquire the taste habits that we now have. Let's face it, people:

Have you ever tasted a jar of baby food? I don't mean the fruits, but the greens, green beans, spinach, and so forth. I used to feel sorry for my children as I stuffed what I considered tasteless slop down their throats. I would have preferred to eat the jar. Nonetheless, babies eat this stuff as if it were fried pork chops with mashed potatoes and gravy. WHY? Because we are born pure and perfect, each and every one of us, but then we develop unhealthy eating disorders. The laws of the universe were created in our souls. Then we learn and develop another way other than the purpose for which we were created.

We humans learned the ways of the carnivorous beast. These beasts were created to catch their prey and rip its flesh apart with fangs. How many humans do we know with fangs? The pointed cuspids in front of the mouth on the outside of the incisors, although considered canine, are far from the sharp-pointed fangs of flesh-eating animals. Compare the lion, dog, or bear families, then look at the teeth of horses, monkeys, and cows. Humans were created with molars, incisors, and cuspids instead of fangs. Take an honest look at the other earth specimens with molars like the cow, horse, and so forth. They all eat only vegetables, just like the natural human diet. Nonetheless, we were given free will. Man has the authority to step outside of the universal law of higher evolved creatures and he has the power to manipulate the universe according to his will (regression into the lower worlds).

### Chakras

The human body has seven major chakra centers that are located in a straight line up and down the middle of the torso and out the head and pelvic area. These centers look like little rotating wheels of color energy. When all is well with the body, then the chakras rotate clockwise and are well defined in color. When there are problems within a chakra, its rotation slows down considerably. Sometimes the problem may be so severe that the chakra center stops, or worse, begins spinning counterclockwise. If left spinning counterclockwise for a long period of time the area which that chakra represents will eventually become diseased.

The word chakra is ancient and comes from the East Indian Sanskrit language; it literally means wheel. The chakras are simple and basic aspects of the human body. They are as definable and provable as electricity in our wall sockets. You can go to your nearest occult bookstore and they will either be able to sell you a chakra-locating pendulum (used for energy healings) or point you in the right direction as to where one may be obtained. However, one can make a simple device by taking a 12-to-15-inch-long common sewing thread and tying a paper clip on the end. Now to observe the chakra invite a friend in on the experiment. Ask your friend to lie down, and clear your mind of any thoughts as to what should happen or anything else. Place the pendulum (paper clip device) inside any chakra of your friend about 2 to 4 inches above the body. It may take a minute for the pendulum to move with the motion in the chakra, but if you are patient you will then be able to observe the motion of the chakra. The chakra may cause the pendulum to appear to move in a circular, elliptical, or pendulum-type motion.

The first chakra, also known as the root chakra, is located in the pelvic area at the base of the spine and extending out into the aura. It is red and is responsible for creating conscious desires of sustaining life and well-being in the physical world. The physical survival instincts take over through the root chakra. Stimulation of this chakra can also increase sexual desire. The sexual energy from this chakra appears to be more of masculine energy. "Purely physical wild animal sex" is inspired through the root chakra. More than likely, as our society frowns on the nastiest of nasty, many Americans will experience blockage in this chakra. The gland in the body associated with this chakra is the adrenal. However, some texts state that this chakra is associated with the gonads. A person with an affected root chakra will typically be very anxious. Everything in life will be of the utmost urgency at nearly every moment of this person's life, resulting in an over-stimulation of the chakra. The results can lead to disease of the kidney, high blood pressure, and, if left untreated, eventually mental disorders of disassociation can occur.

The second chakra, commonly called the sacral seat chakra, is located just above the navel and is orange. This chakra houses much of the emotions, both balanced and off balance. Sexual desire can arise from this chakra also, only more feminine than masculine sexual energy. Remember that originally the soul is androgynous and therefore is capable of experiencing both masculine and feminine sexual energy within either the male or female body. It is similar to humans possessing both male and female hormones simultaneously. The gonad gland is associated with this chakra. Sometimes the adrenal gland may be interchanged between the root and sacral chakra.

The third chakra is the gut of emotion, power, and ego, all of which are produced from knowing or the intellect. It is located just below the breast line and is represented by yellow. A blow to the solar plexus can rapidly take one out of commission; a person will generally lose the ability to breathe, see, smell, and all the senses will fail for a few seconds. The solar plexus has also been credited with regulating the metabolic rate. A person with the solar plexus blocked may tend to be overweight and may be unable to have orgasms, especially women, while the individual with a hyperactive chakra may look anorexic and tend to be sexually over-stimulated. This chakra is associated with the pancreas.

The fourth chakra is the first chakra to begin leaving the physical plane of existence. It is located in the center of the breast and is green. Metaphysically speaking, the human body and all its contents are an exact replica of the universe or creation and all its contents. From the first through the third chakras we receive a manifestation solely of the physical worlds. Do not forget though that the spiritual delivers the "thought" and "will" within the physical to be carried out physically. Thus spiritual awareness, communications, and intuitiveness may pass through the lower worlds via the lower chakras. It is impossible to generate any physical reality without it originating in the spiritual. However, spiritual may coexist or solely exist as pure spiritual with no physical whatsoever. The heart chakra, on the other hand, seems to be associated fully with both the physical and spiritual worlds. The ultimate purpose and will of this chakra is to generate love and relationships. This can be accomplished fully and solely in either the physical or spiritual realms, unlike sexual or physical desire, which can have only a spiritual encounter from the onset but requires the physical to fully experience the total act. An example of this would be when a body is dehydrated and the spiritual guides may stimulate a desire to drink. We can see that the stimulation of desire in the lower chakras is spiritual while the actual practice requires a physical body. The activation of love does not require a physical body to complete this task.

In the heart chakra one may choose to activate and carry out love in the spiritual only. An example of this can be an open meditation with the Creator and universe on cycling love energy. Tibetan monks practice this act routinely. A physical example would be the love of relationships in the physical world, for example loving your family members, friends, pets, adopting children, and the earth, etc. A blocked heart chakra will result from the inability to love freely without expecting anything in return. The thymus gland is associated with the heart chakra.

The fifth chakra, sometimes called the throat chakra, can, like the fourth, represent either solely physical or spiritual communication. It is located in the center of the throat and has a bluish color. Originally, this chakra may have been used in telepathy, the communication by mere thought. The throat chakra also has the ability to resonate in vibratory pitch with the sound of the universe (both physical and spiritual sound). A blocked throat chakra may result in the inability to communicate efficiently, such as transmitting scattered, disorganized thoughts, or stuttering.

Spiritual communication in meditation and prayers may also be hindered. This chakra is associated with the thyroid gland.

The sixth chakra, also called the third eye or the brow chakra, is located right between the eyes on the forehead above the eyes. As this chakra represents spiritual intuitiveness, the actual color is hard to physically comprehend. The color that the texts all give is indigo, which is sort of a deep blue-violet. They always show it with more blue than violet. I see it with more violet/fuchsia than blue. The Indians and gypsies physically draw a circle in this area in manifestation of the existence of the third eye. This chakra generally represents the understanding of actual universal reality. A person with his third eye fully opened would automatically know that it is the earth that revolves around the sun even though she physically observes the sun moving across the sky. This is the method by which Einstein developed his theory of relativity. Not knowing where and how the information is received is due to a partially opened brow chakra. The third eye makes it possible to receive and transmit information, somewhat like a radio. In other words, everything that is knowable is available in the universe and it is through the third eye that this information may be tapped into, by directing "will" or by "involuntary" unintentional reception. The majority of human beings are functioning with a partially closed third eye, some more closed than others. There are exercises that help to open the third eye so that an individual may become more intuitive. If you are interested in doing so, look for books on developing the psyche and seeing auric energy. The more blocked the third eye the less intuitive a person will be. Those who sense absolutely no spiritual or divine presence have a severely blocked brow chakra. These people are the minority by far. The majority of people can relate to a spiritual experience even if nothing more than on the intellectual level. A few may have an emotional block where by they experience the spiritual but will not recognize it as such, due to emotional damage. This chakra is associated with the pituitary gland.

The final major chakra, the seventh, is called the crown chakra, and it is through the crown chakra that the heavens are created (the origination of thought). It is located in the top of the head and is recorded with both colors of white and purple. The crown chakra represents total connectedness to the All-That-There-Is. The wholeness of the being in all aspects of physical, emotional, mental, and spiritual are all represented within the crown chakra. It is the most spiritual aspect of the human body and for this purpose the ancients always kept their heads covered as an attempt to shelter the crown from any outside or negative unwanted interference. Another reason may have been to better attune themselves to the highest source. If you notice, in most any ancient garb the head is always covered. The Bible refers to covering the head; in the New Testament it is only the women who must remain wholly attuned and keep their heads covered. Many black Muslims require their women to cover their heads and wear ancient, traditional clothing while their men wear modern styles of clothing. This is a combination of masculine superiority (the men can wear what they wish) along with the ancient practice of maintaining as pure a crown chakra as obtainable (woman must be pure in the traditional way). The funny thing is that they don't even know why their tradition requires that the head should be covered. In ancient times the human will was much more forcible, individuals both male and female covered their heads in order not to allow other individual's energy fields to penetrate their own will. Even today, if one knows that he or she will enter a situation where tensed, angry, confused emotions and energy will be generated, then it would be highly recommend that he or she wear a hat or turban. The gland associated with the crown chakra is the pineal gland.

### Chakra Balancing and Cleansing

Once you have maintained a state of relaxation for at least a minute you may wish to begin a basic cleansing of the chakra system. When cleansing the chakra system it is always best to begin from a very relaxed state. The mind should be directed and opened to the universe for the intent of cleansing and balancing chakras. You must be seated comfortably in a chair or on the floor, but whichever way you choose your back must be as straight as possible. It is through the spine that the human energy is vitalized. The spine connects the spiritual energy back and forth to God, in a similar fashion as the heart furnishes blood back and forth to the body.

We will start cleansing from the lower worlds of our vessel up into the heavens. The first chakra, the root chakra, is red and located right in the pelvic area at the base of the spine (tailbone). In cleansing this chakra we will imagine a bright white light, as bright as the mind can imagine, coming in from the heavens and brought right up through the pelvic area into a clockwise rotating red circle. We choose clockwise rotation because a healthy chakra rotates clockwise. A chakra in distress will slow down in rotation and when it is totally blocked can actually develop a counterclockwise rotation. As the white light meshes with the red circle it makes the circle brighter and brighter red, cleansing the chakra. In balancing the chakra say to yourself silently or aloud, "I am cleansing and balancing my root chakra. I am aware that I am grounding and balancing my physical body with the energy of Mother Earth. I am currently in the state of empowerment, safety, and security. I now possess all that I desire from the physical plane. I create through my will/God's will." See the ever-so-bright red glowing ball balanced and cleansed. Now remove the white light and bring it up though the second chakra.

The sacral seat controls creativity and self-worth. Imagine the white light merging into the orange ball and becoming one. Say silently or aloud, "I am created perfect in my eyesight/God's eyes. I will spend time today reflecting and expressing my divine purpose. I balance and cleanse my sacral chakra and see the ball rotating clockwise and glowing bright orange." Know your divine purpose as you see the orange ball glowing brighter and brighter and then know that the sacral chakra has been cleansed and balanced. Now remove the white light and bring it up to the third chakra, the solar plexus.

See the white light entering into a yellow rotating wheel just below the breastbone. Give the affirmation of knowing that you have access to the libraries of the universe. Know that all things that you desire to accomplish are at your disposal. Say to yourself, "I am balancing, charging, and cleaning my chakra," as you continue to watch the yellow wheel glowing brighter and brighter yellow. Finally, recognize that you have a clean and balanced chakra glowing bright yellow and rotating clockwise. Move the white light up out of the yellow chakra and on to the fourth chakra.

See the white light enter into the green heart chakra in the center of the chest area. In your mind's eye see the chakra turn brighter and brighter green as the all-highest light massages, energizes, and cleanses. Give the affirmation of unconditional love. Say to yourself, "I possess all the love of the universe. I am capable of giving love and I do receive and accept love unconditionally. I ground myself in the loving green healing energy of Mother Earth." Take time to feel the affirmation taking effect throughout the universe. See the green wheel glowing brighter and brighter. Say to yourself, "I am aware that my heart chakra is thoroughly cleansed, energized and balanced, glowing bright green and rotating clockwise in the center of my chest." See the white light move up out of the heart chakra up the center of the body into the fifth chakra.

See the white light enter into the light blue throat chakra. See the white light becoming one with the chakra, cleansing it brighter and brighter. Say to yourself, "I am capable of communicating well with others. My speech is perfectly understandable. My body language vibrates on a positive note. I communicate well on the mental and emotional planes. I see the white light cleansing my chakra brighter and brighter blue and causing it to rotate clockwise in perfect balance and harmony with the universe." See the white light move out of the throat chakra and up the middle of the face into the sixth chakra.

See the brow chakra being thoroughly cleansed, energized, and balanced as the white light mixes in with the indigo wheel spinning clockwise. Give the affirmation of being intuitively aware of universal knowledge and wisdom. Unlike the intellect in the sacral seat, which knows from its physical senses, the third eye knows higher knowledge through intuition or channeled universal information. Give the positive affirmation of intuitively knowing all that your soul desires to know from the universal libraries. Say to yourself, "I know that I have the past, present, and future all here with me right now; I choose to know all necessary influences and events which may directly or indirectly affect my well-being. I see my chakra being massaged and cleansed thoroughly with the bright white light enhancing the indigo-colored chakra brighter and brighter as it is balanced and spins in a clockwise direction." See the white light leave the third eye and move up into the top of the head.

See the white light spinning in a clockwise direction in the top of the head. Know that the crown chakra in the human body represents Kether, the highest heavens of our universe. Feel connected to all there is. The crown possesses the capability of all knowing, all feeling, and all willing in the universe. Say to yourself as you visualize the white light becoming brighter and brighter, "I possess all knowledge at any time I require it. I feel connected to all there is. I am one with the universe. I AM THE UNIVERSE." Know that your crown chakra has been cleansed, energized, and balanced as you bring the white light up out of the crown chakra and burst it open to shower over the body as the lights of the fourth of July. See your entire auric field being cleansed and energized as the spray of white light showers over it.

This meditation technique is one that I have practiced. It is not a prerequisite to salvation or sweet bliss. I think of it as something that the mental body needs to reassure itself of the divinity that exists within every soul. I hope that you may find peace and joy in this activity but more so I hope that you will know that you can change and add to the technique as your inner self gives guidance.

There is no one set answer on this earth. The answer lies within us as collective beings—the many, many species throughout the universes. I have started with myself and I hope that this concept is one that might catch on—let us be one with the Divine.

1. Crown Chakra
2. Third Eye & Psychic Center
3. Throat Chakra
4. Heart Chakra
5. Solar Plexus Chakra
7. Sacral Seat Chakra
8. Root or Base Chakra

### *The Kabbala*

How many of us can count ourselves fortunate enough to have ever heard the word Kabbala, let alone knowing the meaning and practice of its wisdom? It is the teachings of the Kabbala that Jesus tried to bring to his disciples for applications into his Father's kingdom, along with ancient Hindu teachings. Jesus' youth and livelihood between the ages of 12 to full adult are unrecorded in the Bible. However, every living soul, every master of the universe, every god has had teachings of wisdom. Where did Jesus get his? All that needs to be done is to study his true teaching by filtering out contradicting statements that confuse and blaspheme the truth. Then we are left with a concept of non-contradicting information, the same information that Jesus gave to his disciples, and that I will try to give to you in part. I say in part for so very much of the information has been lost, but I will share with you as I have learned it.

"In the beginning was the Kabbala and the Kabbala was Karmic Consciousness," WHICH GAVE BIRTH TO GOD. (We must remember that God is simply all of creation collectively. To get a better understanding of this information one must have read the Ezzrath Theory on the Creation of the Universe. You will be totally lost without it.) Now let's simplify this. "In the beginning was the WORD . . . " I am sure that we Bible readers can all live with this one. See the Gospel according to John 1:1 for guidance.

The ancient letters, words, and speech were and are living and actively creating our universe as we speak today. All energy, light, and matter was produced through the Aleph, Beth, and Gimel in the consciousness of God.

For your convenience in becoming familiar with the Hebrew alphabet, you will notice that each letter has its own meaning, number, sound, and unique definition of character. The definitions of character have come through my higher guides; all the other information is basically found in any Hebrew teaching text. As we have touched on a little in the chapters on Christianity we know that the Kabbala, the Sepher ha Zorah, was passed down orally or in informal writings by the Talmudist Simeon Ben Yohai around 400-200 B.C. A Spanish mystic by the name of Moses of Leon put it in writing for the first time around A.D. 1275. Prior to this period the Kabbala was primarily taught orally. Its most widely known teaching of today is the philosophy of the ten worlds, known as the Sefiroth of which Kether represents the upper kingdom, heaven, God, the head and Malkuth represents the lower kingdom, earth (not hell originally! simply a lower state of existence), Satan, the bottom. All ten of these worlds represent **our** entire universe of existence. (See figure) Once we have mastered complete understanding of the Kabbala, we are no longer bound to the conditions of this universe and our souls will move on to the next world and whatever may be contained there. The soul will begin learning, experiencing, winning and/or losing (depending on the reality of the universe in which the soul visits) all over again for ever and ever, amen.

| THE MAGICAL HEBREW ALPHA-BET | | | | |
|---|---|---|---|---|
| ALEPH | א | ONE | SILENT LETTER | OX, mystically representing the wind or the breath, oneness the unity in God-Soul /conscious |
| BETH | ב | TWO | B | House, mystically representing the yin/yang or duality, which our collective consciousness chose to create our universal reality. |
| GIMEL | ג | THREE | G | Camel, the matrix or pathway |
| DALETH | ד | FOUR | D | Door, opening, or opening of the matrix |
| HE | ה | FIVE | HE | Window |

| | | | | |
|---|---|---|---|---|
| WAW | ו | SIX | WH | Hook |
| ZAYIN | ז | SEVEN | Z | Sword, represents completion for the patriarchal energy influence on our universe. |
| CHETH | ח | EIGHT | CH from the throat | Fence |
| TETH | ט | NINE | T | Snake, which has always represented wisdom and knowledge. The number 9 represents total completion of our universe. |
| YOD | י | TEN | Y | Hand, the smallest yet most powerful letter whose utterance with true and proper pronunciation opens the portal to connect earth and heaven by the ladder which Jacob used in the Bible when combined with he, waw, he. |
| CAPH | כ | 20 | K | Palm |
| LAMED | ל | 30 | L | Goad-ox, represents that all beings are students of the universe. All intelligence evolves through learning. |
| MEM | מ | 40 | M | Water, Mother womb of the earth and the human female impregnated womb. |
| NUN | נ | 50 | N | Fish |
| SAMECH | ס | 60 | S | Support, prop, holder on a spiritual tip; this letter represents that all beings are helpers in one form or another. |

| AYIN | ע | 70 | SILENT LETTER | Eye, the all-seeing eye of the universe. |
|---|---|---|---|---|
| PEH | פ | 80 | P | Mouth, the opeing or path in which the soul travels "IN," THE MERKABAH |
| TZADDI | צ | 90 | Ts | Fish hook |
| QOF | ק | 100 | K | Crown, protection of knowledge |
| RESH | ר | 200 | R | Head, Knowledge |
| SHEEN | ש | 300 | S | Tooth, foundations of the trinity mother, father and child/children. |
| TAW | ת | 400 | T | Completion/Perfection |
| FINAL CAPH | ך | 500 | Used at the end of a word "CH" | Palm |
| FINAL MEM | ם | 600 | Used at the end of a word "M" | Water |
| FINAL NUN | ן | 700 | Used at the end of a word "N" | Fish |
| FINAL PEH | ף | 800 | Used at the end of a word "F" | Mouth |
| FINAL TZADDI | ץ | 900 | Used at the end of a word "M" | Fish Hook |

If we carefully study the Bible and ancient mythology we learn that the majority of all Bible characters who became great had traveled to Egypt. What was in Egypt? Could this be one of the centers where higher knowledge was taught? All of the Patriarchs were required to train in Egypt. Father Abraham almost lost his wife in order to gain the needed wisdom of the Egyptians. As a great magician Father Abraham was able to exercise wisdom in a way that would save his life and his marriage simultaneously. Today men show superiority through physical brute strength and wit, but in ancient times men and women used magical incantations, manipulations of the worlds of the Kabbala (gaining spiritual aid), and physical metamorphosis. In order to become strong in the applications of these techniques one must possess the correct formulas and pronunciation in opening the connector portal between heaven and earth. In ancient Sumeria it was called DUR AN KI, meaning literally to bond heaven and earth.

I have found that the so-called name of God, or the Tetragrammaton, was the name used to open this portal. This is the reason that once the Jewish people (**non-Jews**) entered our land they refused even unto this day to ever attempt to pronounce the name Yod "He wav He." They learned the correct pronunciation of the Tetragrammaton and experienced all the glory of God, but not knowing what to do with it they outlawed it in their religion. Although the majority of the scholars say that Yahweh is the correct pronunciation of YHWH, no one really knows how to evoke the portal using the correct vowel sound and accent. The ancient Hebrews continually called upon the name of Yod He wav He, but the Jewish people will get nervous even if others around them call on this name. I have done it. They now teach that it is blasphemous to call on the name of Yahweh. This is another reason why in our Bibles today the name has been practically wiped out as compared to how it originally appeared in the Bible.

## Create a New Mindset
## for the Physical Body

Would you get into your car parked uphill, facing downhill, place the gears into drive and then scoot over to the passenger's seat and watch your car drive away with you in it? Yet how many of us place our souls into a vehicle called the human body and sit back and let the body drive us? This section represents the most important aspects of salvation for the physical body. You may have heard the saying, "you are what you eat." Indeed, the physical body represents all that you decide to put into it. Do you feed your body huge, greasy, fried burgers and fries regularly or foods of that caliber? Do you take in harmful chemicals such as tobacco, liquor, and drugs and so forth? What about hidden chemicals in your environment? They can usually be found in the air you breathe or the water you drink. Many have faced life-threatening situations from lead or asbestos poisonings from the paint on the walls or the dirt in the backyard. These are all substances which can be tested through a local chemical lab. Many water departments will test the water or at least will list an analytical report of all the compositions of chemicals within your drinking water.

How about stress? Are you taking in stress and preserving it in the body? Do you spend a lot of time being angry, hurt, a victim? Does the world generally walk all over you? How about worry? Are you the first-prize winner of a worrier's contest? During your participation in the role of victim do you choose to remain in the state of victimization for long periods of time? If you have answered yes to any one of these questions you may be in the process of breaking down the life force of your physical body.

The body, of course, does possess a strong elimination system for toxins and waste through the kidneys, liver, skin (the largest body organ), and human energy seat, but continuous long periods of abuse will begin to take their toll on the body, resulting in dis-ease and possibly death. Your physical and spiritual connectedness to the All-That-There-Is will determine the amount and length of time of physical wear and tear that you can get away with. A second factor that will enter into play as to how much destruction your body will accept before it goes into failure (dis-ease or death) is your individually encoded species' DNA, your genetic structure. There are cases where the body will allow unreal abuse, which will depend on the primary purpose of the incarnation of the soul into physical existence. This is how you may witness a gross exception to the rule, where a man smokes, carries excess weight of 50 pounds or more, hates, remains angry, hurt, and a victim. He will usually suffer aches, pains, and difficulty breathing. Some people may suffer from this and that and make numerous trips to the doctor, but it seems as if they will never die. These people, I believe, came into this life with a preconditioning will to learn to love and trust the universal love schematics. The family members of this person will wonder how it is possible that this individual could have possibly lived so long. They will wonder why it is that God is forcing this suffering creature to continue its unhappy plight on earth. Nonetheless, these souls appear to be here as a product of God's love, learning Her will in the midst of the shadows.

## Mindset for New Eating Habits

The first and most important thing that one must learn to maintain a healthy flesh vehicle is that the fuel you use must generate high efficiency. The fuel for the human body is nutrition. The body requires a certain amount of vitamins, minerals, and other necessary nutrients. Without them the body will fail (you may call this act death). Therefore, if you choose to avoid failure and achieve longevity then your goal requires that you should eat healthy. I myself have just recently made the conscious decision to eat healthier and I believe that this is the place to begin. If you do not begin with the conscious mental will to make a change in your daily habits, then it will be impossible to make any change at all.

After making the conscious decision to change your eating

habits the next step is to think about to what degree you are willing to make a change. I will discuss the most severe and the most lenient changes that I believe will still result in fulfilling our primary goal of increasing longevity.

The most severe change in the average diet today will consist of becoming a "TRUE VEGETARIAN." This is the ultimate truth in fueling the human body's everyday needs for nutrition. Many people often express conflicting views as to what one eats when she says that she's a vegetarian. The wide range of understanding can run from abstaining from meat, dairy products, toxic foods such as sugar, white flour, coffee, alcoholic beverages and so forth to the eating of all foods including chicken and fish but no red meats.

I cannot make the suggestion for you as to how strictly you will decide to change your habits, but, as in any given situation, the greater the efforts the greater the productivity. Little effort will produce little change. I personally chose a moderate change because I wanted to be comfortably happy for the rest of my life on this plan. Whichever plan you choose, if you are to be successful, go into this plan with the mindset that this is for the rest of your life! See this change as a prescription that you are giving yourself for longer life, a younger disposition and appearance, healthier physical vitality, and increased mental awareness. The benefits are so great and the sacrifice should be close to zero. Since this is an important statement let me repeat myself. It is of the utmost importance that you do not feel as if you are in need of anything.

After we decide which level of change best suits our individual preference, if any change at all, then the next step is to stop buying foods that are not consistent with the plan of action we have just implemented. For example, in my moderate plan of change I have decided to change to a non-strict vegetarian diet. In other words, I have eliminated all meat from my diet. I no longer buy sugar, and substitute honey for sweetener. Honey actually promotes physical improvements when taken in small quantities. The recommended dosage is a half teaspoon three times daily. My personal intake is twice the recommended for I use a teaspoon of honey in my herbal teas. I purchase only brown flour. The white flour has all of the nutrients stripped out of it to make it white. The enriched flour is white flour with a small quantity of nutrients replaced. It is simply better to receive all the nutrition for your caloric intake that you can obtain. Remember to always be conscious of what you are doing. See this in your mind's eye. You are building a superhuman body.

You may decide that you will simply reduce the amounts of meat servings from your plate. If you were eating an average of 4 ounces daily change it to only 2 ounces daily. This will still make a beneficial difference in your physique while enhancing your psyche. However, to decide not to make any change in eating heavy amounts of flesh will, on the average, lead to premature body failure. I found it advantageous to include my children in the change. There was less than one week of grumbling due to my decision to inhibit the consumption of meat, perhaps because children roll with life's bumps and punches better than most adults. They understand better than we grown-ups that it is not that serious and thus they take life one day at a time as the universe dishes the days out in accordance with their wills.

If you choose a more strict diet you should give up all dairy products. Milk was produced for the consumption of a 250-pound calf which has four stomachs that are required to aid in the digestion of milk. The eggs are very high in cholesterol as is cheese, which leads to constipation, all of which shows that these foods are not ideal for human consumption. They are tyranny on the digestive system. Dairy products require a high level of destructive wear and tear on the body and may produce allergies. I have decided that I will in the future eliminate this food but at this point in time I will limit or reduce the amount of consumption of these foods. I rarely drink the 2% cow's milk that I may use from time to time in preparing baked meals like corn bread or macaroni and cheese.

For those of you who are able to plunge into the higher reality truths, the purchase of a vegetarian cookbook may prove advantageous. There are so many substitutes for dairy products that come very close to near taste-alikes. I would describe a taste-alike to be any healthy food substitute that you can produce that satisfies the urge or desire of the unhealthy food choices. The best product to substitute for dairy products is soy. Tofu works wonders, tasting somewhat like you are eating an egg. Soymilk can be substituted for cow's milk. I have experienced some degree of lost consistency within the corn bread texture when using soymilk instead of milk. However, it is not to the degree that I could not eat it and enjoy it. I have decided not to do it just now. I will in the future.

It is also important to eliminate fat. Those like myself with the problem of maintaining their ideal weight should seek to eliminate fat, because fat makes you fat. The only oil that I purchase is olive oil, used lightly to prevent sticking when browning foods. The replacement that I use to eliminate butter, margarine, shortening, and vegetable oil is a spread that tastes like butter but is made from yogurt (watch dairy). This low-fat spread cannot be used to fry an egg for it is not fat and the egg will stick to the pan. I found this out the hard way.

The last point I want to make about nutrition is in the drinking of beverages. I have decided to eliminate soda, coffee, caffeinated teas, and alcoholic beverages. They can be replaced with herbal teas, fruit and vegetable juices, and water. Juicing is another book in itself, for all of the rewards and benefits it produces are indispensable for the true vegetarian. Do not confuse buying a bottle of juice made from concentrate with JUICING! There is absolutely no comparison; if you are truly interested in producing a super body you should really consider juicing. READ MORE ABOUT IT!

Meditate on your individual body type needs. Is there any dis-ease taking place in the body already? If so, study and know everything there is to know about your dis-ease. Learn which foods and herbs retard and perhaps eliminate the disease. There are many health, herbal, and nutritional books out there; get them and read them. Remember that you should never go on one person's opinion unless deep inside a voice is telling you to do one thing or the other. In this case one can never ever go wrong. Always follow intuition.

There are several types of natural healing paths that assist the body in healing itself. If you are interested in a total healing then you should look up these key words: Aruvedic medicine, energy and chakra balancing and healings, acupuncture, acupressure, reflexology, iridology, shamanism, healtheology, and so forth. All of these healing techniques from various ancient cultures promote wellness of being and have been the only source of recovery for some terminally ill people.

Upon knowing your body type, begin the process of choosing which supplements will best fit your dietary plan. Let me share with you my body type and how I deduced the information that I am putting forth to you. You see, for me it was much better to do this work myself, for then I know all the assumptions. A doctor or health representative may assume or be misinformed about my state of being, but I know what works well for me. This does not mean that you should exclude your family doctor. I use him as a check on self. You will know that you are doing all the right things to promote wellness when your doctor gives the clean bill of health.

My foremost concern in my body is the dis-ease of hypertension, most commonly called high blood pressure. Both avenues of bad fuel intake and the encoded DNA of my species have produced this dis-ease. After identifying both contributing factors I must then make a conscious effort to become consciously aware of my part in creating this dis-ease in my body. My greatest contributing act in creating high blood pressure began when I was a baby. I never attempted to correct it for I never knew that it was killing me. As a baby, near a year old, I was taking in every poisonous food the mind can imagine for my mother knew no better and she, too, was consuming foods that were harmful to the body. By the time I was in college my daily diet consisted of fried chicken, pork chops, neck bones, or fast-food burgers and french fries. Vegetables were always dripping in grease from fatback and ham hocks. I would treat myself to chitterlings (hog intestines). I would not have dreamed of a baked, broiled, or steamed dish and God forbid anyone to think of serving my food without first drowning it in a ton of fat. I now recognize that my eating habits did not suit my goals for longevity.

My anger was equally if not more of a downfall as far as living a long, healthy lifestyle. Bad eating habits, plus anger, plus worry, equals decreased life expectancy and this I did to myself. What destructive behaviors have you used against yourself? Recognize them and learn all the right patterns of behavior to create a change in your physical existence.

Most of us require a multivitamin supplement. Buy them and take them. Now how hard was that one? Most women prior to menopause will require an iron supplement. For mental awareness some people take ginkgo biloba. For energy they take ginseng. You will also need to purchase an herbal directory with vitamin and mineral information.

Look at my profile. I take a multivitamin, my regular blood pressure medicine, and several herbs to help reduce blood pressure: **valerian** to calm the mind, **black cohosh**, and **cayenne pepper**. I also use **aloe vera** and **goldenseal** as cure-alls. My diet consists of fresh fruits and vegetables. I eat absolutely no meat, but I do eat small rations of dairy foods; they are not needed, but I simply am not ready to let them go at this point in my life. I keep my diet plan in my mind both day and night for I remind myself that I am building a super body. When I prepare my meals and juice I keep in mind that I desire to feed my body nutritiously more so than delight in the mere pleasure of eating. I put this in my mind—I AM FUELING MY VEHICLE FOR LONGEVITY!

At times I allow myself to bend the rules that I have set for myself. The reason that I allow the bending of my own rule is because you must never feel as though you are sacrificing anything.

It is acceptable to go without as a free choice or to feel some desire to eat the foods you have already promised that you would refrain from eating and stick to your made-up mind. However, when there is a calling in the gut that makes you go back and forth to the kitchen and living room to sit it out until dinner, stop and allow yourself the snack. Now here is the trick: Promise yourself not to have seconds and require yourself to have a smaller piece than you would have ordinarily. Of course, this process is slow depending up on how much you stick to the plan, but if you keep at it results will happen. Since you never sacrifice you are always satisfied. **You will have a workable plan for the rest of your life.**

## Mindset for Losing Weight

Whenever you are not hungry make a mental note of it and give thanks to the Creator for allowing you not to feel hungry, if you are overweight. Never eat when you are not hungry no matter how long you have been waiting to take in food for the day. However, if it is late before you feel hungry take in a light meal like a fruit salad or vegetable soup. Your body knows when it is in need of nourishment and will tell you so. If you wake up in the morning and are not hungry, skip breakfast. Make the heaviest meal of the day lunch or the middle meal. Mentally prepare all the green leafy foods with awareness. Say to yourself, "I am building a super body." Leave the kitchen and go to the bathroom and look into your eyes and repeat the above statement in the mirror. "I am building a super body." Say it several times before returning to the kitchen. Now literally see all the nutrients in the foods which you are about to prepare and give thanks to Mother Earth for providing every healthy nutrient that your body needs. As the food is cooking take long, deep breaths in anticipation of the consumption process about to take place. Remember, you are not a human seeking a spiritual experience, but **YOU ARE A SPIRIT SEEKING A HUMAN EXPERIENCE.** Fulfill the purpose of your being in this existence. Take control of the driver's wheel in your body and become aware of every move, every step, and every thought that you take your vehicle through. YOU ARE THE MASTER OVER YOUR VEHICLE—begin your mastery.

Once the food is prepared plan on chewing at least two to three times as long as you would have normally chewed. Take breaks in between bites. Meditate on your marvelously new healthy body in the making. Thank the Creator for granting this desire in your heart to create a new body. Read these sections a couple of times and solo it along as God leads you in your thinking process. THIS WORKS, PEOPLE! I AM A LIVING TESTIMONY. The weight loss is slow, but you can see a health improvement in the appearance of your skin within a week, easy. Talk yourself into loving you. Consciously inform yourself that you are eating slower, chewing longer and taking breaks to take in deep breaths. Taste the food over every inch of your tongue. Notice what the food tastes like from the tip of the tongue and from the sides and back of the tongue. Smell its aroma. Is it sweet, spicy, or pungent? In completing these exercises you are creating an awareness of yourself and your needs. You are creating a different physical being. Create your own mental affirmations to build happy eating habits. IT'S ALL UP TO YOU. As long as you are not suffering or sacrificing you will do this for the rest of your life. However it all depends on how serious your desire for change will weigh in over procrastination and false priorities. Some prefer sitting in the passenger's seat and allowing their vehicle to drive off with them. That's fine, just as long as they understand that when they smash head on into a cement wall of earth reality they chose it. Good Health.

Make a conscious decision that you will eat healthier.
1. Decide the level of change and stick with it.
2. Become fully aware of your physical body's needs and wants. Treat it as if it were your spouse. Make love to your body daily by seeing it evolve into a truly highly advanced individual on earth. SMILE A LOT!

3. Identify the factors that caused your body to be in a lesser state of existence other than excellent.
4. Identify your contribution in creating the above factors.
5. Make a conscious mindset of creating the change that produces enjoyment and excitement while eating and preparing foods.
6. Use affirmations to convince your physical body to allow the soul's body its way and it will happen as you eat your way to health. Follow your inner voice with this concept and individualize it for yourself.

YOU SHOULDN'T WAIT UNTIL AFTER CHRISTMAS OR AFTER THE FAMILY REUNION OR SUCH. It will never happen and these are always excuses to STUFF the face full of everything we ever wanted and gain weight.

Remember that this plan is not a diet; it is awareness. There is NOTHING that you can't have. To begin, you may simply start by learning to become aware that you are allowing your vehicle to drive you around. This is an excellent start. It may seem like nothing to you but I promise that you will discover that your vehicle has been getting away with more trips to the mouth than you would have imagined. Plant it into your heart and your soul that you are aware that you are eating. Notice that foods that are being prepared and never taste quite right are requiring far too many samplings from you. Have you actually eaten your meal while you were preparing it?

> What textures does the food have? Is it smooth, gritty, wet, dry, slippery, hot, cold, warm, sticky, crunchy or what? Come up with some ideas on your own. Perhaps after mastering awareness when eating, tasting, smelling, and feeling the food in your mouth you may desire to master awareness in controlling or eliminating certain foods altogether. This choice can be based only on individual needs and desires.

## Eating to Health (Ancestrial Diet)

Without a doubt our ancient ancestors did not eat as the majority of Americans today do and thus if we are to return to our immortal state we must return to the ways of the ancestors. They never indulged in the poisonous foods that kill humans.

1. I am sure that meat is a primary definite contributor to toxins in the body! All the other foods that will be listed are not suspected of cutting off immortality directly, but indirectly. The state of amnesia has directly cut us off of immortal life according to what the ancients say. MEAT SHOULD BE ELIMINATED.

2. White sugar, white flour, and white rice are the next in line to eliminate. They are easy to remember for they are all white and contribute little to no nutritional value to the human system. If you were to pick only one of the above, eliminate WHITE SUGAR! Sugar causes your joints to crystallize and ache or become brittle and easy to damage.

3. The third assailant to kick out of your home, and I bet you would have chosen it first is . . . can you guess? That's right, it's FAT.

4. Another food group that we can substitute higher qualities of food for to improve overall general health would be DAIRY PRODUCTS.

5. Finally, eliminating all beverages containing alcohol and caffeine is an excellent choice.

6. What's left to eat? The answer is that there are plenty of foods that the earth provides to the animal species known as man. If you simply seek out a health store they will tell you most of the same things that I have said; they may simply leave out the spirituality behind it.

## Exercising to Health (Ancestral Exercise)

The physical body requires some degree of exercise in order to massage the body organs and rejuvenate the system. Exercise yields a longer life expectancy, which is most important, and secondly, a shapelier body. For a slight few the priority will be reversed. There are so many rewarding benefits to exercising the body:

1. increased stamina and energy
2. increased mental awareness
3. increased organ productivity
4. healthier skin
5. easier breathing
6. The body requires less sleep.
7. a better overall outlook on life
8. less stress and anxiety
9. more vitality (you will look younger)
10. People will notice that you are looking healthier and younger.

As long as you choose the workout that supports your body type and needs there are absolutely no negatives other than investing a half-hour to forty-five minutes per day. For many of us a half-hour is too much time to ask simply to yield a longer possible life span. Those of you with this mentality should not even read further for it will be a waste of precious time. However, if you can see a benefit or two worth setting goals and making an attempt at changing the daily habit, I would like you to explore this exercise program.

First, you will need to choose the exercise schedule that best caters to your physical and emotional makeup. Let's consider four groups of people.

1. people who exercise by lifting forks and spoons to their mouths and walking from one seat in the home to another seat elsewhere

2.  people who exercise moderately by doing aerobic exercise two or three times weekly and moderate stretching
3.  people who exercise with advanced aerobics five times weekly and stretch daily
4.  people who exercise vigorously daily for hours

Regardless as to who you are, if you are physically able then you fit into one of these groups or somewhere in between. Choose a group or midway between a group that sounds most like you. Before I started working out I was just a little above the first group. I did no exercise whatsoever, but I did have farther to walk than from one seat to the next, so I would have classified myself as just above step one. After classifying yourself establish whether or not your daily exercise activities are as they should be. That means either you are a member of group two, three, or four or that you are comfortable with your body deteriorating as it is and have decided to let it go. This is fine also. For those of us who fall below group two, as I did, and wish to manifest a change in our behavior, let"s consciously make that decision today. And regardless of how often we may fall off the band wagon, let us promise ourselves that we will immediately pick ourselves up the same day and eat and exercise sensibly the rest of the day. You have got to promise yourself, and stick with this, that just because you sneak an unscheduled piece of pie does not mean that, "OK, I get off my plan and start tomorrow." Making promises to oneself to start after this or that will NEVER work—just do it now!

I have found that flexibility is the key to sticking it out to the end; therefore, when you choose your workout make sure that it is not too strenuous to begin. You see, regardless of what physical fitness level you are at right now you can become fit. Maybe you can start out with five minutes a day. After a week or two you will be bored stiff and you will naturally add on because you will feel as if you are not getting a workout or that you haven't done anything. In fact, the opposite is quite true.

## Relaxation Meditation (Ancestral Thought)

Another step to caring for the physical body is relaxation and quieting the mind's tense effects on the body. Sit in a comfortable position either in a chair or on the floor with your back straight. Emphasis is placed on sitting with your back erect and straight. Start with the tips of your toes in your mind and relax the tips of the toes, the feet, the ankles. Breathe normally. Bring in waves of relaxing calm from the universe into your calves, knees, and thighs. Feel the sinking into a heavy nothingness as if they have joined to be one with God. Now bring that same universal calm up into the abdomen: relax the intestines, stomach, pancreas, kidney, and liver. Say it in your mind, "I am relaxing my abdomen and inward parts." Feel each organ being massaged and relaxed through your creative mind's eye with pulsing white cleansing light. Breathe normally as you relax the chest area, shoulders and arms. Allow the neck to relax. The jaw slightly opens as the tongue begins to feel heavy with relaxation. Relax the face and the scalp. As you are in this relaxed state, the universe is yours! You may now practice breathing exercises, affirmations, chanting, healings, transformations, or simply relax for as long as it is enjoyable to you.

# TEN

# People on the Path

## Sathya Sai Baba

Of all the knowledge and wisdom of human consciousness that I have found, the best expressed nearly full open (raw God consciousness) is located in a human living in India. I have never met Sai Baba, but I have followed reports of his God access and of all the people of the earth, the closest human life form that I find in the description of the Christ or Messiah consciousness is Sai Baba. It even appears that Sai Baba is prophesied to come as the Christ in the book of Revelation. Turn in your Bible to Revelation 1:13-17, "*And in the midst of the seven candle sticks ONE LIKE UNTO the son of man, **clothed with a garment down to the foot**, and girt about the paps with a golden girdle. His head and his hairs were white **like wool** (he is not old enough for his hair to be white yet), as white as snow; and his eyes were as a flame of fire; And his feet like unto fine brass, as if the burned in a furnace (denoting brown skin); and his voice as the sound of many waters (his voice would reach many nations of people). And he had in his right hand seven stars (keys of knowledge of the Universe): and out of his mouth went a sharp two-edged sword: (TRUTH) and his countenance was as the sun shineth in his strength (and those who meet* him face to face will see God). *And when I saw him, I fell at his feet as dead. And he laid his right hand upon me, saying unto me, Fear not; I am the first and the last (As he shared God consciousness* with the writer of Revelation he was engulfed in AWE)."

Although, I have never met Sai Baba, I have followed the reports of all the messiahs of our planet. (God has always placed a messiah amongst the humans. If we are elevated in consciousness we will always seek to know where the messiahs are located in case of a life-or-death human crisis, but not to worship!) It is only that I cannot find any firm evidence in the information reported on Sai Baba to rule out his position on our planet as god in absolute consciousness of GOD. The majority of us are god and unaware of our God consciousness. Unfortunately, the tiny minority of us that are aware of our god consciousness lack knowledge and wisdom to enforce God consciousness in our individual universes. The person closest to fulfilling this capability of knowing, accessing, and applying God consciousness is Sai Baba. And even Sai falls short of my personal expectations of full God consciousness because he ages as a mortal, instead of the original process that we humans (the spirit consciousness entrapped inside lower world animal species) used to make our grand entrance into the material world.

Originally we appeared on the planet through the use of the MERKABAH. (The topic of Merkabah is another book in explanation, but here's a clue to begin your own research.) Sai's expressed ability to possesses the exact same spirit of Christ consciousness can be theorized or assumed through my following observation. He:

1. ELIMINATED DESIRE'S CONTROL.
2. EXPRESSED GOD CONTROL OVER ALL SEVEN T-TRACTS. In other words, Sai appears to have mastery over hate, anger, fear, jealousy/covetousness, uncontrolled desire, condemnation (of others and/or self), and dishonesty which cause murder, stealing, fighting, adultery, cheating, etc. resulting in the disease of the mind, body, and soul. In all practical senses number one takes care of all these.

3. EXPRESSED ABILITY TO MATERIALIZE MATTER FROM PURE CONSCIOUSNESS. Sai can materialize matter before your very eyes and hand you the desires of your heart.

4. HEALS THE SICK.

5. HAS HELPED PEOPLE TO SEE GOD CONSCIOUS-NESS. People have actually expressed that they have met Sai (as a skeptic forced by a spouse) and requested in skepticism the knowledge of the universe. They received exactly that. One person reported knowing every step made by all of creation and including every step made by the ants. He was one with the universe and until that awe wore off was unable to individualize his self, like John in Revelation.

6. NEVER SEEKS MONETARY REWARD.

7. SEEKS PEACE AND TRANQUILLITY WITH ALL WHO MEET HIM. He is in harmony with the universe. (I have never heard one interviewee who has known Sai state any negative report of Sai Baba, and in this world an angel cannot accomplish that.) I am the greatest critic of anyone who professes to be a Christ. However, I have NEVER found anything on Sai Baba reporting to the world as to who he is (the Christ), nor have I found anyone who has reported that he is the Messiah of the human race in the flesh. But my higher consciousness has revealed this man to be one of the messiahs here on earth for the benefit of mankind. His service is not to himself and as a result he has MILLIONS of supporters and students. I say supporters and students, not follow-ers, because anyone seeking to be a leader actually serves the lower worlds. Messiahs will not deal with leadership recognition. I have found no evidence of Sai saying, "Follow me and I will lead the way" or "My way is the only way for mankind today." ANYONE who

makes statements like these or seeks to lead another human soul other than their own higher consciousness serves the lower worlds and will take anyone connected with them in to the lower worlds of existence.

Sai Baba, raised an East Indian Hindu, now advocates no religion. His teachings and beliefs for the evolution of mankind are very similar to mine. Perhaps this has made me somewhat biased in my opinion of him. But it is not just his teachings that convince me that he is a Messiah, but it is his capability to actually perform higher world spirituality. Many, like myself, talk of its existence and can perform the most simple spiritual practices such as energy healing, psychic intuition, transmitting and receiving communications from the fourth and fifth dimension (channeling), astral travel, and so forth. However, the more difficult higher sensory skills go lacking in even the most highly spiritual individual such as:

1.  physical transformation—the ability to physically develop our bodies into any image that we desire
2.  physical transportation—the ability to speed up the vibratory rate of the physical body (not astral travel) and travel across dimensions and/or galaxies to escape the earth's genetically encoded DNA for the mortality of the species (creation of the Merkabah)
3.  psycho/ telekinesis—movement of objects without physical means
4.  levitation—the ability of the physical body to defy the law of gravity by means of transcendental meditation

## John Edgar Cayce

Known as the sleeping prophet, John Edgar Cayce appears to be the leading pioneer prophet (the trailblazer of the West) of the Western world in the teachings of the higher worlds. As we have learned, there is no such thing as good and bad or right and wrong within the Ezzrath Theory. There is only the state of being. When applying right knowledge we learn that there is only an existence and service of either the higher or lower worlds, not right and wrong. I believe that Cayce had this understanding and developed a type of channeling which brought the higher worlds of frequency within his grasp of communication. Cayce had learned to communicate and receive higher conscious information through accessing the universal libraries available to all individuals. The universal libraries are encoded in our DNA; as the earth enters a new cycle the information already within will awaken. Through this information, Cayce was enabled to accurately predict diseases in individuals. He could suggest natural healing herbs for his clients. He could predict future events; after all, he could see them as they were taking place. The past, present, and future all run parallel in one existence and are here in the present with us. We are able to go into the past and heal our own wounded heart and thereby heal our present and even change our future. We can work on our future by creating it from our present or repairing the past. Cayce was clearly an example of a being with the understanding of his multidimensional selves and he nourished and gained information from all of his selves. All of my information regarding Cayce has been found in reference material from the library and TV documentaries of his legacy. The best source of information on Cayce can be obtained via satellite on the Wisdom Channel. The Wisdom Channel supports the Cayce legacy and advocates his primary teachings:

1. We are not victims of change, we are creators of change. We are helping to create our future.
2. We are privileged to be here now as the collective consciousness to make the quantum leap into a new way of thinking.
3. We are not alone in the procreation task that we are undertaking. We are in a partnership with the divine.

The Wisdom Channel has programming designed to cater to higher knowledge and wisdom. It appears that this station tries to stay clear of any negative or judgmental representations of the truth and focuses on simply informing humanity. I cannot recommend any programming higher for the soul's resurrection of its encoded DNA of universal knowledge and wisdom than the Wisdom Channel. If there are any out there that are better I have not found one. For convenience, the Wisdom Channel has a web-site located at http://www.wisdomchannel.com. This site lists programming for both television and radio. It also has a live site for viewing on the web, a bookstore and many other rewarding avenues for the purpose of obtaining higher knowledge. These people are wholly committed to the practice of the spirit of love and unity to influence the universe into right knowledge and they are doing an excellent job at it. Their favorite quote that is broadcast quite frequently is by the late Mother Teresa, which says, "Rather than being against evil, BE FOR LOVE."

Without doubt there is a contrast between being against evil and being for love. Believe it or not, when we practice being against evil we are serving the lower worlds. I must admit to you that even the first part of my book is somewhat against evil. Some of the language is a put-down of the false religion. If I choose to serve solely the higher worlds can I speak out against false religion simultaneously? With the information that you have read thus far can you figure out WHY being against evil will be of a service to the lower worlds? Take the time to ponder this question. Can I be against evil while simultaneously yielding to my higher self-energies? NO, not if it brings devastation and confusion to my fellow brother more than peace and harmony. Therefore, even though I am telling the truth I have hurt my fellow man in the process, thereby serving the lower worlds.

In a sense I am speeding up your evolution (those who investigate this information) when you have your experiences and many lifetimes to get this information without my snatching the illusions away like Santa was snatched away from me. Eventually after getting my head beat in or getting tired of beating others heads in, I would have discovered the deceit without my mother telling me. In order not to be in violation of universal law all souls should be allowed to evolve naturally without the influence of any negative talk or actions. I would have had to speak exclusively on what my salvation chapter contains. However, I choose to fulfill this desire within me of allowing people to have a chance to be knocked over the head with the brutal truth instead of subtle truth. I suppose that this comes from my desire to have known truth sooner myself. So when I see others in darkness I haven't chosen the wisdom of knowing, and allowing that one day all people will come to this same conclusion. I must also feed my ego. Now we know that this is lower world service. The ego that I speak of is the desire to defeat Satan. I still hold anger for the deceit of all humanity with the creation of all these damnable religions even though I know that all is well. Ego and anger both serve the lower worlds regardless of the purpose. The great thing is that it is my choice, and I have promised myself that I will give up both within a couple of years after the publication of this book.

Another website besides the Wisdom Channel's that I find very rewarding to the spiritual researcher is the Spiritweb. It produces loads of information on spirituality. It also gives dates and scheduling of events with speakers on spirituality. There are also several chat rooms and private chat rooms for the convenience of the Internet surfer. You are sure to find spiritual insight here. Remember that not everything that you hear from any one person will be all true. Take the information that rings true to you and keep it in your soul and heart. If you have thoroughly researched an issue and know that it is unfounded, release it back to the universe. Moreover, if you do not have any information on a topic, NEVER release it until you can obtain more information. However, at the same time, DO NOT ACCEPT THAT INFORMATION AS KNOWN TRUTH until you verify it for yourself. I believe this theory not to be only the Ezzrath Theory, but also the theory or reality of the enlightened souls of universe.

# ELEVEN

## The Ezzrath Theory

### General

In general the Ezzrath Theory of life can be summed up simply in two words: "Just be!" If we chose to sum it all up in one word then that word is "be!" There is absolutely one thing within the human experience in which I believe humans are incapable of practicing free will, and that is the free will NOT to be. We can never **NOT** "be." It would be much easier for us to fly in the sky or live in the sea than to end life. God has created all creation within our universe with the free will to do all things within the capacity of its individual creation's creation. For example, a cat may decide to love and care for its master or it may decide to be finicky or attack its master. It has free will to scratch, lie down, jump up, eat, meow, purr, or hiss. However, a cat will never bark, growl, or snarl. Nor will you see the average human fly like a bird or live under the sea as a fish with gills. This is how I am proving to you that creatures, including humans, are only free within the specifications of their creation. I know of absolutely no humans that can exist without food or sleep. They all must eat and sleep or die. Therefore they are not free to permanently practice not eating or not sleeping without suffering the ramifications. Moreover, humans, like all animals, plants, fish, and any other creation, is free to act out as God has empowered them to conduct themselves.

Therefore, when a lion is on the prowl for prey, it catches a rabbit and takes its life, God is not offended. God understands that She created the lion to require prey for its consumption. But let's look at the situation from the rabbit's point of view. The rabbit feels totally violated by the lion as its flesh is ripped away piece by piece resulting in ultimate victimization, the loss of life. This is how we humans look at all insults, injuries, and loss of life in our lives. We are very similar in our thought patterns as the rabbit's thoughts when we ourselves become victims.

If we are to be perfectly honest with ourselves, we must admit that we can understand both the victim and his assailant's points of view and neither of them are condemned as anything less than what they are: a lion and a rabbit. Yet if the same situation takes place in our lives, where our child has been victimized by an assailant. (I use this example because I am a mother and I know that in average human consciousness this is the ultimate victimization.) We are quick to feel like the rabbit. I would be totally grief-stricken; I would imagine all the suffering that my child went through. I could never imagine God sending angels to comfort my child as her assailant took her life. I could not see that angel in the lion's den with my son. I would sit and wonder, "God why couldn't it have been me instead of my child?" I know even with all that I know about ultimate reality, from the onset it would have never crossed my mind that God could remotely have any good plan out of the hurt of my child. I would immediately become the rabbit instead of one with as much intelligence as even we humans have in understanding the picture of the rabbit and the lion. I would be a grief-stricken victim, stripped of all that is dear to me.

Or would I? We fail to realize that humans who victimize need to victimize. Stop to think of when you have hurt a friend by lying or perhaps just not showing up for an engagement that you have promised to attend. These acts, too, create victims, but since we all are guilty of these types of victimization they are more acceptable. We do not realize that at times there are younger souls placed among us who are trying to evolve. The young souls are like the lion and our children are like the rabbit. These losses will create a universal evolution in which we will all evolve into a perfect world once the younger souls have caught up. Evolution may cost us who consider ourselves upright, law-abiding citizens **"victimization."**

When God sees these things, in my theory, he sees the human murderer as no different than the lion murderer. The need and reasoning for the kill may be different, nonetheless the **urge** (LACK OF CONTROL OF DESIRE) to commit the act is of the same level or else it would not take place. Do you believe that it is possible to commit murder without first having an inspiration or desire to do so? If you can believe that a murderer has a passion or desire to commit murder, where does this passion come from? Is it a desire that God could not help creating from the beginning of time? Do you wish to believe that man is so powerful through his hateful heart, man out-powers God and seeds murderous thoughts and desires against God's will? Think about it. It is within that urge and its fulfillment that one learns evolution through the KARMIC universe. Various precious souls of light have agreed upon being a victim so that another soul might inherit insight. In my theory that is why we are evolving now as a society that would never legalize cannibalism, human sacrifice, or even slavery. WE HAVE OUTGROWN THIS CRAP AND IT IS NOW TIME TO MOVE ON! It is only the human race that places incantations of condemnations and fear as a prerequisite for being ("Just be") good. Who said that you must be good? Is there truly any such thing as ultimate good in the physical world? Seriously, anytime that we do "good" isn't there always but always someone who can do better (more good)? Does this make my good any less good than theirs? Who is the judge? What of a dog in heat as she is passed around from dog to dog and standing still right there for the entire line of dogs to have their way? Is there a doggy hell for that sin? Can a dog sin? Let's reason, now that you have a concept of my reasoning, to compare with the concept of the world's religions (your religion if it has a name).

## The Shadow Comparison Listing

Whether it is to kill or to be pro-life.

Whether it is to harm or to care.

Whether it is to hate or to love.

Whether it is to take or to give.

Whether it is to be a victim or to be an assailant.

Whether it is to be a Christian or to be a witch.

Whether it is to choose Allah or to choose Jesus.

Whether it is to be righteous or to be a sinner.

Whether it is to give praise or to bellow criticism.

Whether it is to create disharmony or to create harmony.

Whether it is to stink or to smell as a rose.

Whether it is to create discord or to create peace.

Whether it is to lie or to tell the truth.

Whether it is to take advantage or to be considerate.

Whether it is to destroy or to create.

Whether it is to commit adultery or to remain faithfully loyal.

Whether it is to worship idols or the Creator alone.

All these things and more have been granted to me as my birthright into a free-will universe from my Mother/Father God. And it is your birthright to be genuinely free, also. So if you choose to bind your soul up from birth as a filthy, disgusting, hopeless sinner from the moment of conception that, too, is your free will and so it shall be. If you choose to burn in hell for "doing wrong" then the Creator grants you free will. The one and only request that I do seek of my readers is that they do not feel sorrow, anger, or condemning judgment of those who have learned that the opposite of your belief is true. I have learned that I truly have free will and the only consequences are the ones placed within nature or the universe from the beginning of time, the ultimate LAW OF GOD. I hope that my readers can rejoice to know that any soul can actually be filled with peace, happiness, and joy even though it is without the doctrines of their religion (such as, "You must be born again"). If you take the time to read through all shadow listings you will find that most of you will choose one side and totally avoid the other (that is the shadow) with the exception of one phrase. Can you find the one phrase that is opposite yet we choose neither side? Return to the top and read over the few listed choices again. Take a guess before I give you the answer.     STOP!

Did you notice that a victim and the assailant are direct opposites yet no one wants to be either one? Why not? What is wrong with being a victim or, for that matter, an assailant? If you now go back through the list above and get creative and think of some "evils" yourself you will find that each and every one of them creates a victim. For example, if I lie to you and you receive it you have been victimized. If I kill, steal, hate, etc. another, then they, too, have been victimized. And if the act of killing, stealing, hating, and so forth creates a falling into lower and lower states of amnesia (hell of the human soul) then have I not in turn become a victim of the universal reality (that is the hell of the human soul)? The state of being victimized brings about torture and "hell" to the living soul whether it is a physical, mental, or spiritual victimization. It is out of this torture and "hell" that each and every soul evolves closer and closer to God. Yes, even Satan the devil is a victim of universal reality (that is the reality of living an illusion) and he, too, will eventually evolve. All victims, whether they be physical or spiritual victim, are on the path of spiritual awareness. When a young woman has been raped, her soul has cried out to the universe to teach her endurance and self-empowerment. Everyone will agree that they would love for their daughter to become self-empowered, but no one wants to see the shadow force that will create this reality, including myself! I am not saying that every soul has to be raped to receive self-empowerment. What I am saying is that Romans 8:28 is universal truth. It states, *"and we know that all things work together for good . . ."* The rest of it has a condition requiring that you love God and are called according to His purpose. Nonetheless, the Creator of all existence would never place that requirement on any soul, for in ultimate reality there is only love. For it is in the shadow (negative) that we receive the positive outcome (evolution). This is where man ignorantly placed it in God's mouth that it is good for man to be long suffering. HOGWASH! Suffering is not a requirement for the positive outcome (evolution). It is a **universal elective**. We choose to live in hell (suffering/the shadow) as an individual or collective consciousness process to establish evolution of self.

What I find even more profound is the fact that the acts of a murderer, rapist, or thief are all nothing more than **our perception** of the worst possible acts to commit. One way of seeing one small glimpse of reality is through human dreams. You may feel that you never dream because you forget the dream. Nonetheless, every human soul does dream. In our dreams we will experience all sorts of shadows, such as fighting, arguing, hating, being unfaithful, and so forth. While in the dream we experience every human emotion possible as if it were indeed a reality. At times we may wake up laughing or crying based on the experience of the dreamer. Whether we have yelled at our child, beat the child, or even killed the child in our dreams, when we awaken we feel the emotion for only a moment, and then we take a deep breath and sigh within ourselves, "SPEWWW, it was only a dream." I truly believe that after the **physical** experiences of life on earth this is what we will say in the end of it all. Row, row, row your boat gently down the stream merrily, merrily, merrily, merrily, LIFE IS BUT A DREAM.

People will not accept the truth inside them, telling them that they have the truth if they would only seek to understand their dreams and where they come from. Think of the dream in which you committed your most heinous and repulsive act, one that disgusted you and even when you woke up you were still mad at yourself. So that we can have an image in front of us I will tell you of dreams that I have had where I wake up disgusted with myself. Many times in my dreams I am fighting. I am always very strong and knocking the enemy down, but without fail he always gets back up. I will fight him all the harder, breaking arms off and dismantling the guy. Yet he still gets up and comes for me. I gorge his eyes out and break his neck. I literally hear and feel his bones cracking in my hand. I think that it is over, but as I walk away I hear him getting up. Looking back I see a disfigured, broken-necked guy still charging at me. I wake up out of breath and exhausted from the nightlong battle with this guy. I am disgusted with myself as to why I would stump the guy in his face and literally create all kinds of disgusting avenues to destroy my adversary. My ultimate goal was to stop this guy from charging, by any physical force necessary. In my dream it never dawns on me that I could have tried to reason with the guy. Better yet, what if I had turned the other cheek? I couldn't see myself, but I had to have been huge and strong, because I had no problem whatsoever in dismantling this guy. I remember knowing that I possessed ten times the guy's strength. None of the great teachings that I had taught myself came to mind. It was the animal inside of me that was in control, and she was giving it every physical effort by conjuring up the survival instinct to destroy and conquer.

Now knowing what I know (and I hope that most of you know it, too) fighting just isn't the highest good or in the best interest for human evolution in consciousness, yet in my dream it was all that I could think of. Was this a sin? The person who dreams of murdering someone for no reason: Is this a crime or a sin? There is no disputing it. IT IS NOT A CRIME TO DREAM OF KILLING SOMEONE. But why not? When we experience our dreams are they not indeed at that time REAL to us? In fact, it doesn't stop being real to us until we awaken from the dream.

Life is but a game of "Clue," filled with many passages to finding the path of ultimate truth. Our clues are in the physical life itself. The caterpillar appears to die but then it sheds its cocoon and becomes more beautiful than ever. The ant has strength equivalent to a man carrying a car over his head. Our songs brought forth out of the collective consciousness of man may hint of the hidden. Our novels, stories, movies, and so forth all give man hints of reality and the not so obvious. We say that there are no such things as mermaids, dragons, leprechauns, unicorns, and so forth, but then I ask this question: If they are impossible, HOW CAN MAN THINK OF A CREATION THAT GOD COULDN'T CREATE? I believe that we can only twist the known events to suit our personal agenda but inventing creative non-existent matter is questionable. I am not saying impossible, but questionable. So in my reality I can't dismiss the existence of a creature merely because I haven't seen one. What if the dinosaurs had spiritual powers and never left their large carcasses behind? We would be erroneously insisting that they never existed. What if only five percent of the human race experienced dreams and the rest of us didn't? Wouldn't we classify this reported experience as an illusion on the part of the persons experiencing the process called dreaming, just like we dismiss reported UFO sighting and alien abductions? Nonetheless, lucky for us, the majority of us occasionally or frequently experience dreams. Therefore we are not considered crazy when we mention experiencing another life reality other than our physical life reality.

Notice that with dreams we feel quite comfortable calling them experiences no matter how vile or disgusting they may be. If I said that dream events are real then they are actually happening. They are real. I will lose half of the readers following me now. Why is it that humans will totally lose it if I were to say that in reality you (YOU THERE READING THIS BOOK) are having an experience, and **NOT** reality on the universal God plane where your soul will awake at the point of death or transformation? What if I were to say that there is no such thing as the devil, sin, suffering, hate, evil, misery, love joy, peace, happiness, being content, righteousness or God? What if all of this is simply an illusion similar to the dream state where simply (WE) as creators wanted to create an experience. So we created the state of being. (Row, Row your boat gently down the stream.) Decartes said, "I think, therefore I am." He referred only to a spiritual existence. Just think: What if you could only think? There is no feeling, no touching, no smelling, no seeing, no experiencing at all, because a "thinker only" has no body to feel, touch, smell or see with. When we feel does it require thinking? Yes, we use the brain to access feeling, but we do not think. When you watch a guy drive off in your brand new car you will not sit down and start thinking, "How do I begin this feeling project?" NO WAY. YOU FEEL, MAN, AND I MEAN RIGHT NOW! You are hurt, angry, violated, and a victim almost to the point (for some of us) of physically damaging the guy if you can catch him. Why? Stop and think for yourself: Why would you be angry to the point of a physical altercation simply because a guy took off with your paint, metal, glass, plastic, and rubber? What is a car, more than paint, metal, glass, plastic, and rubber? You know that you have insurance. Let me change that to—**you used to know,** that you have insurance prior to the theft of your new car, but that thought comes nowhere into even the slightest one of the billions of brain cells that you have to think with. WHY? Lost control of desire and individual ownership. EGO.

## Ego

Ego is another byproduct of the lost control of desire. Remember that we as humans suffer only one problem and that is the lack of the control of desire. All other problems, I have found, are simply byproducts of the single worst destroyer of our race. In the beginning, from my understanding, man did not own land, seas, rivers, air space, and so forth. However, now if you fly over some other nation's airspace without its permission you will be shot down once they have given you warning. We humans now possess the air. I do not believe that man was ever supposed to own anything. We were simply to be and the earth was supposed to supply us with food and shelter. What happened? Ego. I won't spend a lot of time on ownership, but I do advise my readers to look into the characteristics of human nature and decipher for yourself whether or not there was less killing, hate, and war when man was one with nature.

Another severe ego problem that needs to be addressed is the desire to lead. Any one seeking to be a leader is serving the lower worlds and is not on the spiritual path back to the Creator. Those of us who keep saying that we need a leader are suffering from lack of self-confidence. That is our problem, now; we have had way too many leaders! We need to pull together as one and stop looking for one martyr to dump all our garbage on. That is how we got into this "murder God's son for our sin" illusion from the outset. We don't want to take responsibility for our own actions. We are looking for someone else to carry our burdens, mistakes, and failures. I do admit that it looks easier, but if we look at the results, we can see that it doesn't work. It never worked. In the first place, if a leader rises and everyone rides on his back, let's say like Martin Luther King, all that has to happen is for the leader to be killed and the entire effort will die with him. But if we all are leaders of ourselves and connected with each other as one in the Divine—in whatever condition, we are joined in one purpose—who can stop us other than nature herself? And if she does, it was worth doing our best to achieve the highest score attainable in the game of life. I truly believe that ultimate truth in obtaining life's foremost destined goal lies in the ability of the species (us—the earthlings) reconnecting as one and becoming as the gods. We have that power within us; all that we have to do is awaken it. Even as you have read my ideas you know that it touches your very essence for it feels perfect, but your illusionary carnal life makes you believe that it is impossible, just as people refused to believe it when Jesus was telling exactly the same philosophy.

## Multidimensional Selves

Is much easier to say that the unseen worlds of angels, demons, gods, and the Creator Herself never existed. The moment man says, "There is a God," then there is a need to know God's character and Her relationship to man. Where does God reside? How do we decide which stories are true? Thus it is with angels, demons, fairies, and so forth. If we cannot see them, how do we know without doubt they do not exist? The most truthful answer is that we don't really know; it is just something in our hearts, let's call it gut instinct, that tells us somehow maybe it could be possible. In the case of God almighty, although none of us has seen God our hearts just know that there is something greater than just one individual soul (self) making everything happening in our existence. This is where I would like to introduce to you multidimensional selves.

Naturally, one would find it most ridiculous to believe it possible for other lives, events, and consciousnesses that are all a part of the same individual self taking place simultaneously and in separate dimensions. I don't know how it is possible. I don't even know whether I fully buy into it. Nonetheless, I just want to throw out things to you that have been thrown to me from the Universe you may call God.

I have met in a dream a male representative of myself and a female. The female is quite more distant and I do not have as much information on her as I do the male. She is a very sexually active individual, very much unlike myself. It is the strangest thing and the strangest feeling to be you and someone else all at the same time. Nonetheless, as my God is my witness, I have experienced it.

I was an East Indian or Iranian/Iraqian thief or terrorist. The man was me. I swear I felt myself running from the authorities, up and down steps and in and out of corridors inside a huge garage-like compound. The theft or violation had already taken place before I became consciously aware of this guy, but I knew I was guilty and about to lose my life. There were many cars around and

I was thinking of where to harbor myself away from the authorities. The sweat and stench of fear bombarded my heart. At the same time, me, who I am now, Ezzrath, told my conscious self as Ezzrath that this idiot is going to get himself killed. As Ezzrath, I/he was like my beloved child, brother, or dad who was about to get himself killed. My soul tried to advise him, kind of like how you may want a character on TV to escape. I could see the bad guys and him, too. I could see the entire picture, but as him all I could see was sweat pouring into my eyes, darkness, and the fear as to where the men who were after me could be. As him, I could not hear myself (Ezzrath) warning him (the Indian) myself that the authorities were just on the floor above me (the Indian) and that there were some nearer me (the Indian) to my far front. As Ezzrath, this was creating great panic because he couldn't hear me, and he didn't know that these men were close enough to possibly catch him. I saw him running for the stairwell and I saw the men spot him and I woke up.

Do multidimensional selves exist? I cannot say one way or the other. More of my life experiences say it is impossible for there to be any such thing as multidimensional selves. However, I cannot erase the fact that I have experienced a dream where I literally felt what it was like to be two vastly different people simultaneously. It was one of the weirdest feelings that I have ever experienced. I had heard about multidimensional selves and, to be quite candid, at first I thought that this theory was too far out in left field to even be considered worthy of mention in my book. Had it not been for this dream I would not have mentioned it. I quickly forgot my own philosophy on how to avoid an ultimate deceit. The idea of multidimensional selves was presented to me and my common sense, which primarily accepts only physical evidence (somewhat like science), took over the driver's seat. I did not ponder the possibility, because it was just too silly of an idea. After my dreams, needless to say, now I must regard the possibility that perhaps we humans may be multidimensional beings.

I have left out several other pieces of information like this one because they just don't add up for me now. I don't know how to put the pieces together, but I felt that as often as I dream and experience myself being two people simultaneously that I would have done you a great injustice not to mention it. I do apologize to you for not being able to put everything into words about how it felt to be more than one conscious person at the same time, yet I did experience the feeling of not just being more than one person, but also feeling knowing that I was two conscious minds dwelling as one. CRAZY!—I AM STILL HUMAN.

## Religions

It is not my intention to condemn any religion. However, and I am not proud of this, I do judge the religions. It is without doubt a service of the ego that I desire to bust wide open the lies, illusions, and entrapment of most religions. As I write, I pray to you, my reader, and to my Creator, my higher self, that I in no way offend you. Keep in mind this is only an opinion of a being that is suffering from amnesia of my true goddess identity. If you have names for your religions or belief systems, know that it was NOT the original way of worshipping the Creator. What was the name of the ORIGINAL religion? I can guarantee that you will have no name to offer, and it is this original belief that we should seek in our search for God. All others have added their twists and personal agendas to the curriculum. What were the names of the Israelite religion, or the Canaanite religions, or the Sumerian religions? Does the Creator require worship? Think about this question a moment. Where did the word worship come from? The original worship of the so-called "creator gods" was digging for his gold, serving him (making a barbecue—sometimes a sacrificial animal, sometimes a human), and bowing to him/her. This was not the Creator of our souls. These beings that all the myths, including the Bible, speak of are our parents from another planet. They brought our physical bodies into existence—**not the**

**soul**—much like our mom and dad brought our bodies into existence today. Would we worship our mom and dad? It was these god fathers who got jealous and needed man to worship them. It was our God/Goddess-fathers/mothers that influenced and in many cases forced us to create human religions.

Nonetheless, these gods have been driven off the planet for a spell, thus giving us the time to evolve, without fear of being blown up, hexed, diseased, or worse. Will they be back and if so will they place us in bondage again as Jehovah required of Israel? I can only offer advice for this question and that is to evolve! EVOLVE AND KNOW WHO YOU ARE! Yet, do not evolve out of fear. If you are content and feel no desire to evolve, and you feel good staying right where you are, then by all means do so. If you decide that you are in need of something more than what your traditional religions have offered, then I would suggest knowing your true inheritance. Seek it for the love of yourself, or the love of God. Then I advise that you start by knowing the origins of your religions. That is how I began, by a process of elimination. Be sure to identify basic truths, and then call anything that does not fit into these basic truths *ultimate deceit.* Now remember when you make up your assumptions that there should be no physical evidence to give you clues that you may be wrong. For example one of my assumptions was that the Bible was absolute truth and that nothing could possibly get in the Bible that wasn't truth. That was a set-up for *ultimate deceit* because I didn't investigate the origins of the Bible. Some examples of religious types of basic assumptions that I have not found substantial evidence to deny as truth:

1. God is.
2. God is a loving and compassionate God.
3. God created Creation.
4. God never fails or make mistakes.
5. God is ALL-KNOWING and ALL-POWERFUL.

I have tried to establish a belief system based on ALL the information presented to me from our ancestors that does not allow contradiction in the belief system. It was important that the concept of my belief not have any contradictions. When a contradiction is found I automatically weigh both concepts and finally compare them to the basic assumptions of truth. Always remain open-minded so that an ultimate deceit does not take place.

These days the only influence of the gods on humans is primarily within the human emotions through the psyche. There are some of us, both good and bad, who escape and return in human form for more of an impact on the human race. We seek to fulfill our desires on the human race rather than as a member of the human race. We usually make a grand entrance of a great uniqueness in our births. Some of us are born on significant days and times, other should have died at birth but live (babies that are living miracles). Some of us are born to barren mothers, some of us are born with an unusual attraction for healing the human race (people are hopelessly drawn to these individuals without understanding why) more than experiencing human delicacies. I believe the most popular days for the rebirth of the gods/goddesses are Sundays and Thursdays. The Chinese hold the sacred time of a special birth baby as 1 a.m. Sunday. The days of the deaths are more frequently on Saturdays.

The mothers know that the child is unique even if they never speak of it. Society will, for the most part, see them as leaders, strange, and/or in some ways they are deemed mentally or emotionally incompetent/crazy. These people have a drive for whatever purpose they came here to fulfill. If they themselves or anyone else stifles them it is a life and death situation. This is where the craziness comes in. Some of the people who I suspect are gods and goddesses in human form are the Pope, Lauryn Hill (she may not know), Erikah Badu, (she writes it in her music—get the title "On and On" and you will learn more of what I have been telling you), Adolf Hitler, and Billy Graham (hopelessly in a state of amnesia). Notice one thing that all these people have in common: A MESSAGE! The second reason I chose these people was the unexplainable, awesome feeling that I get when I look into their eyes; it's as if I see me. Many of the gods and goddesses are trying to set the score straight with the human race. Keep in mind that the human spirit is of a higher essence (perhaps higher than the gods and goddess) that entered into animal flesh.

The gods/goddesses set the human race up so that it would hopelessly and perpetually self-destruct. Their perfect plan to bind man in knots for many millennia was to divide and conquer. Have you ever heard of that plan? It is the best way to defeat a mighty species. If they are great and powerful, you may devise a working tactic that divides the great and powerful. What do you think will be the end product? You are that living product every day. It is a constant part of human life, wars and rumors of wars. People are afraid that one religion may become more powerful than the other religion or one race may outdo the other race. Many people would not allow their children to ever learn the teachings of another person's religion.

Religion was not enough to totally separate mankind for he had learned to tolerate foreign gods. Humans all spoke one language and were black; even though the gods would appear from one nationality to the other establishing diverse cults among the nations, the gods could not separate us in spirit. From the onset of religion, the only thing that separated humans was their religious beliefs, or more correctly, their customs and traditions, often confused with religion, which was an institution established later. There was no separation until the interference of the gods and goddess with the everyday activities of man. The reason that I state that customs and traditions are different from religion is that religions seek converts and in general anyone who follows the cult is considered a member. Customs and traditions were the way of life for a particular race of people. That is why today there is so much confusion with the Jewish religion. In the Jewish religion anyone can become a Jew, including the late Sammy Davis, Jr. One needs only to practice the religion. People get the Jews confused with the ancient black Hebrew Israelites who practiced their customs and traditions. THE ONLY WAY TO BE A HEBREW ISRAELITE ORIGINALLY WAS THROUGH BIRTH! That is why when we speak of Hebrew Israelites we are speaking of a race of people. When speaking of Jewish people, they can be considered both a white race of people who have converted to Hebrew customs, or the Jewish religion based solely on converts regardless of race. Many times we wonder if the Jewish people consider themselves as a race or a religion. The ones I have talked with say that it is both or the more knowledgeable ones admit that it is their adopted religion only.

The final breaking point of separating the humans forever was the creation of races through mutating the melanin gene in the black Africans, and race mixing. One evidence of mutation can be found in what is known as the duffy factor. Pure Africans have been tested to have zero duffy factor while all other races on the planet possess higher levels, the races containing the highest level being Asian. This duffy factor or measure of relative mutation is one of the proofs that link Europeans closely to their African ancestors in genetic makeup. Or perhaps more correctly, it is the race that remains closest to African than any other race. Another source validating mutation in American whites can be found in lactose tolerance. Between 90 and 100 percent of whites are lactose tolerant while African-Americans are closer to 30 percent, and Africans were found as a race to be totally intolerant to lactose. Using lactose intolerance reports it can be assumed that African-Americans now carry as much as 30 percent of the mutated gene from race mixing. The scientists report that the contributing factor, which made whites highly tolerant of lactose, was a gene that mutated long ago.

Once the gods had established a color difference, fear of the opposite color race was placed in man. Man was told that if he did not do as the gods told him he would be cursed like his brother Canaan. The African man fell for this lie and believed that Canaan had been cursed and thereby banished him from CIVILIZATION (as the gods had commanded). Over a period of time various groups of men became afraid of associating with other groups. They began to individualize into smaller units known as tribes, which later developed many diverse languages as led by their individual gods. All of these power systems, in general, employed one scare tactic: FEAR! Another account that we should not forget regarding this establishment of religion is that it may have been possible that the African did not have a choice other than to turn on his albino brother. The gods, such as Jehovah, may have given the order against them; had anyone dared to go against the order, the gods may have had the challenger blown up.

After fear was installed and men had fallen over and over for the tricks of the gods, they became perpetually lost in the knot of fear and delusion. Today, for the most part, the gods no longer have the physical advantage over humans that they had in ancient times. Nonetheless, their scare tactics remain forever reincarnated in the human soul through the taking on of customs and traditions, which today we have made into religions that we kill for, religions that teach us that the moment we lose faith in a savior will be the moment that our souls are condemned to burn in hell forever. If we were to count the bodies of people who have died in the name of Christianity they would number far more than the population in the United States today. Just imagine Americans killed four times OVER in the name of Christianity. If it were to be Americans killed instead of people of other nationalities we would call the act barbaric.

I have stated that all religions originated with the goddesses and gods and not the Creator. Today's religions have the twist of man's imaginations upon ancient practices handed down by the gods and goddesses. Does that mean that all religions are destructive and should not be practiced? Absolutely not; actually, quite the reverse is true. Religion has its advantages. Most religions use positive affirmations of peace and blessings for soul edification. However, the religions that I am speaking out against are the ones that teach you to fear. I have no desire to curb my ego by not talking against this practice at this time in my life. If in your religion you were born a worm and a sinner, if you are taught that you were born and shaped in iniquity, then it is this form of doctrine that creates all our problems. If you deviate one way or the other from the structured belief are you considered a sinner? If you fail to attend communion or Sunday school service or Sabbath worship have you failed your religion? If you can answer yes to any of these questions then you are in a religion that is preparing your soul to reap the fruits of the lower worlds, for all of the above acts are serving the lower worlds. It is impossible for you to evolve fully with these hindering belief structures, even if you could manage to keep all of their ridiculous demands. (We won't mention what effect this has on the psyche.) You would be forced to mentally or verbally begin judging. You will judge yourself and begin condemning others, which is just as much hindrance in the evolution of our species as any vile act.

An excellent example of people who condemn continuously are those Christians who maintain and support the verse in the Bible that state the people are already condemned for not believing in God's son Jesus. SAYS WHO? NOBODY KNOWS. THEY WILL SAY THAT JESUS SAID IT AND ST. JOHN RECORDS EVERYTHING JESUS SAID WORD FOR WORD **THIRTY YEARS LATER!** For Pete's sake, I can't even remember in perfect detail word for word what someone said hours ago, but we are to believe that the author of St. John remembered perfectly thirty years later. We hold to it so strongly that we condemn others, because Jesus said that people were already condemned for not believing. The people who wrote of the grace and the power of doing things in Jesus' name as found in the book of John are the anti-Christ. Jesus would never have directed people to call on his name and to lift him up. As a matter of fact, it directly contradicts Jesus saying there is none good but the father. Jesus only wanted people to uplift the Father, Most High God. This situation hurts mankind terribly if it is man's goal to evolve. For now people look outside themselves for the kingdom of God (where it does NOT exist). They try to go through Jesus Christ instead of going within. If we don't go within we will go without! There is absolutely nothing wrong with believing that Jesus is your savior if you so choose. Nor is there any harm in practicing the positive ways of worship that Jesus taught.

As I have said all along, it is not religions that are bad (causing the human race to fall), it is the fear, hate, and destructive teachings that come along with the religion as baggage which cause us to fall collectively. If you are honest, within your soul you know that fear, hate, and destruction belong nowhere in your life. Why buy into it, then? The worst fear tactic that comes into play is the threat that you are going to burn in hell forever because of lost faith. The argument is that the Bible says it "therefore they believe it." Nonetheless, have you studied the origin of the Bible? The Bible is not an authorized and perfect word of God. It is a forever-changing book with various people's and/or god's agendas at play. The Bible simply says the things that gods and people who had the power to influence it wanted it to say, and then you adopted it as GOD'S WORDS. Seriously consider this statement.

# TWELVE

## Real-Life
## Biographies

Our universe so perfectly proves blatant reality if one steps out into the world of creation and sees the world absent of the blinders. The first reality that people should see is that the physical human existence is a BLINDER in itself! This is why I have decided to include accounts of six people who have either experienced the unseen directly or been totally ignorant of it. One is from a little girl by the name of Amanda Daniels who from the age of two began rambling on and on to her mother and others about the experiences of her life as an alcoholic, and the experiences of heaven when she used to be a grownup. The second will be the story of my uncle, who remains faithful to Christ today, regardless of all the facts that I have shown him which he cannot explain away. He says you don't have to understand it, just believe it. Although he truly loves me, he believes that as long as I fail to accept Jesus Christ as my personal savior, I am doomed to the eternal fiery pit of hell. It is his beliefs and those of my aunt Orine Johnson, who is just like him, that inspired me to complete this book. The third biography will be about a gentleman by the name of Darrick Jemison, to whom I was once married. Aliens abducted him at the age of seven from an alley on Chicago's South Side. He is without a doubt the best psychic I have ever known.

The fourth story is about a white Indian Monk, Bavani, who

remembers a vast majority of her past lives and claims to have known me in ancient times. The fifth and sixth accounts are both near-death experiences, where Diana was pronounced dead at the scene of the accident and Katy Gray's heart stopped beating on the operating table.

## Amanda

The story of Amanda is one of unique circumstances. I will start with the circumstantial meeting of Amanda's mother and myself. I had left my position with the City of Chicago's water department as a sanitary engineer and spent much of my time in my hometown. I had run an ad in the newspaper advertising that I was interested in baby-sitting children. Amanda's mom, Jennifer, responded to my ad with her baby daughter, Alicia. I met with both Jennifer and her mom in my home and they both decided that my home and I would work out for Alicia's day care.

I began baby-sitting for Alicia and when Jennifer would come to pick her up she began to share stories with me. She told me of her older daughter who had spoken of another life here on earth and of her experiences after she died and went to heaven. When I learned this, needless to say I was frantic to meet the little girl to get firsthand information from someone who actually remembered experiencing what I have said all along happens to each and every human soul. I told Jennifer that I had to meet her daughter. Jennifer went on to explain how Amanda had begun shutting down as a self-defense technique in order not to be teased by the kids in school or others who would find her stories a joke. My heart and soul felt for the little girl, for I knew that she was unusually unique in that she crossed over into the physical realm with a memory of life before her new physical experience. I have heard of people who have discovered past lives through hypnosis, but never had I heard of anyone knowing of their life before birth from birth.

I insisted to Jennifer that she had to let me meet with her daughter and she agreed, but then Alicia caught pneumonia and had be hospitalized. The places where Jennifer worked wouldn't accept her taking off to be with her daughter in the hospital and let her go. I had decided that baby-sitting was not something that worked out for my situation either, so Jennifer and I agreed that we would stay in touch, and I believe we engaged in about two more phone conversations after that. I had lost her number and I thought I had lost my only chance to talk to a soul who remembered what I believed to be reality. The thought that as easily as we met the first time it could happen a second time was totally and quickly abandoned.

## Uncle Kenny

As time went on, my mom retired and moved into her dream home. My aunt, who took care of my uncle, got sick and had to be admitted into the hospital. My Uncle Kenny had multiple sclerosis and had lost all mobility from the neck down. After my aunt went into the hospital and was no longer capable of caring for my uncle, he came to live with my mother. I had to help mom on many occasions and it was during these occasions that I would look into my Uncle Kenny's eyes and see remorse for my soul. He felt that God would allow me to go to hell because I was not a Christian. My Aunt Orine, on the opposite side of the family, also had the same look. The looks got much worse as I began to share with them some of the information that is contained in this book. Blasphemy, they proclaimed in all sincerity. How could I say such things? How was it possible to form and shape my lips to proclaim my ideas? "How many people will you lead to hell with this God-awful learning?" they worried. My aunt went as far as to say that too much learning had driven me quite mad. She borrowed that one from Paul. It is these conversations with my uncle and aunt that inspired me to allow the ego to take over and share my theory with the world.

I told my Uncle Kenny of the little girl (Amanda) whom I had never met, who experienced life after death. He still insisted that the Bible stated that there was no such thing as reincarnation and that it was impossible. I would tell Uncle Kenny that the Bible also encoded to him that it wasn't all truth in II Timothy 2:15. It clearly says that we must divide the word of truth in order to find truth. When I pointed out that Jesus gave us a condition as to when we could do away with the law in Matthew 5:18, he told me that Jesus fulfilled the law and that now we are under grace. I then said, "But Uncle Kenny, the verse clearly stated that not until heaven and Earth passed away." I would ask my uncle, "Has the earth passed away?" He would reply, "No." "Has heaven passed away?" "No." "Then how do you justify Jesus' death as fulfilling the law and placing you under grace?" He would then faithfully answer. "Sandy, I don't know, I'm just going to believe it regardless." Then he would instruct me that all I have to do is just believe, too. But I would ask my uncle how I could leave all the tons of information, such as the *Enuma Elish* and *Gilgamesh* epic. These stories totally bust out the Bible as nothing more than the Hebraic culture of our ancestors plagiarizing a more ancient story that was written in cuneiform many years previous. Uncle Kenny asked me why I couldn't just forget the first story and hold on to the Bible. I simply smiled and shook my head to Uncle Kenny. I told him that his religion and traditions are much more important to him than the truth and God, for him to ask me to forget the original story and get back into the Bible. I promised my uncle that there was absolutely no way I would ever return to serve a lie.

Then he asked me how I knew that what I believed was truth. I told him that he would never hear me proclaim that I have absolute truth until I am able to possess the powers of the all-knowing. Anyone who cannot manifest 100 percent of his/her desires without karmic back-splash does not possess all knowl-edge. This is what Jesus meant when his disciples came running to him on the boat because of the storm and Jesus had to manifest their desires by calming the sea. This was a simple task of control-ling the elements, so Jesus wondered how long he would have to suffer with their lack of knowledge. Jesus went as far as to state that greater things than he had done shall his followers do. Unfortunately, none of his followers followed his teachings, but instead followed the teachings of the Antichrist so no Christians to this date have been capable of doing greater works than Jesus' miracles. Christians know that Jesus told the disciples that they shall do greater works, but they do not look at why they are not doing the greater works! Their entire lifestyle contradicts these words that Jesus said himself. The Antichrist taught many to go astray, seeking the kingdom of God without. Now, they look outside of themselves to Jesus' grace instead of remembering that Jesus said that the kingdom of God was within.

However, I do know what is not true. I know that Santa Claus is not true, yet he is real to those who believe. Likewise are the many inventions and imaginations of men's minds not true in the Bible. For example, I said to my Uncle Kenny, "We all agree that Israel fell short and worshipped many other gods, with their most-talked-about idol god being Baal." Even my uncle agreed with this statement. Then I asked, "Uncle Kenny, where are the praises to BAAL?" I am not talking of telling the story that Israel worshipped Baal, I am talking of the **ACTUAL** PRAISES TO BAAL. After all, if Israel began to worship Baal then assuredly they had to say praises to their god. Where are the praises? Where are the orders of thus saith the LORD BAAL? "Uncle Kenny," I said, "Baal has appeared to Israel under the name of Yahweh." I then told my uncle as I am telling you, I offer $10,000 to anyone who can prove that the Hebrew god of the Old Testament was anything more than one of the gods of ancient times—more than likely Baal himself. Better yet, if anyone can prove that the creation stories in the Bible (the so-called word of God) are anything more than plagiarism. He told me that he would have to turn me down because he couldn't prove God, he could only believe. I have sent out offers to several ministers to send in proof that the Ezzrath theory is bogus with respect to the Christian religion and I have recorded their responses as they wrote them, or more than likely avoided them. All of these organizations received a synopsis of my book requesting that they explain how they could justify the worship of Christianity:

The 700 Club/CBN, Attn. Evangelist Pat Robertson
Oral Roberts Evangelistic Association, Attn. Oral
   and Richard Roberts
Jerry Falwell Ministries, Attn. Jerry Falwell
Billy Graham Evangelistic Associations, Attn. Billy Graham
Kenneth Copeland Ministries, Attn. Kenneth Copeland
T. D. Jakes Ministries, Attn. Bishop T. D. Jakes
Crenshaw Christian Center, Attn. Pastor Frederick Price
Seventh-day Adventists, Attn. Headquarters Senior Director
Jehovah's Witness, Attn. Kingdom Hall Senior Director
St. Paul Baptist Church, Attn. Rev. C. L. Adams
Christ Church Cathedral, Attn. Senior Pastor
Sunnycrest Baptist Church, Attn. Pastor Garland A. Morrison
College Wesleyan Church, Attn. Senior Pastor
Allen Temple A. M. E. Church, Attn. Rev. Frederick L. Greene
Westside Assembly of God, Attn. Senior Pastor
Rising Star Baptist Church, Attn. Rev. T. A. Hunter

I already knew that the majority would not answer the letter nor could they possibly address the verses that prove that Christianity is the worship of the Antichrist. However, to my surprise, two organizations did answer my letter: The 700 Club and Bishop T. D. Jakes. I have copied them just as they were sent to me.

Dear Friend,

On behalf of Bishop T.D. Jakes, we want to acknowledge receipt of your correspondence and express our deepest appreciation for your kindness.

Please know we commit to you our prayers for the work that you do for the Kingdom.

The Executive Office of
The Potter's House/T.D. Jakes Ministries

AND

In my synopsis I did not include my race or gender. Notice the mistaken identity assumed by The 700 Club. I obviously had to be a male because only a man could have come up with this degree and class of information. As for the information showing sound scriptural evidence that proves the Ezzrath Theory wrong there is absolutely NONE!

One day I was visiting my uncle's and peeked my head in as he

377 CENTERVILLE TURNPIKE, VIRGINIA BEACH, VIRGINIA 23463-0001   (757) 226-7000

The
Christian
Broadcasting
Network
Inc.

December 3, 1999

Mr. Ezzrath Baht Shem
P.O. Box 3132
Marion, IN   46953

Dear Ezzrath,

Thank you for writing to Pat Robertson.  We apologize that Pat is unable to respond to you personally.

In regard to the comments you shared with us, comments are always welcome at CBN.  They help us understand the concerns and interests of those who are touched by this ministry.

If we can serve you in any other way, please do not hesitate to let us know.  Thank you and God bless you.

Yours in Christ,

Ruth Kastberg
CBN Partner Correspondence

was preparing for the day. I saw that he had a new nurse with a familiar face. I told her that I had seen her before. Then she asked what my name was and she reminded me that I had baby-sat Alicia. This was remarkable, I quickly boasted; out went the ego, and I smiled at Uncle Kenny. "Remember that I told you there was a little girl who had remembered her reincarnation? Here it is two years later, Jennifer and I live in different towns, and of all the people in the world Jennifer becomes your nurse." As always, my poor Uncle Kenny gave a smile and began to realize that his new nurse was the mother of the child that I had told him about, the one who remembered her past life before this life. I asked Uncle Kenny if he believed it was just a coincidence. He told me no, he didn't think it was a coincidence. I set aside time to interview Jennifer's daughter while in my uncle's presence.

## Amanda

Jennifer agreed to bring her daughter, the lovely brunette fair-skinned ten year-old. She puts you in mind of a Snow-White look-alike. You may judge from her picture your-self. When I first met Amanda she was really shy and bashful. I told her to come into the dining room area where we would have plenty of light, and of course my uncle and her mother would be behind her. I began the conversation with the fact that I was so sorry that she had to hide the reality of her experience due to the narrow-minded ignorance of people. I tried to inspire Amanda to be proud of her experience. I found it rather sad to learn that Amanda had been so ridiculed, stared at, and jeered that she very seldom speaks of her experience now that she is ten. It is sad to think that simply because we may not have experienced a situation we can easily condemn, tease, and put to shame another human soul who has. I asked her if she was aware that she was very special and that most of us never remember anything prior to our births. She nodded that she was aware. I could still see that she was very nervous and so could her mom, who also tried to break the ice. Jennifer told Amanda to ask me what I had learnt about others like herself. I told her that I had never met nor heard any testimony of any black person who could remember their past lives. Amanda asked me why did I think it was that I could not find any blacks who had remembered their past lives. I told her that in my opinion, I believe the rules in the game of life were established from the beginning that all human souls would enter into the physical world via a state of amnesia. In her case and others who can remember, they have been chosen as the few to tell their story to the rest of us so that we who choose to remember can begin doing things in our lives to invoke the memory. I told her that white people rule the physical universe (all of the world power) and as such it seems that they are the ones who receive more of the alien abductions, psychic channeling, and memories of the afterlife. However, it could be that blacks do not get as much publicity about their experiences, yet for me to have never met one black who can remember past lives leads me to believe that it is very rare among black people.

I do believe that the fate of establishing the unity of one God, one people, one love, will all be in the hands of those with the authority, white people. However it can only happen once that the white people remember that the original first man was AFRICAN. Therefore in all honesty we are all linked into one common ancestry and that is AFRICAN! Furthermore, it is time that the African-American, and all other races step up to the mike and claim our fair share of responsibility for the destruction of the world. We all made the world as it is today, whether actively or passively. The goal is not to find fault and blame, but to accept responsibility for where we were, where we are, and where we will be. We must respect and love every one of our fellow humans' personal experiences with God, whether they call God Zeus, Jesus, Allah, Yahweh, Jehovah, Buddha, or whatever, so long as in their hearts they are reaching for the ultimate, the Creator of their soul. Who are we to say that our God is God and your God is not? For in the Ezzrath theory it is to my understanding that the Universe/God focuses on INTENT. When you call on Jesus do you intend to seek help from God? THEN THAT IS WHAT YOU WILL RECEIVE. When you call on Allah do you intend to seek help from God? THEN THAT IS WHAT YOU WILL RECEIVE. I believe that even if you are calling out to a rock and sincerely with all your heart believe that you are calling out to the Universe/God for assistance, THEN THAT IS WHAT YOU WILL RECEIVE.

The assistance may come in the form of suffering so that you will learn to seek higher truth than you have now. God may send teachers your way to point you in the closer direction of your goal. God may use both situations like with my Uncle Kenny who, crippled with MS, is now forced to live with non-Christians who will care for him and love him. My mom and I share ideas with Uncle Kenny all the time because he feels like that gives him the chance to win our lost condemned souls from the depths of hell. So my uncle suffers, and God has sent him teachers and he will continue to pray "Jesus, keep me and show me the way, lord." I sincerely believe that God has kept him and is showing him the way if it kills him, requiring life after life to get it right.

I asked Amanda to tell me about her experience in her other life before she became Amanda. I learnt that Amanda has very little memory of her past life. It appears that she is more aware that it happened than of actual living day-to-day experiences. She explicitly remembers being a heavy drinker, smoking, and doing drugs. She is always in the kitchen smoking and drinking herself into an oblivion. Amanda says that she does not have a memory of parents and that it feels as if they had either abandoned her or died when she was young. She had no children, nor did she have a husband. In my imagination it appears that she was simply a lonely soul who had slipped through the physical cracks (family and friends) of no one to care for her. If not in her true reality, it appears that in her fabricated world this had to be true. Amanda has no memory of how the drugs felt. She only remembers the act of doing it.

Amanda remembers driving a black car and it appears to be in this black car that she lost her life through drunk driving. From the digging around in Amanda's memory it seemed as if she had to have lived here in America in an all-white area. She seems to have lived sometime after the sixties and before the mid-seventies, based on her description of her car and the fact that she had never seen blacks until this lifetime.

More than her last life, Amanda explicitly remembers her life after she died and went to a place she calls "heaven." We must always remember that as people tell their stories they are relating them as best as they can to what they KNOW most about an experience. For example, A Christian who is met by a Being, will say that she saw Jesus, a Muslim will say that she saw Allah, and a Buddhist would say that she saw the Buddha, not realizing in all actuality that she saw a spiritual representative, a Guide, an Angel. Amanda described heaven as bright blue light. She says it's kind of like our bright sunshiny days but brighter. When Amanda's mom and others would ask her how she got to be so pretty Amanda would reply, "because God put glitter in my hair." She told me that she would go down to visit earth by thinking it and she would be there. She was never too cold nor too hot. She did not require food or drink. She says that she felt neither hungry nor thirsty. She did however sleep. I asked her to describe sleep in heaven. It seemed that she did not get sleepy, she would think it was time to sleep, close her eyes, and be asleep. She doesn't remember dreams from this sleep. She remembers going to school while in heaven and learning, but can't recall any detail of the events.

What about God, does Amanda speak of God while she was in heaven? Yes, Amanda gives a detailed description of a being whom she calls God. After Amanda continued to beg God for the chance to return to earth, she was told that she would get a second chance. God took Amanda on a trip to earth to pick out her parents. She visited several households and narrowed her choice down to two couples. One of the couples that she really liked apparently had two children already. Amanda felt that was the tie-breaker. The parents she chose had no children. She says that they looked as if they really loved one another and that they would take good care of her. So she told God that she would pick Jennifer and Gary.

Does Amanda tell what God looks like? Maybe I should save this one for my next book. You know they say that you shouldn't give away everything you got with one blow. However, I have never followed the rules thus far in my life and I have no intention following them now. Part of me has a desire to canonize Amanda's story because I believe that I know what has happened, which is different from what she actually experienced. However, seeing what the canon of the King James Version of the Bible has brought the world, I can promise the world that I will NEVER do that.

Here it is. Amanda's adamant description of God is that God was a male, half-white and half-black. I asked her if she meant God looked mixed, she said no. She said that half of God's face was white while the other half was black, "like you guys," she said, as she pointed to me. Then I took my hand and placed it next to her hand and I said, "Are you telling me that the God you saw looked like our hands setting together here on the table?" She giggled and replied, "Yes except the eyes, nose, and mouth are missing." Amanda continued on to describe God's clothing. She says that God wore a full-length white robe. His head was covered with a white hood or turban-type covering. The garment that God wore was described as one that was similar to the one that I had on. I wore white robes from head to toe with a hood for the covering. Amanda seems to express that the head covering was very similar to the hooded garment that I wore, but in some way different. The garment had buttons all the way from top to bottom. I guess that even God can get with the times. Amanda also told me that people in heaven appeared to float more than walk.

Now I will seize this opportunity to expound on some of the experiences set forth by Amanda, applying the Ezzrath theory. The first thing we can realize is that this is a little girl who from the age of two has been telling this story as well as she can describe the events which happened to her. The place that Amanda calls heaven may have been heaven, but it may also have been a midway holding area for souls that departed before what some would say is their time, although there is no such thing. God has planned out all the events of mankind so that nothing can remotely happen out of order. Even if the earth is totally destroyed it all works out beautifully to plan.

The human soul cannot be destroyed. We are all given two angels, a recording angel and a guardian angel. Both of these angels are with us at all times. Sometimes they are relieved, according to Oahspe, and replaced with other guardian and recording angels similar to relief operators on the job. When Amanda reported the seeing a half-black, half-white God, I believe that in all actuality it was her soul guardian angel—NOT GOD. Her guardian angel appeared to her as both black and white so as not to totally confuse Amanda. I believe that for the most part a spirit like Amanda would have experienced seeing a guardian who was white like herself. I believe that all or the vast majority of all **human** guardians are black-skinned like the original HUE-man— BUT IN SPIRIT THEY ARE ACTUALLY LIGHT FORM, meaning that when our guardian angels actually appear to us the skin color does not exist. They generally appear in a form that will be most comfortable for the soul to bond with. If the soul sees itself as a white person it will show its self to be white. If it sees itself with straight hair, long nose, and big eyes, then that is how it generally appears. Guardians and masters who help us evolve, on the other hand, are different. They will appear to us as we will best receive them, not as they are in true form. An excellent example of this fact can be found in the *Oahspe*, which talks of man's need to name the Great Spirit and how Jehovih allowed it to be so.

It appears that in order to present a side of himself that Amanda could still relate to in her mind and yet also reveal the actual blackness of the guardian angels (most ancient ancestors), her guardian chose to appear as both sides black and white. Perhaps if we could realize that in all actuality the whites, reds, yellows, and browns are all of AFRICAN DESCENT, then we could unite as one in HUE-manity!

Regardless of the fact that Amanda saw a being half-white and half-black, common sense tells us that that is next to impossible. I choose not to believe that the little girl is lying or confusing the colors, black and white, although understandable if dismissed by others.

## Darrick Jemison

People of all walks of life have reported alien abductions from the four corners of the earth. Most of them report that the one thing in particular these aliens do is to make sure that their specimens (humans) feel no fear or anxiety during their captivity. When they are being examined like lab mice, they describe a laboratory/clinic-type setting. Many say that the aliens talked to their minds for their lips did not move, but their minds heard the thoughts of their captors. I have had the privilege of hearing one person's firsthand account about his abduction by aliens. He is my ex-husband, Darrick Jemison, also called Yesha'yahuwa, his chosen Hebrew name.

Darrick says that when he was approximately seven years old, one day after school as he was walking home through an alley he saw two little boys. As the little boys approached him he thought that they wanted to play, but one of them took out a rope and laid it across his neck. Darrick said that the rope caused him to black out and when he awoke he was in a clinic on a table unable to move. He says that a six-foot-tall man all in black entered the room and assured him that he would be all right. He told him that one day he would return and then took out the rope and placed it on Darrick's neck again.

When Darrick came to, he was in the alley again, but the only difference was that every sound around him echoed with great amplification. The sound of all the ants marching could be heard like soldiers headed for combat, the buzzing of bugs was like a bugle call. He discovered a green rash around his neck. That has never been analyzed or defined as to where it came from or what it was. When Darrick would lie in his bed at night he could hear his mom and dad as if they were in the very room where he rested. I asked him if it could have been because they were arguing with raised voices. He replied, "No, they didn't want us kids to hear and they were whispering, but I could here it as if they were in the room whispering to me."

I don't know whether Darrick's psychic gift had any role in the choice of the alien's abduction or not, but without doubt with all that I know to be real; Darrick does possess psychic intuition beyond imagination. These are real stories told by real people; there are hundreds of thousands of stories just like these. All that one has to do is research, read, and begin to ask people about their personal experiences. People in general love to share "weird," "spooky," and the supernatural circumstances that happen to them. Collect your own personal portfolio of data. We could assume that all of these people are liars or we could assume that they are having a mass illusion. Nonetheless, the only thing that really makes sense is the assumption that these people are reporting real experiences, although the accounts may have been a little misunderstood or misinterpreted. That is where each individual must put into account his or her interpretation as given by divine inspiration.

To give an example, as Hebrew Israelites we used to discuss experiences of revelations from Yahweh, the god of the Hebrews.

One brother very excitedly shared that God revealed that he was an Israelite while he was sleeping in a homeless shelter. He said that God told him that he was not understanding the name Israel and according to him it was revealed by God that he should say, "Its not Israel, for God **is real** (Israel) to me." We all laughed at the guy at first, but then the more I listened to him, the more I began to realize that many demons were appearing to him and revealing information so that he was inspired to much knowledge, but little wisdom. He called himself Yeshua, a version of the true name of Jesus, and he knew that he was an Israelite through fourth-dimension influences. He said that the system was watching him and that the government had offered to buy his silence. What was scary was the fact that he presented documentation of correspondence between himself and the government where he had been seeking reparations of over one trillion dollars and he had turned down an offer of around fifteen thousand dollars. All that he owned was these letters and a few items of clothing. Stories like these, I keep in my memory as having little merit or validity. Nonetheless, as far-fetched and unbelievable as the story may be, the moment that I seal it in my consciousness as impossible instead of "for now I don't buy into this story," I have eliminated many chances of recovery from deceit, had it been truth, thus creating a possible Ultimate Deceit. The unbelievable is just that and nothing more. It should not become a fact of impossibility nor should the believable become a fact of "infinite possibility" (100 percent believable). There are no absolutes in reality, only shades and variance.

## Bavani

Bavani was a person whom Darrick and I both met at a spiritual boutique on Chicago's North side, who was sort of spooky to talk with. She was a white monk who had traveled to India and other exotic places. She never worked for pay, but traveled from one spiritual spot to the next sharing her wisdom. She did most of her spiritual learning in India. Her appearance was that of a very lively older woman with white hair, but not elderly. She quickly ran up to me and asked how I had been as if she had known me all of my life. She asked if I ever got that anger under control. How on God's green earth did she know that of all the types of problems in the universe my greatest problem was anger? I had not spoken more than a greeting of "Hi, how are you." Remember that this is a woman that I had never met before. She told us (Darrick and myself) that we were ancient souls from way back and that she remembered us from then. I must admit that a huge lump was caught inside my throat for anger is my foremost shadow, but how did she know? Darrick and I were both concerned over the controversy that earth would end between 2000 and 2012 or that something drastic would take place. She counseled us with information regarding her work and the work of others. She said that there are many like herself, who spend large fractions of their lives in spiritual meditation for the salvation of the earth. Then she told us that we must learn not to judge what we called the darkside. She had once been troubled by a spirit and started to perform an exorcism, but before she completed it she learnt that the demon was her son. She told us that she was the mother of demons and that they too seek love and guidance; moreover, that they are lost in a tighter knot than we humans. That was a deep penetrating story, I thought to myself, and then even a more selfish thought came to mind, and that was: had I mothered a demon would I tell it? That would be a hard question to answer. I can't understand how such a kind benevolent soul that gave us free readings and did not get paid to work at the establishment other than travel, room, and board would mother demons.

Today I realize that we all have mothered and fathered demons, which is the reason that mother Teresa's statement makes a lot of sense, **"rather than being against evil, be for love."** This is the only answer for the survival of the human species.

## Deanna Daugherty and Katy Gray

Both Deanna and Katy experienced an Out of Body Experience (OBE) when their hearts had stopped beating. In Deanna's case she was only fifteen and out on a wild night with her friends when tragedy struck. The driver of the car lost control, causing a terrible crash. The ambulance attendant found Deanna dead at the scene. Deanna found herself outside her body and looking at the terrible crash and all the excitement around her, when all of a sudden she saw the attendant look in her direction as the new arriving attendant asked what to do with her. The attendant told him that she was dead and not to bother. Deanna yelled at the men, "No I am not, here I am," but they couldn't hear her. When she looked back she saw her body on the ground and in fear ran back to it and sat down and squeezed herself into a tight ball. Deanna's mother later told her that she was dead on site, but that somehow her body had started convulsing and they brought a helicopter to airlift her to the nearest emergency medical care hospital.

Today Deanna has no memory of a life prior to fifteen years of age. It was wiped out in the car accident. If you look closely at her picture you may be able to see her scars from her trachea surgery performed on site at the accident. She suffers from anxiety attacks, depression with uncontrollable crying, memory loss, and other mental problems that make her a social misfit. To me she is a beautiful soul, stamped on, belittled, and much taken advantage of by our society due to her situation. She is in desperate need of a soul revival, someone to heal her by finding her soul that is lost out in the universe.

Katy's story is a little different. She is an older African-American woman who has been through an emotional cyclone. Her body began to show the signs of dis-ease at a young age. Barely able to walk and in excruciating agonizing pain, Katy finally consented to a hip replacement surgery. This was to be a standard ordinary hip replacement. Katy suffers

from diabetes and asthma. Her asthmatic condition has her hopelessly dependent on steroids.

The time had come for her surgery and everything was normal, until Katy noticed that she was watching the surgery from above. She could hear them talking to each other. Something had gone terribly wrong with the anesthetic. She had flat-lined and could see the medical personnel doing all that they could to revive her. They brought out the paddles and applied them to her chest at least twice while performing CPR in-between the jolts.

When Katy awoke, personnel repeatedly asked her if she was okay or if she was having any problems. To her amazement, none of them ever mentioned that they had botched up the surgery and killed her. Katy informed me that she plans to see an attorney and get the medical records. They never knew that she had witnessed the entire blundered portion of the surgery.

These are all real people whom I have personally encountered in my life. All that is in this book is only shared information for you to know that it is out here. What you do with the information is entirely up to you. I wrote it because I never could have imagined that this knowledge existed and that there could be others out there who like myself are unwilling participants in the illusions of our world.

It has been said that we are nothing more than mere viruses (like cancer) running our course of vast destruction across the planet until we no longer have a host (the earth), ultimately becoming extinct ourselves. It is my prayer and intention that this book opens the door to reason and question of our very soul's existence and purpose. From a physical point of view, where and how did the human race appear on planet earth? From a spiritual point of view, who are the souls of human incarnations and where do they come from?

GIVE IT A THOUGHT.

Shalom and may the peace of God, the All-Highest Light, emanate radiantly, freely, and openly all the days of your life. PEACE,

— *The White Satin*
*Sentinel,*
*Ezzrath Baht Shem*

# Appendix

## ASTROLOGY

| Sign | Symbol | | Date |
|------|--------|---|------|
| Aries | Ram | ♈ | March 21—April 20 |
| Taurus | Bull | ♉ | April 21—May 21 |
| Gemini | Twins | ♊ | May 22—June 21 |
| Cancer | Crab | ♋ | June 22—July 22 |
| Leo | Leo | ♌ | July 23—Aug. 22 |
| Virgo | Virgin | ♍ | Aug. 23—Sept. 22 |
| Libra | Scales | ♎ | Sept. 23—Oct. 22 |
| Scorpio | Scorpion | ♏ | Oct. 23—Nov. 22 |
| Sagittarius | Bow | ♐ | Nov. 23—Dec. 22 |
| Capricorn | Goat | ♑ | Dec. 22—Jan. 20 |
| Aquarius | Water | ♒ | Jan. 21—Feb. 19 |
| Pisces | Fish | ♓ | Feb. 20—March 20 |

## Whose god is GOD?

| Ancient Events | Summerin 3000 BC | Babylonian 2500 BC — OLD | Babylonian 2500 BC — NEW | Egyptian 2500 BC | Canaan | Bible Old Test. (Phoneci-Canaan 2500 BC, Biblical 1500 BC) | Bible New Test. |
|---|---|---|---|---|---|---|---|
| Father God | AN | ANU | Marduk | Ptah/Ea? | Anu/Ea El | El Jahovah | God |
| Son or Sun God | Enlil/Ea | Enlil/Enki | Marduk | Ra/Marduk? | Enlil/Marduk Baal | n/a | Jahshua/ Jesus |
| Requested permission to create man | Ea | Enki | Marduk | gods | gods | Elohim (gods) | God |
| Creator of humans | Ea | Enki | Marduk | gods | gods | Elohim (gods) | God |
| Tricked man out of immortality | Ea | Enki | Marduk | Ra? | ? | Serpent | Serpent |
| Caused flood | Enlil/gods | Enlil/gods | Marduk | gods | gods | Jehovah | God |
| Saved one human family | Ea | Enki | Marduk | | | Jehovah | God |
| Sole survivor of flood | Atra/Hasis | Utanapishtim | Utanapishtim | ? | ? | Noah | Noah |
| Offered sacrifice to God/gods | Atra/Hasis | Utanapishtim | Utanapishtim | ? | ? | Noah | Noah |
| Attended the sacrifice | Ea/Inanna/ Enlil/gods | Enki/Ishtar/ Enlil/gods | Marduk | ? | ? | Jehovah? | God? |
| Showed compassion for his/ her part in killing mankind | Inanna | Ishtar | Marduk | ? | ? | Jehovah | God |
| Fought Leviathan | n/a | Marduk | Marduk | Re, Ra? | Baal/El? | Jehovah | God |
| Supreme God—"God of gods" | n/a | n/a | Marduk | Re, Ra | n/a | Jehovah | God |
| god—who liked humans | Ea | Enki | Marduk | Osiris, Isis | El | Jehovah | God |
| god—who disliked humans | Enlil | Enlil | Marduk | ? | Baal | Jehovah | God |
| Trinity | n/a | God the Father, Son, Nimrod and his mother—2500 BC | n/a | Father, Osiris Son, Horus Mother, Isis | n/a | n/a | God, Father God, son God, Holy Ghost |
| Salvation and gods of resurrection | n/a | Nimrod | Marduk | Osiris | n/a | Jehovah | Jesus |

# EVOLUTION OF THE HUMAN RACE

## RAMAPIHROUS
The first possible ape known
to man evolving into man.
As early as 14 million B.C.

## AUSTRALOPITHECUS AFRICANUS
Appeared next in line
in 6 million B.C.

## HOMO-HABILIS
Appeared in 3 to 4 million B.C.

## NEANDERTHAL MAN & LATER CRO-MAGNON MAN
200,000 B.C. and 20,000 B.C.
respectively

## HOMO-ERECTUS
Appeared as early as one and a half
million years B.C. Anunnaki begins
genetic manipulations in efforts to create
a primitive worker race of beings.

## ❶ THE AFRICAN RACE
(Black-skinned people)
The ORIGINAL SOURCE OF
ALL HUMANITY (HUE-MANS)

## THE PLEIADIANS
(Anunnaki) TRICKS a race of angels
known as Seraphim (clothing
themselves in animal skins) into entering
the babies of an animal called man,
thus creating the man of color
(HUE-MAN), THE ADAM KADMON

## ❻ AFRO-AMERICANS
Black, brown, red, and yellow skin—
Mixed with all races with a minimal
change to the outward appearance

## ❶ AFRICANS
Black skin

## CAUCASIAN RACE
Produced by two routes

1. The African Japhethic race migrated
to the Caucasus mountains, lost its
civilization, became the first
hue-man cavemen, due to breathing
colder more dense mountain air and
lack of exposure to the sun. Over
generations their noses became slim
and their skin turned white.

## AFRICANS, INDIANS AND ASIANS
(Chinese, Japanese, Korean,
Vietnamese) BLACK SKIN

## ARYANS
A superior race from the Orion Belt
(a star constellation) mixed in with
both the Indians and the Asians,
in an attempt to overtake the superior
race called Anunnakis (see Pleiadians).
According to myth they lose the war.
THIS IS THE RACE THAT ADOLPH
HITLER TRIED TO REVIVE. Blond,
blue-eyed people. THE ARYAN NATION

2. Long after the first process had taken
place many Black Canaanites were
targeted by their enemy god Marduk/Ba-al
who used bio-chemical warfare to cause
the loss of melanin to the human genetic
structures. Introduced a new reason for
men to war against each other instead of
religious differences only. Now humans
fought over their skin difference too.

## ❷ INDIAN RACE
Brown people

## ❸ ASIAN RACE
Yellow people

## ❺ HISPANICS
Mexicans, Puerto Rican, etc.
(Mixed with Indian, Caucasian, and African)

❌ Order of appearance of the
races with respect to each other.

# CHRONICLE PERIODS FOR MORTAL MAN

| | |
|---|---|
| **GEMINI**<br>**6000 - 4000**<br>**B.C.** | • Due to the fact that written languages were in the process of being developed during this era, very little is known about it with scientific asurety. However, it is known that civilization was indeed on the earth at this time.<br>• The earth functioned in a matriarchal society with telepathic communication.<br>• The beginning of the first mortal humans |
| **TAURUS**<br>**4000 - 2000**<br>**B.C.** | • Religions are in full bloom in the form of worship of the mother goddess.<br>Wicca, Ancient Hindu, Egyptian, Chinese religions (The govemment destroyed their feminine ruling Documentation.)<br>• Communication changes from telepathic to oral.<br>• Matriarchal society begins to disappear and the patriarchal society begins to rise to power. |
| **ARIES**<br>**2000 - 0 B.C.** | • Man develops written languages.<br>• Patriarchal society is in full bloom with only a few cults in support of both the masculine and feminine entities.<br>• Cult centers are established to worship the various gods and goddesses.<br>• The sacrificial Sun/Son God is created.<br>• Written laws are established under the religions—Hammurabi, Ancient Hebrews, Brahmins (caste system).<br>• Human consciousness is severed from its original self, creating division, wars, famine, destruction, cannibalism, racism rampantly ruling the planet. |
| **PISCES**<br>**0 - 2000 A.D.** | • Human race hits all time low in consciousness. They serve the religions of fallen gods.<br>• Masters/teachers/leaders are born out of the transient age from Aries to Pisces to undo the damaged consciousness of mankind caused by the fallen spirits. Many are executed and martyrs with most of their teachings adulterated through man-developed religions: Confucius, Jesus, Zoroaster, Mohammed, Nostradamus, M. L. King, Gandhi, and many others.<br>• Patriarchal society rules the planet. |

| | |
|---|---|
| | • Harsh laws requiring death for the most insignificant offenses, tortures, executions and cannibalism with nationwide acceptance, dissipate from the consciousness of the masses.<br>• Illusion veil of man made religions place mankind in an ultimate deceit.<br>• Humans seek God in the sky or outside of themselves. In general, they believe in a condemning vengeful god who promises a fiery burning hell for ali souls who fall short of his expectations. |
| **AQUARIUS 2090 - 4000 A.D.** | • HUMANS ARE INDIVIDUAL AND SEPARATE FROM EACH OTHER. Religion is obtained by faith.<br>• Mankind discovers the ultimate deceit. They begin seeking the kingdom of God from within, thus abandoning man-made religions.<br>• Individualism fades out.<br>• Humans find more love, respect, and concern for all life forms through seeking the kingdom of God from within. Religion is obtained through research.<br>• This era will bring a conscious shift as never before witnessed by humans. Mankind will collectively by the masses find itself compelled to unite as one. |

# ULTIMATE UNIVERSAL TIMELINE

| TIME | EVENT |
|---|---|
| In the beginning—more than countable time—eternity or infinity (Before time) | Our universe was nothing more than karmic consciousness. This consciousness at some point collected itself forming the tiniest piece of a particle unimaginable to humans with their miscroscopes. This was the creation of the most high of our universe (GOD) US. |
| BIG BANG AND THE ONSET OF THE CREATION OF TIME. Time (0) | God decides to create our universe. The mere thought and decision to create something more than self caused an enormous blast which scientists now call the Big Bang.<br>God separates. Her/His karmic energies divide into two (yin/yang). (Biblical Gen. 1:3) LIGHT AND DARKNESS—this point is the making of the dualistic universe. |
| Eons pass. Creative energy and intent to create matter begins here at time = ? | Disorder and chaos—The universe begins expanding. **God establishes order by first ranking the children of light and the children of darkness.** Each world instinctively begins establishing the worlds of the universe according to the talent of the individual light and dark consciousness. The subatomic worlds are defined along with the conscious energy required to produce matter. $E = mc^2$. |
| Perhaps hundreds of billions of years ago B.C.—In the theory of an expanding universe scientists place the beginning of our Universe sometime around 20 to 15 billion years ago. The Ezzrath theory supports the expanding universe thought moreso than the collapsing universe or the theory that the Big Bang never happened. | **Thus We/God created the heavens and the heavenly bodies.** Through Quantum materializing the debris from the blast with the capability to produce conscious matter, forming the dimensions and waters of the Heavens, some billions of years later our solar system took on form. Its dimension for which it exists and its appearance originally looked nothing like it does today.<br><br>By now, many species in other dimensions and planets have developed superior physical evolution—some continue on today, others have destroyed their own evolutionary process (somewhat like the current path of mankind, which should shift with the new conscious shift). Members of these physical creatures became gods—JEHOVAH—SLAVE MASTER, of the human race. |

| Many billions of years ago—Science estimate at 5-4.6 billion B.C. | **The formation of our solar system**—Earth becomes a ball of hot molten lava during the formation of our solar system. <br> **Creation of Earth**—A large hot mass of molten matter cooled, producing oceans over the entire planet from condensate. At some point earth was hit by another object (relatively the size of a planet—Marduk?) creating the asteroid belt, moon. It created such a huge unearthing that the waters gathered to fill the abyss, thus exposing land. |
|---|---|
| Science estimates at 3.5 billion B.C. | The first signs of physical life appears— one cell amoeba, protozoa |
| Prior to 60 mill. B.C. | Extinction of dinosaurs |
| Prior to 12 mill. B.C. | Ramapithecus -The first non-ape ancestors |
| 450,000 B.C. | The Anunnaki arrive on planet earth and begin mining the earth's gold for their planet Nabiru. Enki was the first to arrive. Nonetheless lots were cast for who would become the commander of the Earth. Enlil wins the lots causing Enki to be set over Egypt alone. Later more and more Anunnaki arrived on earth. |
| 400,000 B.C. | The Igigi were the young gods who would mine the earth's gold for Nabiru. They become tired of the tedious work and complain, to the higher gods for relief, causing mutiny and rebellion. |
| 300,000 B.C. | A primitive worker race is created through the manipulation of genetics of ape females. Enlil creates his own workers of a higher species known as *Homo sapiens*, who are instructed not to procreate (partake of the tree of life). |
| 100,000 B.C. | The sons of god had sex with the daughter of man, creating human gods capable of transfiguration. |
| 75,000 B.C. | Human life regresses through changes in earth's climate. |
| 50,000 B.C. | Enki and his half-sister Ninharsag establish humans of Anunnaki descent to rule in Shuruppak. Enlil becomes furious and conspires to destroy the human race. |

| | |
|---|---|
| 13,000 B.C. | Enlil plots against the human race in the flood of which Noah is the sole survivor. |
| 10,000 B.C. | Man begins to repopulate the earth; Japheth migrates into the Caucus Mountains, losing melanin, thus creating white men. |
| 9,800 B.C. | Ra/Marduk is given dominion over Egypt. |
| 9,000 B.C. | Horus launches the first pyramid war, avenging the demise of his father Osiris by Seth. The Enlilites were against the control of the Enkites space facilities. Ninurta, the son of Enlil, wins the war. |
| 8,700 B.C. | Ninharsag calls for a truce and establishes Thoth as the ruler over Egypt instead of Ra. |
| 3,800 B.C. | Eridu and Nippur are established in the land of Sumer. |
| 3,700 B.C. | Mankind begins to establish kings. |
| 3,400 B.C. | Hierarchy is established with Marduk in Babylon. Confusion of the languages during the fall of the tower of Babel. Creation of the white race through genetic mutation. |
| 3,100 B.C. | Marduk (Jehovah) imprisoned in the pyramids of Egypt. |
| 2,100 B.C. | Father Abraham is born. The gods deceive humans and trick them into doing acts that would eventually mean losing immortality. |
| 1,500 B.C. | Moses establishes the law through the Levitical priesthood against the human race. Among the Hebrews it is established that there is only one race chosen of God. Many of the other races are taught to be vile sinners worthy of death, even their babies, in Hebrew Israelite culture. |
| 800 B.C. | Total barbaric living among humans—humans begin to die the physical death. End of the dark ages or the rule of the black man and the beginning of the rule of the white man. |

# BIBLICAL CONTRADICTIONS

| Reference: | CONTRADICTIONS |
|---|---|
| | **GOD IS AGAINST KILLING?** |
| Exodus 20:13 | Thou shall not kill |
| Leviticus 24:17 | He that killeth any man shall surely be put to death |
| Revelations 13:10 | He who kills with the sword must be killed with the sword. |
| | **GOD ENCOURAGES KILLING?** |
| Numbers 31:17-18 | Jehovah orders, "Now therefore kill every male among the little ones, and kill every woman that hath known a man by lying with him, but keep alive for yourselves . . ." |
| Ezekiel 9-6 | Utterly slay old and young, men and maidens and little children and women . . . |
| Numbers 15:32-36 | God orders a man stoned to death by the children of Israel for picking up sticks . . . |
| Exodus 22:24 | ". . . I will kill you with the sword . . ." |
| | **WE MUST RESPECT OUR PARENTS** |
| | Jesus states that we must honor our mother and father . . . |
| Matthew 19:19 Exodus 21:17 | "And he that curses his father or his mother shall surely be put to death." |
| | **WE MUST HATE OUR PARENTS** |
| Luke 14:26 | Jesus states that anyone who does not hate his father and mother . . . can not be his disciple. |
| Matthew 23:9 | Jesus requires that you call no man your father upon the earth . . . |
| Matthew 10:35 | Jesus states, "I am come to set a man at variance against his father, and the daughter against her mother . . ." |
| | **THE BIBLE IS FOR THE LAW** |
| Matthew 5:17-19 | Jesus states that the law will be in effect as long as heaven and earth exists. |
| Roman 7:1 | Paul states, "Know ye not, brethren, how that the law hath dominion over a man as long as he lives." |
| Deut. 27: 26 and Lev. 19:37 | Cursed be he that confirmeth not **all the words of this law** to *do* them. |
| Lev. 3:17, 6:18, 6:22; Num. 19:21 | "and it shall be a perpetual statute for ever" |
| Leviticus 24:22 | "Ye shall have one manner of law, as well for the stranger, as for one of your own country (an Israelite): for I am Yahweh Elohim." |

| | |
|---|---|
| Leviticus 7:1 | Likewise this is the law of the trespass offering: it is most holy. |
| Romans 7:12 | "Wherefore the law is holy, and the commandment holy, and just, and good." |
| Genesis 17:7 | "And I will establish my covenant between me and thee, and thy seed after thee in their generations for an everlasting covenant." |
| Leviticus 16:34 | And this shall be an everlasting statute . . . |
| | **THE BIBLE IS AGAINST THE LAW** |
| | Christians believe that Jesus' resurrection ended the law bringing about grace. |
| Romans 4:15 | Paul accuses the law of creating wrath (anger) he goes on to say that, "where no law is there is no transgression." |
| Romans 3:20 | "Therefore by the deeds of the law there shall no flesh be justified in his sight: for by the law is the knowledge of sin." |
| Galatians 3:13 | Paul states that Jesus has redeemed us from the curse of the law. |
| Galatians 2:16 | Knowing that a man is not justified by the works of the law, but by the faith of Jesus Christ . . . "for by works of the law shall no flesh be justified." |
| Galatians 3:11 | But that no man is justified by the law in the sight of God, it is evident: for, the just shall live by faith. |
| | **GOD IS MERCIFUL** |
| Psalms 136:1-24 | God's mercy endureth forever. |
| | **GOD IS NOT MERCIFUL** |
| Numbers 14:16 | "I the Lord thy God am a jealous God, visiting the iniquity of the fathers upon the children unto the third and fourth generation". |
| Malachi 1:3-3 | "I loved Jacob and I hated Esau." |
| Ezekiel 9:5-6 | " . . . let not your eye spare nor have pity. Slay utterly old and young, both maids and little children and women." |
| | **PAUL'S CONVERSION TO CHRISTIANITY HAS CONFLICTING TESTIMONY** |
| Acts 9:3-5 | It states that Paul saw a light and fell down to the ground and those who accompanied him stood speechless, hearing the voice, but seeing no man. |
| Acts 22:6-9 | It states that Paul saw a light and fell to the ground, but in this case those who were with Paul saw indeed the light, but heard not the voice of the man speaking. |

| Acts 26:13-14 | It states that every body fell down to the ground instead of only Paul. |
|---|---|
| | **JESUS AND GOD ARE NOT ONE** |
| Numbers 15:32-36 | God had a man stoned to death for picking up sticks on the Sabbath. |
| Matthew 12:1-8 | Jesus excuses disciples' actions of picking corn on the Sabbath. |
| Exodus 21:24 | God allows "eye for an eye and tooth for a tooth." |
| Matthew 5:38-39 | Jesus states that it is not an eye for an eye or a tooth for a tooth, but that man should turn the other cheek. |
| I John 4:12 | No man has seen God at any time. |
| Exodus 33:11 | Moses talked face to face with God as a man speaks to his friend. |
| Genesis 32:30 | Jacob saw God face to face. |
| Numbers 14:14 | God was seen among the Israelites face to face. |
| John 15:16 John 3:35 | Jesus states that all things that the father has are his. The father has given all things into Jesus' hand. |
| John 10:30 | "I and my father are one." |
| Matthew 20:23 | Jesus states, " . . . but to sit on my right hand, and on my left, is not mine to give." |
| Mark 13:32 | Jesus states, "But of that day and that hour knoweth no man, no not the angels which are in heaven, neither the son of man, but the Father." |
| | **MISCELLANEOUS** |
| John 14:12 | JESUS STATES THAT HIS FOLLOWERS SHALL DO GREATER WORK THAN HE DID. |
| | CHRISTIANS CAN NOT WORK NEAR THE MIRACLES THAT JESUS WORKED LET ALONE GREATER. |
| John 1:29 | John the Baptist knows that Jesus is the one who would save the world from the very beginning. |
| Matthew 3 | John the Baptist has absolutely no idea as to whether or not Jesus is the savior of the world. |
| Matthew 15:21-22 | A woman of Canaan requests help from Jesus and is compared to a dog. |
| Mark 7:26 | A Greek woman requests help from Jesus, and is compared to a dog. Note: The Greeks and Canaanites are without doubt different races! |
| John 10:30 | Jesus states, "I and my Father are one." |
| Matthew 19:17 | Jesus states that none including himself is good, but the Father. |
| Matthew 11:14 | Jesus states that John the Baptist is the prophet Elijah returned. |
| John 1:21 | John the Baptist states that he is not the prophet Elijah (Elias). |
| Isaiah 26:13 | Although the people promise to keep God as number one, God loses power over his chosen people to other gods. |

| | |
|---|---|
| I Corinthians 12:3 | Paul states that anyone who calls Jesus a curse does not speak by the spirit of God. |
| Galatians 3:13 | Paul calls Jesus a curse. |
| John 10:28 | Jesus shall never lose one of his sheep. |
| I Timothy 4:1 | In the latter times some shall depart from the faith. |
| John 3:16-17 | Jesus states that he is sent to save the world. |
| Matthew 15:24 | Jesus states that he is sent only for the lost sheep of Israel. |
| Genesis 1:3-5 | God created daylight on the first day. |
| Genesis 1:14 | God created daylight on the fourth day. |
| Luke 4:5-9 | Jesus is tempted by Satan first on a mountain and then at the temple. |
| Matthew 4:5-8 | Jesus is tempted of satan first at the temple and then taken up to the mountain. |
| John 14:12 | THE GOSPEL (according to the Bible) CLEARLY STATES THAT JESUS' DISCIPLES WILL DO GREATER WORKS THAN JESUS DID. |
| | ABSOLUTELY NO KNOWN CHRISTIAN (or past disciple) CAN DO GREATER WORKS THAN THOSE WRITTEN IN THE GOSPEL REGARDING JESUS' WORK. |

# FEMININE VS. MASCULINE VS. UNIVERSAL ENERGY

| Feminine | Masculine | True God/ Goddess |
|---|---|---|
| Spiritual | Physical | Etheric |
| Light | Darkness | Unthinkable (simultaneous light with darkness) |
| Human Soul (Spiritual) | God Soul (Spiritual) | Masculine/Feminine Illumination |
| Goddess (Physical) | God (Physical) | N/A |
| Woman | Man | N/A |
| Earth | Sun | N/A |
| Intuition | Intellect | All knowing |
| Nurturer | Provider | Perfection |
| Submissive | Control | Abundance |
| Creation | Destruction | Universal Reality |
| Will (Desire) | Power (Ego) | Collective Will |
| Individual Will | Individual Will | Esoteric |
| Mystical | Knowing | TBA |

# Further Reading

Abingdon, *Interpreters Bible Volume 1*, Abingdon Press, 1991.

Agrippa, Henry, *Fourth Book of Occult Philosophy*, Kessinger Publishing Company, 1992.

Ammi, Ben, *God, the Black Man, and Truth*, Communicators Press, 1990.

André and Lynette Singer, *Divine Magic the World of the Supernatural*, _____, _____.

Armstrong, Karen, *History of God*, Ballantine Books, 1994.

Asimov, Isaac, *Collapsing Universe*, The Story of Black Holes, Walker, 1977.

Asimov, Isaac, *Universe from Flat Earth to Quasar*, Walker, 1971.

Baba, Sathya Sai, *Sathya Sai Speak, Vols. 1 and 2*, Bhagavan Sri Sathya Sai Baba Book Center, _____.

Baba, Sathya Sai, *Ramakatha Rasavahini, Part 1*, Sathya Sai Baba Book Centers, _____.

Bacon, Francis, *New Atlantis*, Kessinger Publishing Company, _____.

Ballou, John, *Oahspe: A New Bible in the Words of Jehovih and His Angel Embassadors*, Oahspe Publishing Association, 1882.

Barker, Dan, *Losing Faith in Faith: From Preacher to Atheist*, Freedom from Religion Foundation, 1992.

Biaggi, Cristina, and Marija Alseikaite Gimbutas, *Habitations of the Great Goddess*, Knowledge, Ideas, & Trends, 1994.

Blavatsky, H. P., *Essays*, Kessinger Publishing Company, _____.

Blumberg, Harry, *Modern Hebrew Grammar and Composition*, Hebrew Publishing Company, 1955.

Bonnor, William, *Mystery of the Expanding Universe*, Macmillan, 1964.

Boslough, John, *Stephen Hawking's Universe, An Introduction to the Most Remarkable Scientist of Our Time*, W. Morrow, 1985.

Bramley, William, *Gods of Eden*, Avon Books, 1993.

Brennan, Barbara Ann, *Hands of Light*, Bantam Doubleday Dell Publishing, 1993.

Bryan, C. D. B., *Close Encounters of the Fourth Kind—Alien Abduction, UFO's, and the Conference at M. I. T.*, Alfred A. Knopf, New York, 1995.

Buckland, Raymond, *Complete Book of Witch Craft*, Llewellyn Publications, 1986.

Budge, E. A. Wallis, *Gods of the Egyptians, Vols. 1 and 2*, by Dover Publications, 1969.

Ceram C. W., *Gods Graves and Scholars*, Vintage Books, 1986.

Childe, Vere Gordan, *Aryans,* Routledge (London Import), 1996.

Childe, Vere Gordan, *New Light on the Most Ancient East,* W.W. Norton & Company, 1969.

Childe, Vere Gordan, *Piecing Together the Past,* London, Routledge, 1956.

Childe, Vere Gordan, *The Aryans, a Study of Indo-European Origins,* London, Kegan Paul, Trench and Trubner, 1926.

Childe, Vere Gordan, *The Dawn of European Civilization,* Routledge (London Import), 1957 (6th edition)/1996.

Chopra, Deepak MD, *Ageless Body, Timeless Mind,* Three Rivers Press, 1993.

Choquette, Sonia, *Psychic Pathway,* Crown Publishing, 1995.

Christopher Ehret, *The Archaeological and Linguistic Reconstruction of African History,* Berkeley, University of California Press. 1982.

Clow, Barbara Hand, *Pleiadian Agenda,* Bear & Co, 1997.

Comay, Joan, *Who's Who the Old Testament,* Oxford University Press, 1993.

Condron, Barbara, *Kundalini Rising, Mastering Creative Energy,* School of Metaphysics, 1994.

Conway, D. J., *Ancients and Shining Ones,* Llewellyn Publications, 1994.

Dillon, Mayles, *The Celtic Realms, London,* Weidenfeld and Nicolson, 1972.

Dolfyn, *Angel Directory,* Earthspirit, Inc.,1993.

Dolfyn, *Crystal Connection, Finding Your Soulmate,* The Sacred Circle.

Dolfyn, *Praying with Fire Communication with Fire Spirits,* Dolfyn, _____.

Dolfyn, *Shamanism and Nature Spirituality: The Sacred Circle,* Dolfyn, _____.

Drury, Allen, *A God against the Gods, Return to Thebes,* Doubleday and Company, Inc., 1976.

Drury, Nevill, *Occult Experience,* Avery Publishing Group, _____.

Edey, Maitland A., *Missing Link,* Time Life Books, 1972.

Eisenman, Robert and Michael Wise, *Dead Sea Scrolls Uncovered,* Penguin USA, 1993.

Epperson, A. Ralph, *New World Order,* Publius Press, 1990.

Fatunmbi, Awo Fa'Lokun, *Obatala Ifa and the Spirit of the Chief of the White Cloth,* Original Publications, _____.

Fatunmbi, Awo Fa'Lokun, *Ochosi Ifa and the Spirit of the Tracker,* Original Publications, _____.

Fatunmbi, Awo Fa'Lokun, *Ogun Ifa and the Spirit of the Iron,* Original Publications, _____.

Fatunmbi, Awo Fa'Lokun, *Oshun Ifa and the Spirit of the River,* Original Publications, 1993.

Fatunmbi, Awo Fa'Lokun, *Shango Ifa and the Spirit of the Lightening,* Original Publications, _____.

Finley, Mark A., *Almost Forgotten Day*_____, , _____.

Fraser, Antonia, *King James the VI of Scotland and I of England,* Random House, 1974.

Fritzsch, Harald, *Creation of Matter, The Universe from Beginning to End,* Basic Books, 1984.

Georgiev, B. I., *The Arrival of the Greeks in Greece: the Linguistic Evidence,* R. A. Crosslands and A. Birchall, 1973.

Gimbutas, Marija Alseikaite, *Goddesses and Gods of Old Europe, 6500-3500 BC: Myths,* and Cult Images, (The earliest European cultures before the infiltration of the Indo-European peoples.), University of California Press, 1990.

Gimbutas, Marija Alseikaite, *The Language of the Goddess,* Harper San Francisco, 1995.

Ginzberg, Louis, *Legends of the Bible,* Jewish Publication Society, 1992.

Goldsby, Richard A., *Race and Races,* Macmillan, 1977.

Gomez, Luis O., *Land of Bliss, The Paradise of the Buddha of Measureless Light,* Sanskrit Chinese Versions of the Sukhavativyuha Sutras, 1996.

Graham, Lloyd M., *Deceptions and Myths of the Bible,* Carol Publishing Group, 1975.

Gribbin, John, *Unveiling the Edge of Time Black Holes, White Holes, Wormholes,* Harmony Books, 1992.

HaGadol, Prince Gavriell and Odehyah B. Israel, *Impregnable People,* _____, _____.

Hall, Manly P., *Secret Teachings of All Ages,* Philosophical Research Society, 1988.

Hawking, Stephen, *Black Holes and Baby Universes, and Other Essays,* Bantam Books, 1994.

Herion, Gary A., *Anchor Bible Dictionary,* Doubleday, 1992.

Hillegess, Cliff, *Cliffs Notes on Old Testament,* Cliff Notes Inc., 1965.

Hoffman, Enid, *Develop Your Psychic Skills,* Schiffer Publishing, Ltd.1997.

Hogue, John, *Nostradamvs the New Revelation,* Element Books, 1994.

"*Holy Bibles*"; KJV, NIV, Jerusalem, Lost Books of the Bible and The Forgotten Books of Eden, Open Bible, and the Oahspe Bible.

Hooker, J. T., *Reading the Past,* Barnes and Noble Books, 1998.

Hopkins, Budd, *Missing Time,* _____, 1988.

Hulse, David Allen, *Key of It All,* Llewellyn Publications, (Book One), 1995.

Hurtak, J. J., *Book of Knowledge, Keys of Enoch,* The Academy for Future Science, 1977.

Icke, David, *The Biggest Secret: The Book That Will Change The World,* Bridge of Love Publications, 1999.

Jackson, John G., *Introduction to African Civilizations,* Citadel Press, 1994.

James, G. M. George, *Stolen Legacy: Greek Philosophy is Stolen Egyptian Philosophy,* Africa World Press Inc., 1992.

Johanson, Donald & Maitland Edey, *Lucy the beginnings of Humankind,* Touchstone, 1990.

Johnson, Christopher Jay and Marsha G. McGee, *How Different Religion View Death and Afterlife,* The Charles Press, Publishers, 1998.

Jordan, Michael *Encyclopedia of Gods,* Facts on File, Inc., 1993.

Kinley, Henry Clifford, *Elohim the Archetype (Original) Pattern of the Universe Vol. I, II,* Institute of Divine Metaphysical Research, Inc., 1960.

Kinley, Henry Clifford *Elohim the Archetype (Original) Pattern of the Universe Vol. III IV,* Institute of Divine Metaphysical Research, Inc., 1960.

Kloss, Jethro, *Back to Eden,* Benedict Lust Publications Inc., 1981.

Knappert, Jan, *Encyclopaedia of Middle Eastern Mythology and Religion,* Element. 1993.

Krapf, Phillip H., *Contact Has Begun,* Hay House, 1998.

Kwok, Man-Ho, with Joanne O'Brien, *Elements of Feng Shui,* Element, 1997.

Lalou, Etienne, *Orion Book of the Sun,* Orion Press, 1960.

Landweber, Laura F. and Andrew P. Dobson, *Genetics and the Extinction of Species,* Princeton University Press, 1999.

LaRouche, Lyndon circulate, *The Ugly Truth about the ADL,* Editors of EIR, _____.

Lerner, Eric, *Big Bang Never Happened,* Vintage Books, 1992.

Lewis, C. A., *An Encounter with A Prophet,* Amadon Publishing, 1997.

Lewis, Jack P., *English Bible From KJV to NIV a History and Evaluation,* _____, _____.

Lipp, Frank J., *Herbalism, Healing and Harmony Symbolism, Ritual and Folklore Traditions of East and West,* Duncan Baird Publishers, 1996.

Lowenstein, Tom, *Vision of Buddha,* Duncan Baird Publications, 1996.

Lubicz, R. A. Schwaller de, *The Egyptian Miracle,* Inner Traditions International, Ltd. Rochester, Vermont, Flammarion, 1985.

Mack, Burton L., *Who Wrote the New Testament the Making of the Christian Myth,* Harper San Francisco, 1996.

Mahesh, *Yogi Maharishi, Transcendental Meditation,* _____, _____.

Mantak, Chia, *Iron Shirt Chi Kung I,* Healing Tao, 1991.

Marciniak, Barbara, *Earth: Pleiadian keys to the Living Library,* Bear & Co, 1994.

Martin, William C., *Layman's Bible Encyclopedia,* _____, _____.

Melody, A., *Love in the Earth – A Kaleidoscope of Crystals,* Earth Love Publishing House, 1995.

Michell, John, *Dowsing the Crop Circles,* _____, _____.

Montagu, M. F. A., *The Concept of Race,* New York, Free Press, 1964.

Morgan, Keith, *Have You Been Cursed,* Pentacle Enterprises, _____.

Morgan, Keith, *Making Magikal Incenses and Ritual Perfumes,* Pentacle Enterprises, 1991.

Mumford, Dr. Jonn, *Chakra and Kundalini,* Llewellyn Publications, 1994.

Narby, Jeremy, *Cosmic Serpent, DNA and the Origins of Knowledge,* J P Tarcher, 1999.

Nigel, Calder, *Einstein's Universe,* Viking Press, 1979.

Nourse, Dr. Alan E., *Universe, Earth, and Atom: The Story of Physics,* Harper and Row, 1969.

Pang, Chia Siew and Goh Ewe Hock, *Tai Chi Ten Minuets to Health,* CRCS Publications, 1988.

Peniel, Jon, *Lost Teachings of Atlantis,* Network Publishing Inc., 1998.

Peterson, Ivars, *Newton's' s Clock: Chaos in the Solar System,* W. H. Freeman and Company, 1993.

Pinney, Roy, *Vanishing Tribes.*

Raymond, Andrew, *Secrets of the Sphinx,* U. N. I. Productions, 1995.

Richards, Steve, *Levitation,* The Aquarian Press, 1980.

Rodgers, Dr. John, *New Age Bible,* Inner Light Publications, 1992.

Rogers, J. A., *Sex and Race: Negro - Caucasian mixing in All Ages and All Lands,* Helga Rogers, 1970.

Roman, Sanaya and Duane Packer, *Opening to Channel, How to Connect with Your Guide,* H. J. Kramer Inc., 1987.

Rosenberg, Donna, *World Mythology,* NTC Publishing Group, 1993.

Rosenfield, Israel Edward Ziff and Borin Van Loon, *DNA for Beginners,* Writers & Readers, 1983.

Russell, Bertrand Arthur, *Why I am Not a Christian,* Simon & Schuster, 1977.

Sakya, Jnan Bahadur, *Short Description of Gods, Goddesses and Ritual Objects of Buddhism and Hinduism in Nepal,* Handicraft Association of Nepal, India, 1994.

Schmandt-Besserat, Denise, *Before Writing Vol. 1, From Counting to Cuneiform,* University of Texas Press, 1992.

Seabook, Myles, *I Ching for Everyone,* Barnes and Noble Books, 1998.

Sertima, Ivan. Van, *They Came Before Columbus,* Random House, 1976.

Sforza, Luigi Luca, *Great Human Diasporas, The History of Diversity and Evolution,* Cavalli Perseus Press, 1996.

Shcwaller, Isha, *The Opening of the Way,* Inner Traditions Intl Ltd., 1995.

Sheldon, H. Horton, *Outline of Science, Part 1, Man and His Environment,* Funk and Wagnalls Company, 1929.

SHIN, ABD-RU, *In the Light of Truth,* Grail Foundation Press, 1998.

Silverman, David P., *Ancient Egypt,* Oxford University Press, 1997.

Sitchin, Zecharia and Associates, *Of Heaven and Earth,* Avon Books, 1996.

Sitchin, Zecharia, *Twelfth Planet, Avon Books,* 1983.

Sitchin, Zecharia, *Wars of Gods and Men,* Avon Books, 1999.

Sitchin, Zecharia, *When Time Began, The First New Age,* Avon Books, 1993.

Sorotzkin, Rabbi Zalman, *Insights in the Torah,* Mesorah Publications, Ltd., 1991.

Stringer, Christopher and Robin McKie, *African Exodus, The Origins of Modern Humanity,* Henry Holt, 1996.

Strong, S.T.D., LL.D. James, *Strong's Exhaustive Bible Concordance,* Thomas Nelson, 1997.

Suares, Carlo, *Cipher of Genesis,* Samuel Weiser, 1992.

Sutton, William Josiah, *Antichrist 666,* Teach Services, 1999.

Sutton, William Josiah, *Illuminati 666,* by Teach Services, 1995.

Taube, Karl, *Aztec and Maya Myths,* University of Texas Press, 1994.

Time Life Books, *Mind and Brain,* Time Life Books.

Toohey, William, *Life After Birth,* Seabury Press, 1981.

Unger, Merrill F., *Unger's Bible Dictionary,* 1957, Moody Press.

Vitebsky, Pier, *The Shaman,* Duncan Baird Publishers, 1995.

Walsh, Neal Donald, *Conversations with God an Uncommon Dialogue Parts 1 and 2,* Putnam Publishing Group, 1996.

Wasserman, Debra, *Lowfat Jewish vegetarian Cookbook,* Vegetarian Resource Group, 1995.

Webster, Merriam, *Webster's New Collegiate Dictionary,* G. and C. Merriam Company, 1977.

Wheeler, John Archibald, *Geons, Black Holes, and Quantum Foam,* W.W. Norton & Company, 1998.

Wheless, Joseph, *Forgery in Christianity,* Kessinger Publishing Company, 1997.

Wheless, Joseph, *Is It God's Word,* Kessinger Publishing Company, 1997.

White, E. G., *Great Controversy,* _____, 1950.

Williams, Chancellor, *Destruction of Black Civilization: Great Issues of a Race from 4500 to 2000 AD,* Third World Press,1992

Wilson, Colin, *From Atlantis to the Sphinx, Recovering the Lost Wisdom of the Ancient World,* International Publishing Corporation, 1996.

Windsor, Rudolph, *From Babylon to Timbuktu,* Windsor Golden Series, 1988.

Windsor, Rudolph, *Valley of Dry Bones,* Windsor Golden Series, 1988.

Yin, Amorah Quan, *Pleiadian Perspectives on Human Evolution,* Bear & Co, 1996.

Young, Robert, *Young's Analytical Concordance to the Bible,* Hendrickson Publishers, Inc, 1993.

# Index

# ORDER INFORMATION
# AND MANUSCRIPT SUBMISSION

If you would like your personal copy of the *Ultimate Deceit of the Human Race* please mail $39.95 (hardcover) or $24.95 (softcover) per book, plus shipping and handling of $3.50 per book and $1.00 for each additional book. *Residents of Indiana please include an additional 5% sales tax to your order.*

Send this form and your payment to:

**Anath's Enterprises Inc.**
**P. O. Box 3132, Marion, Indiana  46953**

Choose Payment Method: ❑ Check  ❑ Credit card:
❑ Visa  ❑ MasterCard  ❑ Discover  ❑ American Express

Check number: _____

Credit Card Number: _____

Name: _____

Address: _____

City: _____State: _____Zip:_____

---

**Book signings, seminars, speaking engagements, workshops, consultation: please phone toll free for more information.**

**1 (800) 363-0799**

**Or visit our website at http://www.ezzrath.com**

---

*Anath's Publishing Company is currently seeking authors:*
To submit manuscripts send an entire manuscript or at least two sample chapters and the table of contents. Related subject matter: Mythology, Metaphysics, Nontraditional Biblical Enlightenment, World Religions, Energy Healings, Auric and Psychic Readings, The Tarot, The Occult, Wicca, Kabbalah, Taoism, Confucianism, Vedas, Tantra, and all ancient teachings. Material will not be returned without a SASE. Currently we answer all submissions within two weeks. This may change without notice.

# ORDER INFORMATION
# AND MANUSCRIPT SUBMISSION

If you would like your personal copy of the *Ultimate Deceit of the Human Race* please mail $39.95 (hardcover) or $24.95 (softcover) per book, plus shipping and handling of $3.50 per book and $1.00 for each additional book. *Residents of Indiana please include an additional 5% sales tax to your order.*

Send this form and your payment to:

**Anath's Enterprises Inc.**
**P. O. Box 3132, Marion, Indiana  46953**

Choose Payment Method: ❏ Check  ❏ Credit card:
❏ Visa  ❏ MasterCard  ❏ Discover  ❏ American Express

Check number: _____

Credit Card Number: _____

Name: _____

Address: _____

City: _____State: _____Zip:_____

---

**Book signings, seminars, speaking engagements, workshops, consultation: please phone toll free for more information.**
**1 (800) 363-0799**
**Or visit our website at http://www.ezzrath.com**

---

*Anath's Publishing Company is currently seeking authors:*
To submit manuscripts send an entire manuscript or at least two sample chapters and the table of contents. Related subject matter: Mythology, Metaphysics, Nontraditional Biblical Enlightenment, World Religions, Energy Healings, Auric and Psychic Readings, The Tarot, The Occult, Wicca, Kabbalah, Taoism, Confucianism, Vedas, Tantra, and all ancient teachings. Material will not be returned without a SASE. Currently we answer all submissions within two weeks. This may change without notice.

# ORDER INFORMATION
# AND MANUSCRIPT SUBMISSION

If you would like your personal copy of the *Ultimate Deceit of the Human Race* please mail $39.95 (hardcover) or $24.95 (softcover) per book, plus shipping and handling of $3.50 per book and $1.00 for each additional book. *Residents of Indiana please include an additional 5% sales tax to your order.*

Send this form and your payment to:

**Anath's Enterprises Inc.**
**P. O. Box 3132, Marion, Indiana  46953**

Choose Payment Method: ❏ Check   ❏ Credit card:
❏ Visa  ❏ MasterCard  ❏ Discover  ❏ American Express

Check number: _____

Credit Card Number: _____

Name: _____

Address: _____

City: _____State: _____Zip:_____

**Book signings, seminars, speaking engagements, workshops, consultation: please phone toll free for more information.**
**1 (800) 363-0799**
**Or visit our website at http://www.ezzrath.com**

*Anath's Publishing Company is currently seeking authors:*
To submit manuscripts send an entire manuscript or at least two sample chapters and the table of contents. Related subject matter: Mythology, Metaphysics, Nontraditional Biblical Enlightenment, World Religions, Energy Healings, Auric and Psychic Readings, The Tarot, The Occult, Wicca, Kabbalah, Taoism, Confucianism, Vedas, Tantra, and all ancient teachings. Material will not be returned without a SASE. Currently we answer all submissions within two weeks. This may change without notice.